D1196786

THE PSYCHOLOGY OF VALUES:
The Ontario Symposium, Volume 8

ONTARIO SYMPOSIUM ON PERSONALITY AND SOCIAL PSYCHOLOGY

E. T. HIGGINS, C. P. HERMAN, M. P. ZANNA, EDS.
Social Cognition: The Ontario Symposium, Volume 1

M. P. ZANNA, E. T. HIGGINS, C. P. HERMAN, EDS.
Consistency in Social Behavior: The Ontario Symposium, Volume 2

C. P. HERMAN, M. P. ZANNA, E. T. HIGGINS, EDS.
Physical Appearance, Stigma, and Social Behavior: The Ontario Symposium, Volume 3

J. M. OLSON, C. P. HERMAN, M. P. ZANNA, EDS.
Relative Deprivation and Social Comparison: The Ontario Symposium, Volume 4

M. P. ZANNA, J. M. OLSON, C. P. HERMAN, EDS.
Social Influence: The Ontario Symposium, Volume 5

J. M. OLSON, M. P. ZANNA, EDS.
Self-Inference Processes: The Ontario Symposium, Volume 6

M. P. ZANNA, J. M. OLSON, EDS.
The Psychology of Prejudice: The Ontario Symposium, Volume 7

C. SELIGMAN, J. M. OLSON, M. P. ZANNA, EDS.
The Psychology of Values: The Ontario Symposium, Volume 8

THE PSYCHOLOGY OF VALUES:
The Ontario Symposium, Volume 8

Edited by

CLIVE SELIGMAN
JAMES M. OLSON
University of Western Ontario

MARK P. ZANNA
University of Waterloo

 LAWRENCE ERLBAUM ASSOCIATES, PUBLISHERS
1996   Mahwah, New Jersey

Lawrence Erlbaum Associates, Inc., Publishers
10 Industrial Avenue
Mahwah, New Jersey 07430

Library of Congress Cataloging-in-Publication Data

The psychology of values / edited by Clive Seligman, James M. Olson,
Mark P. Zanna.
      p.   cm. — (The Ontario symposium ; v. 8)
   "The Eighth Ontario Symposium on Personality and Social Psychology
was held at the University of Western Ontario, August 18–19, 1993"—
Pref.
   Includes bibliographical references and indexes.
   ISBN 0-8058-1574-0 (alk. paper)
   1. Values—Psychological aspects—Congresses.   2. Moral
development—Congresses.   3. Social values—Congresses.
I. Seligman, Clive.   II. Olson, James M., 1953–   .   III. Zanna,
Mark P.   IV. Ontario Symposium on Personality and Social Psychology
(8th : 1993 : University of Western Ontario)   V. Series.
BF778.P76   1996
155.2—dc20
                                                          96-8016
                                                             CIP

Books published by Lawrence Erlbaum Associates are printed on acid-free paper, and their bindings
are chosen for strength and durability.

Printed in the United States of America
10 9 8 7 6 5 4 3 2 1

Contents

Preface   vii

1. Value Priorities and Behavior: Applying a Theory of Integrated
   Value Systems   1
   Shalom Schwartz

2. Revising the Value Pluralism Model: Incorporating Social Content
   and Context Postulates   25
   Philip E. Tetlock, Randall S. Peterson, and Jennifer S. Lerner

3. The Dynamics of Value Systems   53
   Clive Seligman and Albert N. Katz

4. Morality and the Self: Implications for the When and How of
   Value-Attitude-Behavior Relations   77
   Connie M. Kristiansen and Alan M. Hotte

5. On Creating Value-Expressive Attitudes: An Experimental
   Approach   107
   Sandra L. Murray, Geoffrey Haddock, and Mark P. Zanna

6. Social Values and Consumer Behavior: Research From the List of
   Values   135
   Lynn R. Kahle

189595

7. Values and Prejudice: Toward Understanding the Impact of
    American Values on Outgroup Attitudes   153
    Monica Biernat, Theresa K. Vescio, Shelley A. Theno,
    and Christian S. Crandall

8. Toward a Theory of Commitment   191
    John Lydon

9. Values, Deservingness, and Attitudes Toward High Achievers:
    Research on Tall Poppies   215
    Norman T. Feather

10. Value Transmission in Families   253
    Meg J. Rohan and Mark P. Zanna

11. Making Choices: Media Roles in the Construction of Value-Choices   277
    Sandra J. Ball-Rokeach and William E. Loges

12. What Values Do People Prefer in Children? A Comparative
    Analysis of Survey Evidence From Fifteen Countries   299
    Douglass Baer, James Curtis, Edward Grabb, and William Johnston

Author Index   329
Subject Index   339

Preface

The Eighth Ontario Symposium on Personality and Social Psychology was held at the University of Western Ontario, August 18–19, 1993. The topic of the symposium was the psychology of values, and the presentations covered a wide variety of issues in this area. As has become the fortunate custom of Ontario Symposia, the papers generated many interesting discussions among participants, as well as many productive interchanges with the approximately 75 additional audience members (20–25 faculty and 50–55 graduate students) from more than a dozen Canadian universities.

The current volume consists of the expanded and updated versions of papers presented initially at the conference. The span of time between the conference and the publication of the book is the result of the practice of giving the authors an opportunity to revise their chapters based on, among other things, feedback obtained from other participants and audience members at the conference. Also, as has become customary, contributors provided comments on preliminary drafts of other participants' chapters—an undertaking for which we, as editors, are grateful.

The chapters in this volume are roughly organized in the following categories: conceptualizations of values, value systems, and value–attitude–behavior relations (chapters 1 to 4); methodological issues (chapters 5 and 6); the role of values in specific domains, such as prejudice, commitment, and deservingness (chapters 7 to 9); and the transmission of values through families, media, and culture (chapters 10 to 12).

Specifically, in chapter 1, Schwartz demonstrates how value systems can be treated as integrated motivational types that form predictable relations with various behaviors. In chapter 2, Tetlock, Peterson, and Lerner revise Tetlock's earlier, influential value pluralism model through consideration of additional factors, such as the social content of values and the social context of decision-making. In chapter 3, Seligman and Katz present a dynamic conceptualization of value systems, and argue that individuals may construct value systems in the context of specific issues and not simply apply some general value system to issues as they arise. In chapter 4, Kristiansen and Hotte suggest that moral reasoning, moral development, and self-conceptions may be important moderators explaining when and for whom values will be used as guides for attitudes and behavior. In chapter 5, Murray, Haddock, and Zanna demonstrate a laboratory procedure for producing value expressive attitudes, in the hope that others will be encouraged to use experimental approaches to study the causal relation between values and attitudes and between values and behavior. In chapter 6, Kahle reviews his research program using the List of Values (LOV), describing the conceptual and methodological advantages and disadvantages of this approach. In chapter 7, Biernat, Vescio, Theno, and Crandall present several theories of racism and show the relevance of values in facilitating or inhibiting the expression of prejudice. In chapter 8, Lydon explores the relation between values and commitment, and tests the idea that we are most committed to goals and projects that express core values. In chapter 9, Feather examines how the connection between value priorities and deservingness influences attitudes toward people of very high status. In chapter 10, Rohan and Zanna investigate how values are transmitted from parents to children and show that parental authoritativeness and responsiveness are crucial to successful value transmission. In chapter 11, Ball-Rokeach and Loges suggest that, in most cases, information about social choices, such as health care, reach individuals after a process of value framing by media. In chapter 12, Baer, Curtis, Grabb, and Johnston provide data from a cross-national survey of child-rearing values to assess the extent to which the United States subscribes to a modern system of values relative to other countries.

We believe that these chapters illustrate both the diversity and vitality of research on the psychology of values. Our hope is that this volume will stimulate further research and theorizing in this area.

Seven previous Ontario Symposia on Personality and Social Psychology have been held. The series is designed to bring together scholars from across North America—and, in the case of the present symposium, the world—who work in the same substantive area, with the goals of identifying common concerns and integrating research findings. Participation by Canadian faculty and graduate students in the symposia has been gratifying. We hope that the symposia have contributed to (and will continue to stimulate) the growth of personality and social psychology in Ontario and Canada.

The first Ontario Symposium, held at the University of Western Ontario in August 1978, dealt with social cognition (see Higgins, E. T., Herman C. P., and Zanna, M. P. (Eds.) (1981). *Social Cognition: The Ontario Symposium.* Vol. 1. Hillsdale, NJ: Lawrence Erlbaum Associates); the second, held at the University of Waterloo in October 1979, had the theme of variability and consistency in social behavior (see Zanna, M. P., Higgins, E. T., and Herman, C. P. (Eds.) (1982). *Consistency in Social Behavior: The Ontario Symposium.* Vol. 2. Hillsdale, NJ: Lawrence Erlbaum Associates); the third, held at the University of Toronto in May 1981, addressed the social psychology of physical appearance (see Herman, C. P., Zanna, M. P., and Higgins, E. T. (Eds.) (1986). *Physical Appearance, Stigma, and Social Behavior: The Ontario Symposium.* Vol. 3. Hillsdale, NJ: Lawrence Erlbaum Associates); the fourth, held at the University of Western Ontario in October 1983, was concerned with relative deprivation and social comparison processes (see Olsen, J. M., Herman, C. P., and Zanna, M. P. (Eds.) (1986). *Relative Deprivation and Social Comparison: The Ontario Symposium.* Vol. 4. Hillsdale, NJ: Lawrence Erlbaum Associates); the fifth, held at the University of Waterloo in August 1984, dealt with social influence processes (see Zanna, M. P., Olson, J. M., and Herman, C. P. (Eds.) (1987). *(Social Influence: The Ontario Symposium.* Vol. 5. Hillsdale, NJ: Lawrence Erlbaum Associates); the sixth, held at the University of Western Ontario in June 1988, focused on self-inference processes (see Olson, J. M., and Zanna, M. P. (Eds.) (1990). *Self-Inference Processes: The Ontario Symposium.* Vol. 6. Hillsdale, NJ: Lawrence Erlbaum Associates); and the seventh, held at the University of Waterloo in June, 1991, examined the topic of prejudice (see Zanna, M. P., and Olson, J. M. (Eds.) (1994). *The Psychology of Prejudice: The Ontario Symposium.* Vol. 7. Hillsdale, NJ: Lawrence Erlbaum Associates).

Once again, primary financial support for the Eighth Ontario Symposium was provided by the Social Sciences and Humanities Research Council of Canada, whose continuing support has been the backbone of the series. We are also deeply indebted to the Department of Psychology and the Faculty of Social Science at the University of Western Ontario for their financial and administrative support. In particular, we would like to thank Anne Baxter for paying the bills, and the social psychology graduate students at the university of Western Ontario for arranging transportation for the speakers. Finally, we would like to thank Larry Erlbaum for his continuing support and editorial guidance.

Clive Seligman
James M. Olson
Mark P. Zanna

1 Value Priorities and Behavior: Applying a Theory of Integrated Value Systems

Shalom Schwartz
Hebrew University of Jerusalem

A major goal of research on values has been to relate individual differences in value priorities to differences in attitudes, behavior, and background variables. Past research most commonly adopted one of two approaches. Much research has selected a few single target values whose priorities were postulated to associate with the attitude, behavior, or background variable of interest and then examined empirical relationships (e.g., obedience and social class—Alwin, 1984; world at peace and pacifism—Mayton & Furnham, 1994; equality and civil rights—Rokeach, 1973). Other research has been more exploratory. It has related lists of values to various other variables and then discussed the significant associations that emerged (e.g., with personality inventories—Furnham, 1984; with race, nationality, and age—Rokeach, 1973; with quality of teaching— Greenstein, 1976). The associations with single values that emerge can, of course, almost always be interpreted as making sense, post hoc.

The focus on relationships with single values makes both these approaches unsatisfying. It leads to a piecemeal accumulation of bits of information about values that is not conducive to the construction of coherent theories. Three noteworthy problems beset these approaches. First, the reliability of any single value is quite low. Hence chance may play a substantial role in the emergence or nonemergence of significant associations with single values. Second, absent a comprehensive set of values or of a broad theory to guide selection of target values, values that were not included in a study may be equally or more mean-ingfully related to the phenomenon in question than those studied (e.g., the almost total absence of power values in the literature on values and political orientations).

Third, and most important, these single-value approaches ignore the widely shared assumption that attitudes and behavior are guided not by the priority given to a single value but by tradeoffs among competing values that are implicated simultaneously in a behavior or attitude (Rokeach, 1973; Schwartz, 1992; Tetlock, 1986). Indeed, values may play little role in behavior except when there is value conflict—when a behavior has consequences promotive of one (or more) value but opposed to others that are also cherished by the person. It is in the presence of conflict that values are likely to be activated, to enter awareness, and to be used as guiding principles. In the absence of value conflict, values may draw no attention. Instead, habitual, scripted responses may suffice.

My work has sought to overcome these three problems. It has derived what may be a nearly comprehensive set of different motivational types of values, recognized across cultures. Because the value set is nearly comprehensive, it is unlikely that important types of values will be overlooked in analyses of the relations of values to other variables. Each of these value types is represented by a number of single values that are combined to form relatively reliable indexes of value priorities. Most importantly, the theory conceptualizes the set of value types as an integrated system. Consequently, the full set of value priorities can be related to other variables in an organized, coherent manner rather than in a piecemeal fashion.

This chapter illustrates how value systems can be treated as integrated wholes in their relations with behavior and, thereby, encourages researchers to abandon the prevailing single-values approaches. For this purpose, it discusses three examples of the relations of value priorities with a diverse set of behavioral variables: cooperative behavior, voting in national elections, and readiness for contact with members of an out-group.

OVERVIEW OF THEORY

Influenced heavily by Rokeach (1973) and Kluckhohn (1951), the theory defines values as desirable, transsituational goals, varying in importance, that serve as guiding principles in people's lives (see Schwartz, 1992, for a fuller elaboration of the theory). The crucial content aspect that distinguishes among values is the type of motivational goal they express. I derived a typology of the different contents of values by reasoning that values represent, in the form of conscious goals, three universal requirements of human existence: biological needs, requisites of coordinated social interaction, and demands of group survival and functioning. Groups and individuals represent these requirements cognitively as specific values about which they communicate in order to explain, coordinate, and rationalize behavior.

Ten motivationally distinct types of values were derived from the three universal requirements. A *conformity* type was derived, for example, both from the prerequisite of smooth interaction and of group survival—that individuals re-

TABLE 1.1
Definitions of Motivational Types of Values in Terms of Their Goals and the Single Values
That Represent Them

POWER:	Social status and prestige, control or dominance over people and resources. (Social Power, Authority, Wealth) [Preserving my Public Image, Social Recognition]*
ACHIEVEMENT:	Personal success through demonstrating competence according to social standards. (Successful, Capable, Ambitious, Influential) [Intelligent, Self-Respect]
HEDONISM:	Pleasure and sensuous gratification for oneself. (Pleasure, Enjoying Life)
STIMULATION:	Excitement, novelty, and challenge in life. (Daring, a Varied Life, an Exciting Life)
SELF-DIRECTION:	Independent thought and action-choosing, creating, exploring. (Creativity, Freedom, Independent, Curious, Choosing own Goals) [Self-Respect]
UNIVERSALISM:	Understanding, appreciation, tolerance and protection for the welfare of all people and for nature. (Broadminded, Wisdom, Social Justice, Equality, a World at Peace, a World of Beauty, Unity with Nature, Protecting the Environment)
BENEVOLENCE:	Preservation and enhancement of the welfare of people with whom one is in frequent personal contact. (Helpful, Honest, Forgiving, Loyal, Responsible) [True Friendship, Mature Love]
TRADITION:	Respect, commitment and acceptance of the customs and ideas that traditional culture or religion provide the self. (Humble, Accepting my Portion in Life, Devout, Respect for Tradition, Moderate)
CONFORMITY:	Restraint of actions, inclinations, and impulses likely to upset or harm others and violate social expectations or norms. (Politeness, Obedient, Self-Discipline, Honoring Parents and Elders)
SECURITY:	Safety, harmony and stability of society, of relationships, and of self. (Family Security, National Security, Social Order, Clean, Reciprocation of Favors) [Sense of Belonging, Healthy]

*Values in brackets are not used in computing the standard indexes for value types because their meanings are not consistent across samples and cultures (Schwartz, 1992, 1994). For example, self-respect is found almost equally frequently with achievement and with self-direction values. Additional values included to measure a possible spirituality value type that was not found were: a Spiritual Life, Meaning in Life, Inner Harmony, Detachment.

strain impulses and inhibit actions that might hurt others. There is substantial, cross-cultural, support for the distinctiveness of these ten types in research with samples from 41 countries (Schwartz, 1992, 1994; Schwartz & Sagiv, 1995). Table 1.1 lists the value types, each defined in terms of its central goal, and followed, in parentheses, by specific single values that primarily represent it. A specific value represents a type when actions that express the value or lead to its attainment promote the central goal of the type.

In addition to propositions regarding the content of values, the theory specifies dynamic relations among the types of values. Actions taken in pursuit of each type of values have psychological, practical, and social consequences that may conflict with or may be compatible with the pursuit of other value types. The total pattern of relations of value conflict and compatibility among value priorities gives rise to a circular structure of value systems. This structure, represented in Fig. 1.1, has also received substantial support in cross-cultural research (Schwartz, 1992, 1994; Schwartz & Sagiv, 1995).[1] Competing value types emanate in opposing directions from the center; complementary types are in close proximity going around the circle.

The nature of the compatibilities among value types is clarified by noting the shared motivational orientations of the adjacent value types. Viewed in terms of these shared orientations, the adjacent types form a motivational continuum around the circular value structure of Fig. 1.1:

Power and achievement both emphasize social superiority and esteem.

Achievement and hedonism both express self-centeredness.

Hedonism and stimulation both entail a desire for affectively pleasant arousal.

Stimulation and self-direction both involve intrinsic motivation for mastery and openness to change.

Self-direction and universalism both express reliance upon one's own judgment and comfort with the diversity of existence.

Universalism and benevolence both entail concern for enhancement of other and transcendence of selfish interests.

Benevolence and tradition/conformity all promote devotion to one's in-group.

Tradition/conformity and security all emphasize conservation of order and harmony in relations.

Security and power both stress avoiding or overcoming the threat of uncertainties by controlling relationships and resources.

In contrast, the motivational goals of the value types in opposing positions around the circle cannot easily be pursued at the same time. For example, the pursuit of achievement values may conflict with the pursuit of benevolence values: Seeking personal success for oneself is likely to obstruct actions aimed at enhancing the welfare of others who need one's help.

Two major value conflicts that structure value systems have been found in over 95% of samples I have studied in 41 countries (Schwartz, 1994). This enables us to conceptualize the total structure of value systems as organized on

---

[1]The near universality of the structure of relations among value types indicates that the meaning of each type is similar in the vast majority of samples. However, the importance of the ten value types varies substantially across samples. It is the similarity of meaning that makes it possible to interpret the differences in value importance.

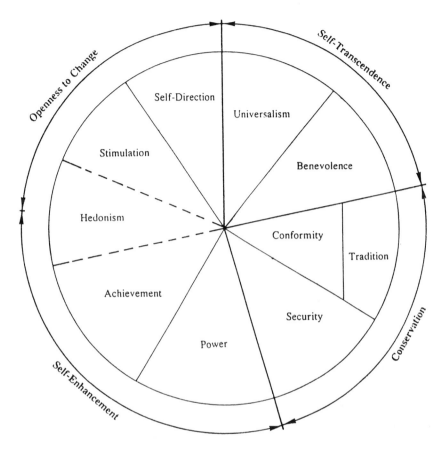

FIG. 1.1. The prototypical structure of value systems.

two basic dimensions. Each, as also shown in Fig. 1.1, is a polar opposition between two higher order value types.

One dimension opposes Openness to Change (combining the self-direction and stimulation value types) to Conservation (combining security, conformity, and tradition). This dimension reflects a conflict between emphases on own independent thought and action and favoring change versus submissive self-restriction, preservation of traditional practices, and protection of stability. The second dimension opposes Self-Transcendence (combining benevolence and universalism) to Self-Enhancement (combining power and achievement). This dimension reflects a conflict between acceptance of others as equals and concern for their welfare versus pursuit of one's own relative success and dominance over others. Hedonism shares elements of both Openness and Self-Enhancement.

This view of value systems as integrated structures facilitates the generation of systematic, coherent hypotheses regarding the relations of the full set of value priorities to other variables (e.g., behaviors). It also facilitates interpretation of the observed relations of sets of values to other variables in a comprehensive manner. Two statements summarize the implications of the interrelatedness of value priorities for generating hypotheses and interpreting findings:

1. Any outside variable tends to be associated similarly with value types that are adjacent in the value structure.
2. Associations with any outside variable decrease monotonically as one moves around the circular structure of value types in both directions from the most positively associated value type to the least positively associated value type (Schwartz, 1992).

Statement one implies that the associations for value types that are adjacent in the value structure may not differ significantly from one another, unless the sample size is large. Statement two implies that order of these associations is, nonetheless, precisely predicted. Although the order of the value types is set by the theory, it is not necessarily the case that the types most and least positively associated with an outside variable are those in exactly opposing positions in Fig. 1.1. As illustrated in study three below, this is because the specific characteristics of the behavior in question make particular motivational goals more or less relevant to a decision. I now apply these ideas to explain behavior.

INTERPERSONAL COOPERATION

Single behaviors are influenced by a large variety of factors specific to the situation in which they occur. Hence it is difficult to predict single behaviors from a transsituational variable like values. Nonetheless, it should be possible to relate value priorities systematically to a single behavior if the setting is controlled in a manner that reduces random variation and eliminates overwhelming situational influences. This allows individual differences in motivation to have a major impact. Liron Natan, Gary Bornstein, and I chose cooperation in an experimental game as a likely behavioral variable (Natan, 1993). Such games are constructed to tap behaviors that express relatively pure motivations straightforwardly.

Ninety Hebrew University students (45 male, 45 female), recruited for a decision-making experiment, participated in small groups. They first completed a 56-item value survey (Schwartz, 1992) in which they rated the importance of each value "as a guiding principle in my life" on a 9-point scale ranging from 7 (of supreme importance) to 0 (not important) to −1 (opposed to my values). Indexes of the importance of each value type were computed by averaging the importance ratings of the values representative of that type (see Table 1.1).

Each participant then read that, for this task, he or she was paired with another student from their group, whose identity was not revealed. Participants were each given the matrix in Table 1.2, without the labels "cooperation, noncooperation, competition, and individualism." This matrix was adapted from games like the decomposed prisoner's dilemma in order to measure cooperation versus noncooperation (Messick & McClintock, 1968; Pruit, 1967).

Participants were asked to choose one of the three alternatives for allocating money between self and a member of their group. They learned that each person would receive the amount of money he or she allocated to self plus the amount their partner allocated to him or her. The cooperative choice entailed taking 2.5 shekels (about $1) for self and giving 2 shekels to the other. Compared to the other choices, this meant sacrificing a little of what one could gain (not taking 3 shekels) and giving the maximum to the other. The other two choices were both noncooperative, maximizing either one's absolute gain (individualism) or relative gain (competition).

In order to derive hypotheses, we consider the consequences of each allocation option for attaining or expressing the motivational goal of each of the ten types of values. In a task of allocating resources between self and other, the relevant value dimension, as shown earlier in Fig. 1.1, is Self-Enhancement (including power and achievement values) versus Self-Transcendence (including benevolence and universalism values). Analyses of the fit between the consequences of cooperative and noncooperative behavior and the goals of the value types yields the following set of hypotheses:

1. The strongest predictor of failure to cooperate is the importance attributed by the individual to power values. This value type emphasizes competitive advantage. Power values legitimize seeking to maximize own gain even at the expense of others. Achievement values also predict noncooperation because they promote self-interest as well. But they are a weaker predictor because obtaining resources through noncooperation would probably be a weak source of social admiration, the core goal of achievement, as defined

TABLE 1.2
Matrix of Allocation Choices in Cooperation Experiment

	Cooperation	Noncooperation	
Allocation to:		Competition	Individualism
Self	2.5 SH	2.5 SH	3 SH
Member in own Group	2 SH	0 SH	1 SH

in the values theory. Hedonism also predicts noncooperation because cooperation would entail some self-sacrifice inimical to hedonistic goals.

2. The strongest predictor of cooperation is the importance attributed by the individual to benevolence values, with universalism second. The experimental setting probably makes cooperation more an expression of conventional decency and thoughtfulness than of basic commitment to social justice. Thus it is more relevant to the goals of benevolence than of universalism values. Conformity also predicts cooperation because cooperation is the normative, conventional behavior in society.

3. Self-direction, stimulation, security, and tradition are all less relevant to this decision, so we expect correlations near zero for them.

These hypotheses can be viewed as predicting the correlations with cooperation of ten separate value types—three negative correlations (hypothesis 1), three positive (hypothesis 2), and four near zero (null hypothesis 3). If, however, the structure of values is considered as an integrated whole, the predicted correlations with cooperation form a systematic pattern that reflects the structure of dynamic relations among the value types.

Specifically, the predicted pattern of correlations shows the two earlier noted characteristics regarding the associations of the system of value priorities with any outside variable: Cooperation is similarly related with value types that are adjacent in the value structure; and its associations decrease monotonically as one moves around the circular structure of value types in both directions from the most positively associated value type (benevolence) to the least positively associated value type (power).

Unfolding the value structure circle yields an integrated prediction of values–cooperation correlations with a sinusoidal shape. The observed point-biserial correlations between cooperation (scored 0–1) and the importance attributed to each value type are shown in Fig. 1.2.[2] The hypotheses were largely confirmed. Benevolence was most positively correlated and power most negatively. More important, the order of the correlations followed the order around the value circle from benevolence to power. The fact that self-direction, stimulation, security, and tradition had correlations near zero leads to more than merely accepting the null hypothesis in this context. It conveys information about the systematic relationship of the whole system of values to cooperation.

The six value types hypothesized to be relevant to cooperation in this setting had a multiple correlation of .53 with the dichotomous behavioral variable. They thus accounted for 28% of its variance, a very respectable proportion for a single behavior.

Although the curve relating value priorities with cooperation is sinusoidal, it

---

[2]Correlations are partialled for each person's mean response to all 56 values, in order to control for differential use of the response scale (see Schwartz, 1992).

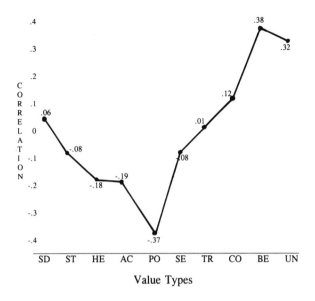

FIG. 1.2.   Point-biserial correlations of value priorities with cooperation versus noncooperation.

is not symmetrical. For example, power is much more negatively related to cooperation than is security, which is adjacent to it. This illustrates the fact that the theory of value structure provides a baseline only for the order of associations. More precise hypotheses about differences in the absolute strength of associations require analyses of the specific relevance of each value type to the behavior in question. The brief explications of the hypotheses presented earlier suggested that power is much more relevant to cooperation than is security.

Another view of the data further clarifies the joint impact of power and benevolence—the two value types that were postulated to be most relevant to cooperation, to have the strongest influence, and to operate in opposing directions. We split the sample at the median on each of these value types and compared the proportion who cooperated in the four subsamples formed by the 2 × 2 cross-classification. Table 1.3 shows that cooperation was twice as frequent among those who attributed high importance to benevolence and low importance to power values (87%) than in any of the other subsamples (35%–43%). That is, a commitment to values that promote cooperation (benevolence), in the absence of conflict with a commitment to values opposed to cooperation (power), was necessary to elicit a high level of cooperation.

The next example of how value systems relate, as integrated wholes, to behavior takes us outside the laboratory to the study of voting behavior. Voting is the outcome of a complex of causes, one of which might be the person's value priorities.

TABLE 1.3
Proportion of Cooperation as a Function of the Importance of Benevolence and Power Values

		BENEVOLENCE	
		Low	High
POWER	Low	.43 (N = 14)	.87 (N = 30)
	High	.35 (N = 31)	.43 (N = 14)

VOTING BEHAVIOR

Political psychologists and political scientists have often downgraded the importance of value priorities as predictors of voting (e.g., Campbell, Converse, Miller, & Stokes, 1960; see Sears, 1987). No doubt, other variables such as group membership, special interests, and the character of the candidates are influential (Kinder & Sears, 1985). But parties do convey broad ideological messages that are not entirely obscure and confusing; and the public has some understanding of these messages (Himmelweit, Humphreys, Jaeger, & Katz, 1981). Thus people can form an impression of possible consequences of voting for one party rather than another for the attainment of their values. By identifying the stands of parties on basic ideological dimensions, it should therefore be possible to specify some systematic, predictive relations of values to voting.

Students of politics (e.g., Himmelweit et al., 1981; Janda, 1980; Lipset & Rokkan, 1967; Seliger, 1975) have identified two major dimensions of political ideology on which parties in various countries are differentiated. One dimension is concerned with issues of civil liberties, law, and order, and the other with economic issues. We refer to these as classical liberalism and economic egalitarianism, respectively. In Israel, where this study was conducted, the first dimension, classical liberalism, is critical for discriminating among parties, the second of relatively little importance (Arian, 1989; Arian & Shamir, 1990). We therefore focus on the classical liberalism dimension.

On this dimension, parties differ in their emphases on individual freedoms, minority rights, readiness for social change, and in their views on whether government should give primacy to its role as the guardian of civil rights or as the protector of society against the threat of deviant behavior from within or enemies from without. In contemporary Israel, the problems of security and the Arab–Israeli conflict make this dimension especially salient.

Relations between religion and state constitute a subdimension of liberalism in Israel (Liebman & Don-Yehiya, 1984). Many religious citizens wish to ground all aspects of public life in Israeli society in Jewish religious law. Other citizens oppose this religious conception of the Israeli state. Ideologically, opposition to the penetration of religion into civil law is based in commitment to individual freedoms, hence the link to liberalism. Support for religious penetration into the state emphasizes conformity to religious norms in order to preserve a sacred social order, even at the expense of individual freedoms—a nonliberal position.

Experts were asked to rate Israeli parties on each of the dimensions of political ideology, as they presumably are seen by the public. Ratings of the parties differed little on the economic egalitarianism dimension. They differed substantially on both the classical liberalism and state/religion dimensions. Moreover, ratings on the latter two dimensions were very similar, as expected. Therefore, in our study of values and voting, Marina Barnea and I focused on the liberalism dimension, combining ratings of parties on the two related dimensions. This gave special emphasis to the parties' ideological stances on freedom of expression for individual ideas and life styles.

Column 1 of Table 1.4 orders eight Israeli political parties from the one rated most liberal to the one rated least liberal.[3] The religious parties rated lowest because they favor imposing religious law, thereby limiting individual freedom in all domains of life. Following each party name is the number of respondents in a representative national survey done in 1990 who had voted for the party in the 1988 national elections.

In order to derive hypotheses, we consider the consequences of electing parties with various stands on the liberalism dimension for attaining or expressing the motivational goal of each of the ten types of values. Because the parties are primarily discriminated according to their views on freedom of individual expression versus maintenance of order and control of "deviance," the relevant value dimension for predicting voting, as shown earlier in Fig. 1.1, is the Openness to Change (including self-direction and stimulation) versus Conservation (tradition, conformity, security) dimension of values.

The associations with the importance attributed to tradition and to self-direction values should be strongest, because the attainment of their core goals is most affected by policy differences on individual freedoms versus order and control. The more a party is seen as emphasizing order and control of deviance at the expense of individual freedoms, the more likely are those for whom tradition values (humility, devoutness, moderation, accepting ones portion in life, respect for tradition) are of great importance and self-direction values (creativity, freedom, independence, choosing own goals, curiosity) of little importance to vote for it.

Giving priority to conformity and to security values should also promote

---

[3]Religious parties include four different religious parties. Mapam-Ratz includes two parties with similar platforms emphasizing civil liberties. Parties that received fewer than 10 votes in our sample were not included in the analyses.

TABLE 1.4
Order of Israeli Political Parties on Classical Liberal Ideology

According to Judges' Ratings		According to Group Centroids on Value-Based Discriminant Function 1
(1) Mapam-Ratz	(n = 55)	1.012 (1)
(2) Shinui	(n = 19)	.831 (2)
(3) Labor	(n = 248)	.381 (4)
(4) T'hiya	(n = 17)	.490 (3)
(5) Likud	(n = 310)	-.103 (6)
(6) Tsomet	(n = 14)	-.032 (5)
(7) Moledet	(n = 10)	-.259 (7)
(8) Religious	(n = 94)	-1.482 (8)

support for parties that favor order and control, because both these value types emphasize preservation of social order and maintenance of harmony in relations. Giving priority to stimulation and hedonism values should promote support for parties that emphasize freedom, because both value types stress the individual's pursuit of pleasant arousal in novel ways and according to personal preference. A concern for opportunities to pursue social recognition for distinctive individual achievements may also lead those who give priority to achievement values to support parties that emphasize freedom.

The remaining value types (benevolence, universalism, and power) are more relevant to the economic egalitarianism dimension of political ideology on which Israeli parties are not strongly discriminated. They are less relevant to the liberalism dimension. We therefore did not anticipate that they would be related to party support in Israel.

As with the hypotheses for cooperation, the hypotheses for voting can be viewed as predicting the relations of ten separate value types with behavior. Here too, however, considering the structure of values as an integrated whole reveals that the hypothesized relations with liberal voting preferences form a systematic pattern that reflects the structure of dynamic relations among the value types (cf. Fig. 1.1). Associations with the priority given to self-direction values are predicted to be most positive, and associations with the other value types are hypothesized to be progressively less positive as one moves in both directions around the circular structure of value types to tradition, the most negatively associated value type.

The hypotheses were tested with data from a representative sample of the Jewish population in Israel above age 19, who responded to a survey in their homes during the summer of 1990. They first completed an abbreviated version of the value survey that included 37, rather than the usual 56, single values selected to represent all ten value types. The values representing benevolence and universalism did not separate empirically in the multidimensional scaling analysis (SSA; Guttman, 1968) on these data. They were therefore combined to form a single Self-Transcendence value type.[4] Because both benevolence and universalism values were expected to have no association with voting, this combination posed no problem. At the end of the survey, respondents indicated the party for which they voted in the most recent national elections (1988). The 769 respondents who voted for parties with at least ten supporters in the sample were included in the analyses.

Discriminant function analysis was used to assess the associations of values with voting. We derived the functions that discriminate significantly among supporters of the eight political parties, using the nine value types as discriminant variables. Two significant discriminant functions were found. The first accounted for 74% of the common variance, the second only for 21%.

As noted earlier, the prevailing view of Israeli politics assumes that the liberalism (freedom of expression) ideological dimension is paramount. Hence, if values are relevant to voting, one would expect the first, value-based function to tap variation among parties essentially on this dimension. To establish if this was so, we examined the ordering of the parties on the group centroids of the first function. We compared the order of the parties on these centroids (Table 1.3, col. 2) with their order on the liberalism dimension based on the a priori, judges' ratings (Table 1.3, col. 1). As shown in the table, the centroids ordered the groups in almost exactly the same order as the judges' ratings (Spearman rank correlation .95). Thus this value-based function ordered the parties on their perceived policies toward classical liberalism.[5]

Because the first function can be interpreted as representing party differences on liberalism ideology, we can test the hypotheses for the specific value types by examining the associations of each value type with this function. We ask, do the value types hypothesized to promote support for parties committed to individual freedoms associate positively with the function? And, do value types hypothesized to promote support for parties that emphasize order and control associate negatively? And, is the order of associations of the nine value types the same as the order predicted from the integrated structure of value relations?

The most accurate measures of the association of discriminant variables (here, value types) with functions are the total structure coefficients (Klecka, 1980). For each value type, the total structure coefficient, indicating its association with function 1, is indicated on the graph in Fig. 1.3.

The four value types hypothesized to associate positively (self-direction, stimulation, hedonism, achievement), and two of the three types hypothesized to

---

[4]This combination corresponds to a higher-order value type found almost universally with the original 56 value survey (Schwartz & Sagiv, 1995).

[5]The much weaker second function was largely unipolar and defined mainly by positive associations with achievement, security, conformity, and power values. The group centroids for this function were unrelated to any of the judges' ratings, suggesting no clear ideological interpretation of this weak function.

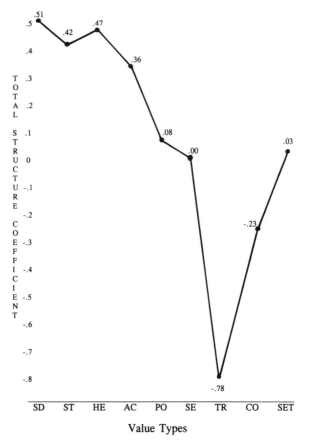

FIG. 1.3.   Total structure coefficients for the association of value priorities with function 1 for discriminating among party voters.

associate negatively (tradition, conformity, but not security) with classical liberalism showed significant associations ($p < .01$) in the predicted direction. No
significant associations emerged for the value types for which none was expected
(power and self-transcendence [benevolence plus universalism]).

Most important, as shown by the sinusoid curve, the order of coefficients was
almost exactly as predicted by the integrated hypothesis for the whole structure
of values (small reversal for Stimulation/Hedonism): Self-direction was most
positive, with the coefficients progressively less positive as one moves around
the structural circle (Fig. 1.1) in both directions toward power.[6]

[6]The security situation in Israel probably led to the absence of an association for security.
Regardless of party preference, respondents rated security values much more important than is
common across nations (unpublished data).

The relationship between value priorities and party voting is also revealed in the comparison of individuals who voted for the two most extreme groups on the liberalism dimension—Mapam-Ratz and Religious. The mean ratings of the importance of value types for these individuals, as well as for supporters of the two major parties, are shown in Table 1.5.

Self-direction, stimulation, and hedonism values were rated more important by supporters of Mapam-Ratz (high liberalism) than by voters for the Religious parties (low liberalism). Tradition and conformity values were rated more important by voters for the Religious parties. Voters for the two major parties attributed intermediate levels of importance to these value types. For these five types, differences between the extreme groups all exceeded .75 standard deviations ($p < .0001$). For the remaining types, differences were smaller and less systematically related to the order of the parties on classical liberalism. In keeping with the integrated hypothesis, the size and sign of the differences between the extreme groups followed the order of the value types around the structural circle with a deviation of only one place for stimulation.

Overall, the findings supported the hypothesized relationships between value priorities and party voting. Using the value-based discriminant functions to classify voters as supporters of one of the eight political parties yielded 51% correct classifications. As calculated by Goodman and Kruskal's Tau, knowledge of individuals' value priorities permitted a 32% improvement compared with chance classification ($Z = 10.24$, $p < .01$). Finally, the order of associations supported our argument that value systems relate as integrated wholes to other variables.

TABLE 1.5
Mean Ratings of the Importance of Value Types as a Function of Political Party Preference

Party	*SD*	*ST*	*HE*	*AC*	*PO*	*SE*	*TR*	*CO*	*SET*
					Value Types				
Mapam-Ratz	5.25	4.25	4.59	4.04	2.80	4.83	2.45	3.92	5.15
Labor	4.84	4.09	4.42	4.51	3.46	5.62	3.30	4.73	5.13
Likud	4.51	4.12	4.29	4.71	3.64	5.65	3.87	4.87	4.97
Religious	3.90	3.22	3.21	3.66	3.12	5.48	5.49	5.05	5.08
Difference MR - Relig	1.35*	1.03*	1.38*	.38	-.32	-.65	-3.04*	-1.13*	.07

Note. *p < .01
SD = Self-direction; AC = Achievement; TR = Tradition; ST = Stimulation; PO = Power; CO = Conformity; HE = Hedonism; SE = Security; SET = Universalism & Benevolence

READINESS FOR OUTGROUP SOCIAL CONTACT

The final study examines how the value priorities of individuals help to explain their readiness for social contact with members of an outgroup. Rokeach (1973) reported the only study I know that directly related to this topic. He found that 21 of the 36 single values in his value lists were significantly associated with an index that included both readiness for social contact and attitudes toward Blacks. In his post hoc discussion, Rokeach portrayed his findings as consistent with descriptions of prejudiced people, but he offered no framework to organize them. The theory of value contents and structure can be used to develop an integrated set of hypotheses to relate the comprehensive system of value priorities to readiness for outgroup contact.

Lilach Sagiv and I applied the theory to study the readiness of Israeli Jews and Israeli Arabs for social contact with one another (Sagiv & Schwartz, 1995). Because the meaning of contact is different for dominant and minority groups, it is important to note that Jews are the dominant group in Israel and Arabs are a minority. Members of dominant groups are likely to understand contact as entailing acceptance of minority group members as fully privileged members of their society. In contrast, members of minority groups are likely to understand broad social contact as implying their own integration into the larger society, or even their assimilation. These different consequences of contact imply different relations with values. I discuss only the dominant group here.

In order to generate hypotheses, we considered the consequences of contact with members of the Arab minority group for the attainment or expression of the motivational goals of the value types by members of the dominant Jewish group. This suggested the following hypotheses:

1. Attributing importance to all three Conservation value types (tradition, conformity, security) correlates negatively with readiness for out-group contact. The most negative correlation is for tradition values because contact entails exposure to divergent traditions and customs, threatening those for whom maintenance of own traditions is important. Moreover, tradition values correlate highly with religiosity (particular among Israeli Jews: Schwartz & Huismans, 1995), and religiosity is related to ethnocentrism (see Wulff, 1991). The negative correlation for conformity values is because contact with culturally different minorities places one in situations where familiar norms do not apply, making it difficult to maintain smooth relations and to avoid violating expectations. The negative correlation for security values is because outgroup members may disrupt the prevailing social order, especially if they feel oppressed and demand change.

2. Attributing importance to both Openness to Change value types (self-direction and stimulation) correlates positively with readiness for outgroup contact. The positive correlation for self-direction values is strong because intergroup

contact provides exposure to new and different ways of life and opportunities to learn about and explore them. Moreover, people who emphasize self-direction values are more likely to reject negative stereotypes of outgroups because they prefer to make independent judgments based on their own experience. A positive correlation is expected for stimulation values because contact with outgroups provides opportunities for novelty and excitement. But, in the context of conflict between Jews and Arabs, the correlation should be weakened because outgroup contact may threaten another goal of stimulation values—enjoyable arousal.

3. Attributing importance to both Self-Transcendence value types (benevolence and universalism) correlates positively with readiness for contact. The most positive correlation among all ten value types is for universalism values because they emphasize understanding, accepting, and showing concern for the welfare of *all* human beings. This value type, with its goal of tolerance and acceptance even of those with different ideas and life styles, is most relevant to outgroup contact. A positive correlation is expected for benevolence values because they also emphasize concern for others. But benevolence values are mainly expressed in everyday relations with close others, not with outgroups. This should weaken the correlation, especially because the Jewish–Arab conflict makes group boundaries salient.

4. We expected correlations near zero for the Self-Enhancement value types (power and achievement) and for hedonism. Social contact is relevant to power values both positively and negatively. Contact may provide members of a dominant group opportunities to exercise power and experience superiority over minorities of inferior status. But accepting minorities into society may endanger the current dominance hierarchy, especially if the minority is struggling to gain status. The correlation will depend on the relative strength of these opposing processes. If they are balanced, it may be near zero. Social contact with Arabs is not especially relevant to attaining the goals of achievement values, hence no correlation is expected. This is because, in Israel, the Arab minority has little impact in the occupational and educational arenas where members of dominant group compete for success and recognition (Chemansky, Guvran, & Hmaisi, 1984; Graham-Brown, 1984). Because outgroup contact is not relevant to the goals of hedonism, no correlation is expected.

When the findings reported by Rokeach (1973) are classified according to our value types, the directions of the correlations are compatible with these hypotheses, with the exception of hedonism. This set of hypotheses also forms an integrated whole that reflects the structure of relations among value types. The predicted correlations are progressively less positive as one moves in both directions around the circle from universalism (most positive) to tradition (most negative) values.

The order of associations implied by the set of hypotheses forms the usual sinusoid curve, but this curve is not symmetrical. For example, an especially sharp drop in correlations is expected from universalism to benevolence, despite the fact that these are adjacent types in the structural circle. This reflects the special relevance to the behavior of outgroup social contact of tolerance for *all* (universalism) in contrast to concern for one's ingroup (benevolence).

The types predicted to have the most and the least positive associations with readiness for outgroup social contact are not located in polar opposition in the theoretical structure of value relations. This reflects the most critical motivational issue related to this behavior in this setting—tolerance versus intolerance. On this issue, universalism and tradition are the most opposed. The prototypical opposition of universalism is with power. The issue central to this opposition, protecting the interests of others (universalism) versus exploiting them for personal advantage (power), is less critically relevant here.

Jewish public school teachers ($n = 151$), in Grades 6 through 10, from schools around the country, provided the data to test these hypotheses. They first completed the 56-item value survey. Subsequently, they indicated their readiness, on a 5-point willingness scale, for 7 types of contact with Israeli Arabs: (1) occasional superficial social contact; (2) business or trade relations; (3) living in the same neighborhood; (4) inviting as a guest to your home; (5) having as a close friend; (6) having as a next-door neighbor; (7) having your children play together. Responses to these items were summed to form an overall index (alpha = .95).

The correlations between value priorities and readiness for social contact are shown in Fig. 1.4.[7] The types of values hypothesized to have negative correlations (tradition, conformity, security), and those hypothesized to have positive correlations (universalism and self-direction), were correlated as expected ($p < .01$). The correlations for the two types hypothesized to have weaker positive correlations (benevolence and stimulation) were in the expected direction, but not reliably different from zero. Finally, as hypothesized, the correlation for universalism was most positive and that for tradition most negative.

The order of correlations matched that specified by the integrated hypothesis, as described by a sinusoid curve, with only a slight deviation for achievement. As expected, given their order in the integrated hypothesis, the correlations for power, achievement, and hedonism were close to zero. Together, the seven value types hypothesized to affect readiness for outgroup social contact explained a substantial 39% of the variance in the readiness of Israeli Jewish teachers for contact with Arabs.

Another way to look at these data is to consider the combined effects on readiness for outgroup social contact of the two value types hypothesized to be most relevant and most in conflict in this setting—universalism and tradition. for this purpose, we split the sample at the median on each of these value types. We

---

[7]Differential use of the response scale for values was controlled by standardizing value ratings within individuals.

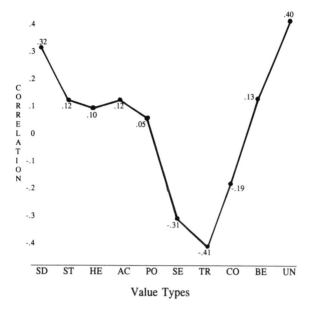

FIG. 1.4.   Correlations of the value priorities of Israeli Jewish teachers with their readiness for social contact with Israeli Arabs.

then compared the readiness for contact of the four subsamples formed by the 2 (universalism: high/low) × 2 (tradition: high/low) cross-classification. The two-way analysis of variance yielded significant main effects for universalism and tradition (F (1,130df) = 21.57 and 15.65, respectively, p <.001), but no interaction. Table 1.6 shows the means for the four subsamples.

The high universalism–low tradition subsample exhibited substantially more readiness for outgroup contact than the low universalism–high tradition subsample (M = 3.98 vs. 2.31). The other two subsamples, whose members were expected to experience value conflict in the face of outgroup contact, showed intermediate levels of readiness. Whereas universalism and tradition values are strongly opposed with regard to the motivation of critical relevance in this setting, they are relatively independent with regard to the broader motivations they express, as described in Table 1.1 and illustrated graphically in Fig. 1.1. This independence is reflected in the almost equal numbers of respondents found in each of the four subsamples in Table 1.6.

Here, I cannot fully discuss the hypotheses and results of parallel studies of the readiness of Christian Arab and Muslim Arab minority groups for social contact with Jews. However, two aspects of these studies are worth mentioning because they highlight points that are crucial when relating value systems to behavior. First, four of the nine hypotheses that we generated for the minority groups differed from those generated for the Jewish group. Second, the set of

TABLE 1.6
Mean Readiness of Israeli Jews for Outgroup Contact With Israeli Arabs as a Function of the Importance of Universalism and Tradition Values

		TRADITION	
		Low	High
UNIVERSALISM	Low	3.01a* (N = 34)	2.31 (N = 37)
	High	3.98 (N = 34)	2.94 (N = 32)

Note. *Response scale: 1 = Not at all willing; 5 = Definitely willing.

hypotheses for the minority groups did not follow the usual order around the value circle.

These differences point to the necessity of analyzing the specific context in which values are expressed or pursued in order to make sense of value–behavior relations. The differences in the hypotheses reflected the different significance of contact for minority and dominant groups, as integration or as assimilation into the larger society, or as acceptance of minorities as full citizens. Clearly, the different meanings of social contact affect its implications for value expression. Moreover, the deviations of the pattern of predicted correlations suggest that the sociopolitical context of Arab minorities in Israel has modified the usual rein-forcement contingencies that link individual value attainment to action in social life. When the order of associations does not correspond to the order implied by the theory of the structure of value relations, it is likely that the "psycho-logic" of conflicts and compatibilities among values is being distorted by externally im-posed social constraints.

For example, for the Israeli Muslim Arab minority, in contrast to the dominant Jewish group, outgroup social contact is relevant to the goal of achievement values—success according to prevailing social standards. The arena for most social achievement in Israel, even for minority group members, is the larger societal world of work in which contact with outgroup members is required. Although minority group members might wish to pursue economic or academic success within their ingroup, there are few opportunities to do so. There is no separate Israeli Arab economy and no Arab university. Hence, in order to demon-strate high levels of competence and success, Arabs are almost entirely con-strained to obtain higher economic and educational positions by active immer-sion in the institutions of the larger society (Smooha, 1984).

The foregoing analysis led to the hypothesis that an emphasis on achievement values correlates positively with readiness for outgroup contact among Israeli

Muslim Arabs. The combination of this hypothesis with an hypothesized positive correlation for benevolence values violates the order of associations implied by the prototypical structure of value relations. Yet, both these hypotheses were confirmed. This observed pattern of associations reflects the unusual organization of social reinforcements to which a weak minority group that seeks to preserve its uniqueness is exposed.

CONCLUSIONS

This chapter began by identifying three problems in past research on the relations of values to other variables: (1) use of unreliable single-item indexes of value importance; (2) use of value lists that fail to cover the full range of motivations expressed in values that are likely to influence behavior; (3) failure to view value systems as integrated wholes with coherent relations to other variables that entail tradeoffs among competing value priorities. I conclude by summarizing the responses to these problems that are provided by the current approach.

The three studies discussed here demonstrate that using priorities for value types rather for than single values permits consistent, theory-based prediction of behavior. When the analyses reported here for the indexes of value types are performed with single values, a much less lucid picture emerges in each study. Of course, many single values do show significant associations with behavior in the directions hypothesized for the value types they represent. However, exactly the pattern expected with unreliable indicators is observed: nonsignificant associations in the predicted as well as the reverse direction for single values from these same types, and a few significant associations for single values from types expected to be unrelated to the behavior.

The same could be demonstrated for the relations of values with attitudinal variables (e.g., environmental attitudes—Grunert & Juhl, 1991) and with background variables (e.g., age—Schwartz, 1992). This gain over single values reflects two advantages of the indexes of value types. First, as multiple-item indicators, they are more reliable than single values. Second, as sets of value items that share a core of meaning across individuals and cultures, their shared variance is a more valid measure of specifiable motivational goals. In contrast, single values are likely to have idiosyncratic meanings.

Use of the full set of value types also offers considerable—though not complete—protection against the second problem identified, overlooking values that are important for understanding behaviors or attitudes of interest. When researchers in various countries added values that they judged to be missing from the survey, these values emerged empirically as exemplars of the existing value types (Schwartz & Sagiv, 1995). It may well be useful to add values of special relevance when studying a particular topic, but the ten value types probably cover most, if not all, the broad types of motivation that are relevant.

Popular instruments currently used to study values, attitudes, and behavior are considerably more problematic. It is possible to form indexes for value types from the items in the Rokeach survey, for example (Schwartz & Bilsky, 1987). These indexes are less well-defined, however, and the coverage is less broad because power and tradition values are omitted. The List of Values (Kahle, 1983) uses single items to measure nine values, and it omits universalism, tradition, and conformity values.[8] These are important types to miss, as evidenced by their substantial relations to behavior in the studies discussed here.

With regard to the third problem, conceptualizing value types as forming a structure that relates as an integrated whole to other variables promotes systematic theory building and testing rather than ad hoc interpretation. The first step required is a close analysis of the consequences of a behavior or attitude for the expression or attainment of the motivational goals of the value types, leading to the identification of the most relevant type. Once this is done, the structure of value types facilitates the generation of hypotheses for the remaining types. With such an approach, the relative sizes of associations of the types are informative, not only their statistical significance. Indeed, even near zero associations provide meaningful evidence regarding the systematic nature of relations of values with an attitude or behavior, because they help to corroborate the coherent pattern of associations with the whole structure of values.

The data reported in all three examples in the current chapter largely followed the sinusoid curves implied by the structure of value systems. True sine curve patterns were not found, however, nor should they be expected. As noted, the specific relevance (e.g., power in the cooperation study) or irrelevance (e.g., hedonism in the outgroup contact study) of each value type to the behavior in question is likely to produce asymmetries in the curve. The order of associations is ordinarily, preserved, however. If it is not, as with the Israeli Muslim Arabs in the outgroup contact study, distortions in the patterns of reinforcement typical of human social relations should be sought.

Finally, viewing value types as an integrated system fits the conception that attitudes and behavior are guided by tradeoffs among relevant competing values (Rokeach, 1973; Schwartz, 1992; Tetlock, 1986). The set of hypotheses typically predicts both positive and negative associations, because the structure of relations among value types is based on oppositions between motivational goals that tend to be mutually exclusive. This chapter calls upon researchers into behavior and attitudes to take competition between the relatively enduring systems of individuals' value priorities into account. The promise of this approach has been described here. It should now face the test of extensive research and the inevitable corrections that will bring.

---

[8]Another problem with the List of Values (LOV) is that 5 of its 9 items are values with cross-culturally inconsistent meanings (Schwartz & Sagiv, 1995). A test of the validity of the LOV in five economically advanced nations rejected the cross-cultural comparability of its items (Grunert, Grunert, & Kristensen, in press).

ACKNOWLEDGMENTS

The research reported here was supported by grant 187/92 from the Basic Research Foundation (Israel Academy of Sciences and Humanities) and by a grant from the Israel Foundations Trustees, and by the Leon and Clara Sznajderman Chair in Psychology.

REFERENCES

Alwin, D. F. (1984). Trends in parental socialization values: Detroit, 1958–1983. *American Journal of Sociology, 90,* 359–382.

Arian, A. (1989). *Politics in Israel.* Chatham, NJ: Chatham House.

Arian, A., & Shamir, M. (1990). *The elections in Israel: 1988.* Boulder, CO: Westview Press.

Campbell, A., Converse, P. E., Miller, W. E., & Stokes, D. E. (1960). *The American voter.* New York: Wiley.

Chemansky, D., Guvran, R., & Hmaisi, R. (1984). Employment potential for university graduates in Arab towns in Israel. In M. Meir-Brodniz, & D. Chemansky, (Eds.), *Economic development in the Israeli Arab sector.* Haifa: The Technion.

Furnham, A. (1984). Personality and values. *Personality and individual differences, 5,* 483–485.

Graham-Brown, S. (1984). *Education, repression and liberation: Palestinians.* London: World University Service.

Greenstein, T. N. (1976). Behavior change through value self-confrontation: A field experiment. *Journal of Personality and Social Psychology, 34,* 254–262.

Grunert, S. C., Grunert, K. G., & Kristensen, K. (in press). On a method for estimating the cross-cultural validity of measurement instruments: The case of measuring consumer values by the List of Values LOV. *Recherches et Applications en Marketing.*

Grunert, S. C., & Juhl, H. J. (1991). *Values, environmental attitudes, and buying behaviour of organic foods: Their relationships in a sample of Danish teachers* (Working paper, Series H No. 60). Aarhus: The Aarhus School of Business, Department of Information Science.

Guttman, L. (1968). A general nonmetric technique for finding the smallest coordinate space for a configuration of points. *Psychometrica, 33,* 469–506.

Himmelweit, H. T., Humphreys, P., Jaeger, M., & Katz, M. (1981). How voters decide. *European monographs in social psychology, Vol. 27.* New York: Academic Press.

Janda, J. (1980). *Political parties.* Glencoe, IL: Free Press.

Kahle, L. R. (Ed.). (1983). *Social values and social change: Adaptation to life in America.* New York: Praeger.

Kinder, D. R., & Sears, D. O. (1985). Public opinion and political action. In G. Lindzey & E. Aronson (Eds.), *Handbook of social psychology, Vol. 2* (pp. 659–741). New York: Random House.

Klecka, W. R. (1980). *Discriminant analysis.* Beverly Hills, CA: Sage.

Kluckhohn, C. (1951). Values and value-orientations in the theory of action: An exploration in definition and classification. In T. Parsons & E. Shils (Eds.), *Toward a general theory of action* (pp.388–433). Cambridge, MA: Harvard University Press.

Liebman, C. S., & Don-Yehiya, E. (1984). *Religion and politics in Israel.* Bloomington: Indiana University Press.

Lipset, S. M., & Rokkan, S. (1967). *Party systems and voter alignments.* London: Free Press.

Mayton, D. M. II, & Furnham, A. (1994). Values, world peace, and political activism. *Journal of Social Issues, 50,*

Messick, D. M., & McClintock, C. G. (1968). Motivational basis of choice in experimental games. *Journal of Experimental Social Psychology, 4,* 1–25.

Natan, L. (1993). *Hashpa'at conflict beyn kvutzati, motivatziot hevratiot u'kdimuyot arachim al shituf p'ula b'dilemmot hevratiot toch-kvutzatiot* [The influence of intergroup conflict, social motivations, and value priorities on cooperation in within-group social dilemmas]. Unpublished master's thesis, The Hebrew University of Jerusalem.

Pruitt, D. G. (1967). Reward structure and cooperation: The decomposed prisoner's dilemma. *Journal of Personality and Social Psychology, 14,* 21–27.

Rokeach, M. (1973). *The nature of human values.* New York: Free Press.

Sagiv, L., & Schwartz, S. H. (1995). Value priorities and readiness for out-group social contact. *Journal of Personality and Social Psychology, 69,* 437–448.

Schwartz, S. H. (1992). Universals in the content and structure of values: Theoretical advances and empirical tests in 20 countries. In M. Zanna (Ed.), *Advances in experimental social psychology, Vol. 25* (pp. 1–65). Orlando, FL: Academic Press.

Schwartz, S. H. (1994). Are there universal aspects in the structure and contents of human values? *Journal of Social Issues, 50,* 19–45.

Schwartz, S. H., & Bilsky, W. (1987). Toward a psychological structure of human values. *Journal of Personality and Social Psychology, 53,* 550–562.

Schwartz, S. H., & Huismans, S. (1995). Value priorities and religiosity in four Western religions. *Social Psychology Quarterly, 58,* 88–107.

Schwartz, S. H., & Sagiv, L. (1995). Identifying culture-specifics in the content and structure of values. *Journal of Cross-Cultural Psychology, 26,* 92–116.

Sears, D. O. (1987). Political psychology. *Annual Review of Psychology, 38,* 229–255.

Seliger, M. (1975). *Ideology and politics.* London: Allen & Unwin.

Smooha, S. (1984). *The orientation and politicization of the Arab minority in Israel.* Haifa, Israel: The Jewish-Arab Center, University of Haifa.

Tetlock, P. E. (1986). A value pluralism model of ideological reasoning. *Journal of Personality and Social Psychology, 50,* 819–827.

Wulff, D. W. (1991). *Psychology of religion: Classic and contemporary view.* New York: Wiley.

2 Revising the Value Pluralism Model: Incorporating Social Content and Context Postulates

Philip E. Tetlock
The Ohio State University

Randall S. Peterson
Northwestern University

Jennifer S. Lerner
University of California, Berkeley

One of life's painful truisms is that difficult choices are unavoidable. This truism holds up pretty well whether we are talking about managing individual lives or complex social systems. At the individual level, we run into a multitude of familiar value trade-offs: obligations to others versus self-interest, self-interest now (consumption) versus self-interest later (savings), autonomy versus intimacy, work versus family versus leisure, and the common dilemma of accountability to conflicting constituencies (in order to please this person or reference group, I must anger this other one). At a societal level, we confront an equally daunting battery of trade-offs. In political economy, there is the classic tension between social equality and economic efficiency. In international relations, there are the contradictory goals of deterrence (be strong enough to resist exploitation) and reassurance (don't be so intimidating that you scare the other side into preemptively attacking you). The list is potentially endless, but we have already made our point: the world can be a very dissonant place. It is impossible to arrange our lives and our values to escape trade-offs completely.

The original value pluralism model of ideological reasoning was an effort to explain how people cope with a wide array of personal and political value trade-offs. We have five objectives in this chapter. First, we present the early version of the value pluralism model and sketch some experimental and archival studies to test the predictions of that model. Second, we note some conceptual and empirical problems with the early value pluralism model. Third, we revise the value pluralism model in two key respects: the addition of the social content and context postulates. The social content postulate asserts that how people cope with value conflict depends on the "social content" of the colliding values—in particular, whether "secular values" have been pitted against "sacred ones." The social context postulate asserts that how people cope with value conflict depends on the social context of decision making—in particular, whether people are accountable for their decisions and, if so, in what ways they are accountable. These postulates also identify a variety of coping strategies that although little studied in the experimental literature, have received considerable attention in political science, law, and moral philosophy—coping strategies such as concealment and obfuscation of taboo trade-offs, buckpassing and procrastination to avoid blame for imposing losses on others, and oppositional posturing to incite resentment toward those who must make trade-offs. Fourth, we examine the subtle question of whether it is possible to have a value-free value pluralism model. We urge social psychologists to resist the temptation to assume that integratively complex trade-off reasoning is either cognitively or morally superior to alternative, simpler, strategies of dodging, ducking, denying and redefining value conflict. Finally, we close by sketching some boundary conditions on the applicability of both the VPM and some of its major theoretical competitors.

THE ORIGINAL VALUE PLURALISM MODEL

Tetlock (1984, 1986) initially proposed the value pluralism model of ideological reasoning to solve a long-standing puzzle in political psychology: namely, "Why are some people and ideological groups much more willing than others to acknowledge that the world is indeed a dissonant place, that cherished values often come into conflict?" The model consisted of three interrelated sets of propositions:

1. Underlying all political belief systems are core or terminal values (Lane, 1973; Rokeach, 1973, 1979) that specify what the ultimate goals of public policy should be (e.g., economic efficiency, social equality, individual freedom, crime control, national security, racial purity, and so on). Values are the backstops of belief systems. When we press people to justify their political preferences, all inquiry ultimately terminates in values that people find it ridiculous to justify any further. Anti-abortion partisans consider "because life is sacred" a self-explanatory explanation for their position just as pro-choice partisans consider "women's liberty" a self-justifying justification for their position.

2. Acknowledging conflict among core values is aversive for three mutually reinforcing reasons. First, it is cognitively costly to make the difficult interdimensional (apples–oranges) comparisons required in trade-off judgments (Einhorn & Hogarth, 1981). Most people do not have carefully calibrated subjective scales that lend themselves to judgments of the form: What loss of liberty would I accept to achieve this increment in public safety? Second, value conflict is emotionally painful (cf. Festinger, 1957). Most people find it dissonant to acknowledge to themselves that they have sacrificed one important value for

another. The more important the value, the greater the potential for anticipatory regret, in which people ponder what would have happened in the counterfactual world in which they chose the "other path." Third, trade-offs are politically embarrassing. Critics can always accuse us of having chosen the wrong path, an especially tempting accusation given the psychophysical tendency for losses on the value we have sacrificed to loom larger than gains on the value we have chosen (Kahneman & Tversky, 1979). Politicians quite rightly see early career changes in their future when they publicly endorse trade-offs that offend substantial segments of the electorate.

3 Given these formidable obstacles, explicit trade-off reasoning should be both difficult and stressful. Whenever feasible, people should prefer modes of resolving value conflict that are simple and require minimal effort. These simple modes of inconsistency reduction are feasible when the conflicting values activated by a policy choice are of markedly unequal strength and value conflict is therefore weak (cf. Abelson, 1959). Under these conditions, the model hypothesizes that people will rely on the simplest of all the cognitive coping strategies: denial and bolstering. They will downplay the weaker value and they will exaggerate the stronger value (a process that dissonance theorists called spreading of the alternatives—Festinger, 1964). As value conflict intensifies, as increasingly important values come increasingly clearly into conflict, people turn to increasingly complex strategies. Initially they shift from denial and bolstering (which allow them to choose on the basis of only one value) to lexicographic strategies (which allow them to screen options on the most important value, eliminating all that do not pass some threshold, and then rely on secondary values to rank the remaining options). On the 7-point integrative complexity continuum (Tetlock, 1986), we observe a progression from the lowest possible level of complexity (scale level 1) in which decision-making is dominated by a solitary value to an intermediate level of complexity (evaluative differentiation) in which people use two or more values to screen options (scale level 3). Lexicographic strategies are still, however, strictly intradimensional decision rules. Decision-makers need only consider one value dimension at a time, thereby eliminating the need for awkward interdimensional comparisons of the form "how much of value x am I willing to give up for this much of value y?" (Cf. Payne et al. 1992; Tversky, 1971.)[1] When value conflict is most intense—when the conflicting values are

---

[1]Lexicographic strategies such as elimination-by-aspects short-circuit the cognitive confusion and emotional angst of complex trade-off reasoning. As long as one has a clear value hierarchy that specifies when value A should trump B and when B should trump C, one can screen options one value at a time until only one option remains. Of course, the closer to equally important values become in one's hierarchy and in the minds of evaluative observers, the more difficult it becomes to use lexicographic strategies. People become increasingly unsure which value is more important in this or that context. As soon as one starts eliminating options using one evaluative standard, one is tempted (or pressured) to re-include them in the option set using another evaluative standard. In principle, one could be trapped in the throes of Hamlet-like ambivalence forever.

not only important, but equally important and equally activated by issue cues, people turn to "conceptually integrated" strategies that specify when, why, and to what degree, one value should prevail over another (scale level 5). People make interdimensional comparisons (How much clean air am I willing to give up for this amount of economic growth?) and try to understand why reasonable people (not just fools and scoundrels) might attach different weights to the same values. Finally, at the highest levels of integrative complexity (scale level 7), we observe not only explicit trade-off reasoning, but self-conscious attempts to think about value conflict in a broader historical, institutional or systemic context. What counts as a reasonable trade-off at one time or in one setting may look patently unreasonable at other times or in other settings.

Figure 1 summarizes the key predictions of the early value pluralism model. The model leads us to expect that "integratively complex" trade-off reasoning is more likely among advocates of pluralistic ideologies—who acknowledge conflicts among core values—than among advocates of monistic ideologies—who insist that core values are mutually reinforcing. For instance, in domestic policy debates, liberals and social democrats are most committed to the often conflicting values of social equality and economic efficiency (cf. Mitchell, Tetlock, Mellers, & Ordonez, 1993). They are therefore under the greatest psychological pressure to take into account the effects of policy proposals on both values as well as to develop criteria for appropriate compromises between the two values—compromises that may take different forms in different economic and political situations. As an example of a highly integratively complex response to value conflict, we paraphrase the comments of a social democratic politician in Sweden who recently observed that a progressive tax code that struck a "reasonable" balance between equality and efficiency in the 1960s looks decidedly "unreasonable" in the 1990s when workers prefer generous unemployment benefits to lowest-paying jobs, firms move plants to lower-tax countries and black

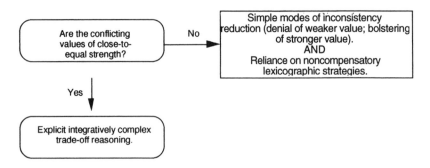

FIG. 2.1.   Original value pluralism model of ideological reasoning.

markets in professional services proliferate. In his view, it is not enough to recognize a trade-off; one must recognize that there is no single equilibrium solution to equality-efficiency trade-offs. To admirers, such integratively complex trade-off reasoning is flexible, multidimensional and sophisticated; to detractors, it is unprincipled, weak, and vacillating.

In brief, the value pluralism of an ideology determines how often people experience value conflicts and how often they resort to complex strategies to cope with such conflicts. This value pluralism model had several noteworthy advantages over earlier formulations of the links between cognitive style and political ideology. As we shall soon see, the model fit existing data better than did its two major theoretical rivals: authoritarian personality theory (Adorno et al., 1950) and the ideologue hypothesis (Rokeach, 1960; Shils, 1956). And it led to novel and testable predictions, some of which were subsequently supported. But the model had serious limitations. Most notably, it underestimated the ingenuity with which both individuals and institutions cope with value conflict.

Empirical Work on Value Pluralism

Over the last twenty years, we have carried out a series of content analytic studies of the policy statements of various political elites, including United States Senators, Supreme Court justices, British Parliamentarians, members of the Soviet Politburo and others. One goal of this research program was to explore the distribution of reasoning styles across the political spectrum. Our earliest studies yielded results quite consistent with authoritarian personality theory (or the rigidity-of-the-right hypothesis). This school of thought posits a special affinity between rigid, self-righteous, and defensive modes of thinking and right-wing political perspectives. Conservative political views supposedly serve ego-defensive functions that permit people to project deeply-repressed hostility toward parents onto socially acceptable scapegoats such as the poor, minorities, and foreign foes. Challenges to this ego-defensive belief structure provoke not rethinking of basic assumptions, but rather anger, intolerance, and resentment (Altemeyer, 1981). In three different samples of U.S. Senators over a thirty year period (1950–1982), we found that conservatives made less integratively complex policy statements (statements that acknowledged the legitimacy of counterarguments and attempted to strike reasonable balances) than did their moderate and liberal counterparts. This result held up after controlling for a variety of possible confounding variables, including age, seniority, and education (Tetlock, 1981b, 1983; Tetlock Micheletti, & Hannum, 1984).

These studies of U.S. Senators were, however, far from the last word on the cognitive style–political ideology relationship. The first problem stemmed from the confounding effects of political role and the reliance on public policy statements. In most of the Congressional sessions studied, conservatives were an out-of-power minority in Congress. The lower integrative complexity of conservative policy statements may have reflected a rhetorical strategy that legislative minorities use to rally opposition to the government (sharp, unqualified criticism—a "give-em-hell" approach). The greater integrative complexity of liberals and moderates may have reflected a rhetorical strategy that dominant legislative coalitions use to justify policies that they are enacting (complex rhetoric that weighs the pros and cons of competing proposals in order to take into account the interests of diverse constituencies). This counter-interpretation gains some credence from the finding that when conservatives held majority control of the Senate and the Presidency, the differences in cognitive style between liberals and conservatives diminished sharply (Tetlock, Hannum, and Micheletti, 1984).[2]

The second complication stemmed from the limited ideological range of positions represented in the U.S. Senate. A defender of the ideologue hypothesis could argue that there simply were not enough representatives of the ideological left to provide a fair test of the hypothesis. In contrast to many advanced industrialized societies, there was no influential socialist or communist party in the United States.

Tetlock (1984) provided a stronger test of the cognitive style–political ideology relationship than did the earlier work on senators. The data consisted of confidential interviews that the political scientist Robert Putnam conducted with 93 members of the British House of Commons. There was good reason to believe that strategic impression management motives exerted much less influence on what politicians said in this setting than in more public settings such as press conferences or in Parliament. The politicians were willing to criticize their own party and even themselves on numerous occasions in these in-depth discussions. In addition, the British politicians represented a wider range of ideological positions than existed in the U.S. Senate. The British MPs included extreme socialists who favored nationalizing all major industries and moderate socialists who favored limited public control of major industries as well as moderate and extreme conservatives.

Complexity peaked somewhat left of center. Moderate socialists were the most integratively complex trade-off reasoners, followed by moderate conservatives, who were, in turn, more complex than extreme socialists and extreme conservatives. Although these latter two groups were least similar in the content of their political beliefs, they were most similar in the integrative complexity of their world view. These relationships between political ideology and integrative complexity remained significant after controlling for a variety of background

---

[2]This narrowing of ideological differences was due however to a sharp drop in the integrative complexity of liberals, not to a rise in complexity among conservatives. Out-of-power liberals look like out-of-power conservatives from a cognitive style perspective but in-power liberals remain more integratively complex than in-power conservatives. A purely impression management explanation is hard pressed to explain this asymmetry.

variables as well as belief and attitudinal variables assessed in the Putnam research.

In some respects, these results vindicate the ideologue hypothesis which posits that, although extremists of the left and right may disagree on almost everything, they exhibit remarkably similar styles of thinking, tending to be contemptuous of other points of view, to subscribe to simplistic views of the causes of societal problems, and to be slow to acknowledge disconfirming evidence. In the British House of Commons, extremists of the left and right were very similar to each other in integrative complexity but very different from politicians closer to the center of the political spectrum. The ideologue hypothesis is, however, inadequate as an explanatory framework. It fails to explain why the point of maximum integrative complexity is consistently displaced to the left of center. The ideologue hypothesis is merely descriptive. It simply asserts that as one departs from an ill-defined political center of gravity, one is increasingly prone to view issues in simple, dichotomous terms. But what determines where this mysterious midpoint lies? Why are liberals and moderate socialists apparently closer to it than conservatives? Why was it necessary to go as far out to the political left as radical socialists to observe a marked decline in integrative complexity?

These objections convinced us that both the rigidity-of-the-right and ideologue hypotheses provided inadequate explanations of linkages between cognitive style and political ideology. The value pluralism model offered an alternative to these static and one-dimensional analyses—an alternative in two key respects. First, the value pluralism model does not force multidimensional belief systems onto a unidimensional left–right measurement scale.[3] It acknowledges that people try to promote many values through political action—values that do not correlate nearly as highly as one would expect if one assumed that people structured their thought along conventional ideological lines. It is not hard, for

---

[3]Tetlock and Boettger (1989) have noted the bizarre consequences of trying to map multidimensional political figures onto a unidimensional scale. They note that, in the final years of the former Soviet Union (1984–1991), reformist Soviet politicians—who advocated political liberalization and economic decentralization—were more integratively complex than traditionalists who opposed these measures. One could construe this finding as support for the ideologue hypothesis. Traditionalists, perhaps, represent the extreme left, which resisted introducing market incentives into the rigidly centrally planned Soviet economy; reformers, perhaps, represent the moderate left, which was willing to compromise Marxist-Leninist principles in order to stimulate efficiency and initiative. As one moves toward the center from the rigid-state-control left, one discovers greater integrative complexity. Alternatively, one could construe the same finding as support for the rigidity-of-the-right hypothesis. Soviet traditionalists, like American conservatives, are more likely to harbor deeply authoritarian commitments to traditional in-group symbols and to resent attempts to tamper with fundamental systemic values (e.g., the Protestant or socialist work ethic, law and order, free enterprise or central planning, support for free-world or progressive regimes abroad). As one moves from the center toward the right (more nationalistic forms of ideology), integrative complexity falls.

example, to identify people (including policy elites) who are liberal on social welfare policy but conservative on defense, conservative on welfare policy but liberal on defense, or conservative across the board except, say, on environmental protection and civil liberty issues. Researchers ignore this multidimensional variation in values at their peril. As we shall see when we discuss ideology-by-issue interactions, the relationships between integrative complexity and political ideology take different forms in different domains.

Second, in contrast to its theoretical rivals, which treat issue-to-issue variation in reasoning styles as random, the value pluralism model asserts that different issues "pull" or elicit complex reasoning from different ideological groups. By focusing on underlying cognitive processes that shaped policy reasoning, the VPM yields specific predictions concerning the forms that complexity–ideology relationships should take in different domains.

The VPM nicely fits early data which indicated that advocates of centrist and moderate left wing causes thought about policy issues in more integratively complex ways than did advocates of conservative causes. In this zone of the political spectrum, we were especially likely to find politicians who valued both social equality and economic efficiency, environmental protection and economic growth, crime control and civil liberties, and deterring Soviet expansion and maintaining good working relations with that country to preserve the peace. From the VPM perspective, the point of maximum integrative complexity was often "left-shifted" because that was the point of maximum value conflict, at least on many issues in that period of history.

The VPM also clarified how far one must go to the left or right for integrative complexity to decline: to the point where conflict between core values begins to diminish sharply. For example, in domestic policy debates in the United Kingdom of 1968, one would expect to find—and one actually does find—a sharp reduction in integrative complexity of reasoning as one moves from moderate socialists who placed nearly equal importance on economic efficiency and social equality to extreme socialists for whom concern for equality dominates concern for efficiency. Similarly, one would expect to find and does find a reduction in complexity of thought as one moves from moderate socialists to moderate conservatives (for whom economic efficiency is a dominant value) to extreme conservatives (for whom economic efficiency is the overwhelmingly dominant value).

The VPM is, however, tricky to test. We need to make assumptions about what values are important to people, the extent to which the world places values in conflict, and the extent to which people perceive values to be in conflict. The VPM becomes a thinly veiled tautology if we are allowed to make empirically convenient ad hoc assumptions about value importance and value conflict. It is trivially simple to "explain" any pattern of data if we proceed down that path.

We have, however, conducted laboratory studies that experimentally control, and archival studies that statistically control, for the influence of value conflict on cognitive style–political ideology relationships. For instance, Tetlock (1986) obtained two types of information from a non-elite (college student) sample: (a) subjects' rank order evaluations of the importance of 18 terminal values from the Rokeach Value Survey (values that included national security, natural beauty, economic prosperity, equality, and freedom); (b) subjects' support for six public policy positions and their thoughts on each issue (e.g., redistributive income policies, domestic CIA activities, defense spending). Each of these policy issues had been selected on the basis of careful pretest scaling data indicating that the issue clearly brought two values from the Rokeach Value Survey into conflict. For instance, the defense spending question was phrased so as to activate tension between the values of national security and economic prosperity. On five of six issues, people reported more integratively complex trade-off cognitions to the degree the policy domain activated conflicting values that people held to be both important in their value hierarchy and close to equally important. This study demonstrated that we should not assume certain ideological groups will always be more integratively complex than others. Although there are main effects, there is also lawful ideology-by-issue variation in complexity of thought. For example, liberals were more integratively complex about raising taxes to redistribute income to the poor (economic prosperity versus equality) but conservatives were more integratively complex about raising taxes to increase defense spending (national security versus prosperity) and violating civil liberties of suspected spies by wiretapping their phones (national security versus liberty). The complexity of one's reasoning in an issue domain is a function of the intensity of value conflict activated by that issue domain.

Several investigators have independently reported findings that reinforce this conclusion. Suedfeld, Bluck, Loewen, and Elkins (1994) show that patterns of value conflict help to explain individual variation in integrative complexity among student political activists of varying ideological loyalties. Suedfeld and Walbaum (1992) also show that intensity of value conflict predicts integrative complexity. Liberman and Chaiken (1991) combine Tesser's (1978) work on thought-induced attitude polarization with the VPM. They hypothesized and found that people develop more extreme attitudes toward a policy as a function of the time spent thinking about the policy, only when they are in a state of low value conflict (one of the activated values is much more important than the other). By contrast, people in a state of high value conflict tend to "depolarize" as a function of how long they think about the issue. The Liberman and Chaiken findings were not, however, completely consistent with VPM. The depolarization effect was somewhat weak and value conflict itself was a function only of differential value ranking and not of average value importance.

Shifting back to archival research, Tetlock, Armor, and Peterson (1994) tested the VPM by assessing both value priorities and integrative complexity in political debates over slavery in pre-Civil War America. With the advice of several historians, these investigators classified 32 prominent political figures of the 1850s into one of four distinct political positions: Radical Abolitionists, Free-Soil Republicans who tolerated slavery in the South but opposed its spread to new territories, Buchanan Democrats who supported Southern states' right to slaves and would permit slavery in new territories if local majorities so favored, and advocates of slavery who favored Southern secession if slavery were not recognized as a constitutionally protected property right. A functional relationship emerged between political ideology and integrative complexity in antebellum America that quite closely mirrored the relationship observed in the British House of Commons during the Prime Ministership of Harold Wilson. Again, integrative complexity peaked somewhat left of center. Integrative complexity was highest among Free-Soil Republicans, followed by Buchanan Democrats, with sharp declines in integrative complexity as we moved either leftward toward Radical Abolitionists or rightward toward fire-eater advocates of slavery. Integrative complexity was also a positive function of endorsing values widely regarded as in conflict in that historical period: especially property rights, state's rights, and domestic peace versus the threat of Southern slave power to free labor and democracy. Once again, value conflict and integrative complexity tracked each other (although there was substantial unexplained residual variance).[4]

THE REVISED VALUE PLURALISM MODEL

Notwithstanding the empirical support for the original value pluralism model, we became convinced that the original formulation was too simplistic. We reached this position for two reasons. First, integratively complex trade-off reasoning is a relatively rare cognitive phenomenon. It is common—in both experimental and archival studies—for 50% to 60% of statements coded for integrative complexity to receive the lowest possible score (1) which indicates a complete denial of ambiguity, uncertainty, or conflict. Although there are some individual difference exceptions, it is also common for less than 10% of thought-sample statements coded to manifest either implicit or explicit awareness of value trade-offs (scores of 4 or higher on a 7-point scale). From these observations, we can conclude

---

[4]In addition to the strong possibility that value conflict is not the only cause of integratively complex reasoning, there are several possible explanations for the unexplained variation. Some raise obvious methodological issues. We failed to measure all the conflicting values or our measures were imperfect. Other possibilities are more theoretically intriguing. The conceptual connections that people forge between abstract values and concrete policy are sometimes startling, at least to those who lack the historian's in-depth knowledge of particular ways of life. For instance, most 20th century observers are startled that "fire-eater" Southern politicians could defend slavery by invoking the values of liberty and equality. Surely those values "belong" to the other side, to the abolitionists. By and large, they do. But some fire-eaters argued (and apparently with great conviction) that restrictions on their freedom to own slaves outside the South violated their equality and liberty as citizens of the republic; after all, Northerners could move their "property" across state lines without fear of forfeiture or confiscation. The key theoretical point is that values are remarkably slippery social constructions that take on different meanings over time and across political cultures.

either that value conflict is a much less pervasive feature of the human condition than we asserted at the outset of this chapter or that people have invented a much wider range of strategies of coping with value conflict. Second, research developments in fields adjoining social psychology—behavioral decision theory, moral reasoning, public policy studies of legislators and government agencies—highlight alternative strategies of circumventing, concealing, and avoiding value trade-offs.

To be specific, whether one responds to value conflict in an integratively complex fashion depends on two classes of moderator variables not specified in the earlier formulation: (a) the social content of the colliding values (in particular, the meaning that people attach to competing values and the normative acceptability of trade-off reasoning); (b) the social context of decision-making (in particular, the types of accountability demands on decision-makers). These moderators influence coping responses to value conflict by affecting the strength of the cognitive, emotional and social-identity obstacles to complex trade-off reasoning identified in the original statement of the VPM. The social-content postulate of the revised value pluralism model reminds us that some value trade-offs are much more emotionally and morally wrenching than are others. Attaching a monetary value to a bottle of wine or house or the services of a gardener can be a cognitively demanding task but raises no questions about the morality of the judge (at least within this political culture); attaching monetary value to human life or familial obligations or national honor seriously undermines one's social identity or standing in the eyes of others (Schlenker, 1980). Proposals to exchange "sacred" values for secular ones (money, time, convenience, . . .) constitute taboo trade-offs and activate their own distinctive set of coping responses. They do so because even contemplating such trade-offs is normatively unacceptable—something to be condemned if one is an observer of the decision process and something to be concealed if one is the decision-maker.

The social-context postulate of the revised VPM reminds us that institutional–political accountability demands can dramatically lower or raise thresholds for complex trade-off reasoning. People do not make decisions in a social vacuum; they live and work in complex webs of accountability in which they frequently wonder "How will others react if I do this or that?" Depending on contextual cues, these accountability demands can either strengthen or weaken each of the hypothesized obstacles to trade-off reasoning. Some forms of accountability heighten concern for minimizing potential blame ("I don't want to think of myself as that type of person and I don't want others to think of me that way"), encouraging decision-avoidance tactics such as buckpassing and procrastination (Tetlock & Boettger, 1994). Other forms of accountability encourage demagoguery and sloganeering (Tetlock, 1981a), as when one is responsible not for making prudent long-term policy but rather for whipping up opposition to trade-offs among people with well-known prejudices and limited knowledge (e.g., mass publics in contemporary democracies). Still other forms of accountability encourage vigilant, self-critical analysis of options, as when one is accountable prior to making a decision to a knowledgeable audience with unknown views or high performance standards (Tetlock, 1983).

The Social-Content Postulate

There is an anti-content bias in much of cognitive psychology (cf. Cosmides, 1989). A good cognitive theory should be comprehensive; it should capture how people think across a wide range of content domains. The original value pluralism model was offered in this parsimonious and universalistic spirit, as an effort to explain when people deny or confront value trade-offs in general. By implication, the identity of the conflicting values was irrelevant. To paraphrase Gertrude Stein, a trade-off was a trade-off was a trade-off.

The social-content postulate backs off from that sweeping commitment. It acknowledges that how people think about trade-offs depends on what they are thinking about. In our political culture, people deem some trade-offs legitimate but reject other trade-offs as contemptible because they treat "sacred values"— life, liberty, justice, honor—as fungible into the "secular values" of money, time, and convenience (cf. Durkheim, 1925/1973). This resistance to cross-domain trade-offs is puzzling from a micro-economic perspective which reduces all values to a single utility metric, but not at all surprising within a value pluralism framework that stresses the qualitative diversity of reasons that people have for liking or disliking things. From the perspective of the value pluralism model, we should expect sharp resistance to reductionist attempts to translate all values onto a common scale (resistance that reminds us of Oscar Wilde's amusing (albeit unfair) definition of an economist as someone who knows the price of everything but the value of nothing). Under certain conditions, people are better thought of not as "intuitive economists" but rather as intuitive theologians who seek to shield sacred values from the universal solvent of money.

What accounts for the sharp resistance to the notion of a unified utility metric on which people weigh all conflicting values? In part, opposition is rooted in the old "incommensurability" problem. People find it cognitively difficult to make apples–oranges interdimensional comparisons. This explanation is, however, inadequate. Such comparisons are hard, but we implicitly or explicitly make them every time we go shopping, or decide not to go shopping. Moreover, we don't find it embarrassing or shameful to admit that we make trade-offs between money and the wine or meat or leisure time that we consume. It is not only acceptable to think in integratively complex trade-off terms about one's household budget; we expect, indeed require, secular-secular trade-offs of all competent, self-supporting adults in competitive market economies. Perhaps for this reason, examination of within-individual, cross-issue variation in integrative complexity often reveals that scores peak when people discuss their household budgets (Tetlock, unpublished data).

Opposition to reducing all values to a single utility or monetary metric runs deeper than mere "incommensurability"; it is rooted in the concept of "constitutive incommensurability" that plays an important role in both modern moral philosophy (Lukes, 1991, Raz, 1982; Williams, 1980) and in classic sociological theory (Durkheim, 1925/1973). The guiding idea is that our commitments to other people require us to deny that we can quantitatively compare the values of certain things. To transgress this normative boundary, to attach a monetary value to one's friendships or one's children or one's academic integrity, is to disqualify oneself from certain social roles, to demonstrate that one is not a true friend or parent or scholar. We run into "constitutive incommensurability" of values whenever treating values as commensurable subverts one or both of the values to be entered into the trade-off calculus. To compare is to destroy. To think about certain trade-offs is to weaken, corrupt, and degrade one's standing as a moral being. In Joseph Raz's words: ". . . it is impoverishing to compare the value of a marriage with an increase in salary. It diminishes one's potentiality as a human being to put a value on one's friendship in terms of improved living conditions." Durkheim (1925/1973) expressed the same sentiment in more sociological language when he observed that in both "primitive religious" and "advanced secular" societies, people ascribe a "transcendental quality" to the fundamental values of their social order. We should not be surprised, therefore, when sophisticated citizens of secular societies tenaciously resist treating sacred values as objects of utilitarian calculation. Their attitude is less one of market or political calculation than it is that of believers to their god, a stance of absolute faith that imposes an "aura" or "mysterious barrier" around social morality. This Durkheimian perspective leads us to expect that violations of sacred values will provoke both moral outrage and cries for punishment. Secular-sacred trade-offs are more than cognitively perplexing; they are deeply disturbing.

The revised value pluralism model treats constitutive incommensurability as a critical moderator of how people respond to value conflict. Confronted by constitutive incommensurability, people will adopt one of two stances, depending on whether they are cast in the role of actors (decision-makers) or observers (judges of decision-makers).

When resource scarcity compels people to make decisions that violate the normative ban on taboo trade-offs, people will make massive impression management efforts to conceal, obfuscate or redefine what they are doing (Calabresi & Bobbitt, 1978; Elster, 1992). Decision-makers will construct institutional buffers between themselves and evaluative observers—buffers that promote secrecy and anonymity (observe the decision-making practices of central banks, many regulatory agencies and, closer to home, affirmative action committees in universities).[5] Decision-makers will also resort to vague rhetorical appeals to shared

---

[5]People who are thrust into roles that require making tragic choices seek secrecy for good reason. The classic example is early demand for kidney dialysis. In 1961, as demand for dialysis soared, the

values that obscure the trade-offs being made. These rhetorical obfuscations—
"the Federal Reserve seeks to maximize long-term prosperity," "OSHA would
never put a price tag on life" or "the admissions committee believes that diversity
is excellence"—disguise the politically unpalatable fact that decision-makers are
prepared to trade off current jobs to contain future inflation, the loss of lives in
work-place accidents to reduce regulatory burdens on business, and the imposi-
tion of higher college admissions standards on some racial groups to compensate
for past and perhaps current discrimination. Our point is not, of course, that these
decision-makers are doing something immoral. The political merits of each
policy can be debated endlessly. Our point is that decision-makers do not like to
acknowledge—in private and especially in public—that they are making taboo
trade-offs. In many cases, to discuss the trade-off openly and honestly is to
commit political suicide.

The revised value pluralism model also predicts that people will resist induction into decision-making roles that require making forbidden trade-offs. Many
people will refuse to respond or will respond indignantly (what kind of person do
you think I am?). Respondents will even challenge the morality and integrity of
the interviewer (what kind of person would pose such a question?). Research on
the contingent valuation method of assessing the dollar value that people place on
public goods illustrates these reactions. When survey interviewers ask people
what amount of money would persuade them to accept more polluted lakes,
dirtier air, or the loss of an endangered species (Mitchell & Carson, 1989), half
or more of the respondents often refuse to state any amount, as though to attach
less than infinite value to such political objectives would be *prima facie* evidence
of immorality.

A recent exploratory study clarifies when trade-off questions spark indignation and punitive responses (Tetlock, unpublished data). Berkeley undergraduates were asked a series of questions that explored their willingness to treat
various values as fungible (possessing a dollar value). Although there were
ideological exceptions (Marxists at one end of the political continuum and libertarians at the other),[6] most people believed it was permissible and moral to buy

---

Seattle Artificial Kidney Center Admission and Policy Committee (otherwise known as the God
Committee) was charged with deciding which applicants would receive the treatment (and therefore
who would live or die). It does not take a lot of political imagination to realize that, no matter what
this committee did, its members should have been prepared for public vilification. When *Life*
magazine revealed that the committee's decision strategy included weighting factors such as sex of
the patient, marital status, number of dependents, income, net worth, emotional stability, educational
background, past performance, and future potential, there was an avalanche of criticism (Calabresi &
Bobbitt, 1978).

[6]Of the 90 participants in this research, we made special efforts to recruit 12 libertarians and 14
Marxists from Berkeley campus political organizations and responses to an attitude questionnaire.
Libertarians allowed the market to encroach into traditionally forbidden domains (surrogate mothers
for hire, payment for one's body organs and one's vote) whereas Marxists were inclined to ban the
market in traditionally permitted domains (the right to profit from the sale of one's property and
labor).

and sell most forms of labor and property, but that it was immoral to attach monetary value to human organs, human lives or basic rights of citizenship. For example, 90% of respondents had no objection to mutually consenting adults entering into contracts to perform such services as cooking, cleaning or painting, or to exchange tangible goods such as housing, clothing, or cars, but support plummeted close to zero when we asked whether it was acceptable to sell one's right to a jury trial or one's vote, or to offer for a fee to go to jail for someone else. The latter transactions fell in the category of "blocked exchanges" (Walzer, 1983). When we asked people for their reactions to possible trade-offs between money and traditionally fungible and non-fungible objects of exchange, we also found sharp, qualitative shifts in emotional and cognitive reactions. People experienced little emotional distress at the prospect of monetizing the skills of a gardener or the value of a house, but they were angered and indeed insulted by questions that explored monetizing organs, lives, and democratic rights ("what kind of person do you think I am?"). In addition to deep emotional distaste, people responded in a punitive attributional fashion to the posing of the question. They often assumed that the questioner must be of dubious moral character. We call this combination of emotional and cognitive reactions—anger, indignation and questioning the character of anyone who could possibly think that way—the "outrage response." We suspect that it is a defining feature of reactions to trade-offs that breach the secular–sacred divide.

In sum, there are some value–trade-off questions that we pay a penalty for even posing. These exploratory data forge a functionalist link between the actor and observer predictions of the social-content postulate: decision-makers (actors) conceal and obfuscate taboo trade-offs because they know that observers will judge them harshly for even contemplating such trade-offs.[7]

---

[7]In addition to the novel predictions noted in the text, the social content postulate of the revised VPM casts a new light on existing effects in the research literature. Consider, for instance, the endowment effect: the tendency for people to demand much more to give up an object than they would be willing to pay to acquire it. The effect is robust and replicable. Reviewing a series of elegant choice and exchange experiments, Kahneman, Knetsch, and Thaler (1991) show that people are often willing to pay only half as much for recently acquired objects as they demand as payment for giving up the same objects (a 2:1 ratio of willingness to accept/willing to pay). This effect generalizes across a wide range of consumer goods (lottery tickets, emblem mugs, pens, and so on) and holds up in even competitive market settings (as even the skeptical behavioral economist, Vernon Smith, 1994, concedes).

Whereas prospect theory traces the endowment effect to loss aversion and the psychophysics of the gain-loss function, the revised VPM traces the endowment effect to the tendency of people to view the objects that the experimenter transferred into their possession as gifts, with all the socio-emotional implications of gifts. In our culture, it is counternormative simply to cash in gifts. Doing so comes dangerously close to attaching a dollar value to the love or respect that the gift expresses. Subjects in endowment experiments may feel constrained by past normative experience from simply turning around and selling something that someone has given them.

This argument suggests that it should be possible to eliminate the endowment effect altogether by experimentally deactivating all norms pertaining to gifts and guaranteeing sellers complete anonym-

The Social-Context Postulate.   Although it is less pronounced than the anti-content bias, there has also been an anti-context bias in cognitive psychology. To be sure, cognitive theories often make strong predictions concerning how contextual cues influence judgment and choice (e.g., framing, priming). Nonetheless, the aspiration has been to identify fundamental laws of human thought (grounded in psychophysics or associative network models or schema theory) that hold true regardless of the context in which people happen to find themselves. The early value pluralism model followed in this universalistic spirit. The social-context postulate retreats from this commitment. It acknowledges that, if we want to understand how people respond to value conflict, we need to locate the decision-maker in a matrix of accountability relationships that strengthen or weaken the three motivational obstacles to trade-off reasoning: the desires to conserve cognitive effort, to protect self-esteem, and to avoid blame.

Research has thus far identified three distinctive ways in which accountability demands moderate responses to value conflict. One is by heightening decision-makers' concern for avoiding blame. If decision-makers believe that they will be blamed by one or another audience no matter what position they take on a trade-off problem, we should expect—following the Janis and Mann (1977) conflict model—that decision-makers will resort to the avoidance tactics of buckpassing (shift responsibility to others) and procrastination (delay decision-making).

The work of Tetlock and Boettger (1994) illustrates how accountability amplifies avoidance of trade-off decisions. The study simulated Food and Drug Administration decisions to admit prohibited drugs onto, or keep approved drugs on, the U.S. pharmaceuticals market. Researchers told subjects that the FDA had the power both to prevent the adoption of drugs and to remove drugs currently in use, and that they wanted subjects to role play FDA regulators whose task was to determine whether a particular anti-clotting drug (Carozile) should either be allowed onto the market (change the status quo) or be allowed to remain on the market (retain the status quo). They also told subjects about the likely risks and benefits of the drug: either no one, 100 people, or 300 people would be killed by side-effects, and either 300, 600, or 900 people would be saved. They then asked subjects to judge the permissibility of the drug under either total anonymity or public accountability. In particular, they assessed the degree of risk from the drug that subjects were willing to tolerate, the tendency to avoid blame by procrastinating or buckpassing, and the degree of conflict or ambivalence that people experienced in decision making through both rating scale and thought-protocol data.

The results revealed how aversive value conflict can be when one is publicly accountable for a decision that requires imposing a loss on one group in order to confer a greater benefit on another. There was a surge of interest in delaying the

---

ity (so they don't have to confront the imagined hurt stares of the experimenter whose gift they have so casually liquidated).

decision for a year (the maximum allowed) whenever subjects were publicly accountable for deciding whether to allow a currently banned drug that would save 300, 600, or 900 lives at the cost of either 100 or 300 lives. Decision-makers did not want to take responsibility for either side-effect casualties or for denying society the benefit of a drug that would save hundreds of lives. Caught in what they perceived to be a no-win political conflict, decision-makers tried to delay the day of reckoning, even though they had been told that the likelihood of finding a breakthrough drug without side-effects in the "permissible delayed-action period" was virtually zero.

Tetlock and Boettger (1994) also assessed the dependent variable of buckpassing. When people believed they had the option of referring the decision to someone else—in this case, a fictitious government agency known as the Agency for Cost Benefit Analysis—they seized upon the opportunity with alacrity. Again, we saw a surge of decision referrals among publicly accountable subjects contemplating admitting a drug that will kill some people but save even more. Subjects (especially integratively complex thinkers) were uncomfortable with both of the options confronting them: taking the responsibility for approving a drug that would kill some people or taking responsibility for rejecting a drug that would have a positive benefit to society as a whole. They sought to escape this discomfort by both procrastinating and buckpassing.

Dilemmas of this sort are by no means unusual; rather, they are the essence of political struggles over resources and entitlements. Given the well-established tendency for losses to loom larger than gains in value trade-offs (by a ratio of 2:1 in prospect theory, Kahneman & Tversky, 1979), it seems reasonable to hypothesize a strong motive among politicians to delay or redirect responsibility whenever decisions require imposing losses on well-defined constituencies (see also Beattie, Baron, & Spranca, 1994). In this political calculus, the friends one gains will be more than offset by the enemies one makes. It should not be surprising that buckpassing and procrastination are common documented patterns of coping among both legislators and regulatory agencies (cf. Wildavsky, 1978).

The second and third pathways of accountability effects alter the incentives and disincentives for integratively complex trade-off thinking. Decision-makers sometimes face accountability pressures that strongly discourage explicit trade-off reasoning; other times, decision-makers face the pressures that demand it. As noted earlier, Tetlock, Hannum & Micheletti (1984) argued from data on senatorial speeches that the role of minority or opposition party created the former set of incentives and the role of majority or governing party created the latter (see also Gruenfeld, 1995). Both the opposition and governing parties seek the approval of a relatively ill-informed audience (the mass public) but do so within radically different political constraints. The majority party must actually govern and is held responsible, rightly or wrongly, for the state of the nation. Accordingly, it has strong incentives to fashion prudent long-term policies that balance the interests of competing constituencies, never completely satisfying everyone and continually having to explain "On the one hand . . . on the other . . . " to each constituency that feels it has been denied its due. The opposition party is much less constrained. It can nurture various constituencies' grievances by engaging in simple rhetorical posturing that depicts the government as foolish, duplicitous, and immoral and that offers plenty of unconditional (and probably unrealistic) promises. It is possible, of course, for the opposition to become too demagogic and to lose credibility, but available evidence suggests that American politicians consider it an advantage to be on the integratively simple offensive (Tetlock, 1981a).

Experimental research makes a similar point about the power of different types of accountability to create incentives or disincentives for complex trade-off reasoning. Accountability manipulations motivate people to recognize trade-offs only when we experimentally foreclose simple strategies of coping with accountability such as "telling people what they want to hear" (the acceptability heuristic). When people are accountable to an audience with known political views, liberal or conservative, they often adjust their opinions in the direction of the audience but show no more awareness of counterarguments or trade-offs. By contrast, when people are accountable to an audience with unknown views or to audiences with conflicting views, there is no simple solution to the accountability predicament and people respond with "pre-emptive self-criticism". In effect, they acknowledge trade-offs and legitimate objections that reasonable critics might raise (cf. Tetlock, 1983; Tetlock, Skitka, & Boettger, 1989).

Taken together, archival work on the effects of political roles and experimental work on accountability sharply qualify the original VPM prediction that decision-makers respond to clear conflicts between important values in an integratively complex trade-off fashion; the revised VPM asserts that complex trade-off reasoning will be activated only when decision-makers are accountable to an audience that cannot be appeased by simple stratagems such as oppositional posturing, ingratiation or attitude shifting. These simple tactics cease to be viable when we are accountable for the long-term consequences of the decisions we make (as occurs when one's political party takes over the government), when we are accountable to especially sophisticated or knowledgeable audiences, and when we are accountable to audiences with unknown or conflicting views.

Figure 2 summarizes the key predictions of the revised value pluralism model. Whereas the original model predicted that people turned to integratively complex coping strategies whenever they confronted a serious value conflict that could not be resolved via denial and bolstering, or lexicographic screening, the revised model identifies a much wider array of options for decision-makers. The social-content postulate alerts us to the fierce indignation that taboo trade-offs trigger. Decision-makers who must make such trade-offs will shroud the process in secrecy and try to conceal what they have done under cover of vague rhetorical appeals to shared values. The social-context postulate alerts us to the powerful role that accountability demands play in selecting strategies of coping with value

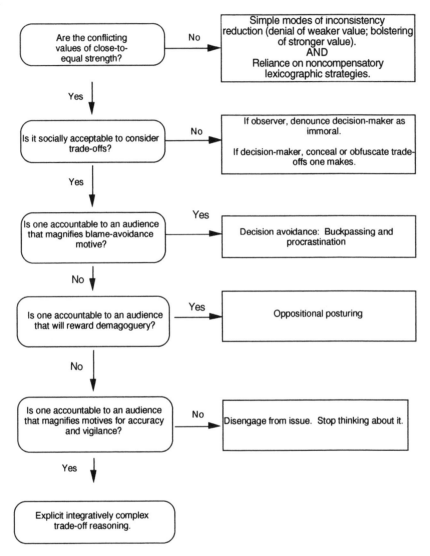

FIG. 2.2. Activating conditions for coping strategies in revised value pluralism model.

conflict. Accountability can promote buckpassing and procrastination by heightening the blame-avoidance motive; it can promote oppositional posturing by giving decision-makers the goal of arousing anger in apathetic and ill-informed audiences; and it can promote integratively complex trade-off reasoning by compelling decision-makers to answer to knowledgeable audiences who cannot be easily appeased by simple ingratiation tactics.

Is a Value-Free Value Pluralism Model Possible?

Although it is tempting to play political favorites and to applaud one coping strategy or to denounce another, the VPM is a descriptive and explanatory theory, not a normative one. We subscribe to the old-fashioned, neo-positivist view that it is possible to document strategies of coping with value conflict, and the conditions for activating those strategies, without taking any stand on the appropriateness of the values involved or conflict resolution strategies employed. We recognize, however, that "value pluralism" is a politically charged phrase, with enthusiastic advocates and detractors.

Perhaps the most eminent proponent of value pluralism in political philosophy is Isaiah Berlin (1969, p. 167–169) who declared that "conflicts of value are an intrinsic, irremovable element in human life: we are continually faced with choices between ends equally ultimate and claims equally absolute, the realization of which must inevitably involve the sacrifice of others . . . the ends of men are many, and not all of them are in principle compatible with each other." For instance, "the extent of a people's liberty to choose to live as they desire must be weighed against the claims of many other values, of which equality, or justice, or security, or public order are perhaps the most obvious examples." Berlin counsels us to be deeply suspicious of Utopian promises of a perfectly harmonious society that reconciles all of our aspirations. Conflicts among values are inevitable and admit of only imperfect compromises and partial, temporary solutions. Our world is one in which legitimate ends clash irreconcilably. To quote Isaiah Berlin again: "should democracy in a given situation be promoted at the expense of individual freedom; or equality at the expense of artistic achievement, or mercy at the expense of justice, or spontaneity at the expense of efficiency; or happiness, loyalty, and innocence at the expense of knowledge and truth? The simple point which I am concerned to make is that where ultimate values are irreconcilable, clear cut solutions cannot, in principle, be found."

Isaiah Berlin is an unapologetic advocate of integratively complex responses to value conflict. In *Four Essays on Liberty,* he notes that

> "If the claims of two (or more than two) types of liberty prove incompatible in a particular case, and if this is an instance of the clash of values at once absolute and incommensurable, it is better to face this intellectually uncomfortable fact than to ignore it, or automatically attribute it to some deficiency on our part which could be eliminated by an increase in skill or knowledge, or, what is worse still, suppress one of the competing values altogether by pretending that it is identical with its rival—and so end by distorting both."

In psychological terminology, Berlin warns us to eschew simple, low-effort modes of dissonance reduction and to embrace complex, emotionally-draining cognitive strategies that specify trade-offs between (among) legitimate competing concerns.

We think it, however, a mistake—one likely to retard scientific progress—to view the value pluralism model as an empirical counterpart to Berlin's normative theory of political pluralism. There is no need to repeat Kohlberg's error in the domain of moral reasoning in the domain of policy reasoning; there is no more psychological justification for positing Kantian categorical imperatives to be the pinnacle of ethical reasoning than there is for anointing integratively complex policy reasoning superior to integratively simple policy reasoning. It is easy to find historical situations or to create laboratory ones in which a resounding majority of "reasonable" observers (social scientists included) will applaud integratively simple responses to value conflict—"value X must trump value Y"— and deplore integratively complex responses—"values X and Y should be weighted in this fashion in this class of situations but in that fashion in that class of situations."

The study of the slavery debate provides an instructive cautionary tale. Most behavioral scientists tend to be more left-of-center than the general population in their political sympathies and more integratively complex than the general population in cognitive style (Suedfeld & Tetlock, 1991). There is thus a double temptation to put a positive value spin on the tendency for integrative complexity to peak in the left-center range of the political continuum on many issues. The slavery debate illustrates how dramatically, over the course of 150 years, value judgments of value conflict can change. The moderate center-left of the political spectrum in antebellum America was occupied by Free-Soil Republicans (foremost among them, Abraham Lincoln) who sought a political compromise that permitted slavery in the South while forbidding it to expand into new territories. A value trade-off that many once judged reasonable (limited slavery in return for national unity and avoidance of war) now looks patently unacceptable. It is a mistake to identify integratively complex trade-off reasoning as inherently more moral than simpler, more absolutist forms of reasoning.

The slavery debate is no isolated example. Many people on both the political left and political right want the Food and Drug Administration to use a simple cost-benefit rule for admitting drugs that treat life-threatening conditions (Tetlock & Boettger, 1994). Their implicit reasoning seems to be: If I am dying and the most effective available drug increases my chances of survival by, say, 25%, I want the doctor to be able to use that drug and not to be second-guessed by an integratively complex panel of deontological bioethicists who wonder whether a drug that kills anyone, under any conditions, no matter how dire, should be permitted in the U.S. pharmaceuticals market. Or, to turn to another historical example, with benefit of hindsight, almost everyone (save a few revisionist naysayers) believes that Winston Churchill was a wiser judge of events, and shrewder framer of options, with respect to British policy toward Nazi Germany in the 1930's than were the advocates of appeasement. Churchill offered a starkly simple dichotomy: prepare to defend the liberty and sovereignty of British allies on the continent or submit to brutal Nazi hegemony over Europe. Chamberlain offered a nuanced integratively complex trade-off between the goals of deterrence and reassurance: build British defenses to communicate resolve but do so cautiously and prudently to avoid provoking Germany (cf. Tetlock & Tyler, in press).

These examples show that our value judgments of value trade-offs are not easily divorced from our judgments of the degree to which situations threaten particular values (subjective probability judgments of the form "If we do X or Y, this or that is likely to happen") and our judgments of the degree to which one value merits priority over another (judgments ultimately grounded in backstop moral commitments that, from the decision-maker's perspective, require no further justification). There is nothing inherently good about integratively complex trade-off reasoning.

The argument does not, however, end here. A committed value pluralist could concede these counterexamples—contexts where value monism seems more appropriate than value pluralism—but still insist that, given the practical realities of human affairs, decision-makers who are incapable of integratively complex trade-off reasoning are not up to the challenge of managing a household budget, less still an entire society for any prolonged period of time. Resource scarcity, volatile expectations, social interdependence, and competing interest groups make trade-offs inevitable. Decision-makers ignore this fundamental feature of social life at their peril. This counterargument is powerful. It persuades us that integratively complex trade-off reasoning must be in the cognitive repertoire of any competent politician, administrator or business executive. Effective decision-makers must decide how to decide, a tricky meta-decision-making task that requires weighing the values at stake, information search costs, accountability demands and procedural constraints. We simply caution against the *automatic* presumption that integratively simple reasoning is either cognitively or morally inferior to integratively complex reasoning.

CLOSING COMMENTS

The revised VPM is open to theoretical challenges from many intellectual directions. In closing, we consider two contradictory criticisms that help to clarify the range of circumstances in which the VPM is likely to be useful. One objection comes from advocates of the standard rational actor model who find all this fuss over value conflict a bit odd. Subjective expected utility theorists reduce the diversity of human values to a single common denominator or utility function. Everything, in their world view, is supposed to be fungible and subject to the inexorable laws of supply and demand (Becker, 1981). Confronted by close judgment calls, one simply identifies the option with the slightly higher expected utility and moves on, with no time for regret over paths not taken. If one confronts a genuine tie, one minimizes further information search and transactions costs by flipping a coin.

The revised VPM concedes that decision-makers occasionally approximate this rational actor ideal—perhaps, for instance, when they find themselves accountable to highly knowledgeable audiences in intensely competitive financial markets. Here we find that complex trade-off reasoning is an integral part of the presupposed background of investment decisions (Malkiel, 1990). Financial analysts have well-rehearsed integratively complex answers to an integratively complex question that their role in a system of market accountability repeatedly requires them to answer: Given this institutional client's time horizon and level of risk aversion, how can we create a portfolio that strikes the right balance between risk and return under current market conditions? This hyper-analytic approach to trade-offs has, moreover, become much more common as executives schooled in economic theory play increasingly prominent roles in corporate and governmental decision-making. From the VPM perspective, however, this rational style of decision-making remains mostly an elite phenomenon and one that even these elites confine mostly to their jobs (most financial analysts balk at monetizing the value of personal relationships). Mathematical decision aids have not yet relegated "value conflict" and related social psychological hypotheses to the status of historical curiosities.

A second objection to VPM comes from the opposite end of the rationality continuum. Drawing upon a potpourri of theories, including cognitive dissonance and self-perception theories in social psychology, psychodynamic theories of political preferences, and classical and operant conditioning theories of political attitudes, one could argue that people often act first and then invoke whatever salient values conveniently justify those acts (Eiser, 1987; Kristiansen & Zanna, 1988; Lasswell, 1948). Far from being the product of careful premeditation and analysis of the impact of each action alternative on internalized values, many people go through much of life on autopilot, responding unthinkingly to salient stimuli of the moment (Langer, 1990; Taylor & Fiske, 1978; Zaller, 1991). It would be foolish to deny that these theoretical perspectives also capture an important slice of life, indeed, quite possibly, the majority of our waking hours.

In a contextualist spirit (McGuire 1983), the challenge is to identify the explanatory range of application of the VPM. We suspect that the VPM is most appropriately invoked at the choice points of our lives where circumstances demand that we make self-conscious decisions that implicate deeply held values that, in turn, cannot be easily quantified and entered into some conditional optimization algorithm. The model thus avoids both maximalist and minimalist assumptions about human rationality. The VPM is a contingency theory of judgment and choice that, like other contingency theories, depicts people as neither rational actors nor cognitive misers, but rather as "mental managers" who like to keep life simple by minimizing cognitive effort, emotional pain, and political embarrassment but who recognize that circumstances sometimes require acknowledging that life is complex.

ACKNOWLEDGMENTS

Revised version of paper presented at the Eighth Ontario Symposium on Personality and Social Psychology: Values. London, Ontario, August 17–18, 1993.

REFERENCES

Abelson, R. P. (1959). Modes of resolution of belief dilemmas. *Journal of Conflict Resolution, 3*, 343–352.

Adorno, T., Frenkel-Brunswick, E., Levinson, D., & Sanford, N. (1950). *The authoritarian personality*. New York: Harper & Row.

Altemeyer, R. (1981). *Right-wing authoritarianism*. Winnipeg, Manitoba: University of Manitoba Press.

Andre, J. (1992). Blocked exchanges: A taxonomy. *Ethics, 103*, 29–47)

Beattie, J., Baron, J., Hershey, J. C., and Spranca, M. (1994). The psychological determinants of decision attitude. *Journal of Behavioral Decision Making, 7*, 129–144.

Becker, G. (1981). *A treatise on the family*. Cambridge: Harvard University Press.

Berlin, I. (1969). Two concepts of liberty. In Isaiah Berlin, *Four essays on liberty*, Oxford: Oxford University Press, 1969.

Calabresi, G., & Bobbitt, P. (1978). *Tragic choices*. New York: Norton.

Cosmides, L. (1989). The logic of social exchange: Has natural selection shaped how humans reason? Studies from the Wason selection task. *Cognition, 31*, 187–276.

diRenzo, G. J. (1967). *Personality, power, and politics: A social psychological analysis of the Italian deputy and his parliamentary system*. Notre Dame, IN: University of Notre Dame Press.

Durkheim, E. (1973). *Moral education*. New York: Free Press.

Durkheim, E. (1976). *The elementary forms of the religious life*, 2nd edition. London: Allen and Unwin.

Eiser, J. R. (1975). Attitudes and the use of evaluative language: A two-way process. *Journal for the Theory of Social Behavior, 5*, 235–248.

Eiser, J. R. (1987). *The expression of attitudes*. New York: Springer Verlag.

Elster, J. (1992). *Local justice: How institutions allocate scarce resources and necessary burdens*. New York: Russell Sage Foundation.

Festinger, L. (1957). *A theory of cognitive dissonance*. Stanford: Stanford University Press.

Festinger, L. (1964). *Conflict, decision, and dissonance*. Stanford: Stanford University Press.

Foa, U. G. (1971). Interpersonal and economic resources, *Science, 171*, 345–351.

Fiske, S., and Taylor, S. (1991). *Social cognition* (second edition). New York: McGraw-Hill.

Gruenfeld, D. H. (1995). Status, ideology, and integrative complexity on the U.S. Supreme Court: Rethinking the politics of political decision making, *Journal of Personality and Social Psychology, 68*, 5–20.

Haan, N. (1985). *On moral ground: The search for practical morality?* New York: New York University.

Janis, I. L., & Mann, L. (1977). *Decision making: A psychological analysis of conflict, choice, and commitment.* New York: Free Press.

Jervis, R. (1976). *Perception and misperception in international politics.* Princeton, NJ: Princeton University Press.

Kahneman, D., Knetsch, J. L. & Thaler, R. (1991). The endowment effect, loss aversion, and the status quo bias. *Journal of Economic Perspectives, 5,* 193–206.

Kahneman, D., & Tversky, A. (1979). Prospect theory: An analysis of decision under risk. *Econometrica, 47,* 263–291.

Kristiansen, C. M., & Zanna, M. (1988). Justifying attitudes by appealing to values: A functional perspective. *British Journal of Social Psychology, 27,* 247–256.

Langer, E. (1989). *Mindfulness.* Reading, MA: Addison Wesley.

Lane, R. (1973). Patterns of political beliefs. In J. Knutson (Ed.), *Handbook of political psychology.* San Francisco: Jossey-Bass.

Lane, R. (1991). *The market experience.* New York: Cambridge University Press.

Larrick, R. P. (1993). Motivational factors in decision theories: The role of self-protection. *Psychological Bulletin, 113,* 430–440.

Liberman, A., & Chaiken, S. (1991). Value conflict and thought-induced attitude change. *Journal of Experimental Social Psychology, 27,* 203–216.

Loomes, G., and Sugden, R. (1982). Regret theory: An alternative theory of rational choice under uncertainty. *Economic Journal, 92,* 805–824.

Lukes, S. (1991). *Moral conflict and politics,* Oxford University Press.

McGuire, W. J. (1983). A contextualist theory of knowledge: Its implications for innovation and reform in psychological research. In L. Berkowitz (Ed.), *Advances in experimental social psychology* (Vol. 16, pp. 2–47). San Diego, CA: Academic Press.

Malkiel, B. G. (Ed.). (1990). *A random walk down Wall Street: Including a life-cycle guide to personal investing.* New York: Norton.

March, J., & Olsen, J. 1988. *Rediscovering institutions.* Oxford: Basil Blackwell.

Mitchell, P. G., Tetlock, P. E., Mellers, B, & Ordonez, L. (1993). Judgments of justice: Compromises between equality and efficiency. *Journal of Personality and Social Psychology, 65,* 629–639.

Mitchell, R. C., & Carson, R. T. (1989). *Using surveys to value public goods: The contingent valuation method.* Baltimore, MD: Johns Hopkins University Press.

Nagel, T. (1979). The fragmentation of value. In *Mortal questions.* Cambridge: Cambridge University Press, 1979, pages 134–138.

Payne, J. W., Bettman, J. R., & Johnson, E. J. (1992). Behavioral decision research: A constructive processing perspective. *Annual Review of Psychology, 43,* 87–131.

Putnam, R. (1971). Studying elite culture: The case of ideology. *American Political Science Review, 65,* 651–681.

Raz, J. (1986). *The morality of freedom.* New York: Clarendon Press, Oxford University Press.

Rokeach, M. (1960). *The open and closed mind: Investigations into the nature of belief systems and personality systems.* New York: Basic Books.

Rokeach, M. (1973). *The nature of human values.* New York: Free Press.

Rokeach, M. (1979). *Understanding human values.* New York: Free Press.

Schroder, H. M. (1971). Conceptual complexity and personality organization. In H. M. Schroder & P. Suedfeld (Eds.), *Personality theory and information processing* (pp. 240–273). New York: Ronald.

Shils, E. E. (1956). Ideology and civility: On the politics of the intellectual. *Sewanee Review, 66,* 950–980.

Skitka, L. & Tetlock, P. E. (1993). Providing public assistance: Cognitive and motivational processes underlying liberal and conservative policy preferences. *Journal of Personality and Social Psychology, 65,* 1205–1224.

Slovic, P., Griffin, D., & Tversky, A. (1990). Compatibility effects in judgment and choice. In R. M. Hogarth (ed.), *Insights in decision-making: Theory and applications.* Chicago: University of Chicago Press.

Smith, V. (1994). Economics in the laboratory. *Journal of Economic Perspectives, 8,* 113–132.

Suedfeld, P. (1985). Cognitive managers and their critics. *Political Psychology, 13,* 435–454.

Suedfeld, P., Bluck, S., Loewen, L., & Elkins, D. (1994). Sociopolitical values and integrative complexity of members of student political groups. *Canadian Journal of Behavioral Science, 26,* 121–141.

Suedfeld, P. & Tetlock, P. E. (1991). *Psychology and social policy.* Washington, D.C.: Hemisphere.

Suedfeld, P., & Walbaum, A. B. C. (1992). Altering integrative complexity in political thought: Value conflict and audience agreement. *InterAmerican Journal of Psychology, 26,* 19–36.

Taylor, S. E., & Fiske, S. T. (1978). Salience, attention, and attribution: Top of the head phenomena. In L. Berkowitz (Ed.), *Advances in Experimental Social Psychology.* (Vol., *11,* pp. 250–289.) New York: Academic Press.

Tesser, A. (1978). Self-generated attitude change. In L. Berkowitz (ed.), *Advances in experimental social psychology* (volume 11, 137–190). New York: Academic Press.

Tetlock, P. E. (1981a). Pre- to post-election shifts in presidential rhetoric: Impression management or cognitive adjustment? *Journal of Personality and Social Psychology, 41,* 207–212.

Tetlock, P. E. (1981b). Personality and isolationism: Content analysis of senatorial speeches. *Journal of Personality and Social Psychology, 41,* 737–743.

Tetlock, P. E. (1983). Cognitive style and political ideology. *Journal of Personality and Social Psychology, 45,* 118–126.

Tetlock, P. E. (1984). Cognitive style and political belief systems in the British House of Commons. *Journal of Personality and Social Psychology, 46,* 365–375.

Tetlock, P. E. (1986). A value pluralism model of ideological reasoning. *Journal of Personality and Social Psychology, 50,* 819–827.

Tetlock, P. E. (1989). Structure and function in political belief systems. In A. R. Pratkanis, S. J. Breckler, & A. G. Greenwald (Eds.), *Attitude structure and function* (pp. 129–151). Hillsdale, NJ: Erlbaum.

Tetlock, P. E. (1991). An alternative model of judgment and choice: People as politicians. *Theory and Psychology, 1,* 451–477.

Tetlock, P. E. (1992). The impact of accountability on judgment and choice: Toward a social contingency model. In M. Zanna (Ed.), *Advances in Experimental Social Psychology* (Vol. 25, pp. 331–376). San Diego, CA: Academic Press.

Tetlock, P. E. (1989). Accountability: A social magnifier of the dilution effect. *Journal of Personality and Social Psychology, 57,* 388–398.

Tetlock, P. E., Armor, D., & Peterson, R. S. (1994). The slavery debate in Antebellum America: Cognitive style, value conflict, and the limits of compromise. *Journal of Personality and Social Psychology, 66,* 115–126.

Tetlock, P. E., & Boettger, R. (1994). Accountability amplifies the status quo effect when change creates victims. *Journal of Behavioral Decision Making, 7,* 1–23.

Tetlock, P. E., Micheletti, P., & Hannum, K., (1984). Stability and change in senatorial debate: Testing the cognitive versus rhetorical style hypothesis. *Journal of Personality and Social Psychology, 46,* 979–990.

Tetlock, P. E., McGuire, C. B., & Mitchell, G. (1991). Psychological perspectives on nuclear deterrence. In M. R. Rosenzweig & L. W. Porter (Eds.), *Annual Review of Psychology* (Vol. 42, pp. 239–276). Palo Alto, CA: Annual Reviews.

Tetlock, P. E., Skitka, L., & Boettger, R. (1989). Social and cognitive strategies of coping with accountability: Conformity, complexity, and bolstering. *Journal of Personality and Social Psychology, 57,* 632–641.

Tetlock, P. E., & Tyler, A. (in press). Winston Churchill's cognitive style: The debate over appeasement of Nazi Germany and self-governance for India. *Political Psychology.*

Tversky, A. (1972). Elimination by aspects: A theory of choice. *Psychological Review, 79,* 281–299.

Tversky, A., Sattath, S., & Slovic, P. (1988). Contingent weighting in judgment and choice. *Psychological Review, 95,* 371–384.

Tversky, A. & Thaler, R. H. (1990). Preference reversals. *Journal of Economic Perspectives, 4,* 201–211.

Walzer, M. (1983). *Spheres of justice.* New York: Basic Books).

Wildavsky, A. (1979). *Speaking truth to power.* New York: Basic Books.

Williams, B. (1981). *Moral luck: Philosophical papers 1973–1980.* New York: Cambridge University Press.

Wilson, J. Q. (1980). *Bureaucracy.* Cambridge, MA: Harvard University Press.

Woodward, C. V. (1983). *American counterpoint: Slavery and racism in the North/South dialogue.* Oxford, England: Oxford University Press.

Zaller, J. (1991). *The nature and origins of mass public opinion.* New York: Cambridge University Press.

3 The Dynamics of Value Systems

Clive Seligman
Albert N. Katz
University of Western Ontario

Several years ago the Parliament of Canada deliberated legislation dealing with capital punishment and abortion. In discussing these issues, a colleague of ours said that he did not understand people who were against abortion, but *for* capital punishment. He couldn't see, he explained, how someone who viewed abortion as killing babies could support the death penalty. Didn't people like that realize, he asked, how inconsistent they were—in support of killing in one case, but against in the other? Neither our colleague nor the rest of us, who were agreeing with him, were aware at the time that we showed the same inconsistency, but in the opposite direction. That is, our liberal beliefs led us to be prochoice on abortion but anti-capital punishment. In other words, we were against the execution of convicted murderers, but for the ending of the lives of fetuses. Why did the apparent inconsistency of others loom so large while our own inconsistency remained hidden?

Part of the answer, we believe, has to do with the value framing of the issues for ourselves and for others. It is understandable that the *sanctity of life* value, which pervades the rhetoric of prolifers, leads those who differ with them to focus on this value, and thus readily see contradictions when prolifers espouse positions on capital punishment. For ourselves, however, we do not feel compelled to frame these two issues with the same value. For us, capital punishment is an issue of *sanctity of life,* but abortion is an issue of women's *free choice.* Quite possibly, prolifers also frame the two issues from two different value perspectives: *sanctity of life* for the abortion issue, and *retribution* for capital punishment. They most likely see us as contradictory, because it appears to them that we argue *sanctity of life* in capital punishment debates, but abandon that value when considering abortion.

This example suggests, among other things, that particular values are associated with specific issues, and that people on opposite sides of an issue may hold different values as important. In fact, there is much research to support these observations (e.g., Kristiansen & Zanna, 1988; Rokeach, 1973; Tetlock, 1986). Which value is considered more important than another to an individual is a result of socialization, parental and peer pressure, and cultural influences (Rokeach, 1973). To us, these diverse social influences on value systems suggest the possibility of frequent changes in individual value priorities as much as they suggest stability. Yet the pervasive (implicit) assumption of values research is that value systems are relatively stable and act as guiding principles in varied situations. The clearest evidence of this assumption of the "stable value system" is the typical method of assessing value systems. Value systems are measured by asking individuals to rank or rate the importance of values "according to how important they are as guiding principles in your life." Value systems are not elicited from individuals in the context of any particular situation, for example, abortion, capital punishment, and the like.

A more interesting implication of the example with which this chapter began, we think, is the idea that, *within an individual,* values may be organized differently for the two issues of abortion and capital punishment. For one issue, sanctity of life may be more important than freedom, and for another issue freedom may be more important than sanctity of life. For example, with regard to abortion, the mother's freedom of choice may be more important than the fetus' sanctity of life; for the same person, with regard to capital punishment, the sanctity of life of the convicted murderer may be more important than the state's freedom to take a life.

One study that suggests individuals might reorder the priority of relevant values, depending on the issue, was conducted by Sparks and Durkin (1987). They showed that conservatives and liberals in Britain alternately supported individual rights over law and order depending on the issue. In one case, involving the rights of workers to vote on an issue decided by union officials, the conservatives supported individual rights of workers to exercise their right to vote, whereas liberals pointed out that the union executive had acted properly within its constitution. On another issue, involving blockading roads to prevent workers from joining the picket lines of other striking workers, conservatives now supported the blockade in terms of law and order, whereas the liberals now supported the individual rights of workers to go where they please. In short, value priorities reversed themselves depending on the politics of the question.

In another study, Kristiansen and Zanna (1988) asked people to rank order their values according to how important they were to them as guiding principles in their lives and also with regard to how relevant the values were to specific issues. For our purposes, the important finding was that values ranked with regard to specific issues (e.g., abortion) independently predicted attitudes toward the issue over and above what was predictable from the importance rankings of the values as general guiding principles.

The purpose of this chapter is to elaborate the view that individuals may have encapsulated, modular, or multiple value-systems associated with different issues. Our basic idea is that individuals may construct value systems in the context of specific issues and not simply apply some general value system to issues as they arise. This perspective challenges the traditional view of the value system as a single ordered set of values that is important to the self-concept and helps guide thought and action. For the traditional value system to serve as an effective guide, it is assumed that it transcends situations. Our view sees value systems as dynamic rather than static and creatively applied in situations rather than rule-bound.

In the remainder of the chapter, we first outline more precisely the major distinction between the traditional view of the value system and the multiple value systems approach. Next, we present data to show that the value system changes with the issue of discussion, and the self-state perspective (actual vs. ought). Finally, we close with some thoughts about how multiple value-systems may operate.

Multiple Value Systems Versus Traditional Value System Approach

In Rokeach's (1973; Ball-Rokeach, Rokeach, & Grube, 1984) theoretical account, values are seen as preferences for desirable life states (freedom, equality) or behavior (honest, logical). For each individual, the values are organized in a value system, which is "an enduring organization of [values] along a continuum of relative importance" (Rokeach, 1973, p. 5). A working assumption of much research on values, conducted in this tradition, is that an individual's value system is fairly stable. Rokeach measured value systems by having people rank order a list of values according to how important the values were as guiding principles in their lives. He has presented evidence that demonstrates high test–retest reliabilities for subjects' rank-orderings of values (Rokeach, 1973). This stability in the value system is understood in the context of the importance of values to the integrity of the self. Values are the standards that the self uses to judge and justify itself; and the stability of value systems is necessary to express the coherence of the self over time and situations.

Rokeach's (1973) perspective of the value–attitude relation suggests that when an attitude issue is raised for an individual, the relevant values are activated in the individual's stable value system, and the attitude is determined by the relative ranking of value(s) in that highlighted cluster. For example, suppose the issue of environmental pollution is raised for an individual for whom the values health, world of beauty, and comfortable life are ranked in that order in that individual's value system. If these are the most relevant pollution values for that individual, then health and world of beauty should be more influential than comfortable life in determining the person's views on pollution. An implicit assumption of this view is that the values relevant to an attitude issue are pulled out of the value system and applied to the attitude issue in the same rank order as they existed originally in the value system. In other words, there is one value system (i.e., one rank ordering of values) for each person, and the individual's attitudes are determined from the ordering of the relevant values in it.

The multiple value-system perspective would suggest that value systems are dynamic and that the value system we construct in any given situation is very much dependent on the context in which we are asked to do it. Recall that Rokeach measures value systems by asking subjects to rank order values as they are important to them as guiding principles in their lives. In other words, people are asked to answer abstractly about how values guide their general evaluations or behavior, without regard to any specific topic or purpose or social relationship. Even though attitudes can be predicted from this method of determining value systems, it does not follow that individuals would rank order values similarly if they were responding to a different request, such as to rank order values as they are important to them as guiding principles in thinking about the issue of the environment.

Let us take another look at our hypothetical person who ranked the values health, world of beauty, and comfortable life in this order as general guiding principles. When that person is asked to consider the pollution issue explicitly, considerations such as job security or cost of consumer products might become more salient and thus affect value priorities. This could affect the rank ordering of the relevant pollution values so that comfortable life may rise to the top.

This alternative view implies that value systems are only stable in a particular domain. For example, if we are interested in value systems with regard to the importance of values as general guiding principles, then we would expect value systems to be consistent over time, so long as the "general, abstract value system" was being assessed. Likewise, we would expect to find that value systems were reliable if individuals were asked to provide them on two different occasions according to their use as guiding principles with regard to environmental issues. But it is an empirical question whether the value systems constructed in the context of general and abstract guiding principles are structured similarly to values systems elicited in the context of environmental concerns. There may well be large discrepancies between the value systems for the general case and for the environmental issue-specific case, suggesting the possibility of value system reconstruction.

In the research presented next, we demonstrate that the traditional approach of conceptualizing value systems—as relatively stable systems that guide thought and action across a multitude of situations—requires reexamination. First, we show that individuals report significantly different value systems when asked to provide their general values systems versus their abortion value systems. Second, we demonstrate that the finding of the first study is replicable with a different issue, in this case, the environment. Third, we show that important, relevant values can be reordered in response to situational manipulations, even when the question directing subjects to report their value systems remains constant. Finally, we demonstrate that many individuals provide significantly different value systems for their ought selves than their actual selves. Further, the results of the fourth study also show that discrepant self-state value systems have important psychological effects.

Research on Multiple Value Systems: Different Issues

Our first two studies examined the extent to which our value systems fluctuate from context to context. Specifically, we looked at how values are ranked when subjects were given the traditional instructions (general) versus when they were asked to rank the values according to guiding principles regarding thoughts and feelings about particular issues. In one study the target issue was abortion, and in the second study, the environment.

Abortion Study 1.   In this study, introductory psychology students were asked to complete a booklet of questionnaires, focusing on their values, attitudes, and personality. The participants completed the booklets individually at their own speed; most took 1 hour to complete the set of questionnaires.

Subjects completed the tasks in the following order: First, subjects completed a modified Rokeach Terminal Value Survey (Rokeach, 1973). The survey consisted of 20 values, 18 from the original Rokeach Terminal Value Survey and two others that are relevant to the issue of abortion: sanctity of life (preciousness of life) and sanctity of one's own body (right to control one's body; protection from unwanted intrusion). The respondent's task was to arrange the 20 values "in order of their importance to YOU, as guiding principles in YOUR life." The values were printed on gummed labels and could be easily moved and rearranged. Second, subjects were asked to write a story about abortion and to complete a 34-item questionnaire about their abortion attitudes. Subjects were classified as prochoice or prolife based on a median split of their abortion questionnaire responses.

Third, respondents filled out a number of personality scales as filler. Finally, the participants completed the same modified Value Survey as before. Subjects in the experimental (or general–abortion) group ($N = 90$) completed the second value survey with new instructions. This time they were asked to rank order their values as guiding principles "in your evaluation and feeling toward the issue of *abortion* . . . The end result should truly show how you really feel about the values that are important to you *regarding abortion.*" Respondents in the control (or general–general) group ($N = 30$) were asked to complete the value survey the second time according to the exact same instructions they were given for the first administration of the survey at the beginning of the session.

A Spearman *rho* was calculated for each subject between the rank-orders obtained on the first administration of the value survey and the second. The average *rhos* for each group are shown in Table 3.1. As can be seen in Table 3.1, when either all 20 values, or only the top five ranked values, are included in the analysis, the *rhos* are lower (and statistically significantly so) for the general–abortion group than the general–general condition.

Although the *rhos* are all positive, clearly some reordering of values occurred when the focus of the value ranking instructions changed from general guiding principles to ranking with regard to abortion. For example, Table 3.2 presents the changes in ranking (in the general–abortion group) for those values that ended up being ranked 1 through 5 for the issue of abortion. At the top of Table 3.2 are the value rankings for the prochoice group and at the bottom are shown the value rankings for the prolife group. It is evident that some values changed rank order dramatically from their place in the general system to their position in the abortion system. For example, sanctity of one's own body for the prochoice group went from rank 15 to rank 4, and sanctity of life for the prolife group moved from rank 14 to rank 1. Additionally, for prolife individuals, freedom is ranked as more important than sanctity of life in the general rank order (rank 3 vs. rank 14), but sanctity of life is considered more important than freedom in the abortion rank order (rank 1 vs. rank 4). These data also show that prochoice and prolife advocates have several different guiding values with regard to abortion, consistent with other studies (see Kristiansen & Zanna, 1988).

Thus far the data show that values are reordered somewhat depending on the

TABLE 3.1
Correlation Between Values Ranked at Beginning and End of Session: Abortion Issue

All Values Ranked	
Group	R
General value rankings only	.84
General and abortion value rankings	.53

Five Most Important Values Ranked	
Group	R
General value rankings	.72
General and abortion value rankings	.30

TABLE 3.2
Is the Value System Preserved as Values are Applied to the Abortion Issue?

Abortion Rankings		General Rankings	
		Prochoice	
1.	Freedom	1.	Happiness
2.	Inner harmony	2.	Self-respect
3.	Self-respect	4.	Freedom
4.	Sanctity of one's own body	8.	Inner harmony
5.	Happiness	15.	Sanctity of one's own body
		Prolife	
1.	Sanctity of life	2.	Family security
2.	Inner harmony	3.	Freedom
3.	Self-respect	4.	Self-respect
4.	Freedom	7.	Inner harmony
5.	Family security	14.	Sanctity of life

issue at hand. But do values predict abortion attitudes differently depending on whether they are ranked according to general instructions or abortion ranking instructions? The pertinent data are given in Table 3.3.

First, we note that 8 values, out of 20, predicted abortion attitudes in at least one ranking task, and four values correlated significantly with abortion attitude in both ranking instruction conditions. Second, the values freedom and sanctity

TABLE 3.3
Predicting Abortion Position From General and Abortion Value Rankings

	Correlation With Abortion Position	
Value	General Rankings	Abortion Rankings
Salvation	-.55***	-.66***
Sanctity of life	-.36***	-.62***
Freedom	-.04 (NS)	+.56***
Sanctity of one's own body	+.03 (NS)	+.31***
True friendship	+.23*	+.23*
A world of beauty	-.01 (NS)	-.22*
An exciting life	+.34***	+.22*
Self-respect	+.21*	+.16 (NS)

Note. Positive correlations mean that the more important the value, the more *prochoice* is the attitude. Negative correlations mean that the more important the value, the more *prolife* the abortion attitude. ***$p < .001$; *$p < .05$; NS = Nonsignificant.

of one's own body showed virtually zero correlations with abortion attitudes in the general condition, but significantly higher correlations in the abortion ranking condition. That is, the more important freedom and sanctity of one's own body were to people, the more prochoice they were. Sanctity of life was also a significantly better predictor of abortion attitude when ranked according to abortion instructions than general ranking ones, as was a world of beauty. The more important the values sanctity of life and world of beauty were to participants, the more prolife their abortion attitudes.

An inspection of the mean ranks provided by the prochoice and prolife groups in the general and abortion ranking conditions for the values freedom and sanctity of life indicates the dynamic movement of values as the ranking instructions change. For freedom ranked in the general condition, prolife individuals gave a mean of 6.70, prochoice, 6.74. In the abortion condition, however, the mean rank for freedom for the prolife condition was 6.87, but the mean for prochoice was 3.52. Freedom became more important for the prochoice people. For sanctity of life ranked in the general condition, the mean for the prolife group was 11.83 and for prochoice, 13.97. However, for the abortion condition, the prolife mean for sanctity of life was 5.37 and the prochoice mean was 11.93. Sanctity of life became much more important for prolife individuals. Taken together, these significant interactions demonstrated that, for these two values, the distinctiveness of the prolife and the prochoice groups only became evident when they were asked to rank order their values from the perspective of abortion.

In sum, these results suggest that values can be ranked differently depending on whether individuals are instructed to rank the values as they are generally important to them versus when the ranking instructions specify the ranking context as abortion. Further, the results showed that the values freedom and sanctity of life rose and fell in importance as the instructions changed from general to abortion-relevant in line with the individuals' attitudes toward abortion. In addition, several values were better predictors of attitudes toward abortion when ranked with regard to abortion than when these same values were ranked according to general guiding instructions.

In this study, as well as in those to follow, we did analyze the personality measures that we included as filler items to separate the two administrations of the value systems measures. Interestingly, there were no meaningful patterns of interactions between the personality measures and the findings relevant to our main argument. In the different studies, we examined a variety of individual difference measures including, dogmatism (Rokeach, 1960), authoritarianism (Cherry, & Byrne, 1977), need for cognition (Cacioppo & Petty, 1982), tolerance of cognitive dissonance (Polak, & Lepper, 1990), self-monitoring (Snyder, 1974), and sex of subject.

It is important to note that the differences between the general–general and general–abortion conditions can not be accounted for only by making abortion values salient, because, in both conditions, prior to the final ranking task, the subjects were asked to write a story about abortion and complete a questionnaire about their attitudes toward abortion. Because the study did not include a no-abortion control condition, it is unclear to what extent the abortion priming increased the size of the correlations between the two value ranking tasks for *both* conditions. However, given the observed differences between the two conditions, something must be important about the domain in which the values are asked to be provided.

It should also be mentioned that whatever overall demand one might have suspected would be present for subjects to be consistent in their two value ranking tasks, the results of the general–abortion condition indicated that the participants did reorder their values.

Environmental Study.   Intrigued by the above results, we wanted to replicate the results with a different issue. In the present study, subjects followed a similar procedure to the one outlined earlier in the abortion study, with the exception that there was no story-writing task.

The subjects were introductory psychology students participating in the study for course credit. As before, the subjects were told that they would be asked to complete several attitude, value, and general questionnaires. Subjects worked on their own and took about an hour to finish.

The participants filled out the questionnaires in the following order. First, they completed a modified Rokeach Terminal Value Survey. The modified survey consisted of the original 18 terminal values plus three others that were added because of their believed relevance to the environment. The added values were: conservation (sustainable development, efficient use of resources), preservation (nonintervention in the natural and built environment), and health (physical well-being). The subject's task was to rank the values "in order of their importance to YOU, as guiding principles in YOUR life."

Second, subjects completed a 16-item environmental concern scale (Weigel & Weigel, 1978) and then a 15-item questionnaire that asked subjects their attitudes toward various possible local environmental policy issues. The results of the policy questionnaire have been reported previously (Seligman, Syme, & Gilchrist, 1994) and are not presented here. Third, the subjects filled out various personality measures as filler. Finally, subjects again completed the modified Rokeach Terminal Value Survey. Subjects in the experimental (or general–environmental) group ($N = 60$) were given instructions the second time to rank order the values as guiding principles "in YOUR evaluation and feeling toward the ENVIRONMENT." Subjects in the control (or general–general) group ($N = 15$) completed the survey according to the same instructions given at the beginning of the session.

When all 21 values are considered, the *rho* between the first and second administration of the value survey for the general–general group is .83, and the *rho* for the general–environmental condition is .36, reliably lower. When only the top five values related to the environment are examined, the *rhos* are .77 for the general–general condition and .20 for the general–environmental condition, again significantly lower.

As with the abortion study, the values were reordered when the ranking instructions changed (see Table 3.4). Because only one participant scored below the midpoint on the environmental concern scale, we refer to participants below the median as being moderate rather than low on environmental concern. As can be seen in Table 3.4, the major shifts in value rankings from the general value system to the environmental value system concern the rise in importance of the environmental values, for example, conservation, world of beauty, and preservation.

Two significant interactions were found between ranking instructions and environmental concern, when one compares high and moderately concerned individuals. For the value *freedom,* the high environmental concern group ranked freedom as significantly less important when responding to environmental ranking instructions ($M = 10.44$) than to general instructions ($M = 6.94$). For moderate environmental concern subjects, there was no difference between environmental ranking instructions ($M = 7.43$) and general ones ($M = 7.00$). For the value *wisdom,* high environmental concern respondents ranked wisdom as more important in the environmental context ($M = 8.06$) than in the general one ($M = 12.06$). There was no difference between the environmental ranking ($M = 9.29$) and the general one ($M = 9.19$) for moderate environmental concern subjects.

Thus the change in ranking instructions seemed to affect high environmental

TABLE 3.4
Is the Value System Preserved as Values are Applied to the Environmental Issue?

Environmental Rankings		*General Rankings*	
	High Environmental Concern		
1.	Conservation	2.	Health
2.	Preservation	9.	A world at peace
3.	A world at peace	15.	Conservation
4.	Health	17.	A world of beauty
5.	A world of beauty	19.	Preservation
	Moderate Environmental Concern		
1.	Conservation	2.	Health
2.	Health	4.	Freedom
3.	A world of beauty	14.	A world at peace
4.	Freedom	17.	Conservation
5.	A world at peace	18.	A world of beauty

concern subjects such that freedom became less important and wisdom more important as the instructions moved from a general ranking task to an environmental specific one. The moderate environmental concern individuals did not change their relative ranking of freedom and wisdom across the two value surveys. Thus the environmental study supports the abortion study in the main finding that value reordering takes place depending on whether individuals are asked to rank order values as they are important to them as general guiding principles or as they are important to them with regard to a specific issue.

Abortion Study 2.   The results of the first two studies demonstrated that value systems can be reorganized as issues change. Although consistent with a multiple value-system perspective, the results of the studies leave open the possibility that the values were reordered for other reasons, having to do with the subjects' understanding of the instructions. Suppose, for example, that the subjects believed that what they were asked to do in the abortion ranking instructions was to consider the implications or relevance of the values for the issue. In other words, perhaps the subjects were merely considering the relative strength of the implications or relevance of each value to the issue of abortion. If so, then the subjects would not necessarily be providing a different value system in terms of the relative importance of the values to their self-concept. Possibly this alternative explanation of the task's ranking instructions would lead to the rank orderings reported above.

One way to address this potential problem is to design an experiment that holds constant the value-ranking instructions while manipulating the salience of the abortion issue. Penny Blackwood (1991) conducted such a study in her master's research, which was supervised by the first author. The intent of the study was to show that relevant values would change their importance rankings in response to an increase in the salience of the abortion issue.

Seventy-eight introductory psychology students were recruited to attend two 1-hour sessions, separated by 3 weeks. In the first session, subjects completed the modified Rokeach Terminal Value Survey, described in the abortion study reported earlier, provided their attitudes toward a number of social issues, including abortion, and, lastly, filled out a number of personality questionnaires. The instructions for the value survey were, "Your task is to rank the values in order of their importance to you." Subjects were classified as prochoice or prolife based on a tertile split on the abortion attitude measure.

Three weeks later, the subjects returned for the second session and were randomly assigned either to the abortion condition or the control condition. In the abortion condition, subjects were asked to write a story based on the lead-in phrase, "Jane is thinking of having an abortion." Subjects in the control condition were asked to write a story in response to the phrase, "Jane is thinking of taking a course." The subjects were told that they would have 10 minutes to write a story of a paragraph or two in length. They were told "Your time is limited, so simply write whatever first comes to mind. Tell the reader what led up to the event and what is going to happen. Also, think about what may be going on in the mind of the main character. . . . " Then subjects were asked to complete the same value survey they were given in Session 1, with identical instructions.

First, we report the results of the coding of values expressed in the stories and, second, we discuss the two significant three-way interactions that were found. Because the stories were expected to prime values, relevant to each issue, it is important to establish that different values were, indeed, evident in the two stories. A coding scheme, developed on an earlier set of stories, similarly elicited, was used. Values were scored as either being expressed or not. Two raters independently scored the stories, with acceptable reliability.

Significantly more subjects writing the abortion story expressed the values, equality, family security, freedom, mature love, sanctity of life, fetus's right to a full life, and sanctity of one's own body than did subjects in the course story condition. Additionally, significantly more subjects writing the course story expressed the values an exciting life, a sense of accomplishment, pleasure, and wisdom than those writing the abortion story. Clearly, the story manipulation was successful in priming different values.

It is also interesting to note, with regard to abortion attitude, that significantly more prochoice subjects expressed the value sanctity of one's own body when asked to write an abortion story than did prolife individuals. However, when asked to write a course story, neither of these two groups mentioned the value sanctity of one's own body. Finally, freedom was expressed marginally significantly ($p = .07$) more frequently by prochoice participants than prolife subjects. Although one might have expected more significant differences in value expression than just for these two, the abortion stories were characterized by a balancing of arguments and were not simply a one-sided presentation in favor of or against abortion. Most subjects showed some awareness of the other side's position. Nonetheless, on these two important values for the issue of abortion, prochoice and prolife individuals were different.

The major analyses involved testing for three-way interactions among the independent variables time of session, abortion attitude, and story. If the story writing task primed values, then we would expect, relative to Session 1, that critical values would change in line with abortion attitudes after writing the abortion story compared to after writing the course story. The only two significant three-way interactions found conformed to prediction. For the value freedom, at Time 1 there were no differences in value rankings between the prolife and prochoice individuals in either the abortion or course story conditions. At Time 2, however, prochoice subjects ranked freedom significantly more important than did prolife subjects in the abortion story condition. There were no differences found in the course story condition. The means are presented in Table 3.5.

Likewise, the pattern of means for the second significant three-way interac-

TABLE 3.5
Freedom: Mean Value Importance Rank as a Functionof Session, Story Condition, and Abortion
Attitude: Abortion Study 2

	Time 1	Time 2
Abortion Story		
Prolife	8.93	11.67
Prochoice	6.17	5.33
Course Story		
Prolife	9.22	8.22
Prochoice	7.00	7.44

tion found, for the value wisdom, was similar (see Table 3.6). At Time 1, there were no differences in the ranking of importance of wisdom between the prochoice and prolife subjects for either the course or abortion story. However, at Time 2, prolife subjects ranked wisdom as significantly more important than did prochoice individuals in the abortion story condition, but not in the course story.

The results of this study showed that asking subjects to write a story about either abortion or taking a course elicited values relevant to each story. Further, the abortion story writing task led to some changes in value importance that were consistent with the subjects' attitudes toward abortion. Moreover, the value importance changes could not be due to different value ranking instructions between conditions, because they were identical. In other words, because the participants were reporting their value systems according to general instructions that did not specify the abortion (or course) issue, any changes in value rankings must be due to some temporary change in context as a result of the story writing task. This result is consistent with what would be expected from the large literature on priming and accessibility (see Higgins, in press).

The previous three studies suggest that subjects may reorder the importance of their values in response to different target issues, which are made salient either through value ranking instructions or by a story writing assignment. In the earlier studies, participants responded to social topics, that is, abortion and environmental issues. In the next study, we examined whether individuals would reorder their value system according to which self-state perspective they were asked to adopt. We thought it would be interesting if it could be shown not only that people could have separate values systems for different societal concerns but that they also have separate value systems for different aspects of the self. The results, if found, would add further evidence that value systems are flexibly attuned to context and are not simply passively applied from a general value

TABLE 3.6
Wisdom: Mean Value Importance as a Function of Session, Story Condition, and Abortion
Attitude: Abortion Study 2

	Time 1	*Time 2*
Abortion Story		
Prolife	10.80	9.53
Prochoice	12.06	13.47
Course Story		
Prolife	11.78	14.22
Prochoice	12.06	11.56

system to specific cases. We also wanted to show that discrepancies in self-state value systems have important implications. We examined two possible consequences of contradictory self-state value systems, for negative affect and memory for earlier stated value systems.

RESEARCH ON MULTIPLE VALUE-SYSTEMS: DIFFERENT SELF-STATES

Our basic question concerns whether individuals have separate value systems associated with different self-states. The idea that normal individuals have more than one self-state, for example, actual, ideal, or ought selves, has been investigated by many researchers (e.g., Higgins, 1989; Markus, 1986; Rogers, 1959). The idea that value systems might be implicated in self-states was intimated by Rokeach (1973) in his work on the value self-confrontation method.

Rokeach's (1973) value self-confrontation technique involves teaching individuals that there are discrepancies between their value priorities and those of others who are important to them. For example, subjects may be asked to rank order Rokeach's terminal values and then to compare their rankings to those of fellow students. Next the experimenter points out a key discrepancy, perhaps that the subjects have ranked "equality" lower than "freedom" relative to rankings of the comparison group. In Rokeach's technique, an individual is forced to confront discrepancies between his or her rankings and those of significant others (e.g., peer group).

It is reasonable to assume that the peer group provides a moral standard against which the individual compares him or herself. Because individuals internalize society's moral standards, as exemplified by significant others, one should be able to find analogous discrepancies within the individual's value system, as the individual moves from one self-state to another. For example, the individual may consider his value system from the perspective of how he actually uses it in everyday situations, and also from the moral standard of how he ought to be using it.

Self-knowledge about one's value discrepancies, induced by the value-confrontation method, apparently results in positive changes in related attitudes and behaviors. In the original study, the technique led to significant reductions in racist attitudes and behavior toward African Americans that lasted at least 74 weeks (Rokeach, 1973). The effectiveness of the technique has been replicated several times (see review by Grube, Greenstein, Rankin, & Kearney, 1977), with behaviors as diverse as weight loss (Schwartz & Inbar-Saban, 1988), exercise (Sawa & Sawa, 1988), teaching effectiveness (Greenstein, 1976), authoritarianism (Altemeyer, 1994), and students' course selection (Ball-Rokeach, Rokeach, & Grube, 1984).

One proposal for why values change as a result of the self-confrontation method is that the technique leads individuals to become dissatisfied with their value priorities (Rokeach, 1973; Ball-Rokeach, Rokeach, & Grube, 1984). Presumably, important discovered discrepancies create dissatisfaction because they call into question the adequacy of one's value system. One possible way to reduce the induced dissatisfaction is for individuals to reorganize their own value system to be more in line with those of significant others.

So one implication of the self-confrontation studies is that individuals who have reported discrepancies in self-state value systems should feel negative affect. Higgins's (1989) findings that discrepancies in personality self-states are associated with negative affect lends credibility to this conjecture. A second implication is that individuals may try to dissipate their negative affect by either reorganizing their actual value system to be more consistent with their ought value system or by misremembering the extent of the earlier discrepancy so as to minimize it.

In the present study (conducted in collaboration with our graduate students, Jon Kovacheff and Nigel Turner), participants rank ordered a set of values from two perspectives, as they used them as guides in day-to-day situations (actual-self) and as they believed they ought to use them (ought-self). At a later date, participants were asked to recall the value hierarchies given at the earlier date. Measures of negative affect were also taken.

First, we expected to find at least some people who showed discrepant value systems associated with different self-states. Second, such discrepancy should be associated with negative affect. Third, because people presumably try to eliminate or reduce negative affect, lower negative affect at Time 2 should be associated with reports of the earlier value discrepancies as being smaller than they actually were.

Sixty-nine subjects, enroled in an introductory psychology course, took part in this study in partial fulfilment of course credit. Subjects were informed that the study involved participation in two 45-minute sessions, the second occurring 1 week after the first. Subjects were told the study involved the completion of several value ranking tasks, a questionnaire to measure their feelings and thoughts, and several individual difference forms.

In Session 1, subjects were asked to complete the Rokeach Terminal Value Survey from the actual and ought self-state perspectives. Specifically, the instructions for the actual perspective emphasized that subjects should rank the values "in order of their importance to YOU as you actually use them as guiding principles in YOUR life . . . and how you actually use the values to make decisions concerning your everyday conduct." The instructions for the ought perspective asked subjects "to arrange the values in order of their importance to YOU, as you feel you ought to or should use them as guiding principles in YOUR life . . . and how you feel obligated or responsible to be guided by these values to make decisions concerning your everyday conduct."

Half of the subjects were also asked to complete the Multiple Affect Adjective Checklist (MAACL; Zukerman & Lubin, 1965), which was used to measure the subjects' mood state. It consists of a list of positive and negative emotional adjectives from which subjects are asked to select those that best describe their current feeling.

At Session 2, 1 week later, all subjects were asked to fill out the MAACL, to complete the personality measures, and finally to recall as accurately as possible their previous week's rank order of both their actual and ought value lists. They were reminded not to rerank the values but to recall their earlier rankings. The major results were as follows:

Value self-discrepancies were measured by Spearman rank correlations (*rho*s) between subjects' actual and ought value systems. The actual/ought *rho*s ranged from $r = -.53$ to $r = .98$, $M = .49$, $SD = .36$. Relative to each other, larger correlations indicated little or low discrepancies; smaller or negative correlations indicated high self-discrepancies. Examination of the distribution of *rho*s indicated that 22 of the 69 participants actually had *rho*s that indicated relationships that were either negative or nonsignificantly positive between the value rankings given under actual and under ought self-conditions. Thus fully 32% of the sample tested here exhibited large discrepancies in value rankings related to different self-states.

As shown in Table 3.7, there were large shifts in rankings for some values. For example, both equality and a world at peace were seen as more important in the ought rankings than in the actual rankings, moving from position 14 to 5 for equality and from position 15 to 2 for a world at peace. Note also that equality and a world at peace reverse their rank order for the two self-states.

Affect.   The value discrepancy measure (*rho*) correlated $(-.48)$ significantly with negative mood at Time 1. *Rho* and negative mood were not significantly

TABLE 3.7
Is the Value System Preserved Across the Actual and Ought Self-States?

Self-State Value Systems: Initial Value Rankings

Ought Rankings	Actual Rankings
1. Family security	1. Happiness
2. A world at peace	3. Family security
3. Freedom	4. Self-respect
4. Self-respect	5. Freedom
5. Equality	14. Equality
6. Happiness	15. A world at peace

correlated ($-.07$) with negative mood at Time 2, suggesting that negative affect noted at Time 1 was dissipated 1 week later.

To test whether subjects would remember their earlier value rankings of actual and ought self-states as more similar than they actually were, we calculated a discrepancy score for the two self-states in the following way. The absolute difference in the value rankings of the top 6 values provided in Session 1 were calculated for each person. The top six values were used because they are the most important and accessible values (see Rokeach & Ball-Rokeach, 1989). Specifically, for each individual, the top six ought values were identified, and then the rankings of these same values in the actual list were determined. The total absolute difference in the two rankings of these six values was then calculated, [total abs(O–A)]. In other words, for each value the difference between its ranking in the ought list and the actual list was calculated.

The Session 2 memory data were scored in the same way. That is, for each individual, the absolute difference in the remembered rankings of the same six values (identified in Session 1) was calculated, [total abs(MO–MA)]. The mean difference between these two scores (i.e., discrepancy found in Session 2 minus the discrepancy found in Session 1) was compared using a correlated t test. Overall, as predicted, participants *remembered* the values associated with their actual and ought self-states as being significantly more similar to one another than they actually were ($M = -.326$). The results are not likely due to regression effects because the size of the initial value self-discrepancies (*rho*) was not significantly correlated with the degree of change between the actual and ought rankings at Time 1 and the memory for them at Time 2.

In order to test whether the degree of memory distortion was associated with less negative affect, the following memory distortion score was calculated for each person: degree of distortion = [abs(MO–MA) minus abs(O–A)]. A negative number indicates that one remembers the value rankings that they had given a week earlier as being more similar to one another than they actually were, whereas a positive number indicates that the value rankings are remembered as more dissimilar. The degree of memory distortion is represented by the size of the difference. The correlation between the memory distortion score and negative affect at Time 2 was significant ($r = .26$), showing that the greater the memory distortion the smaller the negative affect experienced.

In sum, we found, first, that the correlations between value systems associated with how we *ought* to act and how we *actually* behave vary considerably, thus suggesting that there are individual differences in the extent of discrepancies between self-value systems. Second, the greater the discrepancy in value systems between the self-states, the greater the negative affect produced, at least initially, thus confirming the major assumption of why values change. Third, some individuals distorted their memory of their reported self-state value systems such that they remembered smaller discrepancies than actually existed. Finally, the more that participants distorted their memory in favor of consistency between actual and ought value self-states, the less negative affect they reported.

The present study can not unfortunately differentiate between a memory reconstrual explanation of the change in remembered value discrepancies and the possibility that the subjects genuinely changed their value rankings in response to perceived negative affect. However, the main question of whether there are different value systems associated with different self-states that have important implications, for at least negative affect, has been answered in the affirmative.

Discussion

The four studies reported here provide preliminary evidence that individuals reorder their value system or, at least change the importance rankings of some key values, as situations differ. Individuals were found to alter their value systems in response to different instructions for value ranking for different target issues. With regard to both abortion and the environment as target issues, subjects substantially reorganized their value system compared to the value system elicited according to traditional instructions focusing on guiding principles in one's life. When the abortion issue was made salient through a story writing task, rather than through the value ranking instructions, the values of freedom and wisdom became more or less important, in line with the subjects' attitudes toward abortion, compared to their value rankings at an earlier time. In the final study, it was found that subjects reported different value systems associated with their actual and ought self-states. Discrepancies between the actual and ought value systems were related to initial negative affect. Distortions of memory for values discrepancies were related to later negative affect.

The results of the foregoing studies support the view that value systems, when used as guidelines in everyday behavior, are not necessarily immutable. When additional information or contexts are provided, values can be reorganized in a different way to meet the demands of the new situation. To our knowledge, no one has suggested that value systems can not change. For example, the work on the value self-confrontation technique demonstrates that. However, the inference from that research is that an individual's value system changed from one relatively stable system to another. The value self-confrontation research does not argue for a multiple value system perspective that sees an individual as having a number of relatively separate (though related) value systems for various important domains of one's life.

The question for future research is to find the middle ground between a picture of the value system as stable and applicable to all contexts, and one of the value system as everchanging in the face of transient forces. There are arguments for both stability and flexibility in value systems. On the one hand, individuals need to have coherent value systems reflecting their self-concepts. On the other hand, individuals need to be able to respond flexibly as the occasion demands. Just as one may act differently toward one's parents than toward one's friends, one possibly may use different versions of a basic value system in different circumstances.

Taken to its extreme, neither the stable view nor the multiple value system perspective is tenable. An extreme multiple value systems position would treat the traditional concept of the value system as limited to the case when the individual is asked to think abstractly about values. In this view, the general value system would provide no necessary predictive power for behavior or attitudes toward social issues, which would remain entirely issue or situationally driven. Neither our data nor those of other value researchers cited throughout the chapter support such an extreme view.

However, an extreme stability position is just as unlikely because it suggests that the general value system is dominant and that situations only present relevant values to consider within the framework of the general system, that is, relevant values are maintained in the same value importance rank order as in the general system. In other words, the extreme stability position does not allow for a reordering of values, except perhaps in the case of a change over time, from one relatively stable system to another. The essential point is that an extreme stable value system perspective insists on one basic value system at a time. The present results contradict an extreme stability view.

The present discussion is reminiscent of the personality–situation and attitude–behavior debates (see Zanna, Higgins, & Herman, 1982), and the complexity of these debates would also likely apply to the value–attitude issue. For one example, consider one of the main messages of the work of Fishbein and Ajzen (1975) who argue that attitudes are good predictors of behavior when they are both measured at the same level of specificity. As shown in the abortion results of Study 1, values ranked according to an abortion instruction were better predictors of abortion attitudes than values ranked with regard to the general, traditional instructions.

The present view of value systems as dynamic complements Schwartz's

(1992; this book) theory of the circular structure of value systems. In Schwartz's view values are organized into ten value types characterized by motivational goals. Value types that are relatively more adjacent to each other tend to be similarly associated with outside variables. Likewise, opposing value types have opposite relations with outside variables. The relative multiple value system perspective outlined here does not refer to Schwartz's structure of value systems, in the sense of how the values relate to each other along the circle. The multiple value system can accept Schwartz's value structure. However, it still proposes that the different value types may be reordered in different contexts and for different purposes. Indeed, thinking about value types as motivationally driven lends plausibility to the notion that value reordering takes place, because it is entirely likely that peoples' motivations vary across situations, and, thus, may the importance of their value types.

CONCLUDING REMARKS

We should make clear that what we are proposing is not merely that values can be influenced by social situations or context. We think the data reported in the present chapter suggest that the way we think about value systems may be in need of revision. If values or value types do reorder themselves across situations, then we must ask what purpose the general value system serves. It may be the case, on the one hand, that the general value system is truly an organizing system for values, built up over time by the individuals' need to have a set of standards that reflect well on the self-concept and guide thought and action. On the other hand, it seems plausible to us that the general system may largely reflect how we like to think of ourselves—when asked to do so abstractly—which may or may not transcend particular social issues or ethical dilemmas. Our hope is that this chapter will stimulate empirical research to help answer this question.

The present studies provide hints as to how a multiple value system may operate. One way of thinking of it is to use the language of social cognition (see Fiske & Taylor, 1991). Social issues such as abortion may be represented as a schema that has values associated with it. The schema may vary in detail in emotion and content, and may be more or less elaborated. For some people, a particular abortion story may express the schema. For example, some people, when they think of abortion, may think of a poor, single mother, with several children who does not have the resources either to give birth to or raise another child. Another person's abortion story may conjure up a picture of a yuppie unmarried lawyer who decides her pregnancy comes at an inconvenient time. The values associated with these stories may be strongly associated with, indeed dictate, one's attitude.

In the abortion stories collected in Study 3, the majority of the stories involved "boy meets girl, accidental pregnancy occurs, what to do next." The story plots frequently involved the pros and cons of getting an abortion. Yet there still was a value flavor to the stories, at least compared to the taking a course story. In a sample less homogeneous than a first-year university sample, a greater range of abortion stories may be found. It is not known to what extent people have stories for ethical and social issues. For many people, perhaps these issues have fairly incoherent content, even if there is strong affect.

The point to be made is that to the extent that people have well developed schemas for many different social, ethical, political, and personal issues, the more likely the stored values, along with other information, will play a role in attitudes and behavior. A multiple value system would be supported to the extent that values are ordered differently for the various issues and their related schemas. Thus we suggest that when a topic is raised for an individual, the person may not have to consult some general value system, but possibly only deal with the values that are associated with the relevant schema(s) for the issue. Depending on one's socialization, the general value system (as taught by one's parents or peers) may lead to similar value approaches to a number of issues or may lead to very different value perspectives.

Clearly there will be issues for which we do not possess very elaborated schemas and to which we have no particular emotional reaction. For example, one such issue, at least for us, is surrogate motherhood. Quite likely a presentation of surrogate motherhood as either a form of slavery or a typical contractual business deal would have implications for the types of values (and affect) that would arise, assuming that we have either schemas or values associated with both slavery and business deals. Importantly, it is in situations such as these, that accessibility and salience effects of values will be crucial. Future research needs to attend to the way in which values become accessible in ethical and social issues contexts, and the consequences of such situationally created value accessibility for attitudes and behavior. The research paradigm that Fazio (1986) has used systematically to examine attitude accessibility and its effect on the attitude–behavior relation would be a good starting point for values researchers.

One example of such research is Rae Gilchrist's dissertation (1995). He has shown that value importance and value accessibility (as measured by reaction time to judge value importance) are significantly and positively correlated. The more important the value, the more accessible it is. Moreover, a value's accessibility can be increased by frequent presentations of the value. Most interestingly, the manipulated increased accessibility of relevant values leads to significantly increased correlations between values and related attitudes, compared to control conditions. Thus one possible mechanism for how multiple value-systems may work centers on accessibility processes.

In closing, we should note that all values (or value types) are positive. Therefore individuals need not pay a penalty for reordering their value priorities. Probably each of the values is the most cherished in some context.

ACKNOWLEDGMENTS

The research reported in this chapter was supported by a grant from the Social Sciences and Humanities Research Council of Canada to the authors. We thank our colleagues N. Kuiper, G. Maio, J. M. Olson, and M. P. Zanna for their comments on an earlier version of the chapter.

REFERENCES

Altemeyer, R. (1994). Reducing prejudice in right-wing authoritarians. In M. P. Zanna, & J. M. Olson (Eds.). *The psychology of prejudice: The Ontario symposium, Vol. 7* (pp. 131–148). Hillsdale, NJ: Lawrence Erlbaum Associates.

Ball-Rokeach, S., Rokeach, M., & Grube, J. W. (1984). *The great American values test.* New York: Free Press.

Blackwood, P. (1991). *Influencing value importance by increasing value accessibility.* Unpublished master's thesis. Department of Psychology, University of Western Ontario.

Cacioppo, J. T., & Petty, R. E. (1982). The need for cognition. *Journal of Personality and Social Psychology, 42,* 116–131.

Cherry, F., & Byrne, D. (1977). Authoritarianism. In T. Bass (Ed.), *Personality variables in social behavior* (pp. 109–133). Hillsdale, NJ: Lawrence Erlbaum Associates.

Fazio, R. H. (1986). How do attitudes guide behavior? In R. M. Sorrentino, & E. T. Higgins (Eds.), *Handbook of motivation and cognition* (pp. 204–253). New York: Guilford Press.

Fishbein, M., & Ajzen, I. (1975). *Belief, attitude, intention and behavior.* Reading, MA: Addison-Wesley.

Fiske, S. T., & Taylor, S. E. (1991). *Social cognition.* New York: McGraw-Hill.

Gilchrist, R. S. (1995). *An investigation of value accessibility and its role in the value-attitude relationship.* Unpublished doctoral dissertation. Department of Psychology, University of Western Ontario.

Greenstein, T. N. (1976). Behavior change through value self-confrontation: A field experiment. *Journal of Personality and Social Psychology, 34,* 254–262.

Grube, J. W., Greenstein, T. N., Rankin, W. L., & Kearney, K. A. (1977). Behavior change following self-confrontation: A test of the value mediation hypothesis. *Journal of Personality and Social Psychology, 35,* 212–216.

Higgins, E. T. (1989). Self-discrepancy theory. In L. Berkowitz (Ed.), *Advances in experimental social psychology* (Vol. 22, pp. 91–134). New York: Academic Press.

Higgins, E. T. (in press). Knowledge activation: Accessibility, applicability, and salience. In E. T. Higgins & A. Kruglanski (Eds.), *Social psychology: Handbook of basic principles.*

Kristiansen, C. M., & Zanna, M. P. (1988). Justifying attitudes by appealing to values: A functional perspective. *British Journal of Social Psychology, 27*(3), 247–256.

Markus, H. (1986). Possible selves. *American Psychologist, 41,* 954–969.

Polak, R. L., & Lepper, M. R. (1990, August). Personality correlates of the tolerance for cognitive dissonance scale. Presented at the meeting of the *American Psychological Association,* Boston, MA.

Rogers, C. R. (1959). A theory of therapy, personality, and interpersonal relationships, as developed in the client-centered framework. In S. Koch (Ed.), *Psychology: A study of a science. Vol. 3. Formulations of the person and social context* (pp. 184–256). New York: McGraw-Hill.

Rokeach, M. (1960). *The open and closed mind.* New York: Basic Books.

Rokeach, M. (1973). *The nature of human values.* New York: Free Press.

Rokeach, M., & Ball-Rokeach, S. J. (1989). Stability and change in American value priorities, 1968–1981. *American Psychologist, 44,* 775–784.

Sawa, S., & Sawa, G. H. (1988). The value confrontation approach to enduring behavior modification. *Journal of Social Psychology, 128,* 207–215.

Schwartz, S. (1992). Universals in the content and structure of values: Theoretical advances and empirical tests in 20 countries. In M. P. Zanna (Ed.), *Advances in experimental social psychology. Vol. 25.* Orlando, FL: Academic Press.

Schwartz, S. H., & Inbar-Saban, N. (1988). Value self-confrontation as a method to aid weight loss. *Journal of Personality and Social Psychology, 54,* 396–404.

Seligman, C., Syme, G. J., & Gilchrist, R. S. (1994). The role of values and ethical principles in judgments of environmental dilemmas. *Journal of Social Issues, 50,* 105–119.

Sparks, P., & Durkin, K. (1987). Moral reasoning and political orientation: The context sensitivity of individual rights and democratic principles. *Journal of Personality and Social Psychology, 52,* 819–827.

Snyder, M. (1974). The self-monitoring of expressive behavior. *Journal of Personality and Social Psychology, 30,* 212–216.

Tetlock, P. E. (1986). A value pluralism model of ideological reasoning. *Journal of Personality and Social Psychology, 50,* 819–827.

Weigel, J., Weigel, R. H. (1978). Environmental concern: The development of a measure. *Environment and Behavior, 10,* 3–16.

Zanna, M. P., Higgins, E. T., & Herman, C. P. (Eds.). (1982). *Consistency in Social Behavior: The Ontario Symposium, Vol. 2.* Hillsdale, NJ: Lawrence Erlbaum Associates.

Zukerman, M., & Lubin, B. (1965). *Manual for the Multiple Affect Adjective Checklist.* San Diego: Educational and Industrial Testing Service.

4

Morality and the Self: Implications for the When and How of Value–Attitude– Behavior Relations

Connie M. Kristiansen
Alan M. Hotte
Carleton University

At the second Ontario Symposium, Zanna and Fazio (1982) described the evolution of research as a response to three questions. First generation questions ask whether there is an effect to explain. In this regard, this chapter examines the effects of people's values on their attitudes and behavior. Second and third generation questions ask in what situations and for whom these relations hold and how or by what process. As Zanna and Fazio (1982) stated, these latter questions are inextricably linked in that knowledge of when a phenomenon occurs provides information about its underlying processes. This chapter therefore considers for whom and when values are likely to guide attitudes and behavior and suggests that, for moral actions, the nature of both the self and the moral issue affect the process of moral reasoning and thereby value–attitude–behavior relations. A theoretical model derived from Ajzen and Fishbein's (1972) original formulation of the theory of reasoned action is then proposed to capture the relation between the self and morality, on the one hand, and values, attitudes and behavior on the other.

THE VALUE–ATTITUDE–BEHAVIOR RELATION

This review and attempt to integrate seemingly independent literatures was motivated by two factors, namely the magnitude of value–attitude–behavior relations and the extent to which values are used as post hoc justifications of attitudes and behavior. Although intuitively it makes sense to assume that people use their general values in life to guide their more specific attitudes and behavior, a recent study suggested that this might not be as true as one might think (Kristiansen &

Zanna, 1992). In this study, approximately 300 students completed Rokeach's (1967) Value Survey and items assessing their ecology-related attitudes and behavior. A month later, and using the self-confrontation method of changing values, attitudes, and behavior (Ball-Rokeach, Rokeach, & Grube, 1984), these students were randomly assigned to a control or treatment group. Participants in the control group were simply given feedback about the average values of their peers, and invited to compare them with their own values. Treatment participants, in contrast, were provided with additional data indicating that ecologists valued "a world of beauty" highly and more than "a comfortable life." A month following this, all students participated in a supposedly independent study where their posttreatment values, attitudes, and behavioral intentions were assessed. Finally, students' reports of their overt behavior were obtained 2 months later via a telephone survey conducted by a campus ecology group.

The analyses of these data revealed that exposure to the self-confrontation procedure accounted for 6% of the increased valuation of "a world of beauty," but less than 3% of the increased favorability of students' ecology attitudes. And the treatment had absolutely no impact on participants' intentions or their actual behavior. Finally, although treatment participants displayed greater consistency between their values, attitudes and intentions, this enhanced consistency did not extend to their overt behavior.

Given Kristiansen and Zanna's (1992) rather disappointing findings, we looked more closely at the effects obtained in other studies. Tables 4.1 and 4.2 present the effect sizes, or explained variance, for the studies cited by Ball-Rokeach et al. (1984) as evidence for the effects of the self-confrontation procedure on attitudes and behavior. In regard to attitudes, most of the effects obtained in these studies were nonsignificant, and the explained variance ranged from none to 7.2% (see Table 4.1). And in regard to behavior, the explained variance ranged from none to 12.3%, with most effect sizes hovering at less than 1% (see Table 4.2). Similarly, although Ball-Rokeach et al.'s televised self-confrontation, *The Great American Values Test,* changed viewers' attitudes and behavior, as shown in Table 4.3 at most 1% of the variance was accounted for by exposure to the program.

Other experimental and correlational studies, studies that speak more directly to the value–attitude–behavior relation, have documented similar effects. For example, when Grube, Greenstein, Rankin, and Kearney (1977) reanalyzed Rokeach's (1973) data, and Greenstein (1982) reanalyzed his own data, both found that, although some aspect of Rokeach's treatment accounted for 4% of the variance in behavior, less than 1% of this variance was attributable to changes in values. Similarly, as shown in Table 4.4, which presents an unsystematic sample of correlational research, the covariation between values and behavior ranged from 3% to 14%, averaging at 7%. Although some of the latter effect sizes are surely reasonable, one must bear in mind that these surveys are often accom-

TABLE 4.1
Effect of Self-Confrontation Procedure on Attitudes for Studies Listed by Ball-Rokeach, Rokeach,
and Grube (1984)

Study	Attitude Object	Effect Size[a]
Rokeach (1973) experiment 1	Blacks	*ns*
Rokeach (1973) experiment 2	Blacks	*ns*
Rokeach (1973) experiment 3	Blacks	*ns*
	Preference for ethnic studies courses	$\phi^2 = .000$
Hollen (1972)	Ban nonreturnable bottles	$\eta^2 = .063$ to 107[b]
Hopkins (1973)	Minorities	$\eta^2 = .080$
McLellan (1974)	Racism	*ns*
Gray & Ashmore (1975)[c]	*Immediate posttest:*	
	Scaled attitudes to Blacks	$\eta^2 = .052$
	Absolute attitudes	$\eta^2 = .056$
	Job motivation	$\eta^2 = .072$
	Preferential treatment	*ns*
	8 week posttest:	
	Scaled attitudes to Blacks	*ns*
	Absolute attitudes	*ns*
	Job motivation	*ns*
	Preferential treatment	$\eta^2 = .053$
Rokeach & Greenstein (1976)	Blacks	*ns*
Grube (1979)	Ecology	$\eta^2 = .018$
Young (1979)	Career information seeking	*ns*

[a]Nonsignificant findings lacked sufficient information to calculate effect sizes.
[b]Estimated from probability level. Note that Hollen assessed six additional attitudes, all of which were associated with nonsignificant effects.
[c]Based on overall analysis of the 3 treatment and control groups.

panied by pressures toward consistency (e.g., when respondents complete all measures in one sitting).

In sum, then, although values, attitudes, and behavior are related, these relations are often small, albeit equivalent to that of other social psychological phenomena. Cohen (1988), for example, said that "small" effect sizes of $r^2 = .01$ are representative of personality, social, and clinical psychology. Nevertheless, one wonders why people do not express attitudes and actions that are more strongly in line with their values.

The second factor that prompted our interest in potential moderators of value–attitude–behavior relations was research concerning the value justification hypothesis and the possibility that values may play a stronger role as defensive justifications of already established attitudes rather than as guides to the development of people's attitudes (for a review see Kristiansen & Zanna, 1994). This rhetorical use of values was nicely captured in Faludi's (1991) journalistic exposé of the New Right's attempt to appeal to socially shared values to justify attitudes that were really based on their opposition to women's equality. In this regard, Faludi (1991) wrote that the New Right's "Orwellian wordplay . . . [regarding policies designed to enhance women's status, such as the Equal Rights Amend-

TABLE 4.2
Effect of Self-Confrontation Procedure on Behavior for Studies Listed by Ball-Rokeach, Rokeach, and Grube (1984)

Study	Behavior	Effect Size[a]
Rokeach (1973) experiment 2	*Respond to NAACP:*	
	3-5 month posttest	$\phi^2 = .014$
	15-17 month posttest	$\phi^2 = .014$
	Take ethnic course	$\phi^2 = .039$
	Transfer to social sciences	$\phi^2 = .001$
Rokeach (1973) experiment 3	*Respond to NAACP:*	
	3-5 month posttest	$\phi^2 = .031$
	15-17 month posttest	$\phi^2 = .000$
	Transfer to social sciences	$\phi^2 = .102$
Penner (1971)	Eye contact with Blacks	$\phi^2 = .123$
Rokeach & McLellan (1972)	*Join antiracism committee:*	
	Self + Others vs. Control	$\phi^2 = .055$
	Others vs. Control	$\phi^2 = .028$
	Behavioral commitment:[b]	
	Self + Others vs. Control	$\phi^2 = .001$
	Others vs. Control	$\phi^2 = .001$
Conroy, Katkin, & Barnette (1973)	Cigarette smoking	Significant
Hopkins (1973)	Attend antiracism film	$\phi^2 = .017$
	Join Afro-American society	$\phi^2 = .000$
DeSeve (1975)	Cigarette smoking	*ns*
Greenstein (1976)	Teacher performance	$\eta^2 = .040$
Sherrid & Beech (1976)	Attend human relations seminar	ns
Rokeach & Greenstein (1976)	Money to Black artists	*ns*
	Support gay rights	*ns*
Sanders & Atwood (1979)	NAACP solicitation	$\eta^2 = 0.00$
Grube (1979)	*Self-reported actions:[c]*	
	Active in environment movement	$\phi^2 = .000$
	Recycling	$\phi^2 = .000$
	Active in organization	$\phi^2 = .000$
	Behavioral solicitations:	
	Circulate petition	$\phi^2 = .002$
	Other projects	$\phi^2 = .001$
	Return petition	$\phi^2 = .000$
	Percent of favorable responses to all measures	$\phi^2 = .000$
	Mean number of favorable responses	$\phi^2 = .000$
Young (1979)	Talking about career planning with others	$\eta^2 = 0.82^d$

[a]Nonsignificant findings lacked sufficient information to calculate effect sizes.
[b]Based on chi-square analyses including nonrespondents.
[c]Based on comparisons of self-confrontation vs. control group only. Effects opposite to those hypothesized are listed as $\phi^2 = .000$.
[d]Among participants with internal locus of control expectancies.

ment] . . . served to conceal their anger at women's rising independence. This was a fruitful marketing tool, as they would draw more sympathy from the press and more followers from the public if they marched under the banner of traditional family values" (p. 238).

Kristiansen, Gareau, and DeCourville (1994) examined Faludi's backlash hypothesis in regard to people's opinions regarding the "false memory syndrome" (FMS) debate. That is, the claim that adults are erroneously recovering memories of having been abused in childhood. Several researchers (e.g., Terr, 1994) have stated that it is currently impossible to draw a general conclusion regarding the impact of trauma on memory and the validity of recovered memories simply because the experimental research (e.g., Loftus, 1993) lacks external validity and the clinical research (e.g., Terr, 1991) lacks internal validity. In view of this, one wonders what criteria people are using as they vehemently take sides on this issue.

Reading the FMS Foundation's (1993) mission statement suggests that they attempt to justify their challenges to the validity of recovered memories by appealing to socially shared values. For example, they write of their concern with "the consequences of false allegations where whole families are split apart" and offer financial aid and access to legal counsel "to alleviate or remedy damages done by such accusations," thereby drawing values such as family security and law and order into the debate. But given that the vast majority of known incest survivors are women, people may question the validity of recovered memories of abuse not because of their regard for such traditional values, but because of their negative attitudes toward women's equality and independence. Further, authoritarianism seemed potentially relevant to the FMS debate given Faludi's exposé, as well as findings that authoritarians have negative attitudes toward feminists,

TABLE 4.3
Effect of Self-Confrontation Procedure on Attitudes and Behavior
(Ball-Rokeach, Rokeach, and Grube, 1984)

Dependent Variable	Effect Size[a]
Pretest-posttest attitude change[b]	
Attitudes toward the environment	$\phi^2 = .001$
Attitudes toward women	*ns*
Attitudes toward Blacks	$\phi^2 = .001$
Posttest attitudes[c]	
Attitudes toward the environment	*ns*
Attitudes toward women	*ns*
Attitudes toward Blacks	$\phi^2 = .002$
Favorable responses to solicitations[c]	
Environmental group	$\phi^2 = .008$
Women's group	$\phi^2 = .013$
Black group	$\phi^2 = .000$
Monetary donations[c]	
Environmental group	$\phi^2 = .003$
Women's group	$\phi^2 = .006$
Black group	$\phi^2 = .000$

[a]Nonsignificant findings lacked sufficient information to calculate effect sizes.
[b]Based on uninterrupted viewers only.
[c]Based on comparison of uninterrupted viewers versus control city nonviewers.

TABLE 4.4
Correlational Research Examining the Value-Attitude Relation

Researcher	Value(s)	Attitude Object	Effect Size
Furnham (1987)	5 terminal values	Protestant work ethic	$R^2 = .160$
	4 instrumental values	Protestant work ethic	$R^2 = .096$
	5 terminal values	Work ethic	$R^2 = .130$
	6 instrumental values	Work ethic	$R^2 = .180$
Kristiansen & Matheson (1990)	Peace, national security	Nuclear weapons	$R^2 = .103$
Kristiansen & Zanna (1988)	A comfortable life	Nuclear weapons	$R^2 = .123$
	Salvation	Abortion	$R^2 = .248$
Penner (1971)	Equality	Perceived value similarity	$r^2 = .082$
		Perceived behavior similarity	$r^2 = .086$
Rokeach (1973)	Equality	Blacks	$r^2 = .160$
	Equality	Poor people	$r^2 = .053$
Sherrid & Beech (1976)	Equality	Tolerance for nonconformists	$r^2 = .014$

whom they perceive as violating traditional values (Haddock & Zanna, 1994), and ascribe importance to traditional values (Altemeyer, 1994). Authoritarian pedagogy is also hypothesized to underlie child abuse (Miller, 1983).

In their study, Kristiansen, Gareau, and DeCourville (1994) used 26 items derived from the literature of the FMS Foundation (n.d.) and its proponents (e.g., Tavris, 1993) to measure undergraduates' beliefs regarding the validity of adults' recovered memories of child abuse. These "FMS beliefs" included the extent to which students' believed that people could develop false memories from a therapist's suggestions or after reading a book about incest, and whether people were making up stories of abuse to gain sympathy or as excuses for other psychological problems. These students also completed Spence, Helmreich, and Stapp's (1973) Attitudes toward Women Scale, Altemeyer's (1988) Right-Wing Authoritarianism scale, and a modified version of Rokeach's (1967) Terminal Value Survey in which they ranked the personal importance of 18 values, values that included "law and order (maintaining order in society)" and "family security (taking care of loved ones)."

A path analysis of these data revealed that, as expected and as shown by the standardized beta weights in Figure 4.1, students with higher authoritarianism scores assigned more importance to the traditional values "law and order" and "family security." Further, contrary to the FMS Foundation's (1993) expressed concern with maintaining family unity, students who assigned more priority to "family security" were less, rather than more, likely to endorse FMS. Moreover, students' valuation of "law and order" was totally independent of their FMS beliefs. These results, together with the finding that students with higher authoritarianism scores expressed less favorable attitudes toward women's equality, attitudes that were closely tied to students' FMS beliefs, support the application of Faludi's (1991) backlash hypothesis to the FMS debate. They are also consistent with the value justification hypothesis in that people do seem to appeal to values to justify their attitudes toward social issues, even when these values are actually unrelated to their attitudes.

If such rhetorical appeals to values succeed in reframing how social issues are construed, and thereby affect other people's attitudes, it seems that the very notion of *values* is vulnerable to moral exploitation. This, together with the weak value–attitude–behavior relations documented in prior research, motivated us to ask whether there are any other routes to morality besides value-driven deontology. To this end, we asked, "what personality and situational variables affect the magnitude of value–attitude–behavior correspondence?" And our review of the literature suggested that the nature of people's moral reasoning and their self-conceptions, together with the characteristics of the moral issue, may determine when and for whom one might reasonably expect values to be used as attitudinal and behavioral guides.

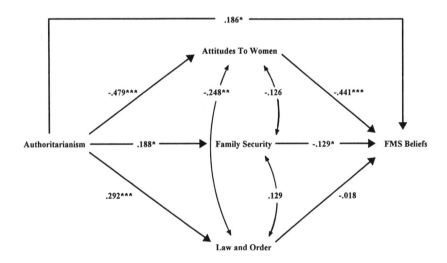

$N = 185$. *$p < .05$. **$p < .01$. ***$p < .001$.

FIG. 4.1. Standardized path coefficients (betas) for relations between authoritarianism, values, attitudes toward women, and "false memory syndrome" (FMS) beliefs.

VARIABLES MODERATING
VALUE–ATTITUDE–BEHAVIOR RELATIONS

No doubt many factors moderate the impact of values on attitudes and behavior, and many of these variables are probably the same as those known to moderate attitude-behavior relations, including the reliability and comprehensiveness of value measures (Braithwaite & Scott, 1991) and the ability of very general values to account for more precisely defined attitudes and behavior (Ajzen & Fishbein, 1977). Specific to values, however, are issues regarding the nature of moral reasoning and the self. In this section we therefore consider the potential implications of moral development, moral reasoning, and self-conceptions for value–attitude–behavior relations.

MORALITY

Morality is an important consideration in the study of value–attitude–behavior relations to the extent that one regards morally relevant attitudes and behaviors as responses to an obligation, founded in some ideal. Values may, at least for some people, provide such transsituational ideals regulating people's beliefs about what they ought to do, and thereby their attitudes and behavior. A conceptual link between morality and values, then, lies in the their mutual concern with obligation and ideals. Given this, two intriguing factors that may moderate value–attitude–behavior correspondence are moral reasoning and moral orientation.

Moral Reasoning. In psychology, moral reasoning has most frequently been studied from Kohlberg's (1969, 1976, 1981, 1984; Kohlberg, Levine, & Hewer, 1983) cognitive developmental perspective. Kohlberg delineated three general levels of moral development, each characterized by different reasoning regarding the factors underlying moral behavior. At the preconventional level, the young child is egoistically concerned with obedience, avoiding punishment, and self-satisfaction. At the conventional level, typical of adolescents and most adults, moral reasoning is concerned with the desire for approval and compliance with social rules, roles, and conventions. Finally, although only attained by some 10% to 20% of adults (Clarke-Stewart, Friedman, & Koch, 1985; Kitwood, 1990), persons engaged in principled, postconventional reasoning are concerned with personal standards and values that they have defined independently of authority figures or society. Thus, it is at this level that people are likely to rely on their own internalized values as guides to their attitudes and behavior. As Kohlberg and his colleagues put it, here "the core of morality . . . is deontological, . . . a matter of rights and duties as prescriptions" (Levine, Kohlberg, & Hewer, 1985, p. 85).

As it turns out, knowledge of a person's stage of moral reasoning is no more able to predict behavior than knowledge of a person's values. In this regard,

Blasi's (1980) review found that moral stage accounted for less than 1% of the variance in moral behaviors such as honesty. Similarly, Rest (1986; Thoma, Rest, & Davison, 1991) reported at best a moderate relation between Kohlberg's postconventional principled reasoning, as determined by his Defining Issues Test (DIT) P-scores, and moral behavior. Indeed, Rest (1979) himself is searching for moderating variables and recognizes the potential role of alternative, nonjustice oriented, routes to morality. Thoma et al. (1991), for example, stated that "the existence of justice reasoning in an individual's decision-making repertoire does not preclude the existence of other interpretive systems or [indicate] that justice reasoning is the preferred system used in solving moral dilemmas" (p. 659).

These small effects in both the value and morality literatures are perhaps not surprising in that, although Kohlberg's model accounts for the development and process of moral reasoning, it in no way considers the content of such reasoning. Similarly, although value research considers the content of people's values and moral standards, it in no way considers the fact that different people may use different processes of moral reasoning. However, just as Smith (1991) and Blasi (1980) have articulated, and even Kohlberg (1969) himself, stage of moral development and values may well have an interactive effect on the production of moral attitudes and behavior: Relative to people who display preconventional and conventional reasoning, those who display postconventional, principled reasoning should be more likely to act in accord with their internalized values, whatever these values may be. Although no study has yet examined the impact of principled moral reasoning on value–attitude and value–behavior relations, Rholes and Bailey (1983) reported that, in two studies of attitudes toward the value-laden issue of abortion, attitude–behavior consistency was greater among university students with higher DIT P-scores.

The distinction between the process of moral reasoning and its content is, of course, fundamental to the suggestion that moral reasoning moderates value–attitude–behavior relations. Although both Kohlberg (1971a, p. 55) and Rest (1979) argue, and present evidence, that the process of moral reasoning is independent of its content, the evidence for this distinction is mixed. In regard to the independence of moral reasoning and attitudes, for example, de Vries and Walker (1986) reported that higher levels of moral reasoning were associated with less favorable attitudes toward capital punishment, and they suggested that this process-content relation stemmed from the liberal ideological bias inherent in Kohlberg's conceptualization of moral development. Contrary to this suggestion, however, Feather (1988) noted that DIT principled reasoning scores were independent of a measure of ideological conservatism. And Rholes and Bailey (1983) found that principled reasoning was unrelated to participants' attitudes toward abortion, thereby supporting the distinction between the process of moral reasoning and its content.

Studies that have examined the process–content distinction as it applies to moral reasoning and values have also yielded mixed results. Parish, Rosenblatt, and Kappes (1979/1980) reported that, although a sample of American college students' DIT P-scores were independent of the priority they assigned to Rokeach's (1967) 18 instrumental values, their DIT P-scores were related to the importance they ascribed to several terminal values: P-scores were higher among those who gave more importance to "equality" and "mature love," and less to "pleasure." Wilson (1983), in contrast, found that the principled reasoning scores of a sample of American veterans varied as a function of the primacy they gave to the instrumental values "ambition," "responsible" and "clean," and the terminal values "a comfortable life," "inner harmony," and "pleasure." And Feather (1988) reported that Australian highschool students' principled reasoning scores were positively associated with the priority they assigned to "inner harmony," "broadminded," and "logical" and negatively related to the importance they gave to being "clean" and "obedient." Finally, we observed that Canadian university students who displayed more principled reasoning placed more importance on "equality" and less on "a comfortable life," with these values sharing 13% of the variance with students' DIT principled reasoning scores (Kristiansen, Hotte, & Mosion, 1995). Although these data might appear to imply that the process of moral reasoning is not independent of its value content, the small size of these relations and the inconsistency of the findings across studies suggest that the process of moral reasoning may be more different from, rather than similar to, the content of such reasoning. Given this, the moderating impact of moral reasoning on value–attitude–behavior relations remains a tenable hypothesis.

Moral Orientation.   Just as the level of moral reasoning may moderate value–attitude–behavior relations, so too may the nature of people's moral orientation. The approach of cognitive developmental theory has been "justice oriented" in that it ascribes to the ideal of an autonomous moral agent who, through a rational and impartial consideration of rights and obligations, determines which principles to follow.

Another moral orientation is the "care orientation" articulated by feminists such as Gilligan (1982, 1987; Gilligan, Ward, & Taylor, 1988) and Noddings (1984). The ethic of care differs from Kohlberg's ethic of justice in at least three ways.

> First, the ethic of care revolves around different moral concepts than Kohlberg's ethic of justice, that is responsibility and relationships rather than rights and rules. Second, this morality is tied to concrete circumstances rather than being formal and abstract. Third, this morality is best expressed not as a set of principles but as an activity, the "activity of care." In Gilligan's different voice, morality is not grounded in universal, abstract principles but in the daily experiences and moral problems of real people in their everyday lives. (Tronto, 1993, p. 242)

Likewise, Meyers and Kittay (1987) wrote that, in the ethic of care, "moral problems do not result from a conflict of rights to be adjudicated by ranking values. Rather, moral problems are embedded in a contextual frame that eludes abstract, deductive reasoning" (p. 7). Relative to the deontology of Kohlberg's justice orientation, then, the ethic of care is a highly contextualized metaethical perspective. Indeed, it is frequently described as "soft" or "contextual" relativism (Crittendon, 1990; Friedman, 1987; Gilligan, 1982; Tronto, 1993) and, in this sense, is similar to Aristotle's moral dispositions and virtue, Hume's focus on moral sentiments, and the inductive, bottom-up reasoning associated with philosophical casuistry (Murray, 1993).

These two processes of moral reasoning may have important implications for our understanding of value–attitude–behavior relations. For one, it seems likely that the attitudes and behavior of care-oriented people will be affected by contextual cues regarding the needs and relationships of the particular people involved in a moral dilemma. If so, such people would display little consistency between their stable, situation-free values and their situationally determined attitudes and behavior. Justice oriented people, by comparison, who engage in postconventional reasoning and objectively appeal to "rational principles" in a deontologic fashion, should be less affected by the parameters of a particular situation and be more likely to express attitudes and behavior derived from their values. Finally, justice oriented people who display conventional reasoning could be expected to attend to societal norms and would therefore be likely to express attitudes and behavior based on their perceptions of these norms.

Before testing whether moral orientation moderates value–attitude–behavior relations, however, one might usefully ask whether this hypothesis makes theoretical sense in terms of the process–content distinction. Are moral orientation and values independent? Some moral philosophers claim that the distinction between justice and care orientations involves different values rather than different processes (e.g., Flanagan, 1991; Tronto, 1993). Indeed, Gilligan (1982) herself waffles on this point, speaking of the values of "care" and "responsiveness to others," while also describing care and justice as different processes, as the ground becoming figure in Gestalt terms. Given that the care orientation, by definition, eschews the use of general principles and values to resolve moral dilemmas, however, it would be logically inconsistent to regard care as simply a different set of values.

Thus far, two studies have examined the process–content distinction as it applies to moral orientation and values. Based on participants' responses to Friedman, Robinson, and Friedman's (1987) four dilemma DIT-style measures of care and justice reasoning, secondary analyses of Kristiansen and Matheson's (1990) data revealed that neither orientation, nor their interaction, was tied to participants' 18 terminal value scores. More recently, Kristiansen, Hotte, and Mosion (1995) observed the same results when a sample of 140 undergraduates completed more refined measures of moral orientation that were derived from exploratory and confirmatory factor analyses of 216 students' responses to three of Friedman et al.'s four moral dilemmas (Hotte & Kristiansen, 1995). Given the preliminary nature of this research, and the fact that only the Friedman et al.

measures have been used, it would be useful to examine the moral orientation-value distinction in more detail, for example, by comparing people's responses to Schwartz's (1992) multiple-item value survey with their responses to a variety of indices of moral orientation (e.g., Ford & Lowery, 1986; Lyons, 1988). Such research would clarify the extent to which care and justice orientations involve different values, different processes, or some combination of both. Thus far, however, moral orientation and values appear to be largely independent, and so, like moral stage, moral orientation may moderate value–attitude–behavior relations.

The Self

Rokeach (1973, 1979) and others (e.g., Smith, 1991) claim that values are integral to self-identity and that people strive to be authentic, moral beings by acting on the basis of values tied to their desired self-conceptions. In this section we therefore review research that addresses the role of the self in value–attitude–behavior relations, and go on to suggest that both the clarity of the self-concept and its schematic structure may be implicated in moral reasoning, and thereby value–attitude–behavior relations.

The Role of the Self.   Surprisingly, in view of the long standing claim that values are intimately tied to the self-concept (Ball-Rokeach et al., 1984; Rokeach, 1973, 1979; Smith, 1991), evidence for the effects of self-conceptions on values, attitudes, and behavior is at best weak. Ball-Rokeach et al., for example, cited nine studies as evidence for the effect of self-dissatisfaction on the value change observed in response to Rokeach's self-confrontation procedure. The magnitude of the effects in these studies is, however, small. Sherrid and Beech (1976), for example, reported a correlation of .17 between how dissatisfied police officers were with their value rankings following exposure to the self-confrontation procedure and subsequent value change. Similarly, in Hamid and Flay's (1974) research, self-dissatisfaction accounted for 1.7% of the variance in value change. More importantly, as Sanders and Atwood (1979) stated, "Self-confrontation is said to produce self-dissatisfaction when one's value rankings are inconsistent with one's conceptions of self. Unfortunately, neither this study, nor any of those referred to earlier, speak directly to this proposition. There are no data here on the conceptions which subjects held of themselves" (p. 239).

Other findings provide indirect evidence for the hypothesized relation between the self and values. In a study of the structure of values, Schwartz and Bilsky (1990) wrote that "the more values there are that serve a given value, the more highly correlated with other values the value should be. . . . Values served by many values would be more central in the multidimensional space" (p. 888). A multidimensional smallest space analysis of data that Schwartz (1992) gathered from 20 nations revealed that "self-respect" was located in the center of the value system, at the point where all the value types converged. This finding suggests that the various value types were instrumental to people's self and self-regard, thereby attesting to the centrality of the self in the value system.

Further indirect support for the hypothesized role of the self in value–attitude–behavior relations includes Steele and Lui's (1983) finding that the opportunity to affirm important values, and thereby the self, eliminated dissonance-induced attitude change and Lydon and Zanna's (1990) data that indicated that people were more committed to values diagnostic of the self. In spite of such support, however, the research necessary to directly assess Rokeach's (1973) claim that inconsistency in the self–value–attitude–behavior system induces self-dissatisfaction that, in turn, motivates the cognitive and behavioral changes necessary to restore consistency, remains to be done. To the extent that the self is involved in value–attitude–behavior consistency, however, at least two aspects of the self merit attention, specifically the clarity of the self-concept and the schematic structure of the self.

Clarity of the Self.   Given the claim that values are integral to the self (Ball-Rokeach et al., 1984; Rokeach, 1973, 1979; Smith, 1991), it is not surprising that Rokeach (1973) speculated that people with more clearly articulated self-concepts would show stronger value–attitude–behavior relations. Suggestive evidence for this hypothesized impact of self-clarity on value–attitude–behavior consistency comes from studies of individual differences, for example in self-monitoring. Low self-monitors have schematic conceptions of themselves, whereas high self-monitors have more clearly articulated conceptions of other people (Snyder & Cantor, 1980) and, consistent with the hypothesized role of the self in value–attitude–behavior relations, relative to high self-monitors, low self-monitors exhibit stronger attitude–behavior covariation (Snyder & Tanke, 1976), are more likely to develop attitudes based on their values (Snyder & DeBono, 1989), and are more likely to appeal to socially shared, positive values to justify their attitudes (Kristiansen & Zanna, 1988, 1994). And similar findings have been observed in regard to self-consciousness. People high in chronic self-consciousness direct their attention toward inner aspects of themselves, and are less compliant, less suggestible, have more accurate self-knowledge, clearer self-schemas, and display greater attitude-behavior consistency (Fenigstein, Scheier, & Buss, 1975; Schrum & McCarty, 1992). In line with the hypothesized relation between the clarity of the self and values, Schrum and McCarty (1992) found that individuals higher in private self-consciousness differentiated more among values when rating the personal importance of Rokeach's (1967) values.

Rokeach's (1973) suggestion that value-guided preferences and behavior are less likely among people with weakly defined self-concepts is also consistent with clinical theory. Kernberg (1975), a psychiatrist who studies disorders of the self, for example, wrote that "the value systems of narcissistic personalities [who have a poorly articulated sense of self] are generally corruptible" (p. 238), and described such people as acting on the basis of social norms and self-interest. Extending such clinical work into the realm of sociology, Lasch (1979) argued that Western society has become narcissistic. And along similar lines, both Smith (1991), from a social psychological perspective, and Campbell (1972), based on his study of mythology, claimed that rapid social change and secularization have removed the symbolic supports and transmitters of values, resulting in the decline of moral behavior to the extent that people rely on socially, rather than personally, required values to guide their actions. Thus, it is perhaps not surprising that researchers often observe weak relations between (Western) people's values and their attitudes and behavior.

In sum, then, it is conceivable that differences in self-articulation, as reflected by individual differences in self-monitoring (Snyder & Gangestad, 1986), chronic self-consciousness (Fenigstein, Scheier, & Buss, 1975) or acute self-awareness (Carver & Scheier, 1981), and narcissism (Raskin & Terry, 1988), moderate the strength of value–attitude–behavior relations.

Independent and Interdependent Self-Schemas.   The postulated centrality of the self in moral behavior, as described earlier, not only presupposes a well defined self, but also assumes a Western conception of the self (Smith, 1991). According to Markus and Kitayama (1991), people in Western societies seek to maintain their independence from others by attending to the self and expressing their unique attributes. In many Asian cultures, in contrast, conceptions of the self are derived from the relatedness of individuals to each other. And, as explained shortly, it seems likely that people with interrelated selves will display less value–attitude–behavior consistency than people who have independent self-schemas.

As evidence for the divergent effect of these self-schemas on cognition, emotion and motivation, Markus and Kitayama reviewed a host of cross-cultural findings. In regard to cognition, for example, and paralleling the differences observed in the self versus other knowledge associated with self-monitoring (Snyder & Cantor, 1980) and self-consciousness (Nasby, 1989), Western students with independent selves had more distinct self-knowledge, while Eastern students with interrelated selves had more elaborate knowledge of others (Kitayama, Markus, Tummala, Kurokawa, & Kato, 1990).

In regard to emotion, Kitayama and Markus (1990) found that, whereas Westerners categorized emotions along two dimensions, namely activation and pleasantness, the Japanese used a third dimension involving the extent to which a person is engaged in an interdependent relationship. Further, the Japanese used this dimension to differentiate ego-focused emotions, such as anger, from other-focused emotions, such as shame, and students with more independent selves more frequently experienced ego-focused emotions whereas those with more interdependent selves more often experienced other-focused emotions.

Most relevant here, Markus and Kitayama's review indicated that these different selves may have different motives. For example, whereas Westerners display self-enhancing biases in their social comparisons and their explanations of success and failure, Easterners exhibit a modesty or other-enhancing bias. And they suggested that, because Easterners do not regard their internal attributes as central to the self, attitude–behavior consistency and notions of dissonance may be nonissues for interdependent people. Rather, interdependent people may regard such consistency as a sign of rigidity and moral immaturity.

In sum, Markus and Kitayama's review suggests that the self-concept and behavior of the independent self are organized and made meaningful by reference to their own internal thoughts and feelings, whereas the interdependent self construes the self and derives meaning by reference to the thoughts, feelings, and actions of others.

Markus and her colleagues (Markus & Kitayama, 1991; Markus & Oyserman, 1989) also speculated that both the Eastern interdependent self and care-oriented people are more connected and responsive to others. In line with this, Lyons (1988) observed that people who described themselves mainly in connected terms adopted a care orientation to the resolution of real-life moral dilemmas, whereas people who used primarily separate-objective terms to describe themselves more frequently used a justice orientation. In view of this relation between the self and moral reasoning, then, it seems likely that the moral attitudes and behavior of those with interdependent selves will vary as a function of their perceptions of the contextual cues regarding the needs and relationships of the people affected by a moral issue. The Western notion of the independent self, on the other hand, is central to Kohlberg's postconventional justice oriented perspective of the moral agent as an autonomous, rational decision maker who expresses "personally required" values (Smith, 1991) that transcend self-interest and social norms (Kohlberg, 1971b). Thus, one would expect people with independent selves to develop value-expressive attitudes and behavior. And these speculations are consistent with Stipek, Weiner, and Li's (1989) finding that Americans experienced guilt after violating a law or moral principle, whereas the Chinese experienced guilt in response to hurting others psychologically. Thus, the very nature of the self in terms of interdependent versus independent self-schemas may be fundamental to care and justice moral reasoning, respectively, and thereby the nature of value–attitude–behavior relations.[1]

---

[1]Not surprisingly, there has been much speculation regarding the antecedents of self-schemas and moral reasoning. Gilligan (1982) suggested that such differences might be tied to gender differences in early infant attachment whereby boys are socialized toward independence whereas girls are allowed to maintain their connectedness with their mothers. This supposition is inconsistent with research that fails to observe gender differences in justice reasoning (Thoma, 1986; Walker, 1991) or moral orientation (Gilligan & Attanucci, 1988; for a review see Larrabee, 1993). There is, however, circumstantial evidence for Markus and Oyserman's (1989) proposal that interdependent and independent selves develop, at least in part, in response to societal power differentials, including inequal-

AN INTEGRATIVE MODEL

This review has stimulated several theoretically derived answers to questions concerning for whom and how values guide attitudes and behavior, answers that implicate moral reasoning, in terms of both the level of justice reasoning and the orientation toward justice and care perspectives, and the self, in terms of its clarity and its independent and interdependent schematic structure. And we suspect that the impact of these variables on value–attitude–behavior relations might be understood within the conceptual framework of Ajzen and Fishbein's (1972) original formulation of the theory of reasoned action.

In this version of the theory, behavior is depicted as a function of what people intend to do, and people's intentions are determined by three factors: their attitude toward the behavior, social norms, and personal norms. Although Ajzen and Fishbein (1972) regard attitudes as stemming from people's evaluations of the salient consequences of an act, attitudes can be conceptualized more simply as people's beliefs about what they want to do or their favorability toward an act (Zanna & Rempel, 1988). The second component, social norms, involves people's motivation to comply with the expectations of significant others, such as family and peers. Finally, personal norms refer to people's own internal beliefs that they ought to perform a given action.

Much research attests to the predictive power of this and more recent versions of the theory of reasoned action. In Schwartz and Tessler's (1972) study of people's intentions regarding six acts of transplant donation, for example, attitudes, social norms, and personal norms accounted for more than 50% of the variance in donation intentions, with personal norms consistently the strongest predictor. Further, when the model was used to predict actual volunteering to become a bone marrow donor 3 months later, personal norms, but neither social norms or attitudes, predicted behavior. Similarly, Gorsuch and Ortberg (1983) reported that church goers' personal norms were more highly correlated with their intentions regarding two moral actions (returning an undeserved tax refund and taking a job that prevented church attendance), whereas their attitudes were better able to predict their intentions regarding two nonmoral behaviors (attending a party and going to a later church service).

---

ities in access to resources and differences in the ability to control one's own fate. For one, less education, lower occupational status, and ethnic and racial minority status are related to both lower stages of justice reasoning and a care moral orientation (Larrabee, 1993; Thoma, 1986; Walker, 1991). Further, the hypothesized impact of power on the nature of the moral self is consistent with social psychological findings concerning the effects of power inequalities on stereotyping. In this regard and consistent with Miller's (1976) earlier assertions, Fiske (1993) presented experimental evidence that "the powerless attend to the powerful who control their outcomes, in an effort to enhance prediction and control, so forming complex, potentially nonstereotypic impressions. The powerful pay less attention, so are more vulnerable to stereotyping" (p. 621). As Schwalbe (1991) pointed out, the impact of power on the nature of the moral self has yet to be examined directly.

Vallerand, Deshaies, Cuerrier, Pelletier, and Mongeau (1992) conducted a confirmatory factor analysis to test the applicability of Fishbein and Ajzen's (1975; Ajzen & Fishbein, 1980) revised theory of reasoned action to moral behavior, a version that excludes the personal norm component. In their study, participants' attitudes had the greatest impact on their moral intentions regarding two hypothetical moral dilemmas regarding sports, and social norms had an indirect impact on moral intentions that was mediated by attitudes. Given this, Vallerand et al. (1992) concluded, "Contrary to much theorizing (e.g., Kohlberg, 1969), that focuses on the person's cognitive development as a prime determinant of moral development, the present approach posits that the main determinant of one's attitude or moral inclination may reside in the social environment" (p. 108). Thus, it appears that moral attitudes can fulfill what functional theorists term a social adjustive function (Pratkanis, Breckler, & Greenwald, 1989). And this is consistent with the fact that most adolescents, the age of Vallerand et al.'s participants, operate at Kohlberg's conventional level of moral reasoning (Kitwood, 1990).

More recently, Beck and Ajzen (1991) found that the theory of planned behavior, which is like the revised theory of reasoned action except that it includes the additional component "perceived behavioral control," was able to account for intentions and behavior regarding three moral actions (cheating, lying, and stealing). Further, a measure similar to personal norms, namely moral obligation, improved the prediction of one of these behaviors.

In view of the applicability of the various formulations of the theory of reasoned action to moral behavior, Azjen and Fishbein's (1972) original formulation of the theory may well capture the relation between moral reasoning and the self, on the one hand, and values, attitudes and behavior on the other. To do so successfully, however, would likely require distinguishing between three different types of social norms. First, like Azjen and Fishbein (1972, 1980; Fishbein & Azjen, 1975), social norms would include the expectations of significant others in a person's own life, such as those of family and peers. Such norms might be described as "personally relevant." A second, more general, type of norm concerns what Devine and her colleagues (Devine & Monteith, 1993) refer to as "societal standards" regarding how one should respond in a situation. And finally, norms may be founded on perceptions of the relationships, expectations and needs of the people involved in a particular moral dilemma. Such norms might be called "contextually relevant." Differentiating between these types of norms, particularly the latter two, is important in that although Gilligan (1982) does not endorse moral absolutism, nor does she endorse moral relativism. Thus, social responsiveness in Gilligan's sense is not merely compliance with societal standards of morality or conventional justice morality in Kohlberg's terms. Instead, it involves being emotionally affected by and responsive to the needs of the people involved in a moral dilemma (Crittendon, 1990; Friedman, 1987), including the self (Gilligan, 1982; Tronto, 1993).

This model also considers people's general values, values that are hypothe-sized to guide people's attitudes and behavior via their impact on personal nor-mative beliefs. In this regard, examining the impact of people's values on their personal norms would test the often made claim that personal norms stem from values (e.g., Devine & Monteith, 1993; Eisenberg, Lennon, & Pasternack, 1986). And the consideration of personal norms may also be useful if measures of personal norms regarding particular behaviors help overcome the difficulties in predicting specific actions from knowledge of people's more general values (Ajzen & Fishbein, 1977).

Finally, although not depicted in the illustrations of the model, people's val-ues, personal norms, attitudes, and social norms may share various reciprocal relations. For one, people's values and personal norms may affect their percep-tions of social norms, for example, through false consensus effects (Ross, Greene, & House, 1977). Or, among those who fall prey to the naturalistic fallacy and believe that "what is" is "what ought to be" (Kohlberg, 1971b), social norms may determine both values and personal norms, producing the 'socially required' values and attitudes associated with Kohlberg's conventional justice reasoning. And of course attitudes may influence values and personal norms through the value justification process described earlier in this chapter (Kris-tiansen & Zanna, 1994).

We suspect that the impact of moral reasoning and the self on the process by which moral dilemmas are resolved will be reflected by the relative weights of the various paths in this extension of Ajzen and Fishbein's (1972) model. Figure 4.2 illustrates the path to morality that is expected to hold for people with independent selves who display postconventional justice reasoning. To the extent that such people attend primarily to their rationally determined, transsituational values, these people's values are likely to have the strongest impact on their

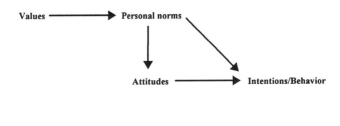

FIG. 4.2.   The route to morality likely among independent selves who engage in postconventional justice reasoning.

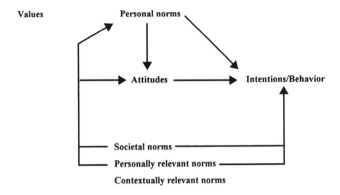

FIG. 4.3. The route to morality likely among independent selves who engage in conventional justice reasoning.

attitudes and behavior. Further, these value–attitude and value–behavior relations may well be mediated by such people's behavior-specific personal norms regarding what they ought to do.

Figure 4.3 presents the moral path that is likely to be followed by people with independent selves who engage in conventional justice reasoning. Rather than relying on their values as attitudinal and behavioral guides, one would expect these people to be responsive to personally relevant and societal-level norms. These norms, in turn, should go on to determine their moral intentions and behavior, either directly or indirectly through their impact on personal norms and attitudes.

Figure 4.4 depicts the route to morality that is expected to be taken by people

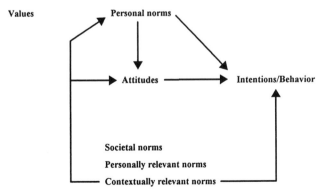

FIG. 4.4. The route to morality likely among interdependent selves who engage in care reasoning, assuming the availability of individuating, contextually relevant information.

with interdependent selves who engage in the contextually driven reasoning associated with the ethic of care (Gilligan, 1982). Like independent conventional justice reasoners, interdependent people are likely to be responsive to external social norms. In this case, however, social norms are likely to be contextually derived from perceptions of the expectations, needs, and relationships of the people most directly affected by the moral issue.

As an example, consider the advice that might be given to a woman who is contemplating having an abortion because she feels emotionally and financially unable to parent the child. As depicted in Fig. 4.2, the personal norms, attitudes, and behavior of an independent person who uses principled justice reasoning should vary as a function of their own general values, values that might include the sanctity of life, religious beliefs, freedom, and equality. As shown in Fig. 4.3, the personal norms, attitudes, and behavior of an independent person who uses conventional justice reasoning are expected to be most strongly affected by their perceptions of societal-level norms regarding abortion and the expectations of the personally relevant significant others with whom they comply (e.g., family and friends). Finally, following the paths outlined in Fig. 4.4, the personal norms, attitudes, and behavior of interdependent care-oriented people are expected to vary as a function of their perceptions of the needs of the people affected by the moral dilemma, such as the woman, the father, and the fetus, as opposed to personally relevant or societal-level norms. In this case, a person could endorse an abortion if they deemed it in the best interests of the people involved, even if this decision contradicted their own guiding values in life or their perceptions of societal and personally relevant norms.

The use of these various routes to morality may, however, be qualified by the relative primacy of justice and care reasoning. That is, whether justice subsumes care reasoning or care subsumes justice reasoning. Although Kohlberg et al. (1983) wrote that "morally valid forms of caring and community presuppose prior conditions and judgments of justice" (p. 92), several moral philosophers have asserted exactly the opposite. Crittenden (1990), for example, wrote that "an ethic of justice, when linked with care, would have to forego its basic claim to provide formal and absolute principles. An ethic of care, by contrast, is marked by tolerance and contextual relativism—it can remain whole, therefore, while embracing the considerations of rights in appropriate contexts" (p. 91). Similarly, Aristotle stated that "when men are friends they have no need of justice, while when they are just they need friendship as well" (Ethics, Book VIII, Chapter 1, cited in Solomon, 1992, p. 119), and, according to Tronto (1993), Hume "argued that if benevolence is sufficiently strong, there would be no need of justice" (p. 256).

If care subsumes justice, the route to morality adopted by interdependent care-oriented people might be contingent on the social versus personalized nature of the moral issue: When personalized information is available, care-oriented people may attend to such information, suspend their value-driven or societally derived judgments, and resolve moral dilemmas on the basis of how best to meet people's interconnected needs. When contextual, individuating, information is lacking, as in the case of public policy issues, interdependent care-oriented people have little recourse but to display the same moral process as either postconventional or conventional justice oriented people. The impartiality and autonomy associated with principled justice reasoning, on the other hand, suggests that people who adopt this stance may tend to ignore contextual information and instead rely on their general, situation-free values to resolve even personalized moral dilemmas. Similarly, conventional justice reasoners may base their moral attitudes and actions on their perceptions of societal and personally relevant norms rather than contextual information. Consistent with this hypothesis, studies of prosocial moral reasoning indicate that more principled reasoning is associated with the resolution of hypothetical, third person dilemmas, in contrast to the conventional, normative reasoning evoked by real-life dilemmas regarding personal relationships (e.g., Eisenberg et al., 1986; Pratt, Golding, Hunter, & Sampson, 1988; Walker, de Vries, & Trevethan, 1987). As Friedman (1987, p. 201) pointed out, however, "what matters is having enough detail for the story at hand," not whether the dilemma is real or hypothetical or public as opposed to private.

Testing the Model.   Several approaches could be used to test the feasibility of this model and the hypotheses it generates. For one, structural equation modelling could test the effects of moral reasoning, the self, and the moral issue on the paths to morality outlined in Figs. 4.2 to 4.4. Because this model is simply an extension of Ajzen and Fishbein's (1972) theory of reasoned action, most of the model's components, specifically personal norms, attitudes, personally-relevant social norms and intentions, could be measured using their methods (see also Fishbein & Ajzen, 1975). The two other types of social norms, namely societal and contextually relevant norms, could be assessed using Devine and Monteith's (1993) methods and items assessing people's perceptions of the contextually relevant needs of the people affected by a moral dilemma, respectively. Values might be readily measured using either Rokeach's (1967) or Schwartz's (1992) Value Survey, and people's stage of justice development could be determined using the Moral Judgment Interview (Colby, Kohlberg, Candee, Gibbs, Hewer, & Speicher, 1987) or Rest's (1979) paper and pencil Defining Issues Test. People's moral orientation might be assessed in a variety of ways, including paper and pencil measures (e.g., Ford & Lowery 1986; Friedman et al., 1987), and content analyses of interviews regarding self-generated, real-life moral dilemmas (e.g., Lyons, 1988) or sentence stem completions (Rogers, 1988). Finally, whether the self is construed as independent or interdependent could be determined using Kitayama and Markus' (1990) items, items that include "Are you the kind of person who holds on to one's own view?" to assess the independent self, and "Are you the kind of person who never forgets a favor provided by others?" to tap the interdependent self.

More basic research, examining various parts of the model, would also be informative. For example, examining the interrelations among values, principled reasoning, moral orientation, and indices reflective of independent versus interdependent self-schemas would allow for the most rigorous test to date of the validity of the content-process distinction as it applies to values, moral reasoning, and moral orientation. Further, examining the relation of people's independent versus interdependent self-schemas with their justice and care orientations would further assess the claim that justice and care moral orientations are rooted in different self-conceptions (Lyons, 1988; Markus & Kitayama, 1991; Markus & Oyserman, 1989).

Next, testing the effects of peoples' morality and self-conceptions on situational attitudinal variance would test the hypothesis that, relative to independent justice oriented persons, interdependent care oriented people are "contextual relativists" whose attitudes are affected by individuating information regarding needs and relationships, thereby causing them to display less cross-situational attitude consistency, and less correspondence between their situation-free values and their situationally determined attitudes. As an example, consider the general social issue of whether a person found guilty of incestuous assault should be incarcerated and/or required to seek therapy. When asked, people will no doubt express an opinion about this issue. Information about the particular parameters of a situation, however, might lead to very different decisions in that people's sentencing preferences may depend on factors such as whether the abuser was abused as a child, as well as the abuser's gender and current age (e.g., 30 vs. 70 years old). And with respect to the needs of incest survivors, their need to affirm their self-worth by seeing justice restored or their desire to establish a positive relation with the abuser might also affect people's decisions, and thereby the magnitude of the value–attitude–behavior relation. Thus, although the nature of the moral violation has not changed, the contextual needs and relationships have, and these changes may affect the value–attitude–behavior relation, especially among interdependent care-oriented people who are inclined to attend to contextual information.

Research might also examine the processes underlying these routes to morality. For one, just as the accessibility of attitudes in memory determines the likelihood that attitudes will guide behavior (Fazio, 1986), the relative accessibility of values and the various types of norms may mediate the effects of moral reasoning and self-schemas on value–attitude–behavior relations. Interdependent care-oriented people's contextual focus suggests that reaching a moral resolution would necessitate substantial "bottom-up" information processing, whereas independent justice oriented people's concern with values suggests that they may engage in relatively more accessible, and hence quicker, "top-down," value-schematic processing. If so, independent justice-oriented people should be able to answer inquires regarding their attitudes toward specific, contextualized, issues more quickly than interdependent care-oriented persons. Further, if care-oriented people are also capable of justice reasoning (Crittendon, 1990; Friedman, 1987; Tronto, 1993), there should be no differences in response latencies for the resolution of general social issues or inquires regarding value priorities. Thus, studies of the effects of morality and the self on response latencies to inquires about these components seem merited, particularly as such findings would speak to the distinction between the process and content of values and moral reasoning.

Although neglected by many modern ethical theories, Oakley (1992) and others (e.g., Frank, 1988) assert that emotions are central to any adequate ethics of character and behavior. Similarly, Aristotle "makes the point insistently that the virtues are concerned with actions and passions, with how we act and how we feel. Moral excellence is a matter of acting and being emotionally affected in the right ways" (Crittendon, 1990, pp. 106–107). Given the differential role of affect in the ethic of care and the interdependent self, in comparison to the the ethic of justice and the independent self (Crittendon, 1990; Friedman, 1987; Gilligan, 1982; Markus & Kitayama, 1991), studies might usefully investigate the affective processes underlying these routes to morality. For example, Higgin's (1987) self-discrepancy theory indicates that people respond affectively to discrepancies between their actual selves and "oughts" with agitation. In the present context, independent justice-oriented people might react this way in response to discrepancies between what they would do and their value-driven personal norms. Conventional justice-oriented people, on the other hand, might react this way in response to discrepancies between what they would do and the oughts of personally relevant significant others or society, whereas interdependent care-oriented people should react this way in response to discrepancies between what they would do and their contextually determined oughts.

CONCLUDING COMMENTS

This review of the implications of moral reasoning, the self, and the moral issue for value–attitude–behavior relations makes it clear that, as others have claimed (e.g., Flanagan, 1991), there is no single, universally endorsed, best criterion of what is "good," what is "moral." Indeed, Markus and Kitayama (1991) suggested that we may overestimate the degree to which Westerners live up to the ideal of an independent self, and Murray (1993) argued that many, if not most, people use contextualized reasoning to resolve moral dilemmas. Certainly, if values can guide our attitudes and behavior and allow some of us to define and express our selves, examining the extent to which values are good for some things, some people, some of the time, is important. If, however, relying on values makes us unresponsive to the needs and perspectives of others, it would support Gergen's (1973) contention that "absolute moral values corrupt absolutely" (p. 108). From this stance, identifying and understanding alternative routes to morality, as well as the factors that affect the paths that people choose, becomes fundamental.

ACKNOWLEDGMENTS

Thanks are extended to Vicki Esses, Morgan Forbes, Jim Olson, Clive Seligman, and Mark Zanna for their helpful comments on an earlier draft of this chapter. The preparation of this paper was also facilitated by grants from the Social Sciences and Humanities Research Council of Canada and the Carleton University Faculty of Graduate Studies and Research.

REFERENCES

Ajzen, I., & Fishbein, M. (1972). Attitudes and normative beliefs as factors influencing behavioral intentions in hypothetical situations involving risk. *Journal of Personality and Social Psychology, 21*, 1–9.

Ajzen, I., & Fishbein, M. (1977). Attitude-behavior relations: A theoretical analysis and review of empirical research. *Psychological Bulletin, 84*, 888–918.

Ajzen, I., & Fishbein, M. (1980). *Understanding attitudes and predicting social behavior.* Englewood-Cliffs, NJ: Prentice-Hall.

Altemeyer, B. (1988). *Enemies of freedom.* San Francisco: Jossey-Bass.

Altemeyer, B. (1994). Reducing prejudice in right-wing authoritarians. In M. P. Zanna & J. M. Olson (Eds.), *The psychology of prejudice: The Ontario symposium* (Vol. 7, pp. 131–148). Hillsdale, NJ: Lawrence Erlbaum Associates.

Ball-Rokeach, S. J., Rokeach, M., & Grube, J. W. (1984). *The great American values test: Influencing behavior and belief through television.* New York: Free Press.

Beck, L., & Ajzen, I. (1991). Predicting dishonest actions using the theory of planned behavior. *Journal of Research in Personality, 25*, 285–301.

Blasi, A. (1980). Bridging moral cognition and moral action: A critical review of the literature. *Psychological Bulletin, 88*, 1–45.

Braithwaite, V. A., & Scott, W. A. (1991). Values. In J. P. Robinson, P. R. Shaver, & L. S. Wrightsman (Eds.), *Measures of personality and social psychological attitudes* (Vol. 1, pp. 662–753). New York: Academic Press.

Campbell, J. (1972). *Myths to live by.* New York: Bantam Books.

Carver, C. S., & Scheier, M. F. (1981). *Attention and self-regulation: A control theory approach to human behavior.* New York: Springer-Verlag.

Clarke-Stewart, A., Friedman, S., & Koch, J. (1985). *Child development: A topical approach.* Toronto: Wiley.

Cohen, J. (1988). *Statistical power analysis in the behavioral sciences.* Hillsdale, NJ: Lawrence Erlbaum, Associates.

Colby, A., Kohlberg, L., Candee, D., Gibbs, J., Hewer, A., & Speicher, B. (1987). *The measurement of moral judgment: Vol. II.* New York: Cambridge University Press.

Conroy, W. J., Katkin, E. S., & Barnette, W. L. (1973, April). *Modification of smoking behavior by Rokeach's self-confrontation technique.* Paper presented at the 81st annual meeting of the Southeastern Psychological Association, New Orleans.

Crittendon, P. (1990). *Learning to be moral*. Atlantic Highlands, NJ: Humanities Press.

DeSeve, K. L. (1975). *An examination of the relationship between values and smoking behavior*. Unpublished doctoral dissertation, Washington State University.

Devine, P. G., & Monteith, M. J. (1993). The role of discrepancy associated affect in prejudice reduction. In D. M. Mackie & D. L. Hamilton (Eds.), *Affect, cognition, and stereotyping: Interactive processes in intergroup perception* (pp. 317–344). New York: Academic Press.

de Vries, B., & Walker, L. J. (1986). Moral reasoning and attitudes toward capital punishment. *Developmental Psychology, 22*, 509–513.

Eisenberg, N., Lennon, R., & Pasternack, J. F. (1986). Altruistic values and moral judgment. In N. Eisenberg (Ed.), *Altruistic emotion, cognition, and behavior* (pp. 115–159). Hillsdale, NJ: Lawrence Erlbaum Associates.

Faludi, S. (1991). *Backlash: The undeclared war against American women*. New York: Anchor.

Fazio, R. H. (1986). How do attitudes guide behavior? In R. M. Sorrentino & E. T. Higgins (Eds.), *Handbook of motivation and cognition* (pp. 204–243). New York: Guilford.

Feather, N. T. (1988). Moral judgment and human values. *British Journal of Social Psychology, 27*, 239–246.

Fenigstein, A., Scheier, M. F., & Buss, A. H. (1975). Private and public self-consciousness: Assessment and theory. *Journal of Consulting and Clinical Psychology, 43*, 522–527.

Fishbein, M., & Ajzen, I. (1975). *Belief, attitude, intention and behavior*. Reading, MA: Addison-Wesley.

Fiske, S. T. (1993). Controlling other people: The impact of power on stereotyping. *American Psychologist, 48*, 621–628.

Flanagan, O. (1991). *Varieties of moral personality*. Cambridge, MA: Harvard University Press.

FMS Foundation (1993, August). *FMS Foundation mission statement*. Philadelphia, PA: FMS Foundation.

FMS Foundation (n.d.). *The false memory syndrome phenomenon*. Philadelphia, PA: FMS Foundation.

Ford, M. R., & Lowery, C. R. (1986). Gender differences in moral reasoning: A comparison of the use of justice and care orientations. *Journal of Personality and Social Psychology, 50*, 777–783.

Frank, R. H. (1988). *Passions with reason: The strategic role of the emotions*. New York: W.W. Norton & Co.

Friedman, M. (1987). Care and context in moral reasoning. In E. T. Kittay & D. T. Meyers (Eds.), *Women and moral theory* (pp. 190–204). Totowa, NJ: Rowman & Littlefield.

Friedman, W. J., Robinson, A. B., & Friedman, B. L. (1987). Sex differences in moral judgments? A test of Gilligan's theory. *Psychology of Women Quarterly, 11*, 37–46.

Gergen, K. (1973). The codification of research ethics: Views from a doubting Thomas. *American Psychologist, 28*, 907–112.

Gilligan, C. (1982). *In a different voice: Psychological theory and women's development*. Cambridge, MA: Harvard University Press.

Gilligan, C. (1987). Moral orientation and moral development. In E. F. Kittay & D. T. Meyer (Eds.), *Women and moral theory* (pp. 19–33). Totowa, NJ: Rowman & Littlefield.

Gilligan, C., & Attanucci, J. (1988). Two moral orientations. In C. Gilligan, J. V. Ward, & J. M. Taylor (Eds.), *Mapping the moral domain* (pp. 73–86). Cambridge, MA: Harvard University Press.

Gilligan, C., Ward, J. V., & Taylor, J. M. (1988). *Mapping the moral domain*. Cambridge, MA: Harvard University Press.

Gorsuch, R. L., & Ortberg, J. (1983). Moral obligations and attitudes: Their relation to behavioral intentions. *Journal of Personality and Social Psychology, 44*, 1025–1028.

Gray, D. B., & Ashmore, R. D. (1975). Comparing the effects of informational, role-playing, and value-discrepancy treatments on racial attitude. *Journal of Applied Social Psychology, 5*, 262–281.

Greenstein, T. N. (1976). Behavior change through value self-confrontation: A field experiment. *Journal of Personality and Social Psychology, 34,* 254–262.

Greenstein, T. N. (1982). A further test of the value-mediation explanation of behavior change following self-confrontation. *Replications in Social Psychology, 2,* 30–32.

Grube, J. W. (1979). *Inconsistencies among values, attitudes and behaviors as determinants of self-dissatisfaction and change.* Unpublished doctoral dissertation, Washington State University.

Grube, J. W., Greenstein, T. N., Rankin, W. L., & Kearney, K. Z. (1977). Behavior change following self-confrontation: A test of the value mediation hypothesis. *Journal of Personality and Social Psychology, 35,* 212–216.

Haddock, G., & Zanna, M. P. (1994). Preferring "housewives" to "feminists": Categorization and the favorability of attitudes toward women. *Psychology of Women Quarterly, 18,* 25–52.

Hamid, P. N., & Flay, B. R. (1974). Changes in locus of control as a function of value modification. *British Journal of Social and Clinical Psychology, 13,* 143–150.

Higgins, E. T. (1987). Self-discrepancy theory: A theory relating self and affect. *Psychological Review, 94,* 319–340.

Hollen, C. C. (1972). *Value change, perceived instrumentality, and attitude change.* Unpublished doctoral dissertation, Michigan State University.

Homant, R., & Rokeach, M. (1970). Values for honesty and cheating behavior. *Personality, 1,* 153–162.

Homer, P. M., & Kahle, L. R. (1988). A structural equation test of the value-attitude-behavior hierarchy. *Journal of Personality and Social Psychology, 54,* 638–646.

Hopkins, S. W., Jr. (1973). *Behavioral and attitude changes produced from dissonance created between interpersonal values and attitudes.* Unpublished doctoral dissertation, University of Texas at Austin.

Hotte, A. M., & Kristiansen, C. M. (1995). *Moral reasoning, moral orientation, and ethical perspective: Underlying structures and interrelations.* Manuscript in preparation.

Kernberg, O. F. (1975). *Borderline conditions and pathological narcissism.* New York: Jason Aronson.

Kitayama, S., & Markus, H. (1990, August). *Culture and emotion: The role of other-focused emotions.* Paper presented at the 98th Annual Convention of the American Psychological Association, Boston.

Kitayama, S., Markus, H., Tummala, P., Kurokawa, M., & Kato, K. (1990). *Culture and self-cognition.* Unpublished manuscript.

Kitwood, T. (1990). *Concern for others: A new psychology of conscience and morality.* London: Routledge.

Kohlberg, L. (1969). Stage and sequence: The cognitive-developmental approach to socialization. In D. A. Goslin (Ed.), *Handbook of socialization theory and research* (pp. 347–480). Chicago: Rand McNally.

Kohlberg, L. (1971a). Stages of moral development as a basis for moral education. In C. M. Beck, B. S. Crittenden, & E. V. Sullivan (Eds.), *Moral education: Interdisciplinary approaches* (pp. 23–92). Toronto: University of Toronto Press.

Kohlberg, L. (1971b). From is to ought: How to commit the naturalistic fallacy and get away with it in the study of moral development. In T. Mischel (Ed.), *Cognitive development and epistemology* (pp. 151–235). New York: Academic Press.

Kohlberg, L. (1976). Moral stages and moralization: The cognitive developmental approach. In T. Lickona (Ed.), *Moral development and behavior: Theory, research and social issues* (pp. 31–53). New York: Holt, Rinehart & Winston.

Kohlberg, L. (1981). *The philosophy of moral development.* San Francisco: Harper & Row.

Kohlberg, L. (1984). *The psychology of moral development.* San Francisco: Harper & Row.

Kohlberg, L., Levine, C., & Hewer, A. (1983). *Moral stages: A current formulation and a response to critics.* Basil, Switzerland: Karger.

Kristiansen, C. M. (1985). Value correlates of preventive health behavior. *Journal of Personality and Social Psychology, 49,* 748–758.

Kristiansen, C. M. (1986). A two-value model of preventive health behavior. *Basic and Applied Social Psychology, 7,* 173–183.

Kristiansen, C. M., Gareau, C., & DeCourville, N. H. (1994, April). *"False memory syndrome:" An authoritarian backlash against women.* Paper presented at the National Multidisciplinary Conference, "Women's Health: Key Research and Health Care Issues," McMaster University, Hamilton, Ontario.

Kristiansen, C. M., Hotte, A. M., & Mosion, N. (1995). *Moral reasoning, moral orientation and values: Process versus content reconsidered.* Research in progress, Carleton University.

Kristiansen, C. M., & Matheson, K. (1990). Value conflict, value justification, and attitudes toward nuclear weapons. *Journal of Social Psychology, 130,* 665–675.

Kristiansen, C. M., & Zanna, M. P. (1988). Justifying attitudes by appealing to values: A functional perspective. *British Journal of Social Psychology, 27,* 247–256.

Kristiansen, C. M., & Zanna, M. P. (1992). [Variables moderating the effects of self-confrontation on values, attitudes and behavior]. Unpublished raw data.

Kristiansen, C. M., & Zanna, M. P. (1994). The rhetorical use of values to justify social and intergroup attitudes. *Journal of Social Issues, 50,* 47–65.

Larrabee, M. J. (1993). *An ethic of care: Feminist and interdisciplinary perspectives.* New York: Routledge.

Lasch, C. (1979). *The culture of narcissism.* New York: W.W. Norton.

Levine, C., Kohlberg, L., & Hewer, A. (1985). The current formulation of Kohlberg's theory and a response to critics. *Human Development, 28,* 94–100.

Loftus, E. (1993). The reality of repressed memories. *American Psychologist, 48,* 518–537.

Lydon, J. E., & Zanna, M. P. (1990). Commitment in the face of adversity: A value affirmation approach. *Journal of Personality and Social Psychology, 58,* 1040–1047.

Lyons, N. P. (1988). Two perspectives: On self, relationships, and morality. In C. Gilligan, J. V. Ward, & J. M. Taylor (Eds.), *Mapping the moral domain* (pp. 21–48). Cambridge, MA: Harvard University Press.

Markus, H. R., & Kitayama, S. (1991). Culture and the self: Implications for cognition, emotion, and motivation. *Psychological Review, 98,* 224–253.

Markus, H., & Oyserman, D. (1989). Gender and thought: The role of the self-concept. In M. Crawford & M. Gentry (Eds.), *Gender and thought: Psychological perspectives* (pp. 100–127). New York: Springer-Verlag.

McLellan, D. D. (1974). *Feedback of information as a determinant of value change and the implication of cognitive-moral development for value theory.* Unpublished doctoral dissertation, Michigan State University.

Meyers, D. T., & Kittay, E. F. (1987). Introduction. In E. F. Kittay & D. T. Meyers (Eds.), *Women and moral theory* (pp. 3–16). Totowa, NJ: Rowman & Littlefield.

Miller, A. (1983). *For your own good: Hidden cruelty in childrearing and the roots of violence.* New York: Farrar, Straus & Giroux.

Miller, J. B. (1976). *Toward a new psychology of women* (2nd ed.). Boston, MA: Beacon Press.

Murray, T. H. (1993). Moral reasoning in social context. *Journal of Social Issues, 49,* 185–200.

Nasby, W. (1989). Private and public self-consciousness and articulation of the self-schema. *Journal of Personality and Social Psychology, 56,* 117–123.

Noddings, N. (1984). *Caring: A feminine approach to ethics and moral education.* Berkeley: University of California Press.

Oakley, J. (1992). *Morality and the emotions.* London: Routledge.

Parish, T. S., Rosenblatt, R. R., & Kappes, B. M. (1979/1980). The relationship between human values and moral judgment. *Psychology: A Quarterly Journal of Human Behavior, 16,* 1–5.

Penner, L. A. (1971). Interpersonal attraction toward a black person as a function of value importance. *Personality, 2,* 175–187.

Pratkanis, A. R., Breckler, S. J., & Greenwald, A. G. (1989). *Attitude structure and function.* Hillsdale, NJ: Lawrence Erlbaum Associates.

Pratt, M. W., Golding, G., Hunter, W., & Sampson, R. (1988). Sex differences in adult moral orientations. *Journal of Personality, 56,* 373–391.

Raskin, R., & Terry, H. (1988). A principal-components analysis of the narcissistic personality inventory and further evidence of its construct validity. *Journal of Personality and Social Psychology, 54,* 890–902.

Rest, J. (1979). *Development in judging moral issues.* Minneapolis: University of Minnesota Press.

Rest, J. (1986). *Moral development: Advances in research and theory.* New York: Praeger.

Rholes, W. S., & Bailey, S. (1983). The effects of level of moral reasoning on consistency between moral attitudes and related behaviors. *Social Cognition, 2,* 32–48.

Rogers, A. G. (1988). *Two developmental voices: A method for identifying a fugue of justice and care themes in sentence completions.* Unpublished manuscript, Harvard University.

Rokeach, M. (1967). *Value survey.* Sunnyvale, CA: Halgren Tests.

Rokeach, M. (1969). Value systems in religion. *Review of Religious Research, 11,* 3–23.

Rokeach, M. (1973). *The nature of human values.* New York: Free Press.

Rokeach, M. (1979). *Understanding human values: Individual and societal.* New York: Free Press.

Rokeach, M., & Greenstein, T. (1976). *Self-dissatisfaction as a determinant of change in authoritarianism.* Unpublished manuscript, Washington State University, Department of Sociology.

Rokeach, M., & McLellan, D. D. (1972). Feedback of information about the values and attitudes of self and others as determinants of long-term cognitive and behavioral change. *Journal of Applied Social Psychology, 2,* 236–251.

Ross, L., Greene, D., & House, P. (1977). The "false consensus effect": An egocentric bias in social perception and attribution processes. *Journal of Experimental Social Psychology, 13,* 279–301.

Sanders, K. R., & Atwood, L. E. (1979). Value change initiated by the mass media. In M. Rokeach (Ed.), *Understanding human values: Individual and societal* (pp. 226–240). New York: Free Press.

Schrum, L. J., & McCarty, J. A. (1992). Individual differences in differentiation in the rating of personal values: The role of private self-consciousness. *Personality and Social Psychology Bulletin, 18,* 223–230.

Schwalbe, M. L. (1991). Social structure and the moral self. In J. A. Howard & P. L. Callero (Eds.), *The self-society dynamic: Cognition, emotion, and action* (pp. 281–303). Cambridge, MA: Cambridge University Press.

Schwartz, S. H. (1992). Universals in the content and structure of values: Theoretical advances and empirical tests in twenty countries. In M. P. Zanna (Ed.), *Advances in experimental social psychology* (Vol. 25, pp. 1–65). New York: Academic Press.

Schwartz, S. H., & Bilsky, W. (1990). Toward a theory of the universal content and structure of values: Extensions and cross-cultural replications. *Journal of Personality and Social Psychology, 58,* 878–891.

Schwartz, S. H., & Tessler, R. C. (1972). A test of a model for reducing measured attitude-behavior discrepancies. *Journal of Personality and Social Psychology, 24,* 225–236.

Sherrid, S. D., & Beech, R. P. (1976). Self-dissatisfaction as a determinant of change in police values. *Journal of Applied Psychology, 61,* 273–278.

Shotland, R. L., & Berger, W. G. (1970). Behavioral validation of several values from the Rokeach value scale as an index of honesty. *Journal of Applied Psychology, 54,* 433–435.

Smith, M. B. (1991). *Values, self and society: Toward a humanistic social psychology.* New Brunswick, NJ: Transaction.

Snyder M., & Cantor, N. (1980). Thinking about ourselves and others: Self-monitoring and social knowledge. *Journal of Personality and Social Psychology, 39*, 222–234.

Snyder, M., & DeBono, K. G. (1989). Understanding the functions of attitudes: Lessons learned from personality and social behavior. In A. R. Pratkanis, S. J. Breckler, & A. G. Greenwald (Eds.), *Attitude structure and function* (pp. 339–359). Hillsdale, NJ: Lawrence Erlbaum Associates.

Snyder, M., & Gangestad, S. (1986). On the nature of self-monitoring: Matters of assessment, matters of validity. *Journal of Personality and Social Psychology, 51*, 125–139.

Snyder, M., & Tanke, E. D. (1976). Behavior and attitude: Some people are more consistent than others. *Journal of Personality, 44*, 510–517.

Solomon, R. C. (1992). *Morality and the good life.* New York: McGraw-Hill.

Spence, J. T., Helmreich, R., & Stapp, J. (1973). A short version of the Attitudes toward Women Scale (AWS). *Bulletin of the Psychonomic Society, 2*, 219–220.

Steele, C. M., & Liu, T. J. (1983). Dissonance processes as self-affirmation. *Journal of Personality and Social Psychology, 45*, 5–19.

Stipek, D., Weiner, B., & Li, K. (1989). Testing some attribution-emotion relations in the People's Republic of China. *Journal of Personality and Social Psychology, 56*, 109–116.

Tavris, C. (1993, January 3). Beware the incest survivor machine. *New York Times Book Review,* p. 1.

Terr, L. (1991). Childhood trauma: An outline and overview. *American Journal of Psychiatry, 148*, 10–20.

Terr, L. (1994). *Unchained memories: The stories of traumatic memories, lost and found.* New York: Basic Books.

Thoma, S. J. (1986). Estimating gender differences in the comprehension and preference of moral issues. *Developmental Review, 6*, 165–180.

Thoma, S. J., Rest, J. R., & Davison, M. L. (1991). Describing and testing a moderator of the moral judgment and action relationship. *Journal of Personality and Social Psychology, 61*, 659–669.

Tronto, J. C. (1993). Beyond gender difference to a theory of care. In M. J. Larrabee (Ed.), *An ethic of care* (pp. 240–257). New York: Routledge.

Vallerand, R. J., Deshaies, P., Cuerrier, J. P., Pelletier, L. G., & Mongeau, C. (1992). Ajzen and Fishbein's theory of reasoned action as applied to moral behavior: A confirmatory analysis. *Journal of Personality and Social Psychology, 62*, 98–109.

Walker, L. J. (1991). Sex differences in moral reasoning. In W.M. Kurtines & J.L. Gewirtz (Eds.), *Handbook of moral behavior and development* (Vol. 2, pp. 333–364). Hillsdale, NJ: Lawrence Erlbaum Associates.

Walker, L. J., de Vries, B., & Trevethan, S. D. (1987). Moral styles and moral orientations in real-life and hypothetical dilemmas. *Child Development, 58*, 842–858.

Wilson, J. P. (1983). Motives, values and moral judgments. *Journal of Personality Assessment, 47*, 414–426.

Young, R. A. (1979). The effects of value confrontation and reinforcement counseling on the career planning attitudes and behavior of adolescent males. *Journal of Vocational Behavior, 15*, 1–11.

Zanna, M. P., & Fazio, R. H. (1982). The attitude-behavior relation: Moving toward a third generation of research. In M. P. Zanna, E. T. Higgins & C. P. Herman (Eds.), *Consistency in social behavior: The Ontario symposium* (Vol. 2, pp. 283–301). Hillsdale, NJ: Lawrence Erlbaum Associates.

Zanna, M. P., & Rempel, J. K. (1988). Attitudes: A new look at an old concept. In D. Bar-Tal & A. W. Kruglanski (Eds.), *The social psychology of knowledge* (pp. 315–334). Cambridge, England: Cambridge University Press.

5 On Creating Value-Expressive Attitudes: An Experimental Approach

Sandra L. Murray
Geoffrey Haddock
Mark P. Zanna
University of Waterloo

Many of the most intriguing and publicized events in the media seem to center around individuals who take radical courses of action in defense of their values. The abortion debate perhaps best illustrates this phenomenon. For example, Michael Griffin, a pro-life activist, shot and killed Dr. David Gunn, a Florida physician who performed abortions as part of his regular practice. Ironically, radical pro-lifers later justified Griffin's actions by appealing to the value they placed on the sanctity of life. Weeks later, Rochelle Shannon, another pro-life activist, shot and wounded another physician who performed abortions. Such extreme expressions of one's values have puzzled both the general public and the psychological community for a number of years.

As the current volume attests, psychologists and sociologists devote considerable attention to questions surrounding how values influence attitudes and behaviors. Of course, in exploring these questions, researchers have necessarily studied more mundane phenomena than the dramatic examples cited here. Psychologists have asked, for example, how more everyday actions, such as signing a petition, joining a political organization, or donating to a charity, reflect one's values.

Researchers have taken many different approaches to explore the links among values, attitudes, and behaviors. But, with the exception of a handful of experimental studies, much of this research has been correlational in nature—examining the relation between holding particular values and endorsing particular positions or acting in particular ways (e.g., Rokeach, 1973). We hope to resurrect enthusiasm for an experimental approach to these questions by presenting our laboratory procedure for creating value-expressive attitudes (i.e., attitudes derived from one's values). By providing the power to test causal hypotheses, an experimental approach may afford greater clarity in understanding the relations among values, attitudes, and behavior.

In this chapter, we first discuss the relation between our manipulation of value-relevance and previous experimental and correlational approaches designed to assess the links among values, attitudes, and behaviors. We then describe our initial attempts in developing our experimental procedure. Finally, we report two studies that explore whether this acute manipulation of attitude function can mirror effects found using more chronic measures, such as self-monitoring (Snyder, 1974). The first study tests a hypothesis derived from an attitude functions framework: Do value-expressive attitudes change most in response to arguments linked to values? The second study tests a hypothesis derived from the values-commitment relation: Does adversity heighten individuals' commitment to value-expressive attitudes?

DEVELOPING A MANIPULATION
OF VALUE-RELEVANCE

Review of Past Research

As we discussed, much of the literature examining the link between values, attitudes, and behavior has been correlational in nature. In developing our experimental induction of value-relevance, we first perused this literature to see if we could adopt any existing approaches to suit our purposes. Chronic individual differences in personality provide one index of individuals' general tendency to link their attitudes to their enduring values. For instance, people who score high on a dogmatism scale may be particularly likely to link their attitudes or behaviors to their personal values (e.g., Miller, 1965). Similarly, self-monitoring might also provide an index of individuals' tendency to link their attitudes and behaviors to their values (e.g., DeBono, 1987). More specifically, DeBono (1987) argues that low self-monitors link their attitudes to their values (i.e., an internal reference point), whereas high self-monitors are more likely to shift their attitudes in accord with situational pressures.

But there are certain difficulties with taking an individual differences approach. For instance, Miller (1965) suggested that more dogmatic individuals may hold more extreme attitudes or possess more knowledge about a particular attitude object. If this is the case, these individuals might resist persuasive attempts to change their attitudes, not because these attitudes reflect their values, but because they hold strong, well-informed positions. Similarly, low self-monitors might resist persuasive appeals, again not because their attitudes reflect their values, but because they pride themselves on being knowledgeable about the issues that are important to them. However, the literature linking low self-monitoring to value-relevant attitudes and behavior left us with an intriguing idea: Find a way to create individual differences in value-relevance in the laboratory. That is, we decided to devise a technique to convince an individual that he or she was the type of person whose attitudes typically reflected their values (or not).

In pursuing this goal, we turned to the literature on attitude functions to see if we could find any clues to devising an experimental procedure for creating value-relevant attitudes. This literature argues that attitudes serve a variety of functions—such as, value-expressive, utilitarian and social adjustive (e.g., Katz, 1960; Smith, Bruner, & White, 1956). Value-expressive attitudes, of course, allow individuals to express their values. Social-adjustive attitudes help individuals behave in ways appropriate to different reference groups. Utilitarian attitudes are based on an analysis of the personal costs and benefits associated with possessing a particular attitude.

The first relevant manipulation of a value-expressive attitude function we found was developed by Ostrom and Brock (1969). They developed a values-bonding procedure whereby they had subjects make logical links between specific statements and specific values. Under the guise of completing a speech interpretation task, subjects were asked to form links between statements opposing the supposed inclusion of Greenland in the Pan-American Bank (e.g., "One leading industry hardly seems adequate to justify the extension of membership") and particular values (e.g., "making one's own decisions"). In this example, a subject would make this link by physically drawing a line from a key idea in the statement (e.g., justify) to a related value (e.g., making one's own decisions). Through this procedure, Ostrom and Brock hoped to link a particular attitude to participants' central values. Furthermore, this manipulation appeared to be successful, in so far as, participants in the values-bonding condition were more resistant to attacks on these "bonded" attitudes. More recently, Johnson and his colleagues have also successfully incorporated a linking procedure within a manipulation of value-relevance (e.g., Johnson, Treadway, & Kahn, 1992). In light of these successes, we decided to incorporate a values-bonding technique within our procedure.

Rather than manipulating the value-relevance of attitudes, Lydon (1987) conducted a series of studies in which he attempted to convince individuals that their personal projects (e.g., volunteer work) were (or were not) a reflection of important values. In various studies, Lydon incorporated procedures such as having participants provide three value-laden reasons for engaging in specific projects and arrange a list of values in terms of their importance for motivating specific projects. Unfortunately, these procedures did not have any impact on experimental subjects' perceptions of the value-relevance of their projects, as compared to controls. Although not any more successful, one component of Lydon's procedures did intrigue us.

He attempted to alter individuals' perceptions of the value-relevance of their personal projects by manipulating the framing of questionnaire items (cf. Salancik & Conway, 1975). That is, experimental or value-expressive (VE) subjects responded to the question, "To some degree this project is relevant to my values," whereas comparison subjects responded to the item, "To a great degree this project is relevant to my values." Lydon hoped this differential framing would elicit stronger agreement for the VE participants, leading them to conclude that their personal projects fulfilled a value-expressive function. Given our goal was to convince individuals that they were the type of person whose attitudes did (or did not) reflect a VE function, we decided to develop a bogus attitude functions questionnaire that utilized differential framing, as we later describe.

At this point in our survey of the literature, we had two of the components we felt were critical for a successful manipulation of value-relevance—a values-bonding procedure and the administration of a bogus attitude functions inventory. We then realized that we would need a comparison group to evaluate the utility of these procedures in altering individuals' perceptions of the link between their attitudes and values. However, in addition to using a baseline control condition, we decided to develop a parallel manipulation to convince people that their attitudes fulfilled a social-adjustive (SA) function.

Upon reflection, we also realized that one critical factor was missing from our procedure—a way to enhance individuals' motivation to believe that they were indeed the type of person whose attitudes fulfilled a VE or SA function. As a result, the initial incarnation of our VE procedure contained three elements: a glowing depiction of individuals who hold VE attitudes, an attitude functions inventory designed to elicit VE responses, and a bonding task. Similarly, the SA procedure contained three elements: a glowing depiction of individuals who hold SA attitudes, an attitude functions inventory designed to elicit SA responses, and a bonding task.

STUDY 1

Overview

Our objective in this first study was to convince experimental participants that they were the type of person whose attitudes typically fulfilled either a value-expressive or social-adjustive function. This study had three conditions: value-expressive (VE), social-adjustive (SA), and control. Experimental participants first learned about the virtues of holding either VE or SA attitudes. They then completed a bogus attitude functions inventory that was purportedly designed to determine whether they were the type of person whose attitudes typically fulfilled either a VE or SA function. After receiving feedback on their responses, experimental participants completed a linking procedure (modeled after Ostrom and Brock, 1969) designed to consolidate their perception that their attitudes fulfilled either a VE or SA function. Finally, both experimental and control subjects completed a manipulation check in the context of completing a variety of personality inventories.

Participants

Forty-two University of Waterloo undergraduates (21 males and 21 females) participated in the study for course credit.[1]

VE and SA Conditions: Materials and Procedure

The experimenter introduced the study to individuals in the VE and SA conditions by explaining that the study examined whether attitudes fulfill different functions for different types of people. In introducing the notion of attitude functions, the experimenter first provided participants with reasonably accurate descriptions of value-expressive and social-adjustive attitude functions, as the following instructions illustrate.

"Our previous research suggests that for different people attitudes might fulfill either a value-expressive or a social-adjustive function. Value-expressive attitudes allow individuals to express their values. Social adjustive attitudes help individuals mediate their interpersonal environments. We have found that some people typically base their attitudes on value-expressive concerns while other people typically base their attitudes on social-adjustive concerns."

Phase 1: Contrasting VE and SA individuals.   The experimenter then expanded upon these depictions, providing individuals with an exaggerated depiction of the virtues and vices of VE and SA individuals. Participants in the *value-expressive* condition learned about the many virtues of people who hold VE attitudes while also learning about some of the vices of people who hold SA attitudes. The exaggerated depiction in the VE condition read as follows:

"People whose attitudes typically fulfill a value-expressive function base their attitudes on their core personal values. That is, they generally adhere to their innermost feelings and beliefs in the expression of their opinions. Thus, the attitudes of value expressive individuals reflect the person they believe themselves to be. This self-expressive style can be contrasted with the more "chameleon" style of people whose attitudes typically serve social-adjustive functions. The attitudes of these conforming individuals are primarily a function of the particular situation in which they find themselves rather than a function of their enduring values. Rather than following their own personal standards, these individuals—in an attempt to

---

[1]There were no gender effects in the analyses we report for Study 1 or 2. Therefore, all reported results for these studies are collapsed across gender. (Only men participated in Study 3.)

ingratiate themselves with others—abandon their own personal beliefs and adopt the opinion of the majority."

In contrast, participants in the *social-adjustive* condition learned about the many virtues of people who hold SA attitudes while also learning about some of the vices of people who hold VE attitudes. The exaggerated depiction in the SA condition read as follows:

"People whose attitudes typically fulfill a social-adjustive function base their attitudes on an integrated consideration of their personal beliefs and those of others. That is, they are generally very responsive to the feelings and beliefs of the important members of their social world. Thus, the attitudes of these open-minded people reflect a desire to incorporate other's views of the world into their own. This style can be contrasted with the more egoistic, dogmatic style of individuals whose attitudes typically serve value-expressive functions. These individuals usually base their attitudes solely on an egocentric consideration of their own personal values and opinions. Without considering why someone might hold an attitude contrary to their own, these more close-minded individuals typically reject others' contrary beliefs as inferior."

Phase 2: Attitude Functions Questionnaire.   After hearing either the VE or SA depiction, experimental subjects then completed a questionnaire that was purportedly designed to determine whether they were the type of person whose attitudes fulfilled either a VE or SA function. Unbeknownst to the participants, we designed the items in this questionnaire to elicit the desired responses. That is, we designed two questionnaires, one for subjects in the VE condition and one for subjects in the SA condition (see Tables 5.1 and 5.2). We designed the items

TABLE 5.1
Value-Expressive Version of the Attitude Functions Questionnaire

1.   My attitudes generally tell others a great deal about my values.
2.   My attitudes are usually based on my moral principles about how the world should be.
3.   A person's values should be one of the most important factors in determining their attitudes.
4.   When my opinions are challenged, I often accept other's contrary opinions rather than sticking to my own attitudes.
5.   Although I sometimes consider others' views when I am formulating my opinion about certain issues, I ultimately adhere to my own personal values or beliefs about what is right and wrong.
6.   My views of the world are simply a reflection of those of my peers.
7.   I would be extremely uncomfortable holding attitudes different than those of my peers.
8.   My attitudes tell others a lot about the person I am.
9.   I usually look to the opinions of others and *not* inside myself in order to decide what my attitude is on a particular issue.
10.   Most often my opinions about world issues are a reflection of my personal standards.
11.   In general, I adhere to my innermost feelings and beliefs in the expression of my attitudes.

Note. Responses were made on a 9-point scale, where 1 = do not agree and 9 = very strongly agree.

TABLE 5.2
Social Adjustive Version of the Attitude Functions Questionnaire

1.	I often try to be sensitive to others' thoughts and feelings about various issues.
2.	I never incorporate others' credible views into my own opinions on issues I find important.
3.	Occasionally, I find myself listening to the well-informed opinions of others when I am evaluating my own beliefs about an issue.
4.	To some extent my opinions are influenced by how important issues are viewed by people I respect and care about the most.
5.	A person's values should be the only factor which influences their attitudes.
6.	Rather than being a sole reflection of my values, my attitudes are often influenced by the opinions of my close friends.
7.	The informed opinions of others are sometimes useful in helping me to articulate my beliefs about social issues.
8.	I ignore other's opinions and base my attitudes only on my own personal values.
9.	To some degree, my parents' opinions about political, moral, and social issues influence my attitudes.
10.	I tend to be dogmatic and consider only my own values and not others' somewhat divergent opinions when I try to decide how I feel about an issue.
11.	I sometimes try to be sensitive to the opinions of others when I am trying to decide how I feel abut issues.

Note. Responses were made on a 9-point scale, where 1 = do not agree and 9 = very strongly agree.

in the VE questionnaire to elicit strong agreement with VE statements (Items # 1, 2, 3, 5, 8, 10, 11) and strong disagreement with SA statements (Items # 4, 6, 7, 9). Conversely, we designed the items in the SA questionnaire to elicit strong agreement with SA statements (Items # 1, 3, 4, 6, 7, 9, 11) and strong disagreement with VE statements (Items # 2, 5, 8, 10).

In each experimental condition, participants were asked to rate, on a 9-point scale, how well each statement in the attitude functions questionnaire described them (1 = do not agree, 9 = very strongly agree). The experimenter then reviewed the questionnaire with each participant, targeting two pro-trait items and one con-trait item. By noting that the subject had scored particularly high (or low) on these items (relative to the test norms), the experimenter attempted to persuade subjects that they were indeed the type of person whose attitudes fulfilled either a VE or SA function.

Phase 3: Linking Procedure.   In the third and final phase of the procedure, VE and SA participants completed a bonding or linking procedure designed to consolidate the perception that their attitudes fulfilled the intended function. Individuals in both the VE and SA conditions first indicated their attitude toward four issues (tuition increases, bilingual services in Ontario, affirmative action, and immigration). We selected these particular attitude objects because of their seemingly multi-functional nature (e.g., a negative attitude toward tuition increases could be linked to the value of equality or to the beliefs of a student's peer group). Participants in the VE condition then indicated which of a number of values (e.g., equality, freedom, social justice) had the greatest impact on their attitude toward each issue. In contrast, participants in the SA condition indicated which of a number of reference groups (e.g., teachers/professors, parents, close friends) had the greatest impact on their attitude toward each issue.[2]

Manipulation Check.   Finally, VE and SA subjects completed a manipulation check in the context of completing a variety of personality measures (e.g., social desirability, self-monitoring). We designed this manipulation check to assess whether participants in the VE (or SA) condition believed their attitudes typically fulfilled a VE (or SA) function. This manipulation check contained two sections. In the first section, participants were asked to indicate which of these four descriptions best described them, (A) My attitudes *almost always* serve a social-adjustive function, (B) My attitudes *generally* serve a social-adjustive function, (C) My attitudes *generally* serve a value-expressive function, and (D) My attitudes *almost always* serve a value-expressive function. In the second section, participants then rated how well each of the four statements described them on a 7-point Likert scale (1 = not at all like me, 7 = very much like me). We attempted to reduce any experimental demands associated with this measure by stressing to participants that our attitude functions inventory was not 100% valid (and actually misclassified people about 20% of the time). Because of our instrument's fallibility, we asked participants to honestly tell us how well they thought their results reflected their self-perceptions. We also assured participants that their responses were anonymous and confidential.

Control Condition: Procedure and Materials

Participants in the control condition were provided with reasonably accurate depictions of individuals who hold VE versus SA attitudes, as the following instructions illustrate.

"Our previous research suggests that for different people attitudes might fulfill either a value-expressive or a social-adjustive function. Value-expressive attitudes allow individuals to express their values. Social adjustive attitudes help individuals mediate their interpersonal environments. We have found that some people typically base their attitudes on value-expressive concerns while other people typically base their attitudes on social-adjustive concerns."

After learning about the VE versus SA nature of attitudes, control participants then completed the manipulation check in the context of completing a variety of personality measures (e.g., social desirability, self-monitoring).

---

[2]In an initial study, we piloted a slightly different version of this linking procedure. We asked participants to describe (in words) the link between their attitudes and values or between their attitudes and the opinions of specific reference groups. Because most participants had difficulty with this task, we resorted to simply asking individuals to indicate the specific values (or reference groups) that had the greatest influence on their attitudes.

Debriefing

At the end of the study, all participants were debriefed. We explained to subjects that we had engineered the procedures to (falsely) convince them that they were the type of person whose attitudes primarily fulfilled a VE or SA function. For example, we showed individuals how we had designed the items in the attitude functions inventory to make it easy (or difficult) to endorse particular items. We then emphasized that people generally hold attitudes that fulfill VE functions and attitudes that fulfill SA functions and that our questionnaires could not reveal any diagnostic information about their personalities. (None of the subjects reported any suspicion about the procedures.)

Results

If our manipulation is effective, individuals in the VE condition should view their attitudes as more a reflection of their values than individuals in the SA condition. Conversely, individuals in the SA condition should view their attitudes as reflecting the opinions of others to a greater extent than individuals in the VE condition. This should be true whether we examine participants' choices among the various descriptors or their individual ratings of each statement. When we examined the results on the manipulation check, we were encouraged to find reasonable support for the strength of our manipulation.

Choice Among Descriptors. When we examined participants' choices among the different descriptions, the predicted pattern of results emerged. Ten out of 12 participants in the VE condition depicted their attitudes as generally (Option C) or almost always (Option D) serving a VE function. Conversely, 11 out of 12 participants in the SA condition depicted their attitudes as generally (Option B) or almost always (Option A) serving a SA function. Among control subjects, 8 out of 12 depicted their attitudes as generally or almost always serving a VE function, whereas 4 out of 12 control subjects depicted their attitudes as serving a SA function.[3] As this distribution illustrates, subjects' responses (i.e., choice among the descriptors) depended on condition, yielding a significant chi-square, χ^2 (2) = 13.51, $p < .01$.

Ratings of Individual Descriptors. Turning now to subjects' ratings of each descriptor, a one-way ANOVA on the value-expressive ratings revealed an overall significant effect, $F(2,39) = 10.11$, $p < .001$ (see Table 5.3). VE subjects were most likely to indicate that their attitudes typically fulfilled a VE function, whereas SA subjects were least likely to characterize their attitudes in this way. More specifically, Newman-Keuls comparisons revealed that VE individuals

---

[3]On the choice task, six subjects did not indicate which descriptor best described them.

TABLE 5.3
Study 1: Ratings of Individual Descriptors by Condition

	Ratings Scales	
Condition	Value-Expressive[a]	Social-Adjustive[b]
Value-Expressive (VE)	5.15	2.88
Social-Adjustive (SA)	2.88	4.88
Control	4.26	3.41

[a]Mean of "almost always VE" and "generally VE" ratings.
[b]Mean of "almost always SA" and "generally SA" ratings.

rated their attitudes as reflecting their values to a significantly *greater* extent than SA individuals. Also, VE individuals rated their attitudes as reflecting their values to a *greater* degree than control individuals, although this effect was not significant. Finally, SA individuals described their attitudes as being significantly *less* a function of their values than did individuals in the control condition.

For the social-adjustive ratings, a one-way ANOVA again revealed an overall significant effect, $F(2,39) = 7.38, p < .01$ (see Table 5.3). The pattern of means was once again quite consistent with our predictions. SA subjects were most likely to indicate that their attitudes typically fulfilled a SA function, whereas VE subjects were least likely to characterize their attitudes in this way. More specifically, Newman-Keuls comparisons revealed that SA individuals rated their attitudes as reflecting SA concerns to a significantly greater extent than VE individuals. Also, SA individuals rated their attitudes as reflecting SA concerns to a significantly greater degree than control individuals. However, VE and control participants did not differ.

Moderating Influences? We also examined whether social desirability (Crowne & Marlowe, 1964) or self-monitoring (Snyder, 1974) moderated the impact of our manipulation. For example, individuals high on social desirability might be most susceptible to the attitude functions manipulation than those low on this dimension. On the other hand, high self-monitors (who typically adjust their behavior to situational demands) might be especially influenced by this manipulation, whereas low self-monitors (who typically adhere to internal standards of reference) might be less influenced. However, when we examined participants' responses in 3 × 2 ANOVAs, we did not find moderating effects for either variable, although the low cell sizes makes this conclusion a tentative one.

Discussion

Overall, the pattern of results provided reasonable support for our manipulation of attitude functions. On both the choice and rating measures, participants in the

VE condition were most likely to indicate that their attitudes fulfilled a VE function, whereas participants in the SA condition were most likely to indicate that their attitudes fulfilled a SA function. Despite this success, we did have some reservations about our manipulation.

Despite the measures we took to reduce experimental demands (e.g., assuring participants' of their anonymity, emphasizing that our attitude functions test was not 100% valid), we were somewhat troubled by possible demands associated with our procedure, although social desirability did not moderate the impact of the manipulation. In the first phase of our manipulation, experimental participants heard depictions describing the virtues of one "type" of individual, while learning the vices of the other "type." We hoped this would heighten participants' motivation to see themselves as either VE or SA individuals. But, in depicting VE and SA individuals in such biased terms, we may have come on a little too strong. For example, participants in the VE condition would almost have to admit they were weak-willed, social chameleons to depict themselves as SA individuals. Similarly, individuals in the SA condition would have to admit they were egocentric dogmatists to describe themselves as VE individuals. As we discuss shortly, we hoped to reduce this pressure to conform to our manipulation in our second study by making our descriptions of VE and SA individuals more even-handed, describing both the virtues and vices of each type of individual.

Second, we wondered whether our acute manipulation of attitude functions can reproduce effects observed using more chronic indicators. Research suggests that individuals respond differently to persuasive appeals depending on the function their attitude fulfills. For instance, DeBono (1987) found that high self-monitors (i.e., individuals whose attitudes are thought to fulfill a SA function) change their attitudes most in response to communications that link particular positions to the beliefs of important reference groups. In contrast, low self-monitors (i.e., individuals whose attitudes are thought to fulfill a VE function) change their attitudes most in response to communications that link particular positions to their personal values. In our second study, we wanted to see whether our manipulation of attitude functions could replicate this effect. That is, individuals exposed to our VE manipulation should change their attitudes most in response to "value-based" communications. In contrast, individuals exposed to our SA manipulation should change their attitudes most in response to "peer-based" communications.

STUDY 2

In our next study, we decided to address these lingering concerns about our procedure. To make our manipulation of attitude functions less demanding, we depicted VE and SA individuals in a more even-handed light, as we describe next. To test the validity of our manipulation, we attempted a conceptual replication of DeBono's correlational findings using our experimental manipulation of attitude functions. Thus, more than simply validating our procedure, Study 2 also presents an experimental test of the functionality–persuasion hypothesis (i.e., that attitudes change most in response to information that addresses the function of the attitude).

Paralleling DeBono's procedure, we exposed our participants to one of two communications advocating the institutionalization of the mentally ill. The values appeal linked a favorable attitude toward institutionalizing the mentally ill to important personal values. In contrast, the peers appeal linked such an attitude to the beliefs of the participants' peers. To summarize, the design of this study was a classic 2 × 2 that manipulated both perceived attitude functions (VE versus SA) and communication type (values- versus peers-appeal).

If our less demanding manipulation is still effective, individuals in the VE condition should describe their attitudes as typically fulfilling a VE function, whereas individuals in the SA condition should describe their attitudes as typically fulfilling a SA function. Furthermore, if our acute manipulation of attitude functions is valid, individuals in the VE condition should change attitudes toward institutionalizing the mentally ill most in response to the values appeal. Conversely, individuals in the SA condition should change attitudes most in response to peers-beliefs appeals. Thus, if our results are to parallel DeBono's, we should get the most attitude change when the attitude function matches the communication type.

Overview

Study 2 contained two main parts: the first, the manipulation of attitude functions; the second, the presentation of the communication. Participants first completed the bogus attitude functions inventory used in Study 1.[4] After receiving feedback that suggested they were the type of person whose attitudes typically fulfilled either a VE or SA function, participants then learned about the virtues and vices of holding VE or SA attitudes. Finally, subjects completed the linking procedure used in Study 1. At this point, the study was interrupted by a second experimenter who asked the subject to participate in a brief survey being conducted by the Psychology Department. In this study, we exposed participants to a communication linking a favorable attitude toward institutionalizing the mentally ill either to important values or the beliefs of their peers. After listening to this communication, participants completed a survey assessing their attitudes toward institutionalizing the mentally ill.

---

[4]We presented the attitude functions inventory prior to the biased depictions, the reverse of the procedure in Study 1. We did this in an additional attempt to attenuate any possible demands in our manipulation.

Participants

Fifty-two University of Waterloo undergraduates (23 males and 29 females) participated in the study for course credit.

Attitude Functions Manipulation

The experimenter introduced the study by explaining that attitudes fulfill different functions for different types of people. The general instructions to subjects were identical to those presented in Study 1.

Phase 1: Attitude Functions Questionnaire. After hearing this general depiction of VE and SA individuals, the participants then completed the attitude functions questionnaire used in Study 1. As you recall, there were two versions of this questionnaire: The VE questionnaire was designed to elicit strong agreement with VE items (and strong disagreement with SA items). In contrast, the SA questionnaire was designed to elicit strong agreement with SA items (and strong disagreement with VE items). Parallel to Study 1, the experimenter then reviewed the questionnaire with the participant, leading them to believe that their attitudes typically fulfilled the desired function.

Phase 2: Contrasting VE and SA Individuals. Upon receiving feedback from the experimenter, participants then learned about some of the virtues and vices of *both* VE and SA individuals. However, we attempted to *tailor* these descriptions for each condition. In the VE condition, we tried to make the virtues of VE people more positive than the virtues of SA people, while making the faults of SA individuals more serious than the faults of VE individuals. Conversely, in the SA condition, we tried to make the virtues of SA people more positive than the virtues of VE people, while making the faults of VE individuals more serious than the faults of SA individuals. The depiction for participants in the VE condition read as follows:

"People whose attitudes typically fulfill a value-expressive function hold attitudes that are derived from their core personal values. That is, they generally adhere to their innermost feelings and beliefs in the expression of their opinions. Thus, the attitudes of value expressive individuals usually reflect the person they believe themselves to be. At times though—perhaps when an issue is particularly important to them—some of these people may tend to be dogmatic and sometimes reject others' contrary beliefs out of hand.

In contrast, people whose attitudes typically fulfill a social-adjustive function are generally very responsive to the feelings and beliefs of others in forming their attitudes. So, the attitudes of these individuals often reflect a desire to incorporate others' views of the world into their own. Often times though, these people can be too easily swayed by others. Sometimes, in the face of social pressure, people whose attitudes serve a social-adjustive function might even change their own personal beliefs and adopt the opinion of the majority."

In contrast, the depiction for participants in the SA condition read as follows:

"People whose attitudes typically fulfill a social-adjustive function base their attitudes on an integrated consideration of their personal beliefs and those of others. That is, they are generally very responsive to the feelings and beliefs of the important members of their social world. Thus, the attitudes of these open-minded people reflect a desire to incorporate other's views of the world into their own. At times though—perhaps when they are faced with an opposing viewpoint held by particularly important others, such as close friends—some of these individuals might tend to modify their position.

On the other hand, people whose attitudes typically fulfill a value-expressive function generally hold attitudes that are derived from their values. They almost always adhere to their innermost feelings and beliefs in the expression of their opinions. However, this can lead to their being quite close-minded or dogmatic. Without considering why someone might hold an attitude contrary to their own, these individuals often reject others' contrary beliefs as inferior to their own."

Phase 3: Linking Procedure.   Next, participants completed the linking procedure used in Study 1 to consolidate their perception that their attitudes fulfilled either a VE or SA function. Individuals in both the VE and SA conditions first indicated their attitude toward four issues (tuition increases, bilingual services in Ontario, affirmative action, and immigration). Participants in the VE condition then indicated which of a number of values had the greatest impact on their attitude toward each issue. In contrast, participants in the SA condition indicated which of a number of reference groups had the greatest impact on their attitude toward each issue.

Exposure to Communication

Once participants completed the linking procedure, they started filling out a variety of personality measures (e.g., social desirability, self-monitoring).

At this point in the study, we introduced the appeals manipulation. A second experimenter interrupted the session and asked Experimenter 1 if the participant would be interested in completing a survey for the Psychology Department.[5] This experimenter explained to the subject that the department was interested in sponsoring a mental health week in the coming term in which various speakers would discuss different mental health issues in introductory psychology classes. The experimenter then asked them to listen to a tape of one of these purported

---

[5]Using two experimenters allowed us to "blind" each experimenter to the manipulation conducted by the other.

talks because the department wanted to determine the types of talks that students would find most interesting. All subjects agreed to listen to one of the 10-minute tapes.

The second experimenter then took the participant to a separate lab room to listen to one of two communications regarding the institutionalization of the mentally ill. Participants in the values-appeal condition heard a recording linking a favorable attitude toward institutionalization to the value of being a responsible and loving person (pretesting revealed this to be an important value for our subjects). Participants in the peers-appeal condition heard a recording indicating that a strong majority of Canadian university students favored institutionalization. (For a more detailed description of the content of the communications and the dependent measure, see DeBono, 1987.) After listening to either the values-appeal or peers-appeal, subjects completed two questionnaires: one assessing their interest in the talk and the second assessing their attitude toward institutionalizing the mentally ill. In presenting these tasks, we explained to subjects that their thoughts and feelings about the issue might influence their interest in the talk, hence the need to collect both measures. DeBono's 26-item attitude questionnaire included statements such as "It is generally not a good idea to care for the mentally ill in hospitals and institutions" and "Mainstreaming the mentally ill into society is generally a bad idea." Subjects responded to each of the 26 items on a 5-point scale (1 = strongly disagree, 5 = strongly agree) in which higher scores represented more favorable attitudes toward institutionalizing the mentally ill. Once subjects had completed the survey, they went back to the original experimenter, where they then continued filling out the personality measures before completing the attitude functions manipulation check.

At the end of the study, individuals were debriefed using the procedures outlined for Study 1. No subject reported any suspicion about a link between the two studies.

Results

If our toned-down manipulation is still effective, individuals in the VE condition should view their attitudes as more a reflection of their values than individuals in the SA condition. Conversely, individuals in the SA condition should view their attitudes as reflecting the opinions of others to a greater extent than individuals in the VE condition. Once again, this should be true whether we examine participants' choices among the various descriptors or their individual ratings of each statement. When we examined the results on the manipulation check, we were encouraged to find strong support for the strength of our manipulation.

Choice Among Descriptors.   When we examined participants' choices among the different descriptions, the predicted pattern of results emerged. Seventeen out of 25 participants in the VE condition depicted their attitudes as generally or almost always serving a VE function. Conversely, 17 out of 23 participants in the SA condition depicted their attitudes as generally or almost always serving a SA function.[6] As this distribution illustrates, subjects' responses (i.e., choice among the descriptors) depended on condition, yielding a significant chi-square, χ^2 (1) = 8.48, $p < .01$.

Ratings of Individual Descriptors.   Turning now to subjects' ratings of each descriptor, a one-way ANOVA on the value-expressive ratings revealed an overall significant effect. VE subjects were more likely to indicate that their attitudes typically fulfilled a VE function ($M = 5.48$) as compared to SA subjects ($M = 3.25$), $F(1,49) = 81.00$, $p < .001$. For the social-adjustive ratings, a one-way ANOVA again revealed an overall significant effect, $F(1,49) = 48.86$, $p < .001$. As expected, SA subjects ($M = 4.58$) were more likely than VE subjects ($M = 2.52$) to indicate that their attitudes typically fulfilled a SA function.

Attitudes Toward Institutionalizing the Mentally Ill.   Our primary goal in this study was to replicate DeBono's (1987) findings using our manipulation of attitude functions. To explore whether our attitude functions manipulation and communication type interacted to predict participants' attitudes, we conducted a 2 (condition: VE versus SA) × 2 (appeal: values versus peers' beliefs) ANOVA using participants' attitude toward institutionalizing the mentally ill as our dependent measure. As displayed in Table 5.4, this analysis revealed the anticipated, significant interaction, $F(1,48) = 5.65$, $p < .05$. VE subjects changed their attitudes most in response to the values appeal whereas SA subjects changed their attitudes most in response to the peers appeal. That is, VE subjects exposed to a values appeal favored institutionalizing the mentally ill more than VE subjects exposed to the peers appeal. In contrast, SA subjects exposed to the peers appeal favored institutionalizing the mentally ill more than SA subjects exposed to the values appeal.

Discussion

Once again, we found strong support for the success of our attitude functions manipulation. In this study, we tried to reduce the "heavy-handedness" of our initial manipulation by depicting the virtues and faults of both VE and SA individuals, rather than simply depicting each type of person in uniformly good or bad terms as we did in Study 1. Encouragingly, on both the choice and rating measures, participants in the VE condition were still most likely to indicate that their attitudes fulfilled a VE function, whereas participants in the SA condition were most likely to indicate that their attitudes fulfilled a SA function. Furthermore, this acute manipulation appeared to produce effects that mirrored those

---

[6]On the choice task, four subjects did not indicate which descriptor best described them.

TABLE 5.4
Attitudes Toward Institutionalizing the Mentally Ill by Attitude Function and Communication Type

	Appeal	
Function	Values	Peers
Value-Expressive	70.23	64.69
Social-Adjustive	61.92	75.31

Note. Higher scores indicate a more positive attitude toward institutionalizing the mentally ill. (Possible range: 26 to 130).

obtained using self-monitoring, which other authors have construed as a chronic indicator of attitude functions (e.g., DeBono, 1987). Individuals who believed their attitudes typically fulfilled VE functions changed their attitudes most in response to values appeals, whereas individuals who believed their attitudes typically fulfilled SA functions changed their attitudes most in response to peers appeals.

In summary, the results on both the manipulation check and our replication of DeBono's (1987) findings increased our confidence that our manipulation was in fact influencing individuals' perceptions of the value-relevant nature of their attitudes. With our new attitude functions manipulation in hand, we proceeded to design a third study that would allow us to explore the interrelations among attitude functions, adversity, and attitudinal commitment.

STUDY 3

Of the varied real-life examples of individuals taking extreme actions in defense of their attitudes, two psychological processes seem critical. First, individuals appear particularly committed to attitudes that reflect their values. In a meta-analytic review of the persuasion literature, Johnson and Eagly (1989) found that individuals resisted persuasive appeals most when their attitudes reflected their enduring values. Second, the experience of adversity—suffering because of one's beliefs—also enhances commitment (e.g., Brickman, 1987; Festinger, 1957). For example, Marlowe, Frager, and Nutall (1965) discovered that individuals were most willing to act on their liberal racial attitudes when they suffered for them. (Upon reflection, this effect runs against lay intuitions about the inverse relation between adversity and commitment.)

The case of the abortion debate illustrates how value-relevance and adversity may interact and actually strengthen the experience of attitudinal commitment. Individuals on both sides of the abortion debate link their attitudes to core, personal values. Adamant pro-lifers justify their behavior by appealing to the sanctity of life whereas pro-choicers justify their behavior by appealing to freedom of choice. In addition, both sides risk considerable public and personal costs in upholding their attitudes. But rather than weakening their zeal, the experience of adversity only seems to strengthen commitment to these value-relevant attitudes, suggesting that individuals should become most committed to value-relevant attitudes when they suffer because of them. In a first, correlational, test of the values-adversity hypothesis, Lydon and Zanna (1990) found that individuals felt most committed to ongoing personal projects when these projects reflected their values and they experienced adversity in the course of completing them.

We designed Study 3 to provide the first experimental test of the values-adversity hypothesis. We reasoned that individuals assess self-integrity by evaluating their attitudes against the standards set by their values (e.g., Steele, 1988). In other words, individuals should feel best about themselves when their attitudes and values are internally consistent. Therefore, abandoning value-relevant attitudes in the face of adversity should threaten self-esteem. In contrast, adhering to value-relevant attitudes in the face of adversity should protect self-integrity. This should be particularly true for individuals who perceive themselves to be the type of people whose values guide their attitudes (i.e., VE participants). Reneging upon a social-adjustive attitude in the face of adversity, however, should not produce as great a threat to the self. (These attitudes are more a reflection of others' beliefs than they are self-defining.) As a result, individuals may be more likely to abandon SA attitudes when they suffer because of them. This should be particularly true for individuals who perceive themselves to be the type of people whose consideration of others' opinions guide their attitudes (i.e., SA participants).

To test the hypothesis that value-relevance moderates the adversity–commitment relation, we incorporated manipulations of attitude functions and adversity within a study that threatened individuals' commitment to their attitudes toward affirmative action.

To create individuals that viewed their attitudes as more (or less) a reflection of their values, we manipulated attitude functions using the procedure we fine-tuned in Study 2. In finding a way for individuals to "suffer" because of their attitudes, our first thought was to expose people to ridicule or censure from others as a result of the beliefs they held. But we hesitated to use this "social" adversity because of its obvious confounds with our SA manipulation. However, in the Marlowe et al. (1965) study, we found a manipulation of adversity that we could adapt to suit our purposes. In the high adversity condition of their study, individuals lost the opportunity to earn $20 because their attitudes toward different ethnic groups were too liberal (i.e., they did not possess the "right" attitudes). In the low adversity condition, individuals only lost the opportunity to earn $1.50 because of their attitudes.

Given Marlowe et al.'s (1965) success, we decided to use this type of manipulation in our first attempt to induce adversity. Paralleling Marlowe et al.'s procedure, individuals in our high adversity or "incorrect attitudes" condition lost the opportunity to earn $20 because their attitudes toward women's issues were too liberal. But in our low adversity or "random loss" condition individuals lost the opportunity to earn $20 by the toss of a coin (i.e., a random loss).

In summary, we manipulated two variables in Study 3: (1) perceived attitude functions (value-expressive versus social-adjustive) and (2) adversity (incorrect attitudes versus random loss). Individuals' commitment to their attitudes towards affirmative action served as our main dependent measure. We expected individuals who believed their attitudes fulfilled a VE function to be most committed to affirmative action when their liberal attitudes towards women's issues cost them the opportunity to earn $20 (i.e., when they suffered precisely because of their attitudes). In contrast, we expected individuals who believed their attitudes fulfilled a SA function to be least committed to affirmative action when they suffered because of their liberal attitudes.

Overview

Study 3 contained two main parts: the first, the manipulation of attitude functions; the second, the manipulation of adversity. Participants first completed the bogus attitude functions inventory. Next, they learned about the virtues and vices of holding VE or SA attitudes. Finally, subjects completed the linking procedure. At this point, the study was interrupted by a second experimenter who asked the subject if he would be willing to participate in a second short study and earn $20. Individuals then lost the opportunity to earn this "windfall" either because their attitudes towards women were too liberal or by the toss of a coin. Participants then completed a series of questionnaires, including one that contained measures of their commitment to a variety of issues, including the critical issue, affirmative action for women.

Participants

Forty-seven University of Waterloo male undergraduates participated in the study for course credit. Six subjects were excluded from the present analyses (four because of suspiciousness and two because they declined the invitation to participate in the second study).

Procedure

To create our "incorrect attitudes" and "random loss" conditions, we introduced a male confederate to our procedures. Throughout the study, the "real" participant believed that this second subject (the confederate) was completing the identical procedures in an adjoining room.

Attitude Functions Manipulation.   In the first phase of the procedure, the participants were exposed to the attitudes function manipulation detailed in the procedure for Study 2.[7] After participants completed the linking procedure, they started filling out a variety of personality measures (e.g., social desirability, self-monitoring).

Adversity manipulation.   At this point in the study, a second experimenter interrupted the session to ask the subjects (the "real" subject and the confederate) if either of them would like to participate in a fifteen minute study for $20 payment, as the following invitation illustrates:

"Hi, I'm conducting a study looking at people's reactions to different types of jokes. Different people find different things funny and so we're interested in looking at some individual differences that might influence what people find funny. The study simply involves looking at some political cartoons and reading some political jokes and then making some ratings about how funny you found them. It's a pretty easy task that only takes fifteen minutes and the people who have taken part so far have really enjoyed it."

In the "*incorrect attitudes loss*" condition, participants were denied the opportunity to participate because their attitudes towards women's issues were too liberal. To accomplish this, Experimenter 2 first made an heartfelt plea for the subjects' help in completing her study:

"The only problem is I just found out from my supervisor that I need to finish running subjects by the end of the day because he wants to present the results at a conference next week. We're down to our last two people, but because we need to finish today, we're willing to pay people $20 for participating. The study really shouldn't take any more than 15 minutes to complete. Would either of you be interested in participating?"

Once the confederate and the "real" subject indicated interest in the experiment, Experimenter 2 then explained that she needed people who held different opinions concerning women's issues.[8] Under this guise, she then asked the subjects to complete a short 3-item questionnaire concerning their opinions about different social policies regarding women (e.g., Women should be more strongly encouraged to pursue careers in mathematics and science). (As this example illustrates, we tried to design items that even more conservative subjects would have difficulty disagreeing with.) She then "scored" each subject's questionnaire. The "real" subject then lost the opportunity to be in the study because of his liberal attitudes toward women. Once she had scored his survey, the experimenter simply stated, rather abruptly, "Oh, I can't use you. I don't want people who

---

[7]In Studies 1 and 2, affirmative action was one of the target issues included in the linking procedure. We removed "affirmative action" from the linking questionnaire in Study 3 because we wanted to minimize any connections between the two phases of the study.

[8]The confederate's enthusiasm induced subjects' willingness to participate in all but two cases.

feel as liberally as you do about these issues." This experimenter then turned to the confederate and invited him to participate in the study because he had the kind of attitudes that she looking for. She then arranged to meet the confederate at the end of the study.

In the *random loss* condition, participants lost the chance to participate in the study to the confederate as a result of a coin toss. To accomplish this, Experimenter 2 first made an heartfelt plea for the subjects' help in completing her study:

> "The only problem is I just found out from my supervisor that I need to finish running subjects by the end of the day because he wants to present the results at a conference next week. Because we have to finish today, we're willing to pay $20 for your participation. The study really shouldn't take any more than 15 minutes to complete. Would either of you be interested in participating?"

Once the real subject and the confederate indicated interest in the experiment, Experimenter 2 then said: "Oh, actually I only need one more person. I guess the fairest thing to do then is just to flip a coin." She then asked the real subject to call the coin. Once the coin was called (e.g., heads), Experimenter 2 selected the opposite two-sided coin (e.g., tails) from her pocket and tossed it. The real subject then lost the opportunity to be in the study because he lost the coin toss. Once she tossed the coin, Experimenter 2 said to the subject: "Oh, it's (*heads/tails*) so I won't be able to use you in my study." She then turned to the confederate and said: "So you'll be taking part in my experiment. I'll come back and get you at the end of this session and then we'll start on my study."

Once Experimenter 2 left, the confederate returned to his room and the real subject continued completing the package of personality questionnaires. The main dependent measures (including the commitment index, an adversity manipulation check and the attitude functions manipulation check) were embedded in this package.

At the end of the study, individuals were debriefed using the procedures outlined for Study 1. Four subjects (one in each condition) reported suspicions about their interaction with Experimenter 2. (These subjects were excluded from the analyses.)

Dependent Measures

Commitment Index.   This measure tapped individuals' commitment to a variety of social policy issues, including affirmative action for women. The other issues were increasing immigration, mandatory AIDS testing for public sector workers, the right to free speech, and the legalization of marijuana. Participants rated their attitudes toward each issue, their commitment to each issue (i.e., How committed do you feel toward this attitude?), and the personal importance of each issue (i.e., How important is this attitude to you?). These ratings were made on 9-point scales (e.g., 1 = not at all committed, 9 = extremely committed). In addition to these global commitment items, we also obtained a behavioral measure. Participants rated how willingly they would engage in a variety of activities in support of their beliefs (e.g., sign a petition, join an organization supporting my beliefs, try to convince others of the merits of my beliefs). Participants indicated their willingness to engage in each of the nine behaviors on a 9-point scale (1 = not at all willing, 9 = extremely willing).

Adversity Manipulation Check.   Just before the debriefing, participants completed a 2-item questionnaire designed to tap how *upset* they were about not being able to take part in the second study (i.e., How upset were you about not being able to participate in the $20 study on political jokes? [1 = not at all upset, 7 = extremely upset]) and their *attributions* for this loss (i.e., I couldn't participate in the study on political jokes for reasons that had . . . [1 = nothing to do with me, 7 = a lot to do with me]).

Results

In describing our findings, we first examine the results for the manipulation checks to see whether they were successful in inducing the desired states. We then explore whether VE subjects became more committed to their attitudes toward affirmative action for women after having suffered because of their liberal beliefs about women's issues.

Attitude Functions Manipulation Check.   When we examined participants' choices among the different descriptions, we again found strong support for the success of our attitude functions manipulation. All of the participants in the VE condition depicted their attitudes as generally or almost always serving a VE function. Conversely, thirteen out of nineteen participants in the SA condition depicted their attitudes as generally or almost always serving a SA function.[9] As this distribution illustrates, subjects' responses (i.e., choice among the descriptors) depended on condition, yielding a significant chi-square, $\chi^2(1) = 19.76$, $p < .001$.

Turning to subjects' ratings of each descriptor, a one-way ANOVA on the value-expressive ratings revealed an overall significant effect. VE subjects were more likely to indicate that their attitudes typically fulfilled a VE function ($M = 4.89$) as compared to SA subjects ($M = 3.12$), $F(1,39) = 22.28$, $p < .001$. For the social-adjustive ratings, a one-way ANOVA again revealed an overall significant effect, $F(1,38) = 18.75$, $p < .001$. As expected, SA subjects ($M = 4.36$) were more likely than VE subjects ($M = 2.68$) to indicate that their attitudes typically fulfilled a SA function.

---

[9]On the choice task, three subjects did not indicate which descriptor best described them.

Adversity Manipulation Check.   Individuals in the "incorrect attitudes" ($M =$ 3.16) and "random loss" ($M = 2.73$) conditions did not differ in how upset they felt about losing out on the $20 study, suggesting that both groups of individuals "suffered" comparably, $F(1,39) < 1$. However, they did attribute this loss to different sources. Individuals in the incorrect attitudes condition ($M = 5.58$) were more likely to attribute this loss to themselves than individuals in the random loss ($M = 2.14$) condition, $F(1,39) = 45.70$, $p < .001$. Taken together, these results suggest that our adversity manipulation was effective in creating the desired state in each group of subjects.

Commitment to Affirmative Action.   Our primary goal in this study was to explore how value-relevance and adversity interact to predict individuals' commitment to their attitudes. We expected individuals in the VE condition to become more committed to affirmative action when they suffered because of their liberal ideology. In contrast, we expected individuals in the SA condition to become less committed to affirmative action when they suffered because of their liberal ideology.

A composite of the global and behavioral commitment items served as the index of individuals' commitment to their attitudes toward affirmative action. To create the global index, we aggregated the "commitment" and "importance" ratings for this issue. (These items were highly correlated, $r(39) = .66$). To create the behavioral index, we aggregated the nine "behavioral" items ($\alpha = 83$). Because these "global" and "behavioral" indices were highly correlated, $r(39) = .64$, we then standardized each index and aggregated these standard scores to form a composite index of commitment.

We then wanted to see whether the manipulations influenced individuals' commitment to affirmative action—above and beyond their general tendencies to express commitment to their attitudes. Thus, we computed an index of individuals' commitment "specific" to affirmative action by subtracting the mean of subjects' self-reported commitment to the filler issues from their score on the composite index of commitment toward affirmative action.[10]

We then conducted a 2 (function: value-expressive versus social-adjustive) × 2 (adversity: incorrect attitudes versus random loss) ANOVA on this "specific" commitment index. This analysis revealed the anticipated, significant interaction, $F(1,37) = 6.02$, $p < .05$. As Table 5.5 reveals, VE individuals became most committed to their attitudes toward affirmative action when they suffered precisely because of these opinions (i.e., the incorrect attitudes loss condition).

---

[10]In calculating this general commitment index, we included the three filler items whose (a) atttitude scores were uncorrelated with expressed attitudes to affirmative action, and (b) commitment scores were significantly correlated with expressed commitment to affirmative action (i.e., immigration, mandatory AIDS testing, the right to free speech). Our manipulation did not affect individuals' commitment to the filler issues.

TABLE 5.5
Commitment to Affirmative Action As a Function of Attitude Functions and Adversity

	Adversity	
Function	Random Loss	Incorrect Attitudes Loss
Value-Expressive	-.41	.59
Social-Adjustive	.16	-.13

Note. Higher scores indicate greater commitment to affirmative action, controlling for individuals' general commitment levels.

More specifically, VE individuals in the incorrect attitudes loss condition expressed more commitment to affirmative action than VE individuals in the random loss condition, $F(1,37) = 7.52$, $p < .01$. (The adversity manipulation did not differentially affect individuals in the SA condition.) Among subjects in the incorrect attitudes loss condition, VE individuals also tended to express more commitment to affirmative action that SA individuals, $F(1,37) = 3.74$, $p < .10$.

Finally, this evidence of heightened commitment among VE subjects who suffered because of their positions was not simply due to attitudes becoming more extreme in this cell. To explore this potential confound, we conducted a 2 × 2 ANOVA on individuals' attitudes toward affirmative action. This analysis yielded no significant effects, suggesting that our manipulations affected perceptions of commitment without changing the extremity of individuals' attitudes.

Discussion

In Study 3, we again found strong support for the success of our attitude functions manipulation on both the choice and ratings measures. Participants in the VE condition came to see themselves as the type of person whose attitudes typically fulfilled value-expressive functions. In contrast, participants in the SA condition came to see themselves as the type of person whose attitudes typically fulfilled social-adjustive functions.

Most importantly, Study 3 yielded reasonable support for this first experimental test of the values–adversity hypothesis. Suffering for their beliefs appeared to heighten VE individuals' commitment to their attitudes toward affirmative action. This heightened commitment was reflected in their global statements as well as their intentions to perform specific behaviors supporting their attitudes.

Our experimental results replicate those described by Lydon and Zanna (1990) who used correlational measures of value-relevance and adversity to explore students' commitment to their ongoing personal projects. Thus, Study 3 provides additional evidence that our acute VE manipulation induces a state that mirrors that obtained using a more chronic index of value-relevance.

GENERAL DISCUSSION

Our primary goal in this research was to develop a manipulation of value-relevance. In Study 1, we developed a three-step procedure to alter individuals' perceptions of the functions their attitudes fulfilled (VE versus SA). After modifying this manipulation, we incorporated it within two different studies, the first exploring the functionality-persuasion hypothesis and the second exploring the values-adversity hypothesis. Study 2 revealed that individuals who believed their attitudes typically fulfilled VE functions changed their attitudes most in response to a persuasive appeal linked to their values. In contrast, individuals who believed their attitudes typically fulfilled SA functions changed their attitudes most in response to a persuasive appeal linked to their peers' beliefs. Study 3 revealed that individuals who believed their attitudes typically fulfilled VE functions expressed heightened commitment to affirmative action when they suffered because of their liberal position on women's issues. As a testament to the utility of our attitude functions manipulation, both Studies 2 and 3 replicated the results of studies using correlational indicators of value-relevance (e.g., DeBono, 1987; Lydon & Zanna, 1990).

Perhaps the greatest advantage of our manipulation of value-relevance is its person-centered nature. We tried to convince individuals that they were the type of person whose attitudes typically fulfilled a specific function (VE or SA), rather than convincing them that a particular attitude fulfilled a specific function (VE or SA). Our approach might reduce some of the potential confounds associated with using the more common, issue-centered manipulation. The value-relevance manipulation in Study 3, for example, did not induce participants to think about their attitudes toward affirmative action (in particular) but this "person-centered" manipulation still affected individuals' responses to adversity. Had we taken an "issue-centered" approach (and explicitly linked participants' attitudes toward affirmative action to their values), demand characteristics could complicate the interpretation of the results.

In future research, our general procedure could be adapted to create individuals who believed their attitudes typically fulfilled more instrumental functions, as one example. This type of person could be described as logical, rational, or possessing an analytical mind. Creating such manipulations would allow us to contrast effects of possessing VE, SA and instrumental attitudes in a variety of different contexts. Extending upon the present studies, the most obvious first step is to compare whether adversity differentially affects individuals who believe their attitudes fulfill value-expressive versus instrumental functions. Indeed, a number of researchers have started to explore questions surrounding the relations among values, attitudes and behavior using an experimental paradigm (e.g., Johnson et al., 1992; Lavine, Robertson, & Borgida, 1993; Maio & Olson, 1994).

To return to our original theme, many of the most intriguing events in the media center around the actions individuals take in defense of their values. The abortion debate provides one vivid exemplar of the role of values in shaping people's everyday behaviors. Although a complete understanding of the link between values, attitudes, and behavior may be elusive, it remains our hope that an experimental manipulation of value-relevance can be used to shed some light on these important phenomena.

ACKNOWLEDGMENTS

Preparation of this chapter was supported by Social Science and Humanities Research Council of Canada (SSHRC) doctoral fellowships to Sandra Murray and Geoff Haddock and by a SSHRC research grant to Mark Zanna. We would like to thank Ramona Bobocel, John Holmes, John Lydon, Tara MacDonald, James Olson, and Clive Seligman for their insightful comments on an earlier version of this chapter. We would also like to thank Dr. Kenneth DeBono for his generousity in providing his experimental materials. We are also indebted to Mary Dooley, James Karr, Renata Snidr, Paul Stuebing, Wendy Telford, and Adam Zanna for their help in conducting this research. Sandra Murray is now at the Research Center for Group Dynamics, Institute for Social Research, P. O. Box 1248, Ann Arbor, MI, 48106–1248. Geoffrey Haddock is now at the Department of Psychology, University of Exeter, Exeter, GB, EX4 4QG.

REFERENCES

Brickman, P. (1987). *Commitment, conflict, and caring.* Englewood Cliffs, NJ: Prentice-Hall.

Crowne, D. P., & Marlowe, D. (1964). *The approval motive: Studies in evaluative dependence.* New York: Wiley.

DeBono, K. (1987). Investigating the social-adjustive and value-expressive functions of attitudes: Implications for persuasion processes. *Journal of Personality and Social Psychology, 52,* 279–287.

Festinger, L. (1957). *A theory of cognitive dissonance.* New York: Row, Peterson.

Johnson, B. T., & Eagly, A. H. (1989). Effects of involvement on persuasion: A meta-analysis. *Psychological Bulletin, 106,* 290–314.

Johnson, B. T., Treadway, C. M., & Kahn, A. R. (1992). *Contrasting persuasive effects of value- and outcome-relevant involvement: The use of value and outcome bonding techniques.* Unpublished manuscript, Syracuse University.

Katz, D. (1960). The functional approach to the study of attitudes. *Public Opinion Quarterly, 24,* 163–204.

Lavine, H., Robertson, B., & Borgida, E. (1993). *Self-interest and value-based involvement: Implications for persuasion processes.* Unpublished manuscript, University of Minnesota, Minneapolis, MN.

Lydon, J. E. (1987). *Going the extra mile: The road to commitment is marked by values.* Unpublished doctoral dissertation, University of Waterloo.

Lydon, J. E., & Zanna, M. P. (1990). Commitment in the face of adversity: A value-affirmation approach. *Journal of Personality and Social Psychology, 58,* 1040–1047.

Maio, G. R., & Olson, J. M. (1994). Value-attitude-behavior relations: The moderating role of attitude functions. *British Journal of Social Psychology, 33,* 301–312.

Marlowe, D., Frager, R., & Nutall, R. L. (1965). Commitment to action taking as a consequence of cognitive dissonance. *Journal of Personality and Social Psychology, 2,* 864–868.

Miller, N. (1965). Involvement and dogmatism as inhibitors of attitude change. *Journal of Experimental Social Psychology, 1,* 121–132.

Ostrom, T. M., & Brock, T. C. (1969). Cognitive bonding to central values and resistance to a communication advocating change in policy orientation. *Journal of Experimental Research in Personality, 4,* 42–50.

Rokeach, M. (1973). *The nature of human values.* New York: Free Press.

Salancik, G. R., & Conway, M. (1975). Attitude inferences from salient and relevant cognitive content about behavior. *Journal of Personality and Social Psychology, 32,* 829–840.

Smith, M. B., Bruner, J. S., & White, R. W. (1956). *Opinions and personality.* New York: Wiley.

Snyder, M. (1974). The self-monitoring of expressive behavior. *Journal of Personality and Social Psychology, 30,* 526–537.

Steele, C. M. (1988). The psychology of self-affirmation: Sustaining the integrity of the self. In L. Berkowitz (Ed.), *Advances in experimental social psychology,* (Vol. 21, pp. 261–302). New York: Academic Press.

Social Values and Consumer Behavior: Research From the List of Values

Lynn R. Kahle
University of Oregon

SOCIAL ADAPTATION THEORY

The major goal of this chapter is to provide an overview to the work in which my colleagues and I have engaged over the past decade, in which we have applied the List of Values (LOV) to issues in consumer psychology. I begin with a description of the guiding theory, followed by a discussion of the methodological research and some specific theoretical and practical issues.

The theoretical approach on which our research on values has been based is social adaptation theory, which has been elaborated and extended to values from its origin in attitude research (Kahle, 1983, 1984a, 1984b; Kahle, Kulka, & Klingel, 1980). Values are the most abstract type of social cognition that people use to store and guide general responses to classes of stimuli. According to social adaptation theory, individuals adapt to various life roles in part through value development and value fulfillment. Value development summarizes previous experience and provides a strategy for dealing with new choices. For example, people who value fun and enjoyment may want a computer to play video games, whereas people who value sense of accomplishment may want a computer to use as a work tool. People who value self-respect may resist any new technology that defies a goal of self-reliance.

Values develop from life experiences. People obtain experiences by interacting with their environments in an attempt to develop optimal interchanges with their environments. As Piagetian theory has so well described, information may be assimilated into existing cognitive structures, such as values, or it may accommodate the existing cognitive structures into the more refined structures that result from additional interaction. Once acquired, information is also organized to coordinate the new information with prior knowledge. This organization can result in changes to both the new and old information, and it should lead to greater integration of information. The integration and specific meanings will be unique for each individual, but similarities in experiences and semantic environments, such as those shared by individuals within a particular demographic category, will lead to measurable similarities and patterns of responses. Situational forces will also interact with cognitive structures such as values in directing behavior (cf. Kahle, 1980; Weeks & Kahle, 1990).

Homer and Kahle (1988) have shown in a structural equation study of consumer behavior a sequence from values to attitudes to consumer behavior. This sequence is consistent with social adaptation theory and is similar to the trend in commercial use of lifestyle information, which use now tends to supplement value information with relevant attitudinal information before trying to predict behaviors. Homer and Kahle surveyed 831 food shoppers regarding their attitudes and behaviors toward purchasing natural foods. They also administered the List of Values, which showed three factors in this sample, consistent with the assumptions that values vary in terms of the importance of self or internal factors (e.g., self-fulfillment), others (e.g., warm relationships with others) and external forces (e.g., security) in value fulfillment. People with internal values tend to want to control their lives; hence, they tend to show greater concern regarding such attitudinal issues as opinions toward food additives in meat and the importance of nutrition. These attitudes in turn lead to greater self-reported behaviors such as frequency of shopping at natural food stores and monthly amount of money spent at natural food stores.

Most comprehensive efforts at behavioral prediction no longer rely on global values alone. Rather, they tend to use values as anchors or cognitive sources from which attitudes may emerge. The attitudes will vary depending upon many contextual factors, and they will be uniquely related to the specific choice at hand. These basic conceptual phenomena demonstrated in the Homer and Kahle article have been replicated several times (Kahle, Homer, O'Brien, & Boush, in press; Madrigal & Kahle, 1994; Rose, Kahle, Shoham, & Batra, 1994). For example, Rose et al. showed in a quota sample of 663 U.S. citizens a sequence from values to attitudes of group identification and need for affiliation. These attitudes in turn led to attitudes toward conformity. Conformity is positively related to fashion behaviors of brand-name purchasing and style, but they are negatively related to purchasing clothing based on utilitarian qualities.

Values have the potential to help clarify the understanding of consumers' motivations and may point to the underlying "rationality" or "psycho-logic" of ostensibly illogical decision processes. For example, Hawkins, Best, and Coney (1995) report that consumers may prefer the taste of one beer over another, in spite of the beers being identical in every respect except the values to which their marketing materials have been tied.

Researchers can use value-behavior linkages or value chains to help measure and understand consumers' adaptive involvement with a product or choice. Value chains can be identified by asking respondents a series of "Why?' questions, much as a 3-year -old might: Why did you buy that? Why? Why? Why? Usually consumers respond with product attributes to the first question, beneficial consequences of the attributes to the second question, and eventually respond with a core value. For example, a person may say that he or she bought a cold remedy because it contains germ-fighting ingredients, because it then fights germs, which promotes a healthy family, to which the respondent wants to belong.Thus, the logic started with the attribute of fighting germs and ended with the fulfilling of the value of "sense of belonging."

Similarly, value chains provide the opportunity to develop advertising and communication programs that tie product or other benefits to consumers' personal meanings and values at several, increasingly meaningful levels of abstraction (Reynolds & Gutman, 1988; Valette-Florence & Rapacchi, 1991). Furthermore, efforts to measure advertising or communication effectiveness may be improved by assessing how successfully the communications tie meanings back to personal values. Even if value and lifestyle information is not directly utilized in communication efforts, communicators can understand characteristics of certain regions or target segments if this type of information is available (Kahle, 1986; Kahle, Liu, & Watkins, 1991), as is discussed shortly.

A number of studies testing social adaptation theory have been published in marketing and psychology journals. Most of these studies in the value sphere have relied on the List of Values (LOV) methodology. Although the theoretical approach has no necessary connection with the methodological approach, it at least is not theoretically contradictory.

VALUE METHODOLOGY

Measuring Values With the LOV

The LOV (Beatty, Kahle, Homer, & Misra, 1985; Kahle, 1983; Kahle, Beatty, & Homer, 1986) can serve as a useful value measurement instrument in the study of consumer similarities and differences across social units ranging from individuals to countries. Table 6.1 presents a form in which the question could be and has been asked on a typical English-language mail, face-to-face, telephone, or real-time survey. This form has been developed as a result of extensive methodological research (cf. Kahle, Hall, & Kosinski, 1995) in both academic and commercial research settings. We have tried various combinations of rating and ranking, conjoint measurement, constant sum scales (Weeks & Kahle, 1990), use or nonuse of term definitions, and a variety of cultural contexts. We have also contrasted the LOV with other approaches to measuring values, such as VALS and the Rokeach Value Survey. Two studies of the LOV showed a test-retest

TABLE 6.1
The List of Values as a Survey Question

The following is a list of things that some people look for or want out of life. Sometimes you find that you have to give up a little of something important because something else is *most* important to you. Please study the list carefully and then rate each thing on how important it is in your daily life, where 1 = important to me, and 9 = extremely important to me.

		Important to me	Most Important to me
1.	Sense of belonging (to be accepted and needed by our family, friends, and community)	1--2--3--4--5--6--7--8--9	
2.	Excitement (to experience stimulation and thrills)	1--2--3--4--5--6--7--8--9	
3.	Warm relationships with others (to have close companionships and intimate friendships)	1--2--3--4--5--6--7--8--9	
4.	Self-fulfillment (to find peace of mind and to make the best use of your talents)	1--2--3--4--5--6--7--8--9	
5.	Being well-respected (to be admired by others and to receive recognition)	1--2--3--4--5--6--7--8--9	
6.	Fun and enjoyment in life (to lead a pleasurable, happy life)	1--2--3--4--5--6--7--8--9	
7.	Security (to be safe and protected from misfortune and attack)	1--2--3--4--5--6--7--8--9	
8.	Self-respect (to be proud of yourself and confident with who you are)	1--2--3--4--5--6--7--8--9	
9.	A sense of accomplishment (to succeed at what you want to do)	1--2--3--4--5--6--7--8--9	

Now re-read the items and circle the one thing that is *most important* to you in your daily life.

---

reliability with a month lag to be 92% and 85%, respectively (cf. Beatty et al., 1985), which compares favorably with the average test-retest reliability of .73 for the Rokeach Value Survey (Rokeach, 1973).

Several studies have used the LOV. In the first study in which it was used within the United States, respondents (2,264 noninstitutionalized adults selected from a probability sample of the coterminous United States) to the original LOV study (Kahle, 1983) were asked, among other things, to select their first and second most important values from a list of nine. This list was culled from Rokeach's (1973) list of 18 terminal values, Maslow's (1954) hierarchy of values, and various other contemporaries in value research (Veroff, Douvan, & Kulka, 1981). Because few respondents select excitement as their first choice, this category has often been collapsed into fun and enjoyment in life, although Pontiac for one has used *excitement* for many years as an effective tag-line for its advertisements ("We built excitement"). Individuals who rank excitement first most often select fun and enjoyment second.

We have now identified literally thousands of correlates with ratings and rankings of the items in the LOV (cf. Kahle, 1983, 1994; Kahle & Kennedy, 1989), which speaks to the validity of the measurement approach. We can provide at least a flavor of those relations here, providing a personality-like description of people who identify each value as especially important. *Self-respect* is the "All American" value, selected by the largest number of Americans and having the least distinctive endorsers. *Security* is a deficit value, endorsed by people who lack economic and psychological security, as manifested in responses to standard survey items used to indicate mental health (cf. Veroff et al., 1981). *Warm relationships with others* is an excess value, endorsed by people, especially women, who have a lot of friends and who are friendly. Likewise, people (mostly men) who endorse *sense of accomplishment* as paramount have accomplished much. People (especially young professionals) who endorse *self-fulfillment* are relatively well fulfilled economically, educationally, and emotionally. *Being well respected* is selected by the Rodney Dangerfields of the world. It's interesting to contrast self-respect, which one can achieve alone, with being well respected, which requires the cooperation of others. People who value self-respect are much better adjusted, according to our survey measures of mental health. *Sense of belonging* also requires the help of others. Similar to warm relationships with others, it is a social value selected more by women than by men. But sense of belonging is less reciprocal than warm relationships and seems to result in greater conformity and dependency. If this value group had not existed, Procter & Gamble would have created it—it's a home and family oriented value. *Fun and enjoyment in life* has been increasing in popularity, especially among young people. We thought that this value would isolate the hedonists in our sample, but the cliché that we now think describes these people is, "Stop and smell the roses." These people respond most favorably to survey items designed to measure involvement with leisure-time activities.

Research has also revealed many findings regarding the relation between consumer behavior and values, particularly a study with a national quota sample of the United States (Kahle, 1994). Clearly, subscription to different values implies differences in consumer psychology and in consumer behavior. Because values influence the way in which consumers react to product offerings, advertising, packaging, pricing, personal selling, and retailing, the effective marketer should be aware of this influence and incorporate it when developing marketing strategy, when planning products, and when communicating with consumers.

Table 6.2 presents several items designed to measure consumer adaptations. Items from this list that are empirically characteristic of value groups from a quota sample of 667 U.S. citizens include the following: People who endorse self-respect as most important engage in social identity purchasing and display high levels of health consciousness. Security is associated with purchasing for self-indulgence and with a desire for quality, convenience, and nostalgia. People who value warm relationships with others are characterized by purchasing for patriotism, by deal proneness, and by the belief that "ads are informative." People who value self- fulfillment make purchases that emphasize quality, self-indulgence, convenience, patriotism, entertainment, conspicuous consumption, and brand loyalty. Sense of accomplishment is associated with conspicuous consumption, purchasing for sex appeal, self-indulgence, and convenience. Being well-respected is associated with a strong desire for quality, company reputa-

TABLE 6.2
Representative Consumption-Orientation Items Related to Social Values

Orientation	Representative Item
Authenticity	I like to buy products made with wood rather than products made with plastic.
Brand consciousness	When I go shopping I chose the brands I buy with great care.
Brand loyalty	When I shop I tend to buy the same brands I bought the last time.
Company reputation	I only buy brands that are made by well-known companies.
Conspicuous consumption	It is important that others think well of how I dress and look.
Convenience	I like to buy products that save me time, even if they cost a little more.
Deal proneness	I use store coupons frequently.
Desire for elegance	How elegant and attractive a product is, is as important as how well it works.
Desire for quality	I always try to buy top quality products.
Endorsements	Knowing that a celebrity backs a product makes me feel safer buying it.
Entertainment attitudes	Entertainment is an important part of my life.
Health consciousness	I watch what I eat very carefully.
Nostalgia	I like to buy things that remind me of time in my past.
Patriotism	I am extremely proud of everything my country has done.
Price pessimism	Prices of things are going to rise quickly, very soon.
Self-indulgence	I deserve the very best in what I buy.
Sex appeal	I like to feel attractive to members of the opposite sex.
Social identity	The things I buy reflect the kind of person I am.
Voluntary simplicity	It is better to live a simple life with a few possessions than a complex life with many.

tion, patriotism, social identity, health consciousness, and brand loyalty. Consumers who value sense of belonging believe that "you get what you pay for"; they admire voluntary simplicity, purchasing for company reputation, patriotism, nostalgia, brand consciousness, brand loyalty, deal proneness, and health consciousness. Excitement is associated with entertainment-oriented consumption, belief in endorsements, brand loyalty, brand consciousness, price pessimism, purchasing for sex appeal, and desire for elegance. Fun and enjoyment in life is associated with purchasing for elegance, convenience, nostalgia, patriotism, authenticity, and brand consciousness.

Ideally values should be measured as systems rather than as individual values. This goal creates complications because of the large number of potential patterns of values and because of the difficulties of data reduction in one context; however, some progress has been made in this area (Kamakura & Novak, 1992; Madrigal & Kahle, 1994). Specifically, advanced statistical techniques are being developed that allow simultaneous considerations of value systems. Madrigal and Kahle, for example, used a principle components factor analysis with varimax rotation to obtain value factor scores. These scores were then used in a cluster analysis algorithm based on nearest centroid sorting to determine value-system segments (Anderberg, 1973)

Alternative Methods of Measuring Values

We have done comparative methodological research on two other popular methods of measuring values, which seem less appropriate for research than the LOV. Because these methods have been frequently discussed elsewhere, we will offer a brief review and summarize our reasons for preferring the LOV.

Values and Lifestyle Segmentation (VALS). SRI International sponsors a values and lifestyle segmentation program known as VALS (Values and Lifestyle Segmentation). Respondents are presented with a set of 34 demographic and attitudinal questions. Responses are classified such that consumers are identified as falling into 1 of 9 lifestyle groups.[1] Although VALS has shown some utility, it relies heavily on demographic variables and does not relate to consumer behaviors as closely as other systems, such as LOV (Beatty, Homer, & Kahle, 1988; Kahle, Beatty, & Homer, 1986). In our research, the LOV related more closely to consumer behavior in virtually all cases. Many of the specific questions in VALS have cultural bias aimed toward the United States. For example, questions about corporate and governmental policy have different implications in Europe and the United States. LOV is far easier to administer and is not tied to proprietary data analysis algorithms. SRI has, in fact, ceased using VALS and now sells VALS II. It is more psychological and less value-based than VALS. With the secrecy shown by SRI any methodology they produce should be considered prescientific (cf. Ziman, 1968). Secrecy is a common problem for methodology research in consumer behavior because for-profit research firms want to protect their competitive advantages.

Rokeach Value Survey (RVS). The RVS is the most popular method for measuring values among social science researchers. Rokeach (1973) asks people to rank 18 instrumental values and 18 terminal values. The LOV does not measure instrumental values in Rokeach's sense of the term. We have a great deal of admiration for the tradition Rokeach has initiated, but we believe that the LOV relates more closely to people's daily lives (Beatty et al., 1985) than the RVS terminal values. For example, most people rank highly the RVS value of "a world at peace," but few people claim to take active steps in any given day to fulfill that value, especially in their consumer roles. The LOV also is simpler to administer because it has fewer values for respondents to assess. The "magic number of 7 $(+/- 2)$"—which is approximately how many items the normal adult can hold in short-term memory—implies that the 9-item LOV is viable for storage in short-term memory but also implies that the RVS exceeds people's

---

[1]The groups in the United States include survivors (4%), sustainers (7%), belongers (35%), emulators (9%), achievers (22%), I-am-me's (5%), experientials (7%), societally conscious (9%), and integrateds (2%).

normal short-term memory capacity. The LOV also avoids or minimizes several other methodological problems related to the RVS (cf. Beatty et al., 1985), such as the tendency to respond to items in a socially desirable rather than a candid manner. Direct correlations between two measures of social desirability and both the LOV and RVS items reveal very few statistically significant relationships. The largest correlation between any (terminal) value and either measure of social desirability was .15 for the LOV and .26 for the RVS.

Notably, because VALS uses nominal analyses and the RVS uses ordinal analyses, both violate a major requirement of the most powerful and advanced techniques of causal analyses—that variables be measured at least at the interval level (Asher, 1976). LOV makes possible the gathering of data that will circumvent this problem by using interval-level rating scales.

Our experiences have led us to believe that ranking does not generally produce superior results to rating. In some instances a "rank then rate" procedure produces ostensibly more careful consideration of the values by respondents. We believe, however, that use of an unbalanced scale (from *important* to *most important* rather than from *most unimportant* to *most important*) maximizes respondent discrimination and provides optimal statistical power. We now believe that use of nominal scales that classify people into value groups has limited utility, although we have frequently used that approach.

Data Analysis Approaches to LOV Research

Regression Analysis.   Since the first study we have developed several approaches to measurement that differ from the previous national LOV study (Kahle, 1983) in several ways. The most notable methodological difference is the measurement of values on both a nominal and an assumed interval level, rather than only on a nominal level as in the earlier study (i.e., "Rate the importance of each of these values on a scale from 1 to 9" as well as the earlier study's "Which of these values is most important to you?"). This refinement in measurement allows us to conduct analyses with statistics that assume interval level data, such as constructing causal models (cf. Asher, 1976), because interval data, but not nominal data, satisfy the minimal assumptions for the most powerful and advanced analysis techniques. We then are able to utilize the important methodological advances from the past several decades by collecting the data in a suitable way.

Conjoint Analysis.   We have experimented with a variety of methods of measuring values. The interval-level method of measuring the importance of values usually employs some form of a rating scale, as in Table 6.1. Although this method is straight forward and simple, people sometimes rate all values as important or very important. As a result, it is much more difficult to differentiate among values and distinguish the ones that are most important. In rating tasks we now use a scale ranging from *important* to *most important* to circumvent this ceiling-effect problem. Rokeach tried to overcome the ceiling-effect problem by asking subjects to rank values.

Another way to overcome this measurement problem is to utilize conjoint measurement (Green & Rao, 1971; Luce & Tukey, 1964). This measurement methodology requires that the respondent make trade-offs between levels of different values. In this way a respondent can not simply rate all values as important but must discriminate his or her preference for different values at different levels of desirability.

For example, consider three value sets, each of which contains three values: fun and enjoyment in life, sense of belonging, and sense of accomplishment. Each value also varies in the degree to which a consumer would endorse that value from a high degree, to a moderate degree, to a lesser degree. As such, one such value set could present a value structure that endorses a high degree of sense of belonging and sense of accomplishment while placing a lesser degree of importance on fun and enjoyment in life. Other value sets could differ dramatically in the way they represent each of the three values.

The conjoint task forces a respondent to make trade-offs among different levels of desirability among values such that more important values will surface. When a consumer evaluates a sufficient number of alternatives the conjoint measurement procedure allows us to derive the underlying relations for each value. For this analysis strategy we measure the values of a sample of people using this procedure. Then we cluster analyze the resulting value profiles such that consumers with very similar value structures are grouped together into segments. When complete we would expect to have N-number of segments, each containing consumers with similar value structures. From this perspective we could explore differences in consumer needs and preferences for types of products within the context of different product positionings.

Kennedy, Best, and Kahle (1987) applied this technique in a study of advertising for the automobile market in the United States. A conjoint analysis followed by a cluster analysis of the data yielded four unique value-based segments. The value structures for consumers within segments were similar and between segments quite different. Based on these results, we can advance the premise of a link between value-orientation and ad-product positioning.

Constant Sum Scales.   We have also tried a variety of constant sum scales. These generally either allocate a number of points (e.g., 100) to be dispersed among the values or they tell a respondent to begin with 100 points for the first-choice value and then to assign a descending number of points based on relative importance (Weeks, Chonka, & Kahle, 1989; Weeks & Kahle, 1990). In spite of the methodological appeal of these approaches, in surveys of the general public a significant percentage of respondents fail to understand the instructions. Thus, the conceptual advantages tend to be canceled out by the practical liabilities, resulting in a slightly lower quality of measurement.

THEORETICAL ISSUES IN VALUE RESEARCH

Values and Demographics

Values in principle provide more information than mere demographics. Demographics often have complex patterns of influence (cf. Mager & Kahle, in press). Consider the demographically similar groups of sense of accomplishment and self-fulfillment. Both share demographic similarity in educational, economic, psychological, and social prosperity. But raising a child has a quite different meaning for these two groups. Taking a child from infancy to adulthood is a major accomplishment, but it does not necessarily contribute to self-fulfillment. For another example, women favor two values more than men, sense of belonging and warm relationships with others. Yet the psychological benefits of a reciprocal, sharing lifestyle, characteristic of women who endorse warm relationships with others, contrasts sharply with the demographically similar women who submerge themselves into being possessions of their family, "belonging" to it. Women who endorse sense of belonging seem more like neurotic housewives, according to the patterns of data (cf. Kahle, 1983).

Two studies have examined the variability of values and geography within the United States. Kahle (1986) predicted that, because of political considerations, histories, loyalties, climates, resources, and other reasons, the values would vary across regions. Kahle (1986) showed that both the 4-level (i.e., West, Midwest, Northeast, and South) and the 9-level (e.g., Pacific, Mountain, etc.) different Census regions of the United States are characterized by different values in a survey of a probability sample of more than 2,000 citizens of the coterminous United States. Garreau's (1981) Nine Nations of North America did not account for as much variance in values as did the nine-level U.S. Bureau of Census regions, which are based on political (state) borders rather than "cultural" borders.

Kahle, Liu, and Watkins (1991) have replicated that finding of geographic variability in values and shown that, in addition, the value-consistent lifestyle differences among regions also are manifested in a national study. In a study of a quota sample of 640 citizens of the United States, Kahle, Lui, and Watkins found evidence of regional variation in values, as described in Table 6.3. In Table 6.3, "region order" means the ascending order of the means in different regions. "Comparison" implies that, given alpha = 0.05, a Tukey multiple pairwise comparison test shows the significantly different pairs of regions. For simplicity, we only list the results in the four regions case, but not the also-statistically-significant 9 regions case.

TABLE 6.3
Value Rating Differences Across the Four Regions

Value	F	Region Order	Comparison
Self-respect	4.43*	W,E,M,S	W-S**
Security	0.92		---
Warm relationships with others	5.54*	E,W,M,S	EWM-S
Self-fulfillment	3.38*		M-S
Sense of accomplishment	2.54*	M,W,E,S	M-S
Being well-respected	3.22*	M,W,E,S	W-S
Sense of belonging	2.74*	W,E,M,S	W-S
Fun and enjoyment in life	1.73	W,E,M,S	---

Note. Reprinted from Kahle, Liu, and Watkins (1991).
$*P < .05$. **E = East, M = Midwest, S = South, W = West.

Using the LOV Cross-Culturally

A strong need for an accepted instrument for cross-national and cross-cultural comparison and contrast of values has slowed progress on research on international values. To the extent that international research can focus on one instrument, multiple studies will become comparable and provide converging information about values. The LOV is one viable nominee for this role, and respondents from a variety of nations have completed it (Beatty, Homer, & Kahle, 1988; Beatty, Kahle, & Homer, 1991; Beatty, Kahle, Utsey, & Keown, 1993; Kahle, 1992; Kahle, Beatty, & Homer, 1989; Kahle, Beatty, & Mager, 1994; Lui & Kahle, 1990; Madrigal & Kahle, 1994; Muller, Kahle, & Chéron, 1992).

A number of challenges exist with cross-cultural surveys. Researchers must convey the meaning of questions accurately and in a way respondents can grasp. They must correctly incorporate subtleties and nuances of language. They must select the most effective method of communication (e.g., mail, telephone, or personal interview). Construction of a representative sample is potentially far more complex for researchers in some countries than in others, because sources similar to the ones used to describe populations in some countries may not be available in others. Finally, certain questions to which some cultures are willing to respond may be considered sensitive or inappropriate by others.

Cross-cultural research using the List of Values (Grunert, Grunert, & Kristensen, 1993; Valette-Florence, 1988) could potentially be a major step toward improved understanding of political and economic ties between the communities and citizens of divergent countries. Table 6.4 shows the distribution of social values in several different countries. Several of the major characteristics of countries include the prominence of self-fulfillment in France and Japan, of sense of belonging in Norway, Russia, and Germany, of self-respect and security in the United States, of warm relationships with others in Russia, and of sense of

TABLE 6.4
Social Values in Several Counries

Value	France	BRD	Denmark	Norway	US	USSR	Japan
Self-fulfillment	30.9%	4.8%	7.1%	7.7%	6.5%	8.8%	36.7%
Sense of belonging	1.7	28.6	13.0	33.4	5.1	23.9	2.3
Security	6.3	24.1	6.3	10.0	16.5	5.7	10.9
Self-respect	7.4	12.9	29.7	16.6	23.0	10.1	4.7
Warm relationships with others	17.7	7.9	11.3	13.4	19.9	23.3	27.6
Fun & enjoyment in life/excitement	16.6	10.1	16.8	3.6	7.2	9.7	7.5
Being well respected	4.0	6.1	5.0	8.4	5.9	8.5	2.1
Sense of accomplishment	15.4	5.4	10.9	6.8	15.9	10.1	8.3
TOTAL	100.0%	100.0%	100.0%	100.0%	100.0%	100.0%	100.0%
N	175	1008	239	413	997	321	387

Sources: Beatty et al., 1993; Grunert and Scherhorn, 1990; Kahle, Beatty, and Homer, 1989; Kahle, Poulos, and Sukhdial, 1988. Reprinted by Kahle, Beatty, and Mager (1994).

accomplishment in France and the United States (Kahle, Beatty, & Mager, 1994).

Maslow's Hierarchy and the List of Values

The LOV provides a unique opportunity to test propositions derived from Maslow's theory about values, if that theory is indeed testable. Maslow's theory, which is still widely cited and influential, hypothesized a hierarchy of values (he used *needs* and *values* interchangeably) through which people pass sequentially. As lower values are satisfied, higher values predominate. Because the LOV items often apply Maslowian terms such as security, respect, belonging, and fulfillment, it is possible to test a number of competing hypotheses between social adaptation theory, which claims values are situationally salient, and hierarchy theory. The results have consistently supported social adaptation theory: patterns of value pairings, inconsistencies between internal and external values, age norms (Kahle, Boush, & Homer, 1988), as well as structural equation models of the competing theories (Kahle, Homer, O'Brien, & Boush, in press; Kahle, Kulka, & Klingel, 1980) consistently fail to support Maslow's theory. For example, if values are distributed according to a particular pattern, then the types of relationships developmental psychologists observe between adjacent categories ought to be evident in adjacent value categories; however, we fail to observe those patterns in a form consistent with Maslow's theory. For another example, values that imply the same Maslowian level (e.g., self-respect and being well respected both imply the same level) ought to exhibit similar patterns of relations to behavior, but in fact they do not. Proponents of Maslow seem to have confused sequences of physiological necessities with sequences of psychological necessities.

APPLICATIONS

Further evidence of the LOV's validity comes from various applications of its measurement to increasing understanding in various consumer contexts. We know that people who endorse the social values of warm relationships with others and self-respect give more gifts and exert more effort giving gifts, both in the United States and in Japan (Beatty, Kahle, & Homer, 1991; Beatty, Kahle, Utsey, & Keown, 1993). We know that a complex interaction exists between sales people's values, the values of their sales managers, and the specific type of selling task in which they engage (Weeks & Kahle, 1990). We know that values relates to numerous other aspects of consumer behavior, including cynicism (Boush, Kim, Kahle, & Batra, 1993), fashion (Goldsmith, Heitmeyer, & Freiden, 1991; Rose, Shoham, Kahle, & Batra, 1994), social normative influence (Kahle, 1995; Kahle & Shoham, 1995), role adaptation (Kahle, 1983, 1995), natural food choice (Homer & Kahle, 1988), mental health (Kahle, 1983), role adaptation (Kahle, 1983), global communications (Kahle, Beatty, & Mager, 1994), human resource management (Kahle & Eisert, 1986), pet ownership (Kropp, Smith, Rose, & Kahle, 1992), vacation activity (Madrigal & Kahle, 1994), segmentation (Kahle, 1986), and lifestyle (Kahle, Lui, & Watkins, 1991). Table 6.5 summarizes the spheres of several of the empirical applications of LOV research.

One topic of interest, for example, has been the relation between fashion and values. Fashion leaders tend to value fun and enjoyment in life more than others (Goldsmith et al., 1991). The most social values of warm relationships with others, sense of belonging, and being well respected are associated with a high need for group identification and affiliation, conformity, and the display aspects of clothing (style and brand name). Conformity is also related to cynicism and trust in information sources (Boush et al., 1993).

Another interesting application of LOV research is as a social monitor. The changes in values can indicate how society is changing across time (Kahle, 1995; Kahle, Poulos, & Sukhdial, 1988; Kahle & Shoham, 1995; Mueller et al., 1992). Sequential cross-sectional surveys can provide snapshots of a social group, such as a country, at a particular point in time. Kahle, Poulos, and Sukhdial found an increase in the United States in the importance of warm relationships with others and a decrease in the importance of security. Kahle and Shoham found increasing evidence in the United States for "role-relaxed" consumers, who care less about

TABLE 6.5
Areas of Applications of LOV

Study	*Application Area*
Beatty et al. (1985)	media preferences, leisure
Beatty et al. (1991)	gift giving, culture
Beatty et al. (1993)	gift giving, culture
Boush et al. (1993)	cynicism
Homer & Kahle (1988)	natural food shoppers
Kahle (1983)	mental health, roles
Kahle (1986)	geographic segmentation
Kahle, Beatty, & Homer (1986)	segmentation
Kahle, Beatty, & Homer (1989)	Norwegian consumers
Kahle, Liu, & Watkins (1991)	geographic variation
Kahle, Poulos, & Sukhdial (1988)	social trends
Kahle & Shoham (1995)	role-relaxed consumers
Kennedy, Best, & Kahle (1987)	car ad positioning
Kropp et al. (1992)	pet owners
Madrigal & Kahle (1994)	vacation activity
Mueller, Kahle, & Chéron (1992)	demand forecasts
Rose et al. (1994)	conformity and dress
Weeks, Chonka, & Kahle (1989)	sales force annual sales
Weeks & Kahle (1990)	salespeople's effort

social roles than other consumers, who care more about product quality and product functional attributes, and who value self-respect more than being well-respected. For example, role-relaxed consumers are willing to spend more money on a product if they believe that they are purchasing increased quality, but they do not like luxury for luxury's sake Mueller, Kahle, and Chéron showed that fun and enjoyment in life is increasing in importance among residents of Ontario in the 25 to 44 age cohort, suggesting that recreational luxury products (e.g., sports cars, home exercise equipment, and sophisticated home entertainment products, such as surround-sound systems, wide-screen televisions, and video cameras, may increase in importance in the next decade.

CONCLUSIONS

A great deal of work remains in research on social values (cf. Kahle, 1985, 1990). We have demonstrated that some understanding and utility can be obtained by studying consumer values, but we need a more sophisticated understanding of the processes by which respondents transform social value knowledge into economic value behavior. Future research should address this domain.

REFERENCES

Anderberg, M. R. (1973). *Cluster analysis for applications.* New York: Academic Press.

Asher, H. B. (1976). *Causal modeling.* Beverly Hills: Sage.

Beatty, S. E., Homer, P. M., & Kahle, L R. (1988). Problems with VALS in international marketing research: An example from an application of the empirical mirror technique. In M. Houston (Ed.), *Advances in consumer research* (Vol. 15, pp. 375–380). Ann Arbor, MI: Association for Consumer Research.

Beatty, S. E., Kahle, L. R., & Homer, P. (1991). Personal values and gift giving behavior: A study across cultures. *Journal of Business Research, 20,* 183–190.

Beatty, S. E., Kahle, L. R., Homer, P. M., & Misra, S. (1985). Alternative measurement approaches to consumer values: The List of Values and the Rokeach Value Survey. *Psychology & Marketing, 2,* 181–200.

Beatty, S. E., Kahle, L. R., Utsey, M., & Keown, C. (1993). Gift giving behaviors in the United States and Japan: A personal values perspective. *Journal of International Consumer Marketing, 6,* 49–66.

Boush, D. M., Kim, C.H., Kahle, L. R., & Batra, R. (1993). "Cynicism and conformity as correlates of trust in product information sources," *Journal of Current Issues and Research in Advertising, 15,* 1–9.

Garreau, J. (1981). *The nine nations of North America,* New York: Avon.

Goldsmith, R. E., Heitmeyer, J. R., & Freiden, J. B. (1991). Social values and fashion leadership. *Clothing and Textile Research Journal, 10,* 37–45.

Green, P. E., & Rao, V. R. (1971). Conjoint measurement for quantifying judgmental data. *Journal of Marketing Research, 8,* 355–363.

Grunert, S. C., Grunert, K. G., & Kristensen, K. (1993). Une méthode d'estemation de la validité interculturelle des instruments de mesure: le cas de la mesure des valeurs des consommateurs par la liste des valeurs LOV [One method of estimation of the intercultural validity of measurement instruments: The case of the measurement of values of consumers by way of the LOV]. *Recherche et applications en marketing, 8*(4), 5–28.

Grunert, S. C., & Scherhorn, G. (1990). Consumer values in West Germany: Underlying dimensions and cross-cultural camparison with North America. *Journal of Business Research, 20,* 97–107.

Hawkins, D. I., Best, R. J., & Coney, K. A. (1995). *Consumer Behavior: Implications for Marketing Strategy* (6th ed). Chicago: Irwin.

Homer, P. M., & Kahle, L. R. (1988). A structural equation analysis of the value-attitude-behavior hierarchy. *Journal of Personality and Social Psychology, 54,* 683–646.

Kahle, L. R. (1980). Stimulus condition self-selection by males in the interaction of Locus of Control and skill-chance situations. *Journal of Personality and Social Psychology, 38,* 50–56.

Kahle, L. R. (Ed.). (1983). *Social values and social change: Adaptation to life in America.* New York: Praeger.

Kahle, L. R. (1984a). *Attitudes and social adaptation: A person-situation interaction approach.* Oxford, England: Pergamon.

Kahle, L. R. (1984b). The values of Americans: Implications for consumer adaptation. In R. E. Pitts Jr. & A. G. Woodside (Eds.), *Personal values and consumer psychology.* (72–86). Lexington, MA: Lexington Books.

Kahle, L. R. (1985). Social values in the Eighties: A special issue. *Psychology & Marketing. 2,* 231–237.

Kahle, L. R. (1986). The nine nations of North America and the value basis of geographic segmentation. *Journal of Marketing, 50,* 37–47.

Kahle, L. R. (1990). Contemporary research on consumer and business social values. *Journal of Business Research, 20,* 81–82.

Kahle, L. R. (1992). Marketing and the new world order. In K. Grunert (Ed.), *Advanced research in marketing*. Aarhus, Denmark: European Marketing Academy.

Kahle, L. R. (1994). Values and behaviors: Can you get there from here? In M. Lynn & J. M. Jackson (Eds.),*Proceedings of the Society for Consumer Psychology*, (43–47).

Kahle, L. R. (1995). Role-relaxed consumers: A trend of the nineties. *Journal of Advertising Research, 35*(2), 66–71.

Kahle, L. R., Beatty, S. E., & Homer, P. M. (1986). Alternative measurement approaches to consumer values: The List of Values (LOV) and Values and Lifestyle Segmentation (VALS). *Journal of Consumer Research, 13,* 405–409.

Kahle, L. R., Beatty, S. E., & Homer, P. M. (1989). Consumer values in Norway and the United States: A comparison. *Journal of International Consumer Marketing, 1,* 81–92.

Kahle, L. R., Beatty, S. E., & Mager, J. (1994). Implications of social values for consumer communications: The case of the European Community. In B. Englis (Ed.). *Global and multinational advertising* (pp. 47–64). Hillsdale, NJ: Lawrence Erlbam Associates.

Kahle, L. R., Boush, D., & Homer, P. M. (1988). Broken rungs in Abraham's ladder: Is Maslow's hierarchy hierarchical? In D. Schumann (Ed.), *Proceedings of the Society for Consumer Psychology,* (pp. 11–16).

Kahle, L. R., & Eisert, D. C. (1986). Social values and adaptation in the American workplace. In E. G. Flamholtz, Y. Randle, & S. Sackman (Eds.), *Future directions in human resource management* (pp. 203–223). Los Angeles: UCLA Publications.

Kahle, L. R., Hall, D. B., & Kosinski, M. J. (1995). *The real-time response survey in new consumer product research: It's about time.* Manuscript in preparation.

Kahle, L. R., Homer, P. M., O'Brien, R. M., & Boush, D. M. (in press). Maslow's hierarchy and social adaptation as alternative accounts of value structures. In L. R. Kahle & L. Chiagouris (Eds.), *Advertising and consumer psychology: Values, lifestyles, and psychographics.* Mahwah, NJ: Lawrence Erlbaum Associates.

Kahle, L. R., & Kennedy, P. (1989). Using the List of Values to measure consumers. *Journal of Consumer Marketing. 6,* 5–12.

Kahle, L. R., Kulka, R. A., & Klingel, D. M. (1980). Low adolescent self-esteem leads to multiple interpersonal problems: A test of social adaptation theory. *Journal of Personality and Social Psychology, 39,* 492–502.

Kahle, L. R., Liu, R., & Watkins, H. (1991). Psychographic variation across United States geographic regions. In J. Sherry & B. Sternthal (Eds.), *Advances in consumer research* (Vol. 19, 346–352). Provo: Association for Consumer Research, 346–352.

Kahle, L. R., Poulos, B., & Sukhdial, A. (1988). Changes in social values in the United States during the past decade. *Journal of Advertising Research, 28,* 35–41.

Kahle, L. R., & Shoham, A. (1995). Role-relaxed consumers: Empirical evidence. *Journal of Advertising Research, 35*(3), 59–62.

Kamakura, W. A., & Novak, T. P. (1992). Value-system segmentation: Exploring the meaning of LOV. *Journal of Consumer Research, 19,* 119–123.

Kennedy, P., Best, R., & Kahle, L. R. (1987). An alternative method for measuring value-based segmentation and advertisement positioning. *Current Issues and Research in Advertising, 11,* 139–155.

Kropp, F. G., Smith, M. C., Rose, G. M., & Kahle, L. R. (1992). Values and lifestyles of pet owners. In M. Lynn & J. M.Jackson (Eds.), *Proceedings of the Society for Consumer Psychology* (pp. 46–49).

Liu, R., & Kahle, L. R. (1990). Consumer social values in the People's Republic of China. In M. Gardner (Ed.), *Proceedings of the Society for Consumer Psychology* (pp. 52–54).

Luce, R. D., & Tukey, J. W. (1964). Simultaneous conjoint measurement: A new type of fundamental measurement. *Journal of Mathematical Psychology, 1,* 1–27.

Madrigal, R., & Kahle, L. R. (1994). Predicting vacation activity preferences on the basis of value-system segmentation. *Journal of Travel Research,* Winter, 22–28.

Mager, J., & Kahle, L. R. (in press). Is the whole more than the sum of the parts? Re-evaluating social status in marketing. *Journal of Business Psychology.*

Mager, J., & Wynd, W. R. (1993). Marketing implications of value differences between Soviet and American Students. *Journal of International Consumer Marketing, 6,* 87–108.

Maslow, A. H. (1954). *Motivation and personality.* New York: Harper.

Mitchell, A. (1983). *The nine American lifestyles.* New York: Warner.

Mueller, T. E., Kahle, L. R., & Chéron, E. J. (1992). Value trends and demand forecasts for Canada's aging baby boomers. *Canadian Journal of Administrative Science, 9,* 294–304.

Reynolds, T. J., & Gutman, J. (1988). Laddering theory, method, analysis, and interpretation. *Journal of Advertising Research, 28,* 11–31.

Rokeach, M. (1973). *The nature of human values.* New York: Free Press.

Rose, G. M., Shoham, A., Kahle, L. R., & Batra, R. (1994). Social values, conformity, and dress. *Journal of Applied Social Psychology, 24,* 1501–1519.

Valette-Florence, P. (1988). Analyse structurelle comparative des composantes des systé de valeurs selon Kahle et Rokeach [Comparative structural analyses of the components of the systems of values according to Kahle and Rokeach]. *Recherche et applications en marketing, 3,* 23–57.

Valette-Florence, P., & Rapacchi, B. (1991). Improvements in means-end chain analysis using graph theory and correspondence analysis. *Journal of Advertising Research, 31,* 30–45.

Veroff, J., Douvan, E. & Kulka, R. (1981). *The inner American.* New York: Basic Books.

Weeks, W. A., Chonka, L. B., & Kahle, L. R. (1989). Performance congruence and value congruence impact on sales force annual sales. *Journal of the Academy of Marketing Science, 17,* 345–351.

Weeks, W. A., & Kahle, L. R. (1990). Social values and salespeople's effort: Entrepreneurial versus routine selling. *Journal of Business Research, 20,* 183–190.

Ziman, J. (1968). *Public knowledge: The social dimension of science.* Cambridge, England: Cambridge University Press.

7

Values and Prejudice: Toward Understanding the Impact of American Values on Outgroup Attitudes

Monica Biernat
Theresa K. Vescio
Shelley A. Theno
Christian S. Crandall
University of Kansas

A number of current theories of racism include a common underlying theme—an emphasis on values as contributors to both White antipathy and sympathy toward Blacks. For example, both the theories of Modern Racism (McConahay, 1986; McConahay & Hough, 1976) and Symbolic Racism (Kinder, 1986; Kinder & Sears, 1981; Sears, 1988) suggest that racism is largely based on Whites' perceptions that Blacks violate their cherished values. For McConahay and Hough (1976), the relevant values are "derived from the secularized versions of the Protestant Ethic: hard work, individualism, sexual repression, and delay of gratification" (p. 41). Similarly, for Kinder and Sears (1981), these values include "individualism and self-reliance, the work ethic, obedience, and discipline" (p. 416).

The Ambivalent Racism perspective (Katz & Hass, 1988; Katz, Wackenhut, & Hass, 1986) suggests that both pro-Black and anti-Black attitudes derive directly from two basic American values: humanitarianism/egalitarianism (communalism), and the Protestant Work Ethic (individualism), respectively. The theory of Aversive Racism (Gaertner & Dovidio, 1986) also points to the effects of an egalitarian value system on Whites' reactions to Blacks. Whereas modern Whites continue to possess primarily negative affect toward Blacks (based on life-long anti-Black socialization), this negative bias may be reduced or reversed in normative contexts that make salient and/or threaten one's egalitarian self-image (see also Dutton, 1976; Jackson, Sullivan, & Hodge, 1993, Study 2).

What do these authors mean by values, and why might values be important to racial attitudes? Although none of these researchers is explicit in defining the value construct, their use of the term seems to be consistent with the conception of terminal values that Rokeach (1973) proposed, and which runs through this volume: Values are generalized standards; they are "desirable end states of existence." The two values that appear most critical to issues of race are Protestant Ethic and egalitarian/humanitarian ideals. The former may be responsible for promoting racist feelings and behavior—to the extent that Black Americans are perceived to deviate from the principles of individualism, hard work, and obedience, White Americans experience antipathy toward them. Egalitarian/humanitarian ideals, however, appear to suppress racist responses—to the extent that White Americans support the principles of equality, social justice, and concern for others' well-being, they either experience feelings of sympathy for Black Americans (Katz & Hass, 1988; Myrdal, 1944) or they work to avoid the threat to self-concept that negative behavior toward Blacks would produce (Gaertner & Dovidio, 1986). In either case, egalitarian values work as brakes on racist reactions (see Dutton, 1976; Feldman, 1983; Lipset & Schneider, 1978).

Although these theories place a strong emphasis on values, there has been surprisingly little research from each perspective that clearly documents the importance of the value construct for understanding Whites' racial attitudes and reactions to particular Black individuals. Our goal in this chapter is to examine these various theories of racism with an eye toward (a) elaborating upon the value component of each theory, (b) surveying the existing literature for evidence describing the import of values, (c) using data from our laboratory to illustrate the role of values in outgroup perceptions from each theory's perspective, and (d) pointing out directions that future research within each perspective might fruitfully take. We do not intend to set up these theories as competing models, nor to work toward a conclusion of which theory is "best." Rather, we hope to point to the validity of each perspective, and to indicate how, via their emphasis on values, these approaches are largely compatible.

The perspectives that we address include Symbolic Racism (Kinder, 1986; Kinder & Sears, 1981; Sears, 1988), Modern Racism (McConahay, 1986; McConahay & Hough, 1976), Aversive Racism (Dovidio & Gaertner, 1991; Gaertner & Dovidio, 1986), and Ambivalent Racism (Katz & Hass, 1988; Katz et al., 1986). In addition to these, we also consider a more general approach to understanding outgroup perception—Rokeach's theory of "belief congruence." This approach suggests that prejudice is based on the assumption that members of another group hold beliefs (attitudes and values) that differ from one's own (Insko, Nacoste, & Moe, 1983; Rokeach, 1968; Rokeach & Mezei, 1966; Rokeach & Rothman, 1965; Rokeach, Smith, & Evans, 1960; Stein, Hardyck, & Smith, 1965), and in more recent theorizing, that perceived discrepancies in value *hierarchies* between groups are responsible for outgroup antagonism (Schwartz & Struch, 1989; Schwartz, Struch, & Bilsky, 1990; Struch & Schwartz, 1989).

Before turning to each of these perspectives, we must also mention that a broader objective of this work is to extend the various theories of racial prejudice in such a way that they encompass attitudes toward a variety of other outgroups.

Given our focus on values, the outgroups with which we concern ourselves are those that are also likely to instantiate value concerns—for example, homosexuals, the overweight, etc. Although racism is likely to have features that distinguish it from other "-isms," we suggest that the general premises of racism theories—and particularly their emphasis on values—can be used to develop a broader theory of outgroup prejudice. In this broader perspective, how do we know *which* values matter when it comes to prejudice? We suggest two propositions that define which values are likely to be implicated in outgroup attitudes. The first proposition is that humanitarianism/egalitarianism will be negatively associated with *all* measures of prejudice and discrimination. This is because it represents a form of antiprejudice that is not specific to any particular group or underlying cause of negative affect toward outgroups; it is a "prejudice antidote." Several studies suggest that endorsement of humanitarian values is negatively correlated with prejudice (e.g., Katz & Hass, 1988; Sears, 1988).

The second proposition is that the values implicated in outgroup rejection will depend on the content of dominant stereotypes of a particular outgroup. That is, if the stereotype of any group suggests that members do not uphold a particular value, then an individual's endorsement of that value will predict rejection of members of that outgroup. For example, homosexuals are often perceived as violating traditional "family values," (see Haddock, Zanna, & Esses, 1993; Jackson & Burris, 1995; Krulewitz & Nash, 1980); fat people[1] as violating aesthetic and moral values concerning discipline, hard work, delay of gratification, and willpower (Crandall, 1994; Crandall & Biernat, 1990). Individuals who strongly endorse these values should therefore be particularly negative toward these outgroups.

One set of values that is implicated in a number of outgroup stereotypes is individualism, as previously discussed. For example, both fat people and Blacks are regarded as lazy, "sinful," and lacking discipline and self-denial (Allon, 1982); in short, they both violate the Protestant Work Ethic. Similarly, homosexuals may be perceived as lacking in the ability to self-deny or delay gratification and repress sexual desires. Because of this value system's central importance in North American society, it is likely to be relevant to the perceptions of many outgroups. Furthermore, perceived failure to conform to this value will be viewed with strong disdain.

In general, then, we predict that endorsement of humanitarian or egalitarian values will be negatively associated with prejudice and discrimination toward virtually all outgroups. The other values that predict prejudice will be based on the stereotypical attributes of a particular outgroup, with Protestant Ethic values

---

[1]The term *fat* is used rather than *obese* or *overweight* because the latter imply a medical condition or known standard of appropriate weight, factors that are not relevant to our concerns. *Fat* is descriptive, and it is the label preferred by the relevant activist group (National Association to Advance Fat Acceptance).

perhaps the most likely to be implicated in a variety of outgroup stereotypes. When the stereotype suggests that a group does not support a particular value, then the endorsement of that value by an individual will predict a higher degree of negative feeling toward that group, for that individual. Before further comment on our general perspective on outgroup prejudice, however, we turn to a review of the racism literature.

SYMBOLIC AND MODERN RACISM

Early theorizing about symbolic racism focused on the distinctions between this "new" form of racism and old-fashioned or dominative (Kovel, 1970) racism (see Sears & McConahay, 1973). Although a number of researchers were noting decreases in blatant forms of prejudice and racism in the late 1960s and early 1970s (Campbell, 1971; Greeley & Sheatsley, 1971; Karlins, Coffman, & Walters, 1969; Schuman, Steeh, & Bobo, 1985; Sheatsley, 1966; Taylor, Sheatsley, & Greeley, 1978), many of these same researchers continued to document anti-Black feeling, even among seemingly nonracist Whites (see also Crosby, Bromley, & Saxe, 1980). Symbolic racism was invoked as a construct to illuminate this phenomenon. In an early paper on the topic, McConahay and Hough (1976) defined symbolic racism as "the expression in terms of abstract ideological symbols and symbolic behaviors of the feeling that blacks are violating cherished values and making illegitimate demands for changes in the racial status quo" (p. 38). For these researchers, the roots of symbolic racism included a) traditional religious and value socialization toward the ideals of "secular American civil Protestantism," b) socialization to political conservatism, and c) unacknowledged negative feelings toward Blacks.

This description was at least partly empirically based. In two surveys of southern California residents, the best predictors of symbolic racism (measured with items similar to the later-developed Modern Racism Scale,[2] McConahay, Hardee, & Batts, 1981) were political conservatism and a variety of religious and secular traditionalism measures (e.g., conventional religious beliefs, the expression of preference for the "old ways" of teaching, and reverence for patriotism). McConahay later opted to use the label "modern racism" instead of "symbolic racism," so as to emphasize the contemporary nature of the beliefs he was describing, and to acknowledge that old-fashioned racism may involve symbolic aspects as well.

Kinder and Sears (1981) offered a similar definition of the symbolic/modern

---

[2]Sample items from the Modern Racism scale include the following: "Over the past few years, the government and news media have shown more respect to blacks than they deserve"; "Blacks are getting too demanding in their push for equal rights."

racism construct.[3] Their work focused primarily on comparing symbolic racism and realistic group conflict theory. Using data from the 1969 and 1973 Los Angeles mayoral election surveys, Kinder and Sears (1981) found that tangible threats Whites might face from Blacks (e.g., having a child who would be bused) consistently did *not* predict preference for the White over the Black candidate, but that measures of symbolic racism (similar to those used by McConahay & Hough, 1976) did (see also Kluegel & Smith, 1983; McConahay, 1982; Sears & Allen, 1984; Sears & McConahay, 1973; cf. McClendon, 1985).

Our concern in this chapter is not with this realistic threat versus symbolic expression debate, nor with the question of whether or how symbolic racism differs from old-fashioned racism. We wish to focus instead on the conceptualization of symbolic/modern racism itself. Kinder and Sears (1981) described symbolic racism as "a *blend* of antiblack affect and the kind of traditional American moral values embodied in the Protestant Ethic" (p. 416; emphasis added). However, they have never clearly measured both the value and affect constructs, specified what form this blend takes (but see Sears, 1988), or indicated whether both components are necessary to explain racial prejudice.

Perhaps the most vocal critics of the symbolic racism approach have been Sniderman and Tetlock and their colleagues (Sniderman & Hagen, 1985; Sniderman, Hagen, Tetlock, & Brady, 1986; Sniderman & Piazza, 1993; Sniderman, Piazza, Tetlock, & Kendrick, 1991; Sniderman & Tetlock, 1986a, 1986b). Their criticisms focus, among other things, on the definitional and measurement shortcomings mentioned above. For example, in discussing the likely causal relationship among the two components of symbolic racism—anti-black affect and traditional moral values—they write: " . . . does anti-black affect lead to support for traditional values? Or is it perhaps the other way around . . . Or are both anti-black affect and traditional values involved, symbolic racism being an additive combination of the two? Or, yet again, is symbolic racism an interactive combination of anti-black affect and traditional values?" (Sniderman & Tetlock, 1986a, p. 132).

Kinder and Sears have largely been satisfied with measuring both aspects of symbolic racism with a single set of items that "deliberately mix racist sentiments and traditional American values, particularly individualism" (Kinder, 1986, p. 156). It seems important, however, to measure traditional values and anti-Black affect separately, as a means of better understanding the "blending" of these constructs, and to untangle the possible causal links described earlier. More importantly, the "double-barreled" nature of Kinder and Sears' construct is sim-

---

[3]McConahay's and Kinder and Sears' definitions of symbolic racism do differ slightly. For example, McConahay's symbolic racist believes that American society is rid of discrimination and that many opportunities exist for Blacks, but this is not part of either Kinder's or Sears' definition (see Kinder, 1986). We prefer to focus, however, on the commonalities in these researchers' perspectives, especially regarding their emphasis on traditional values.

ply difficult to defend from a methodological standpoint. As Sniderman and Tetlock (1986a, 1986b) note, it is possible that traditional values alone may be associated with attitudes toward a variety of racial policy preferences, as well as to nonracial policy preferences. Is the construct of symbolic racism meaningful if this is the case? Can any additional variance be explained if measures of traditional values are conjoined with measures of anti-Black affect?

The only relevant published data we could find on this point appear in Sears (1988). Using data from the 1984 National Election Study, Sears examined the effects of a "feeling thermometer" measure of anti-Black affect, and six-item measures of individualism and equality, on racial policy beliefs, evaluations of candidate Jesse Jackson, and relative evaluation of candidates Reagan versus Mondale. Anti-Black affect and egalitarian values were each significant predictors of racial policy preferences and Jackson evaluations (even after controlling for ideology and party identification), but individualism values were not. Both values predicted the Reagan–Mondale preference, but anti-Black affect did not. Sears (1988) concluded that "these data support the main thrust of the symbolic racism approach: Antiblack affect and traditional values have stronger effects on racial policy than do such conventional political variables as ideology and party identification . . . " (p. 70).

Worthy of note is the fact that in these data, egalitarian values figured more strongly in racial policy preferences than did the values that had been cited as the crux of symbolic racism theory—individualistic (Protestant Work Ethic) values. Others who have noted similar findings include Feldman (1983) and Kluegel and Smith (1983). Sears suggests that this pattern may require some alteration of the symbolic racism perspective—one that focuses on resistance to equality, rather than the perception that Blacks violate individualistic values, as a critical component of the theory. At best, however, these data provide only mixed support for the importance of the "blend" construct.

Evidence From Our Laboratory

We have sought to examine the validity of this *blend* construct in the person perception rather than policy/candidate preference domain. To what extent do anti-Black affect and traditional values—alone and in tandem—predict evaluations of individual Black (as opposed to White) targets? Using scales developed by Katz and Hass (1988), we measured undergraduate subjects' Protestant Work Ethic (PWE) and humanitarian/egalitarian values (EG), as well as their anti-Black attitudes in a pretest session. Several weeks later, individuals who scored particularly high in either PWE or egalitarian values participated in an experimental study that ostensibly involved helping companies improve their employee evaluation procedures. After listening to a prime (an audiotaped speech) designed to elicit either PWE or egalitarian concerns, subjects examined an employee file that contained a job application and insurance forms, and two sets of evaluations provided by supervisors.

The employee was either depicted as Black or White (by use of a photograph attached to the job application), and as either a good, dependable worker or as a lazy, undependable worker (for a description of similar methodology, see Biernat, Vescio, & Theno, 1996). In other words, the employee either supported or violated traditional work ethic values on the job. Subjects later made a series of evaluations of the employee; among these were a 7-item measure of social distance (e.g., "this person appears to be a likeable individual"; "I would like to have this person as a close friend"; see Crandall, 1991), a series of trait ratings, and a recommendation to fire or retain the employee.

Of interest here were the relationships among subjects' previously measured attitudes and values, and their evaluations of the Black or White, dependable or undependable worker. We were particularly interested in the "blend" between anti-Black affect[4] and traditional values that Kinder and Sears describe, and tested for both the multiplicative and additive forms of this blend (see Sniderman & Tetlock, 1986a). We first calculated zero-order correlations between ratings of the employee (trait judgments, social distance, firing) and anti-Black attitudes, PWE values, EG values, and the attitude × value interaction terms; these appear in Table 7.1. Consistent with the symbolic racism approach (see Sears, 1988), these attitude and value measures were not associated with evaluations of the White applicant. In fact, these measures only had an effect on subjects' evaluations of the Black, value-violating (i.e., lazy) employee. Stronger anti-Black attitudes and PWE values produced increased negativity toward the Black value-violator, whereas stronger EG values produced increased positivity; the product terms performed comparably.

However, these correlations do not clearly test for the joint contribution of values and anti-Black attitudes to these target evaluations. To do this, we focused only on the Black value-violating target, and for each dependent measure, computed two multiple regression equations—one including anti-Black attitudes, PWE values, and EG values, and a second that included these factors plus the anti-Black × PWE and anti-Black × EG interactions. Including all three main effects in a single regression reduced all of their effects to nonsignificance, although anti-Black attitudes contributed somewhat more unique variance than did the value factors (squared semi-partial correlations for social distance, trait evaluations, and probability of firing were .05, .09, and .04 for anti-Black

---

[4]We operationalize anti-Black affect here using an anti-Black *attitude* scale. Although we recognize there are distinctions between affect and attitude constructs (see Eagly & Chaiken, 1993; Zanna & Rempel, 1988), we note Katz and Hass' (1988) claim that their anti-Black scale includes "beliefs about deviant characteristics and associated negative affect" (p. 894). Technically, however, we do not use a *pure* measure of affect in this study or in the later reported study concerning homosexuals.

TABLE 7.1
Correlations Between Ratings of the Employee and Anti-Black Affect, Values, and Their "Blend," Race Study

				Predictor Variables		
Target Race & Violation Level	Dependent Measure	Anti-Black	PWE Value	EG Value	AB X PWE	AB (rev) X EG
Black/ no value violation (n = 34)	Soc dist	.15	.21	-.26	.21	-.22
	Trait pos	-.15	.10	-.05	.01	.09
	Prob fire	--[a]	--	--	--	--
Black/ value violation (n = 33)	Soc dist	.41**	.32*	-.35**	.34*	-.44**
	Trait pos	-.30*	-.44**	.37**	-.35**	.40**
	Prob fire	.40**	.40**	-.27	.40**	-.39**
White/ no value violation (n = 30)	Soc dist	-.25	-.23	.19	-.27	-.22
	Trait pos	.17	.23	-.14	.23	-.15
	Prob fire	-.10	.04	.01	-.04	.05
White/ value violation (n = 32)	Soc dist	.23	-.04	-.13	.16	.19
	Trait pos	-.26	.11	.14	-.14	.22
	Prob fire	-.03	-.10	-.10	-.07	-.23

Notes. Soc dist = Social distance, Trait pos = Positive trait evaluations, Prob fire = Probability of firing the employee, PWE = Protestant Work Ethic values, EG = Humanitarian/egalitarian values, AB = anti-Black.
[a]No subjects indicated they would fire the Black nonviolating employee.
*p < .10. **p < .05.

attitudes; .01, .07, and .02 for PWE values; .02, .02, and .0001 for EG values). The addition of the interaction factors did not add appreciably to R^2 (all $ps >$ .25).

These data suggest that each of the relevant variables—anti-Black attitudes, PWE values, and EG values—has some effect on evaluations of the "lazy" Black employee, but these effects appear to be neither additive nor multiplicative in form. This is inconsistent with the Symbolic Racism perspective that the *blend* of these factors reflects racism. At least in the domain of person perception, and specifically subjects' reactions to a lazy Black employee, each construct alone performed as well as its blend with other factors.

As indicated earlier, our broader research goal is to work toward a general theory of prejudice that incorporates reactions toward a variety of outgroups. Toward that end, we conducted a study concerning reactions to homosexual targets that was analogous to the race study just described. Because it is likely that the traditional values implicated in reactions to homosexuals are those concerned with respect for family, this was the focus of our study. We also continued to examine the impact of egalitarian values on evaluations of homosexual targets, given our suspicion that this value acts as a general prejudice "antidote." Extending the Symbolic Racism thesis concerning the blend of anti-Black affect and traditional values, we suggested that reactions to homosexuals may be based on some blend of anti-*homosexual* affect and traditional values. To measure each of these constructs, subjects completed the Heterosexuals' Attitudes Toward Homosexuals scale (HATH; Larsen, Reed, & Hoffman, 1980), Katz and Hass' (1988) Humanitarian/Egalitarian scale, and the terminal values scale of the Rokeach Value Survey (RVS). Preselected for participation in our experiment were those individuals who placed a particularly high (ranking from 1 to 4) or a particularly low (ranking from 13 to 18) value on "family security" on the RVS.

In the experiment, conducted about 8 weeks after values and antihomosexual attitudes were measured, subjects listened to a mock radio interview in which they heard either a homosexual or heterosexual widowed father describe his adjustment to the loss of his wife (sexual orientation was manipulated as the father talked about dating). To manipulate support or violation of family values, in one version of the interview the father was generally a "good parent" who placed his son's needs before his own, and who was careful that his son not see him display signs of affection to his dating partner. In the other version, designed to depict a violation of family values, the father was more selfish about his desire to get on with his life, and the son witnessed the father engaging in sex with his partner (for a full description, see Vescio, Biernat, & Theno, 1996). After listening to the interview, subjects evaluated the father on a series of trait adjectives, and also completed the measure of social distance.

We discuss this study in more detail shortly, but relevant to our purposes now are the associations among antihomosexual attitudes, EG values, and the value for family security, and evaluations of the homosexual and heterosexual, value

TABLE 7.2
Correlations Between Ratings of the Father and Anti-Gay Affect, Values, and Their "Blend," Sexual Orientation Study

Target Sexual Orientation & Violation Level	Dependent Measure	Predictor Variables				
		HATH	Family Value	EG Value	HATH*Family	HATH (rev) * EG
Homosexual/ no viol (n = 43)	Soc dist	.75***	-.06	-.30*	.47**	-.65***
	Trait pos	-.72***	-.08	.29*	-.55***	.64***
Homosexual/ violation (n = 38)	Soc dist	.70***	.24	-.32*	.58***	-.65***
	Trait pos	-.74***	-.23	.39**	-.61***	.75***
Hetero/ no viol (n = 41)	Soc dist	-.02	-.13	-.01	-.10	.01
	Trait pos	.02	.13	.11	.11	.06
Hetero/ violation (n = 39)	Soc dist	.02	.05	-.20	.05	-.14
	Trait pos	-.10	-.05	.18	-.07	.18

Notes. Soc dist = Social distance, Trait pos = Positive trait evaluations, HATH = Heterosexuals' Attitudes Toward Homosexuals scale, EG = Humanitarian/egalitarian values, Viol = Violation, Hetero = Heterosexual target.
$*p < .08$. $**p < .05$. $***p < .0001$.

162

violating and nonviolating, father. These data appear in Table 7.2. Analogous to our report of the race data, we first calculated zero-order correlations between ratings of the father (trait and social distance judgments) and HATH scores, (reversed) family security rankings, EG values, and the attitude $\times$ value interactions. As can be seen in the table, HATH scores and egalitarian values were associated with evaluations of the homosexual father (whether he violated family values or not), but not of the heterosexual father. Family security was generally unrelated in all cases. Not surprisingly, the blend terms also were highly correlated with evaluations of the homosexual father.

Once again, however, when we considered the simultaneous effects of the HATH and values, only the HATH remained a significant predictor (semi-partial $r^2 = .44$ and $.42$ for social distance and trait evaluations, respectively; all semi-partial r^2s for the two value constructs were $< .03$). Similarly, when we added the product of the HATH and values to their main effects, there was no appreciable increase in R^2 ($Fs < 1$). As in the race study, there was no evidence that either the additive or multiplicative construction of the blend factor accounted for subjects' evaluations of homosexual targets.

Overall, the data from both the race and sexual orientation studies suggest that anti-outgroup attitudes were a stronger predictor of target evaluations than were values, or the combination of the two factors. This appears to be inconsistent with symbolic racism theory's emphasis on the *blending* of these constructs.[5] However, these data do suggest that egalitarian and Protestant ethic values alone have some impact on evaluations of an outgroup target, and, as we will later point out, their impact may be stronger when evaluations are made of outgroups as a whole, rather than of individual outgroup members.

BELIEF CONGRUENCE THEORY

The research described earlier was also inspired by Rokeach's theory of belief congruence (Insko et al., 1983; Rokeach, 1968; Rokeach & Mezei, 1966; Rokeach & Rothman, 1965; Rokeach et al., 1960; Stein et al., 1965). This model suggests that prejudice is based on the assumption that members of outgroups hold beliefs (attitudes and values) that differ from one's own. Research from this perspective has involved pitting ethnicity information against manipulated belief similarity, and has found similarity to generally play the larger role in judgments

---

[5]Of course, one could argue that in both studies, our value measures were less reliable than our affect measures, and that this might account for their differential effectiveness. This was not true in the race study, but the single-item measure of family values in the sexual orientation study could be problematic on this point. However, the lower reliability must be balanced against the fact that we selected subjects for participation in both studies based on their extreme value scores, with no regard for their affect scores. If anything, the extremitization on values should increase the likelihood that this measure produce significant effects.

of and behavior toward target individuals (e.g., choices of who to have coffee with).

Our connection with this model developed in part from our reading of symbolic racism theory. In describing the "traditional values" component of symbolic/modern racism theory, McConahay and Hough (1976) wrote, "Persons holding such values would regard anyone, white, brown, or black, who appeared to deviate from these values—e.g., hippies, vagrants, sexual libertines—as immoral" (p. 41). Clearly, these authors were suggesting that deviation from values, and not race per se, is a critical basis of negative responses to outgroup members.

Using this logic in our own work, we hypothesized that outgroup members who are known *not* to violate important values (i.e., those who are "value congruent") will be perceived relatively positively; ingroup members who *do* violate those values will be perceived relatively negatively. In other words, the strongest case for the importance of value violation would be made if value violation, *rather than* group membership, predicted perceptions of individual targets. A weaker case would be made if value violation, *in addition to* group membership, accounted for these perceptions. However, if group membership alone affects impressions, value violation would appear to be a less critical component of outgroup perception.

In the two studies described earlier, we were able to test these predictions, using both race and sexual orientation as group membership cues. In each case, group membership was crossed with a manipulation of value violation (dependable or lazy worker in the race study, good moral parent or poor parent in the sexual orientation study). Our designs were complicated by the addition of two other factors, which have not been explored in past research on belief congruence. First, we selected subjects on the basis of their values as previously described (PWE and egalitarian values in the race study, family security values in the sexual orientation study). Second, we manipulated the salience of these values through the use of supraliminal primes. Specifically, in the race study, subjects listened to one of two speeches designed to evoke the relevant values, and in the sexual orientation study, subjects either attended to or were distracted from listening to a speech concerning the importance of traditional family life (see Vescio et al., 1996 for details). Manipulation of these factors was included because of our suspicion that the relevance of value violation might depend on the extent to which an individual endorses that value, and/or the extent to which an individual is reminded of that value in the immediate context.

Each study, then, was based on a value × prime × group membership cue × value violation design. The last two factors replicate the traditional belief congruence paradigm, and the first two factors allow us to address two additional research questions: How do individual differences in support for traditional values combine with the experimental factors to influence judgement? And how might situational "priming" of a value affect social judgment—for example, does one need to be reminded of a value before its violation is disturbing?

The Race Study

Whether or not the employee violated work ethic values was the only significant predictor of probability of firing, $F(1,125) = 189.89, p < .0001$. A recommendation to fire was made in 1.6% of the nonviolating cases compared to 79.7% of the violating cases. Both race and value violation had independent main effects on social distance and trait ratings of the employee. Interestingly, subjects demonstrated a pro- rather than anti-Black bias. For example, they felt more distance from the White target ($M = 3.98$; 7-point scale) than the Black target ($M = 3.25$; $F(1,126) = 11.08, p < .002$). We have consistently noted this pattern in related research in our laboratory (e.g., see Biernat & Vescio, 1993), and have suggested that it may be based, in part, on subjects' heightened sensitivity to or concern about appearing nonprejudiced (see later discussion of Aversive Racism). Not surprisingly, value violators (i.e., lazy employees) were viewed more negatively than value supporters (Ms for social distance = 4.68 and 2.46, respectively, $F(1,126) = 170.02 \, p < .0001$).

In addition to these main effects, there was also some evidence that the priming manipulation and subjects' own values affected trait evaluations as well. On one subset of trait ratings, which included the attributes corrupt, dislikeable, hostile, immoral, unfriendly, and narrowminded (alpha = .90), the interaction between prime, race, and value violation was significant, $F(1,126) = 3.64, p < .06$. Two points are notable in these data, which are depicted in Table 7.3. First, subjects were more negative toward value violators than non-violators in each race by prime combination. However, the more striking finding was that under egalitarian prime conditions, ratings of the Black value violator were significantly more positive than in each of the other value violation conditions (see top row of Table 7.3). The egalitarian prime served to increase evaluations of the

TABLE 7.3
Interaction Between Priming Condition, Race, and Value Violation on Trait Evaluations of the "Employee," Race Study

| Violation Condition | Priming Conditions and Race of Target | | | |
| | Work Ethic Prime | | Egalitarian Prime | |
	Black	White	Black	White
Violation	6.22[ae]	6.05[bf]	7.20[cefg]	5.59[dg]
No violation	8.34[a]	8.26[b]	8.13[c]	8.19[d]

Note.   Traits included corrupt, dislikeable, hostile, immoral, unfriendly, and norrowminded (response scale = 1 - 9). High numbers indicate more positive evaluations.
    Contrasts were calculated within columns and within rows of this table. Means with the same superscripts significantly differ from each other at $p < .02$.

Black (but not the White) value violator; the work ethic prime did not serve this function, and neither prime differentially affected ratings of the nonviolators of either race.

On a second set of trait evaluations, which included the attributes family-oriented, good parent, intelligent, and kind (alpha = .78), subjects' own value levels (high PWE and high EG) interacted with the prime and violation level of the target, $F(1,126) = 5.34, p < .03$. The relevant means appear in Table 7.4. In this case, although value violators were consistently viewed more negatively than nonviolators, this difference was reliable only among high PWE subjects given the PWE prime, and high EG subjects given the EG prime (see cols. 2 and 5 of Table 7.4). In other words, only subjects whose strong values were primed significantly discriminated between value violators and nonviolators in their evaluative ratings. They appeared to do so by *de*creasing their ratings of the value violator, not increasing their ratings of the nonviolator.

What do these data say about the belief congruence perspective? Consistent with much of Rokeach's own work on the topic, we found that "belief similarity" (value violation) had a very strong effect on subjects' judgments of the "employee." This was generally true regardless of subjects' individual value levels, and regardless of which situational prime they received. However, the effect of race was not completely discounted in judgments: We noted a general tendency to favor Black over White employees. In addition, these data suggest that on some evaluative dimensions, subjects whose own important values are primed are particularly sensitive to value violation. A tendency was also apparent for subjects primed to think of egalitarian values to be more charitable to "lazy" Blacks relative to "lazy" Whites. Apparently, a reminder of important values sensitized our subjects both to value violation, and to race concerns.

TABLE 7.4
Interaction Between Value Profile, Priming Condition, and Value Violation on Trait Evaluations of the "Employee," Race Study

	Value Profile and Priming Conditions			
	High PWE/Low EG		*Low PWE/High EG*	
Violation Condition	*PWE Prime*	*EG Prime*	*PWE Prime*	*EG Prime*
Violation	5.17[ac]	5.54	5.83[cd]	5.30[bd]
No violation	6.82[a]	6.25	6.42	6.55[b]

Note. Traits included family-oriented, good parent, intelligent, and kind (response scale = 1 - 9). High numbers indicate more positive evaluations.

   Contrasts were calculated within columns and within rows of this table. Means with the same superscripts significantly differ from each other at $p < .08$.

The Sexual Orientation Study

In our study on sexual orientation, in which subjects were exposed to a homosexual or heterosexual, "moral" or "immoral" parent, the homosexual father ($M = 3.67$) received higher social distance ratings than the heterosexual father ($M = 2.79$), $F(1,164) = 27.72$, $p < .0001$, as well as more negative trait evaluations, $F(1,164) = 5.22$, $p < .03$. Unlike the race study, subjects in this experiment clearly expressed antipathy toward the outgroup. The value violation level of the target (whether he was a good or bad parent) also affected trait evaluations, such that the violator ($M = 7.15$) was viewed more negatively than the nonviolator ($M = 7.43$), $F(1,164) = 3.90$, $p < .05$. On ratings of social distance, the value violation level of the father affected judgments only when subjects had been primed to think of family values, interaction $F(1,164) = 9.02$, $p < .01$. Subjects who were primed reported significantly greater distance toward the target who violated family values ($M = 3.66$) than toward to the nonviolator ($M = 2.88$); *un*primed subjects did not differentiate between violators ($M = 3.10$) and nonviolators ($M = 3.29$).

In this study, we found no evidence for higher order interactions among subjects' personal endorsement of family security values, situational primes, and our target manipulations. The social distance data suggest, however, that a situational prime alone—regardless of subjects' personal values—resulted in increased sensitization to value violation. Consistent with belief congruence theory, subjects disliked value violators (particularly when primed to think of family values). Analogous to the race study findings, this did not, however, rule out the effect of the father's sexual orientation as a judgment cue. Independent of the effects of value violation, subjects disliked homosexual fathers. Yet in both studies, value violation appeared to play the larger role.[6]

Belief Congruence Revisited

Although Rokeach's original presentation of belief congruence theory suggested that belief dissimilarity is the primary determinant of prejudice, others have delineated the circumstances under which beliefs or group membership will have the larger effect. In their examination of the belief congruence hypothesis, Triandis and his colleagues (Triandis, 1961; Triandis & Davis, 1965; cf. Smith, Williams, & Willis, 1967) suggested that belief similarity is likely to be a more important determinant of judgment or choice than group membership in situations with low intimacy, whereas group membership (e.g., race) may be a more important determinant in more intimate relations. Others (e.g., Insko et al.,

---

[6]One might argue that demand effects are responsible for the priming by violation effects reported here. Yet in an independent study using a much more subtle prime (a photograph of a family on a newspaper page), comparable effects emerged (see Vescio et al., 1996).

1983; Mezei, 1971; Moe, Nacoste, & Insko, 1981; Silverman, 1974) have suggested that belief will be a more important determinant of ethnic discrimination than race in contexts where social pressure is nonexistent or ineffective.

The judgment situation in which we placed our subjects in both the race and sexual orientation studies was clearly of the less intimate variety—subjects had no contact with the targets of their evaluation. Similarly, because our subjects answered questions privately, and were assured anonymity, little or no social pressure was operating. Thus, our finding that value violation or support had the larger, more consistent impact on evaluative judgment is consistent with these authors' predictions. Perhaps if subjects had anticipated interacting with our targets in either a social or work context, or if responses had been publicly made,[7] we would have found stronger effects of social category membership (see Hyland, 1974).

We should also note that our studies did not include experimental conditions in which *no* information regarding value violation was provided. In most social situations in which discrimination is practiced, people do not inquire into the values of outgroup members; rather they are likely to assume value violation (or lack of support for values) in members of disliked groups (see Precker, 1953). Under these conditions, of course, it is social category membership that should carry the most meaning and provide the basis for judgment, particularly among highly prejudiced subjects (Byrne & Wong, 1962; Stein et al., 1965).

Furthermore, it is unclear whether the effects of value violation we've observed are based on *decreased* evaluations of value violators, or on *increased* evaluations of nonviolators (i.e., value supporters; for a debate on a comparable issue in the similarity-attraction literature, see Byrne, Clore, & Smeaton, 1986; Rosenbaum, 1986a, 1986b; Smeaton, Byrne, & Murnen, 1989). In the race study, we found some evidence that the former possibility held true—subjects primed to think of values that were important to them showed increased negativity toward the value violator. In the sexual orientation study, however, we found both increased negativity (distance) toward the violator under primed versus nonprimed conditions, as well as increased positivity (less distance) toward the *non*violator when family values were primed.

In their work critiquing symbolic and modern racism theory, Sniderman et al. (1991) also found support for increased positivity toward value supporters, but only when they were members of the outgroup. These researchers examined conservative and liberal respondents' willingness to offer government assistance to a Black or White, dependable or lazy, laid-off worker. Their findings suggested not that subjects were especially likely to deny assistance to lazy (i.e.,

---

[7]Interestingly, we would predict that social pressure might operate in a direction opposite to that suggested by belief congruence researchers. In today's political climate, social pressure might be expected to work in a pro-outgroup direction (e.g., there may be pressure to treat homosexuals positively).

value violating) workers, or even that they denied assistance to lazy Blacks; rather, conservative subjects were especially likely to *offer* assistance to dependable (i.e., value nonviolating) Blacks. Liberals did not differentially respond to Blacks and Whites, violators and nonviolators. In the same laid-off worker experiment, conservatives also showed favoritism to married Blacks (who, perhaps, are perceived as *supporting* important family values), over married Whites. This research, then, indicates that value violation may be less important to outgroup perceptions than value support. For conservative perceivers in particular, when unambiguous evidence exists that an outgroup member supports one's values, that member is viewed more favorably than a comparable member of one's ingroup. Sniderman et al. (1991) suggest that this may be due to the fact that value nonviolating outgroup members are seen as exceptions, and therefore deserving of extra praise (see Jussim, Coleman, & Lerch, 1987).

Symbolic Racism Theory Revisited

More research is needed to clarify whether perceived value violation or value support is the more critical process in outgroup perception. To address this point, it may be appropriate to back up a step and ask a more basic question: Do Whites perceive Blacks as violating their cherished values? Although this is a basic assumption of symbolic and modern racism theories, we know of no direct evidence that it is so.

To test this assumption, we asked a sample of White undergraduates at the University of Kansas ($N = 442$) to first complete the "terminal values" component of the Rokeach Values Survey (Biernat et al., 1996, Study 1). Specifically, subjects were asked to rank 18 values in order of their perceived importance as "factors that guide" their lives. After this task, subjects were asked to think about the value they had ranked "1" on the list, and to keep that value in mind as they answered four questions about African Americans and White Americans. The questions were designed to measure the extent to which subjects viewed Whites and Blacks as supportive or nonsupportive of their number 1 value. The questions asked to what extent the subject believed each group *shares, disrespects, lives their lives consistently with,* and *violates* their number 1 value. All responses were made on 1–7 scales, with endpoints labeled *not at all* and *very much so.*

Subjects perceived the group "White Americans" as significantly more likely than "African Americans" to *share* their number 1 value, and to *live their lives consistently with* that value, $ps < .0001$. However the differences between perceptions of White and African Americans on the questions concerning value *violation* and *disrespect* were nonsignificant, $ps > .14$. In other words, subjects perceived White Americans as more likely than Black Americans to support their values, but did not perceive the groups as differing in the extent to which they violated those values. This pattern held regardless of which particular values subjects had ranked number one. Relevant means appear in Table 7.5.

TABLE 7.5
Mean Perceptions of Value Support and Violation of Ingroups and Outgroups

	Target Group	
Value Question	White Americans	African Americans
Shares	5.43	5.03
	(1.34)	(1.60)
Lives life consistently with	4.74	4.34
	(1.37)	(1.42)
Violates	2.55	2.45
	(1.48)	(1.53)
Disrespects	2.22	2.13
	(1.36)	(1.44)

Value Question	Heterosexuals	Homosexuals
Shares	5.27	4.94
	(1.38)	(1.91)
Lives life consistently with	5.21	4.25
	(1.43)	(1.79)
Violates	2.46	2.63
	(1.47)	(1.83)
Disrespects	2.33	2.29
	(1.40)	(1.72)

Value Question	Thin/Average Weight	Fat/Overweight
Supports	5.23	4.58
	(1.58)	(1.80)
Violates	2.34	2.60
	(1.57)	(1.71)

Note. Standard deviations in parentheses.

Because of our interest in extending research on race to include perceptions of other outgroups, we also asked the same series of four questions regarding the groups homosexuals and heterosexuals. The same pattern emerged (see Table 7.5). Subjects perceived heterosexuals as significantly more likely than homosexuals to *share* their number 1 value, and to *live their lives consistently* with that value, $ps < .001$. The heterosexual-homosexual difference did approach significance on the value *violation* question, $p < .07$, but was nonsignificant on the value *disrespect* question, $t < 1$.

Finally, in a separate sample of 621 Kansas undergraduates, we examined reactions to an additional outgroup—fat people. Subjects were instructed to think about their values generally, and to indicate to what extent "fat/overweight" people and "thin/average weight" people violated and supported those values. In this case, thin people were perceived as both significantly more likely to support values, and less likely to violate values, than fat people, $ps < .0001$ (see Table 7.5). Once again, however, the fat-thin difference was greater in support for than violation of values.

We conclude from these data that a major premise of Symbolic and Modern Racism theory—that Whites perceive Blacks as violating cherished values—may need modification. It is more likely that Whites perceive Blacks as *less likely to support* their values than Whites, but not as more likely to violate them. This may also hold true for perceptions of homosexuals as compared to heterosexuals, but apparently not for perceptions of fat as opposed to thin people.[8]

This pattern of findings regarding race is consistent with evidence from Gaertner and Dovidio and their colleagues (Dovidio & Gaertner, 1993; Gaertner & Dovidio, 1986; Gaertner & McLaughlin, 1983). In their work, subjects tended not to perceive Blacks more negatively than Whites, but they did perceive Whites more positively than Blacks. More subtle reaction time indicators of association between racial group and evaluations also supported such a pattern. In other words, ingroup-outgroup bias may more readily be located at the positive end of evaluative dimensions (see Brewer, 1979). It is worth noting, however, that for each of the social groups in these studies, subjects were much more likely to perceive support for than violation of their important values.

RACIAL AMBIVALENCE

Katz and his colleagues have suggested that White America's response to Blacks is driven by the construct of "ambivalence." This ambivalence stems from the simultaneous holding of both anti- and pro-Black attitudes (Katz, 1981; Katz, Glass, & Cohen, 1973; Katz & Hass, 1988; Katz et al., 1986). Blacks are seen as disadvantaged by the system, thereby eliciting sympathy and pro-Black sentiments; at the same time, Blacks are seen as deviating from the dominant society's values and norms, which elicits hostility and anti-Black affect. These simultaneous feelings of aversion and hostility, and of sympathy and compassion, toward members of a stigmatized group (Katz, 1979) creates an arousal state, or "high vulnerability to emotional tension" (Katz et al., 1986, p. 45).

---

[8]In a modification of the belief congruence approach, Schwartz and his colleagues have suggested that it is dissimilarity in value *hierarchies,* not individual values, that is, in part, responsible for outgroup antagonism (Schwartz & Bilsky, 1987; Schwartz & Struch, 1989; Schwartz et al., 1990; Struch & Schwartz, 1989). Specifically, value dissimilarity (calculated as a Spearman rank order correlation between ingroup and outgroup value hierarchies) is hypothesized to lead to the perception of "inhumanity" of the outgroup; this construct may mediate the impact of perceived intergroup conflict on outgroup aggression (Struch & Schwartz, 1989). We have not addressed value dissimilarity using this method in our own work, but suggest it as a useful tool in future investigations (see Haddock et al., 1993).

Katz et al. (1986; Katz & Hass, 1988) also propose that the duality of attitudes in most White Americans' thinking about Blacks is the result of conflict between two core American values as they are applied to minority target evaluations. American Whites embrace egalitarian or humanitarian values, stemming from concepts such as social justice, improvement of the plight of the underdog, and so forth. These invoke pro-Black sentiment. On the other hand, Whites also adhere to the other core value that we have already discussed with regard to the theory of symbolic racism—that of individualism; the Protestant Work Ethic. Anti-Black attitudes derive from this value system (see also Sidanius, Devereux, & Pratto, 1992). Using value and affect scales developed for this purpose, Katz and Hass (1988) found that priming of egalitarian values (achieved by having subjects fill out their egalitarianism scale) increased pro-Black scores, whereas priming of Protestant work ethic values increased anti-Black scores.

With this construction of the ambivalence construct, Katz and his colleagues have developed their ambivalence–amplification model, which draws on the psychoanalytic analysis of ambivalence (see also Gergen & Jones, 1963). With regard to race, this model suggests that (a) ambivalence (which is experienced by most Whites with regard to Blacks) arouses negative emotions (see Hass, Katz, Rizzo, Bailey, & Moore, 1992), and (b) to reduce this emotional tension, responses to particular Black individuals are amplified; the direction of the amplification is cued by the situational context (Katz et al., 1973). In general, the model predicts extremitized evaluations of Black relative to White targets. Under conditions fostering negative behavior or providing negative cues, ambivalence leads individuals to behave or react more negatively toward Blacks than toward Whites, and under positive cue conditions, ambivalence results in greater positivity toward Blacks than Whites (see also Gaertner & Dovidio, 1986). Amplified responses are viewed as an attempt by the ambivalent subject to repudiate the contradicted attitude and restore a positive self image.

General support for the hypothesized ambivalence amplification pattern can be found in a variety of research paradigms. For example, Katz, Glass and Cohen (1973) examined reactions to unintentional harm-doing in a teacher–learner shock paradigm. Subjects completed both the Woodmansee and Cook (1967) Racial Attitude Inventory and the Schuman and Harding (1964) scale on sympathetic identification with the underdog. White male subjects who were ambivalent toward Blacks (both high on prejudice and high on sympathy) were more likely to denigrate a Black confederate given strong shocks than a Black confederate given only moderate shocks, or a White confederate in either shock condition. Katz, Cohen, and Glass' (1975) field experiments involving cross-racial helping behavior indicated that Whites gave more support to Black confederates when they displayed socially valued goals or conformed toward White norms and values, and more support to White confederates when the minority behavior did not reflect these same characteristics. McConahay (1983) has used the Modern Racism Scale (MRS) as an indicator of racial ambivalence (for McConahay, an ambivalent person scores fairly high on the MRS and low in old-fashioned racism). Using a simulated hiring paradigm, he found that when the situational context was cued to be negative (i.e., subjects evaluated an "undistinguished" Black applicant *before* viewing any other applications), subjects scoring high on the Modern Racism Scale preferred White over Black candidates. However, when the situation was cued to be positive (i.e., the undistinguished Black applicant was evaluated *after* the subject viewed the superior credentials of two White applicants), high MRS subjects distinctly preferred the Black candidate over the White candidates.

Other researchers have also found evidence for extremitization patterns, but have posited a mechanism other than ambivalence as responsible for these effects. Linville and Jones (1980) asked subjects to evaluate law school candidates who were Black or White, and academically weak or strong. Consistent with the amplification pattern, Black candidates were rated more positively than Whites in the strong application condition, but more negatively than Whites when the application was weak (see also Rogers & Prentice-Dunn, 1981). Linville and Jones (1980; Linville, 1982) have invoked the construct of cognitive complexity rather than ambivalence as responsible for this effect (Whites' lack of complexity in thinking about Blacks relative to Whites leads to extremitization), and recent work has been geared toward testing these alternative explanations (Hass, Katz, Rizzo, Bailey, & Eisenstadt, 1991)

Although the debate over the specific mediating mechanisms continues, there is considerable correlational and experimental evidence supporting the basic predictions of the ambivalence–amplification perspective. Furthermore, this model is perhaps the broadest of the racism theories we've examined, in that it was originally developed to apply to other stigmatized groups as well. For example, Katz, Glass, Lucido, and Farber (1977) found that subjects who encountered confederates in wheel chairs and heard noxious noise (versus moderate noise) were more likely to denigrate these targets relative to nonhandicapped targets. Gibbons, Stephan, Stephenson, and Petty (1980) found that a confederate on crutches who was responsible for a subjects' success or failure on an anagrams task was evaluated more extremely (positively or negatively) than the same confederate who appeared without crutches. We should note, however, that in studies involving both race and other stigmas, the outgroup extremitization pattern appears to be more reliable at the positive end, rather than the negative end, of the evaluative continuum (Carver, Glass, & Katz, 1978; Carver, Glass, Snyder, & Katz, 1977; Jussim et al., 1987; Linville & Jones, 1980; Scheier, Carver, Schulz, Glass, & Katz, 1978).

Ambivalence and the Situational Salience of Values

Although the ambivalence-amplification model applies to a variety of outgroups, it is only with regard to racism that Katz and his colleagues have emphasized the links between values and the attitudes that presumably produce amplified responses toward Blacks. As already indicated, Katz and Hass (1988) have established the association between egalitarian values and pro-Black attitudes, and PWE values and anti-Black attitudes, respectively. Furthermore, in an experimental setting, Hass et al. (1991) found that ambivalence was positively correlated with evaluations of favorable Black targets, and negatively correlated with evaluations of unfavorable Black targets. However, no research has drawn these two findings together, by establishing how priming of the distal variables (Protestant Ethic and egalitarian values) affects ambivalent feelings, which in turn affect evaluations of individual Black targets. The situational arousal of these values might be expected to influence the relationship between ambivalence and evaluations in predictable ways.

More specifically, the link between ambivalence and evaluations should be strengthened under conditions that heighten the salience of the more "latent" affective construct. We suggest that for most White Americans, anti-Black affect is a longer-standing belief system than is pro-Black affect; anti-Black feeling presumably develops relatively early in life in our White-dominant culture, whereas pro-Black feelings may develop only later, through more conscious consideration and liberal influence (see Devine, 1989; Higgins & King, 1981). If this is true, anti-Black affect should be more chronically salient in White American's lives, or as Devine (1989) suggests, more likely to operate automatically than pro-Black attitudes. But the situational arousal of egalitarian values may increase the salience of these less available, pro-Black feelings, and, in turn, make ambivalence a more potent force. Thus, the link between ambivalence and evaluations of Black targets should be strengthened under conditions that arouse egalitarian values (Gibbons et al., 1980).

This is precisely what we found in the employee evaluation study described earlier. We had measured ambivalence using Katz and Hass' (1988) pro- and anti-Black attitudes scales about 9 weeks prior to the conduct of the employee evaluation experiment. To review the study, subjects were first primed to think about either egalitarian or work ethic beliefs by listening to an audiotaped speech exalting the virtues of the relevant value system. They then were asked to review and evaluate the work record of an employee who was depicted as a Black or White, lazy or dependable worker. We correlated subjects' ambivalence scores (standardized pro-Black × anti-Black attitudes) with their social distance ratings of each target, under each value prime condition. Because the ns were relatively low in each condition (from 15 to 17), few of the correlations were significant; nonetheless, the pattern of effects is informative. For ease of description, social distance was reverse scored such that higher numbers indicate a more positive evaluation. The correlations appear in Table 7.6.

It was only among subjects in the egalitarian prime condition that the predicted pattern of correlations between ambivalence and target evaluations was found. Ambivalence was positively (though not significantly) correlated with evaluation of the dependable Black, and negatively correlated with evaluation of the lazy Black worker; these correlations significantly differed from each other

TABLE 7.6
Correlations Between Ambivalence and (Reversed) Social Distance Ratings of Black and White, Lazy and Dependable Workers, Under Egalitarian and PWE Prime Conditions

	Primed Value	
Target Race and Demeanor	Egalitarian	Work Ethic
Black/dependable	.36	-.07
Black/lazy	-.59*	.12
White/dependable	-.44	.45
White/lazy	-.27	.11

*p < .05.

($z = 2.68, p < .008$).[9] Although Katz and Hass suggest that ambivalence should be unrelated to evaluations of White targets, we also found evidence that ambivalence was associated with negative evaluations of both the dependable and lazy White targets under egalitarian prime conditions, but with positive evaluations of the White targets under work ethic prime conditions.

These data appear to be consistent with the theoretical process outlined above. The priming of egalitarian values may increase the salience of relatively latent pro-Black attitudes. This increased salience heightens the effect of the ambivalence construct on evaluations of Black targets, thus producing the pattern of correlations predicted by ambivalence theory. Heightened salience of egalitarian values also led highly ambivalent subjects to evaluate White targets (and particularly dependable White targets) negatively, but when work ethic values were salient, high ambivalence meant for positive evaluations of the White workers. Because this study used a between-subjects design, these effects cannot be attributed to subjects' directly countering a positive evaluation of a Black target with negative evaluations of a White. Nonetheless, there may be some link between ambivalence toward Blacks and attitudes toward Whites. Perhaps the most logical associations are that pro-Black subjects are less pro-White than most Whites tend to be, and anti-Black subjects are particularly pro-White in their attitudes. If this is true, the presumed salience of pro-Black attitudes under egalitarian prime conditions may also prompt relatively negative opinions of Whites; when work ethic values are primed, however, anti-Black and/or pro-White affect may in-

---

[9]More recently, Griffin has suggested an alternative method for computing ambivalence scores that avoids some of the conceptual flaws of the Katz and Hass (1988) "product" computation (see Thompson, Zanna, & Griffin, 1995). When we used that formula in our data set ([pro-Black–anti-Black]/2—|pro-Black–anti-Black|), the produced correlations were very comparable to those reported in Table 6, with one exception: the correlation between ambivalence and social distance for the dependable Black target was −.03 (compared to .36 for the Katz & Hass method).

crease in salience, and make for increased positivity toward value-supporting Whites.

Further work is necessary to gain better insight into the conditions that "activate" or limit the effects of attitudinal ambivalence (see Gibbons et al., 1980). Furthermore, the association between attitudes toward Blacks and attitudes toward Whites is worthy of further exploration: Do anti-Black and pro-White attitudes co-occur, or are these constructs independent? In general, we suggest that ambivalence researchers should continue to include both Black and White targets in their studies so that the conditions and limits of ambivalence effects can be better explicated.

AVERSIVE RACISM

Like symbolic and modern racism theorists, Gaertner and Dovidio (1986) distinguish between two forms of racism. Dominative racists (or Sears,' Kinder's, and McConahay's "old-fashioned racists") display a traditional pattern of anti-Black antipathy—the blatant expression of racial hatred and hostility. Such dominative racists are relatively rare today; Dovidio and Gaertner (1991) estimate that about 20% of White Americans may be characterized as dominative racists. The other 80%, however, are not free from negative feelings and beliefs about Black Americans. Gaertner and Dovidio suggest that given the historically racist American culture, and given human cognitive mechanisms for processing categorical information, racist beliefs and feelings among White Americans are the rule; most Whites have internalized the negative cultural treatment of and beliefs about African Americans (see also Devine, 1989). However, what distinguishes this group of Whites from dominative racists is their endorsement of strong egalitarian values as an important component of their self-concepts. These individuals, who are termed aversive racists, " . . . sympathize with Blacks as the victims of past injustice, support public policies that, in principle, promote racial equality and ameliorate the consequences of racism, identify more generally with a liberal political agenda, regard themselves as non-prejudiced and non-discriminatory, but almost unavoidably, possess negative feelings and beliefs about blacks" (Gaertner & Dovidio, 1986, p. 62).

Because aversive racists have strong egalitarian self-concepts, the negative feelings and beliefs they have about African Americans create conflict. This "ambivalence" is presumably dealt with, in most cases, by attempting to force negative thoughts out of awareness; in fact, negative beliefs are often unacknowledged. When a situation arises in which the negative components of racial attitudes are salient, however, the aversive racist experiences negative arousal, which leads to attempts to rectify these feelings and maintain a positive self-image. This may be accomplished by behaving favorably toward Black Americans. That is, in situations in which an egalitarian image is threatened (by the availability of negative racial beliefs), or when clear norms for appropriate behavior are present, the aversive racist may go out of his or her way to appear as nonprejudiced as possible (see Dutton, 1976; Dutton & Lake, 1973). Consistent with this prediction, Gaertner and Dovidio (1986) have found that White liberals equally helped Black and White individuals requesting assistance in a wrong number telephone call, White female undergraduates equally helped Blacks and Whites who were engaging in a difficult problem-solving task, and White undergraduates accepted help more frequently from Black than from White partners who offered them assistance.

However, Gaertner and Dovidio (1986; Dovidio & Gaertner, 1991) also indicate that in situations in which the interracial aspects of an interaction are not made salient, or in which norms for appropriate behavior are ambiguous, this pattern of response would not be expected. More specifically, in situations that offer nonracist explanations or justifications for negative behavior toward Blacks, or in which the egalitarian self-image is not threatened, relatively anti-Black behavior will result. As McConahay (1986) writes, to legitimize a negative reaction to a Black, the situation must be "characterized by racial ambiguity. That is, a context in which there is a plausible, nonprejudiced explanation available for what might be considered prejudiced behavior or intended behavior" (p. 100). In the helping paradigm that characterizes much of Gaertner and Dovidio's research, not helping may be explained by factors other than prejudice—for example, a study participant might think, "if another subject is not working hard, he is not deserving of my help;" "if other bystanders are present in an emergency, I don't need to be the one who offers assistance."

This type of justification was presumably possible in other conditions of the Gaertner and Dovidio (1986) studies described earlier. That is, (a) White liberals were more likely to hang up prematurely on Black callers than on White callers (hanging up is a legitimate, non-race relevant reaction to a wrong number caller), (b) Blacks who put little effort into a task and then asked for assistance were less likely to be helped than Whites who did the same (not helping is legitimate when the target does not try), and (c) White students were less likely to solicit help from a Black than a White partner (not requesting help is always legitimate, it need not be due to an attempt to avoid subordinate status to a Black).

In sum, the normative context determines whether or not aversive racists will show evidence of their anti-Black feelings and beliefs. When norms indicating appropriate behavior are clear, or when the egalitarian self-image is in danger of being tarnished, positive behavior will result; when there is a lack of normative structure defining appropriate behavior, aversive racists may be able to treat blacks relatively negatively, but to justify or rationalize that treatment by attributing it to something other than race. These predictions obviously have ties to the ambivalence–amplification perspective in their emphasis on overly positive and negative behavior toward Blacks. However, Gaertner and Dovidio's conceptualization of ambivalence is slightly different from that of Katz and Hass (the former posit no genuine pro-Black affect, but rather ambivalence between egalitarian values and negative beliefs), and the aversive racism perspective is unique in its emphasis on the normative context as it determines the form and direction of interracial behavior.

Aversive Racism and the Manipulation of Egalitarian Value Salience

Although Gaertner and Dovidio (1986) have demonstrated that normative contexts affect the extent to which racial bias is or is not demonstrated, there is no direct evidence that threats to an egalitarian self-image are responsible for such effects. That is, in none of their studies have these researchers explicitly manipulated the extent to which egalitarian values are salient or a subject's egalitarian self-image is threatened. The race study described earlier provided us with an opportunity to examine the effects of an egalitarian value prime on liberal and conservative respondents' reactions to Black and White employees. By definition, liberals are the most likely group to be characterized as aversive racists (see also Olson & Zanna, 1993); therefore, manipulated salience of egalitarian concerns should be particularly likely to motivate positive responding to Black relative to White targets.

We divided our sample into conservative ($n = 58$) and liberal respondents ($n = 68$) based on their standing on a measure of political orientation (a two-item index involving liberal-conservative and Democrat-Republican dimensions). In an analysis of social distance ratings using a political orientation (conservative/liberal) × prime (egalitarian or PWE) × race of employee (Black or White) × value violation (dependable or lazy worker) design, we were particularly interested in the significant political orientation × prime × race interaction, $F(1,122) = 7.12, p < .01$. To better interpret this finding, we calculated prime × race × value violation ANOVAs separately for liberals and conservatives.

Both liberals and conservatives were more negative toward value violators than nonviolators, and both tended to rate Black employees more positively than White employees. However, it was only among liberal subjects that the priming manipulation had any effect: the predicted race × prime interaction was significant, $F(1,65) = 4.63, p < .05$. When subjects were primed to think of work ethic values, there was no difference in social distance toward Black ($M = 3.84$) and White ($M = 3.59$) employees. But when primed to think of egalitarian values, which are critical to the aversive racism perspective, liberals evaluated the Black target ($M = 2.77$) more positively (with less distance) than the White target ($M = 4.11$). This interaction was not significant for conservative subjects ($F < .10$), suggesting that egalitarian values were not sensitizing these subjects to race (for conservatives given the egalitarian prime, Blacks and Whites were rated comparably, $Ms = 3.61$ and 4.41, respectively; this differs significantly from the Black-White difference among liberals who received the egalitarian prime, $p < .01$). We observed a similar pattern of effects on subjects' recommendation to fire the employee (i.e., under egalitarian prime conditions, liberals but not conservatives had a lower probability of firing the Black, $M = .26$, than the White employee, $M = .50$; comparable means for conservatives were .47 and .56).

In general, these data provide more direct support for Gaertner and Dovidio's (1986) contention that egalitarian values are critical to White liberals' responses to Black versus White targets (Olson & Zanna, 1993). Being primed to think about egalitarian concerns increased the likelihood of positive responding to Black relative to White employees. When individualistic/work ethic values were primed, liberals were apparently less sensitized to the issue of race, or to how racist they might appear to others. The next step toward testing the aversive racism model might be to not merely lead subjects to think about egalitarian values, but rather to directly threaten their egalitarian or humanitarian self-images. The large literature on cognitive dissonance and self-affirmation theories might provide helpful guidance toward this end.

TOWARD A GENERAL THEORY OF PREJUDICE

Each of the theories of racism we've examined in this chapter involve some form of a "two factor" model of prejudice; in each case, one factor tends to promote prejudice, the other to suppress it. Factors that promote racism include anti-Black affect (present in all of the models), conventional values toward individualism (symbolic, modern, and ambivalent racism), the perception that Blacks violate important values (symbolic racism, belief congruence), and negative normative or contextual cues, such as a value violating Black target, or a situation that okays the expression of prejudice (most clearly evident in ambivalence and aversive racism). Counteracting these prejudice–promotion factors are variables that put the brakes on racism: pro-Black affect (only present in the ambivalence model), egalitarian and/or humanitarian values (all the models, although only present in recent versions of symbolic racism theory), and positive normative or contextual cues—a value supporting Black target, or a situation in which anti-Black responding can readily be interpreted as prejudiced (ambivalent and aversive racism).

Other contributing factors have been noted as well. For example, political conservatism is consistently correlated with outgroup prejudice (Crandall & Biernat, 1990; Sniderman et al., 1991; Weigel & Howes, 1985), as is an authoritarian personality style (Altemeyer, 1988, 1993; Esses, Haddock, & Zanna, 1993; Haddock et al., 1993; Skitka & Tetlock, 1993; Sniderman & Piazza, 1993). In addition, a pattern of attributing negative outcomes (e.g., poverty, illness, unemployment) to internal, controllable causes may also be tied to antagonistic responses to outgroup members (Skitka & Tetlock, 1993; Weiner, 1993).

Our premise is that this set of factors may account for prejudice toward a variety of outgroups, not just toward Blacks. In five replications using two large samples of University of Kansas undergraduates (Ns = 264 and 621), we measured a number of these factors with regard to prejudice toward three distinct groups—Black Americans, homosexuals, and fat people. Racial prejudice was measured using the Modern Racism scale (McConahay et al., 1981), anti-homosexual prejudice using the HATH (Larsen et al., 1980), and antifat prejudice using the "Dislike" scale of the Anti-Fat Attitudes Questionnaire (Crandall, 1994). As predictors of prejudice, we included measures of Protestant Work Ethic values, humanitarian/egalitarian values (both measured using scales by Katz & Hass, 1988), perceptions that each outgroup violated important values relative to the corresponding ingroup (see description of measurement in Table 7.7), and conservative politics (in 3 of the 5 replications only).

Results of multiple regression analyses predicting prejudice appear in Table 7.7, for the two race replications, two sexual orientation replications, and the single weight replication, respectively. The first set of results involve regressions of prejudice on the two value constructs only—Protestant Ethic and humanitarian values. In each of the five replications, both values significantly predicted prejudice—high PWE values were associated with higher prejudice, and high egalitarian values with lower prejudice levels. In the second set of regressions, our measure of perceived value violation was added to the models. In each case, the effects of values remained significant, but the addition of the perception of value violation appreciably increased the amount of variance explained. The more subjects perceived that outgroups violated/did not support their values relative to ingroups, the more prejudice they reported (see also Byrne & Wong, 1962; Schwartz & Struch, 1989).

For the three replications in which the measure was available, we next added conservative politics to the regression equations. In the prediction of racial and antihomosexual prejudice, the effects of conservative politics were significant, the other predictors retained significance, and the amount of variance explained increased somewhat; conservative politics did not, however, predict anti-fat prejudice above and beyond the other factors.

Finally, we return to a point we raised earlier in the chapter regarding *which* particular values are likely to be implicated in people's prejudicial responses. The data just reported suggest that for prejudice toward Blacks, homosexuals, and fat people, both individualistic and humanistic values are implicated in prejudicial responses. However, other values may be involved to the extent that they are relevant to important stereotypes about the outgroups. For example, along with violating work ethic values, fat people may also be seen as violating aesthetic values; in Rokeach's terminology, they may violate the value individuals place on "a world of beauty." This value is not, however, implicated in stereotypes and perceptions of Blacks or homosexuals. Therefore, valuing a world of beauty should be positively correlated with prejudice toward fat people,

TABLE 7.7
Predictors of Prejudice in Five Undergraduate Samples

Prejudice Index, Replication Number, and N

Model	Model R^2 and Predictors	Modern Racism 1 N = 264	Modern Racism 2 N = 590	HATH 1 N = 263	HATH 2 N = 621	Anti-fat 1 N = 616
Model 1: values only	R^2	.32	.22	.25	.17	.11
	PWE	.32***	.24***	.37***	.24***	.15***
	Hum/egal	-.49***	-.45***	-.36***	-.38***	-.33***
Model 2: values + perception of value violation	R^2	.40	.33	.37	.34	.17
	PWE	.31***	.17***	.30***	.14***	.12**
	Hum/egal	-.42***	-.35***	-.28***	-.30***	-.28***
	Out-in vio	.27***	.35***	.37***	.43***	.25***
Model 3: values, perception of value violation + conservative politics	R^2	--	.36	--	.43	.17
	PWE	--	.13***	--	.09*	.12**
	Hum/egal	--	-.28***	--	-.22***	-.29***
	out-in vio	--	.33***	--	.40***	.24***
	Cons polit	--	.19***	--	.28***	.01

Notes. PWE = Protestant Work Ethic Values, Hum/egal = humanitarian/egalitarian values, Cons polit = conservative politics, Out-in Vio = perceived outgroup minus ingroup value violation. In replications Racism 1 and HATH 1, out-in vio was operationalized as follows: (ingroup support - ingroup violation) - (outgroup support - outgroup violation). In replications Racism 2, HATH 2, and Anti-fat 1, a similar construction was used, but "value support" was substituted with a measure of the extent to which each group was perceived to "live their lives consistently with" important values.
*$p < .05$. **$p < .001$. ***$p < .0001$.

181

but not toward Blacks or homosexuals. This is precisely what we found when we added subjects' endorsement of "a world of beauty" from the Rokeach terminal values scale to the Model 3 regression equations described in Table 7.7 (this measure was not included in replications 1 and 3). Support for a world of beauty was nonsignificantly related to racism (beta = .04) and the HATH (beta = .01, $ps > .30$), but *was* positively associated with anti-fat prejudice (beta=.08, $p <$ .05), above and beyond the effects of the other Model 3 predictors.

What we have not included in the regression models just described are situational factors (e.g., priming, normative context) that also contribute to the expression of prejudice and that figure prominently in the theory of aversive racism. Such situational factors may be more relevant to antagonism expressed toward individual members of outgroups, rather than to outgroups as a whole. For example, the experimental studies described earlier in this chapter suggest that the priming of relevant values (humanitarian and PWE values in the race study, family values in the sexual orientation study) may have increased the salience of value violation; that is, subjects were more negative toward value violators when those values had been situationally primed.

CONCLUDING COMMENTS

In this chapter, we have attempted to provide the reader with an overview of several current theories of racism, each of which emphasizes the relevance of values to understanding prejudice. Although the theories differ on a number of points and in their focus of attention, they are similar in that they each suggest that important American values contribute to the expression of prejudice—in either a facilitating (PWE values) or inhibiting (humanitarian/egalitarian values) manner. We have also described some evidence from our laboratory suggesting the need for revision of several points in these theories. For example, symbolic and modern racism theories suggests that Whites perceive Blacks as violating their cherished values. However, our data indicate not that White subjects perceive Blacks as more likely to violate their values than Whites, but that they see Blacks as less likely to *support* their values than Whites. This is perhaps a subtle point, but its implication is that prejudice may be based on ingroup favoritism rather than outgroup negativity (see Brewer, 1979). The theory of ambivalent racism makes predictions regarding the association between individual differences in ambivalence and extremitization of outgroup ratings. Our data suggest that the predicted pattern of judgment—ambivalence positively correlated with evaluations of favorable Black targets and negatively correlated with evaluations of unfavorable Black targets—may be particularly likely to occur under conditions in which egalitarian values are made salient.

Our main purpose in this chapter, however, was to use the theories of racism to develop a broader model of outgroup prejudice. We suggest that many of the premises of racism theories can be used to understand antagonism toward a variety of outgroups—homosexuals, fat people, and so forth—that raise concerns about important personal values. In our data, humanitarian/egalitarian values were consistently associated with reduced levels of prejudice toward Blacks, homosexuals, and fat people, whereas PWE values were associated with increased prejudice toward each of these groups. Furthermore, the perception that an outgroup violates one's values relative to the ingroup contributed to prejudice as well. We also reported some suggestive evidence that the values relevant to prejudice may be those implicated in stereotypes of particular outgroups.

To this point, we have not described the recent work of Esses et al. (1993; see also Haddock et al., 1993), that offers both methodological and theoretical insight into the concept of value violation as we have described it here. These researchers have developed a method for assessing what they call "symbolic beliefs." In their instrument, subjects are asked to generate a list of "values, customs, and traditions" that they believe are "blocked or facilitated by" a target group (p. 149). In two studies, for example "blocking of family" was one of the three most often mentioned "symbolic beliefs" regarding homosexuals (Haddock et al., 1993). Subjects are then asked to indicate the extent to which each value is blocked or facilitated (from − − to + +), and the percentage of group members who do so. The resulting symbolic belief score is based on the mean probability × valence estimate. This symbolic belief measure appears to be an important predictor of anti-outgroup attitudes (including attitudes toward groups such as Pakistanis, homosexuals, and French Canadians), but only among individuals who score high in Right Wing Authoritarianism. This work suggests that our general model of outgroup prejudice as depicted in Table 7.7 could perhaps be improved by additionally considering the effects of an authoritarian personality style on outgroup judgment.

The present work raises a number of additional questions that could profitably be addressed in future research. For example, how is it that egalitarian values "put the brakes" on prejudice? Do such values constitute a chronic, personal norm against prejudice? Do they exemplify an active method for breaking the prejudice habit (Devine, 1989; Devine & Monteith, 1993; Monteith, Devine, & Zuwerink, 1993)? Does the activation of egalitarian values lead people to suppress their outgroup stereotypes? At another level, one might examine more directly the relationship between stereotypes of outgroups and the values implicated in those beliefs. For example, to what extent can our manipulations of value violation in the race and sexual orientation studies be construed as manipulations of stereotype consistency? A lazy Black worker violates PWE values, but he is also behaving consistently with negative stereotypes of Blacks. An amoral homosexual parent violates family values, but also presents an image consistent with homosexual stereotypes. Furthermore, to what extent are these merely manipulations of general positivity or negativity of targets?

Finally, we ask how broadly applicable the values approach to outgroup prejudice might be. We have suggested that any outgroup that is perceived as violating/nonsupporting of important values will be affected by both individual and situational variations in that value's salience. Does virtually every social outgroup fit this description—that is, are all outgroups perceived as threats or challenges to one or more important values? Our guess is that the only outgroups that might be immune are our reference groups—those groups toward which we orient ourselves but of which we are not members. Even positive outgroups may occasionally be seen as living their lives in violation of values. For example, the wealthy or intellectually gifted may act contrary to the values for humility and simple living. Yet certainly some outgroups are seen as more discrepant from important values than others, and some outgroups may be seen as nonsupportive of many values rather than one. Prejudice may derive, in part, from the perception that a group fails to support one's values, and the most consensually derogated outgroups are likely to be widely perceived as violating many important values.

ACKNOWLEDGMENTS

Much of the research reported in this chapter was supported by grants from the University of Kansas Office of Research Support, and the National Institutes for Mental Health (grant R29MH48844) to the first author. We are grateful to the editors and to John Lydon for their helpful comments on an earlier version of this paper.

REFERENCES

Allon, N. (1982). The stigma of overweight in everyday life. In B. Wolman (Ed.), *Psychological aspects of obesity: A handbook*. New York: Van Nostrand Reinhold.

Altemeyer, B. (1988). *Enemies of freedom: Understanding right-wing authoritarianism*. San Francisco: Jossey-Bass.

Altemeyer, B. (1993). Reducing prejudice in right-wing authoritarians. In M. P. Zanna & J. M. Olson (Eds.), *The psychology of prejudice: The Ontario symposium Vol. 7* (pp. 131–148). Hillsdale, NJ: Lawrence Erlbaum Associates.

Biernat, M., & Vescio, T. K. (1993). Categorization and stereotyping: Effects of group context on memory and social judgment. *Journal of Experimental Social Psychology, 29*, 166–202.

Biernat, M., Vescio, T. K., & Theno, S. A. (1996). *Violating American values: A value congruence approach to understanding outgroup prejudice*. Manuscript submitted for publication.

Brewer, M. B. (1979). In-group bias in the minimal intergroup situation: A cognitive-motivational analysis. *Psychological Bulletin, 86*, 307–324.

Byrne, D., Clore, G. L., & Smeaton, G. (1986). The attraction hypothesis: Do similar attitudes affect anything? *Journal of Personality and Social Psychology, 51*, 1167–1170.

Byrne, D., & Wong, T. J. (1962). Racial prejudice, interpersonal attraction, and assumed dissimilarity of attitudes. *Journal of Abnormal and Social Psychology, 65*, 246–253.

Campbell, A. (1971). *White attitudes toward black people.* Ann Arbor, MI: Institute for Social Research.

Carver, C. S., Glass, D. C., & Katz, I. (1978). Favorable evaluations of Blacks and the handicapped: Positive prejudice, unconscious denial, or social desirability? *Journal of Applied Social Psychology, 8,* 97–106.

Carver, C. S., Glass, D. C., Snyder, M. L., & Katz, I. (1977). Favorable evaluations of stigmatized others. *Personality and Social Psychology Bulletin, 3,* 232–235.

Crandall, C. S. (1991). Multiple stigma and AIDS: Illness stigma and attitudes toward homosexuals and IV drug users in AIDS-related stigmatization. *Journal of Community and Applied Social Psychology, 1,* 165–172.

Crandall, C. S. (1994). Prejudice against fat people: Ideology and self-interest. *Journal of Personality and Social Psychology, 66,* 882–894.

Crandall, C. S., & Biernat, M. (1990). The ideology of anti-fat attitudes. *Journal of Applied Social Psychology, 20,* 227–243.

Crosby, F., Bromley, S., & Saxe (1980). Recent unobtrusive studies of black and white discrimination and prejudice. *Psychological Bulletin, 87,* 546–563.

Devine, P. G. (1989). Stereotypes and prejudice: Their automatic and controlled components. *Journal of Personality and Social Psychology, 56,* 5–18.

Devine, P. G., & Monteith, M. J. (1993). The role of discrepancy-associated affect in prejudice reduction. In D. M. Mackie & D. L. Hamilton (Eds.), *Affect, cognition, and stereotyping: Interactive processes in group perception* (pp. 317–344). New York: Academic Press.

Dovidio, J. F., & Gaertner, S. L. (1991). Changes in the expression and assessment of racial prejudice. In H. J. Knopke, R. J. Norrell, & R. W. Rogers (Eds.), *Opening doors: Perspectives on race relations in contemporary America* (pp. 119–148). Tuscaloosa: University of Alabama Press.

Dovidio, J. F., & Gaertner, S. L. (1993). Stereotypes and evaluative bias. In D. M. Mackie & D. L. Hamilton (Eds.), *Affect, cognition, and stereotyping: Interactive processes in group perception* (pp. 167–193). New York: Academic Press.

Dutton, D. G. (1976). Tokenism, reverse discrimination, and egalitarianism in interracial behavior. *Journal of Social Issues, 32,* 93–107.

Dutton, D. G., & Lake, R. A. (1973). Threat of own prejudice and reverse discrimination in interracial situations. *Journal of Personality and Social Psychology, 28,* 94–100.

Eagly, A. H., & Chaiken, S. (1993). *The psychology of attitudes.* New York: Harcourt Brace Jovanovich.

Esses, V. M., Haddock, G., & Zanna, M. P. (1993). Values, stereotypes, and emotions as determinants of intergroup attitudes. In D. M. Mackie & D. L. Hamilton (Eds.), *Affect, cognition, and stereotyping: Interactive processes in group perception* (pp. 137–166). New York: Academic Press.

Feldman, S. (1983). Economic self-interest and mass belief systems. *American Journal of Political Science, 26,* 446–466.

Gaertner, S. L., & Dovidio, J. (1986). The aversive form of racism. In J. Dovidio & S. L. Gaertner (Eds.), *Prejudice, discrimination, and racism* (pp. 61–89). New York: Academic Press.

Gaertner, S. L., & McLaughlin, J. P. (1983). Racial stereotypes: Associations and ascriptions of positive and negative characteristics. *Social Psychology Quarterly, 46,* 23–30.

Gergen, K. J., & Jones, E. E. (1963). Mental illness, predictability, and affective consequences as stimulus factors in person perception. *Journal of Abnormal and Social Psychology, 67,* 95–105.

Gibbons, F. X., Stephan, W. G., Stephenson, B., & Petty, C. R. (1980). Reactions to stigmatized others: Response amplification vs sympathy. *Journal of Experimental Social Psychology, 16,* 591–605.

Greeley, A. M., & Sheatsley, P. B. (1971). Attitudes toward racial integration. *Scientific American, 225,* 13–19.

Haddock, G., Zanna, M. P., & Esses, V. M. (1993). Assessing the structure of prejudicial attitudes:

The case of attitudes toward homosexuals. *Journal of Personality and Social Psychology, 65*, 1105–1118.

Hass, R. G., Katz, I., Rizzo, N., Bailey, J., & Eisenstadt, D. (1991). Cross-racial appraisal as related to attitude ambivalence and cognitive complexity. *Personality and Social Psychology Bulletin, 17*, 83–92.

Hass, R. G., Katz, I., Rizzo, N., Bailey, J., & Moore, L. (1992). When racial ambivalence evokes negative affect, using a disguised measure of mood. *Personality and Social Psychology Bulletin, 18*, 786–797.

Higgins, E. T., & King, G. (1981). Accessibility of social constructs: Information-processing consequences of individual and contextual variability. In N. Cantor & J. Kihlstrom (Eds.), *Personality, cognition, and social interaction* (pp. 69–121). Hillsdale, NJ: Lawrence Erlbaum Associates.

Hyland, M. (1974). The anticipated belief difference theory of prejudice: Analyses and evaluation. *European Journal of Social Psychology, 4*, 179–200.

Insko, C. A., Nacoste, R., & Moe, J. L. (1983). Belief congruence and racial discrimination: Review of the evidence and critical evaluation. *European Journal of Social Psychology, 13*, 153–174.

Jackson, L. A., Sullivan, L. A., & Hodge, C. (1993). Stereotype effects on attributions, predictions, and evaluations: No two social judgments are quite alike. *Journal of Personality and Social Psychology, 65*, 69–84.

Jackson, L. M., & Burris, C. T. (1995). Of Shibboleths and Samaritans: Religious fundamentalism as a moderator of the similarity-helping relation. Manuscript submitted for publication.

Jussim, L., Coleman, L. M., & Lerch, L. (1987). The nature of stereotypes: A comparison and integration of three theories. *Journal of Personality and Social Psychology, 52*, 536–546.

Karlins, M., Coffman, T., & Walters, G. (1969). On the fading of social stereotypes: Studies in three generations of college students. *Journal of Personality and Social Psychology, 3*, 1–16.

Katz, I. (1979). Some thoughts about the stigma notion. *Personality and Social Psychology Bulletin, 5*, 447–460.

Katz, I. (1981). *Stigma: A social psychological analysis.* Hillsdale, NJ: Erlbaum Associates.

Katz, I., Cohen, S., & Glass, D. (1975). Some determinants of cross-racial helping behavior. *Journal of Personality and Social Psychology, 32*, 964–970.

Katz, I., Glass, D. C., & Cohen, S. (1973). Ambivalence, guilt, and the scapegoating of minority group victims. *Journal of Experimental Social Psychology, 9*, 423–436.

Katz, I., Glass, D. C., Lucido, D. J., & Farber, J. (1977). Ambivalence, guilt and the denigration of a physically handicapped victim. *Journal of Personality, 45*, 419–429.

Katz, I., & Hass, R. G. (1988). Racial ambivalence and American value conflict: Correlational and priming studies of dual cognitive structures. *Journal of Personality and Social Psychology, 55*, 893–905.

Katz, I., Wackenhut, J., & Hass, R. G. (1986). Racial ambivalence, value duality, and behavior. In J. Dovidio & S. L. Gaertner (Eds.), *Prejudice, discrimination, and racism* (pp. 35–59). New York: Academic Press.

Kinder, D. R. (1986). The continuing American dilemma: White resistance to racial change 40 years after Myrdal. *Journal of Social Issues, 42*, 151–172.

Kinder, D. R., & Sears, D. O. (1981). Prejudice and politics: Symbolic racism versus racial threats to the good life. *Journal of Personality and Social Psychology, 40*, 414–431.

Kluegel, J. R., & Smith, E. R. (1983). Affirmative action attitudes: Effects of self-interest, racial affect, and stratification beliefs on whites' views. *Social Forces, 61*, 797–824.

Kovel, J. (1970). *White racism: A psychohistory.* New York: Pantheon.

Krulewitz, J. E., & Nash, J. E. (1980). Effects of sex role attitudes and similarity on men's rejection of male homosexuals. *Journal of Personality and Social Psychology, 38*, 67–74.

Larsen, K. S., Reed, M., & Hoffman, S. (1980). Attitudes of heterosexuals toward homosexuality: A Likert-type scale and construct validity. *Journal oj Sex Research, 16*, 245–257.

Linville, P. (1982). The complexity-extremity effect and age-based stereotyping. *Journal of Personality and Social Psychology, 42*, 193–211.

Linville, P. W., & Jones, E. E. (1980). Polarized appraisal of out-group members. *Journal of Personality and Social Psychology, 38*, 689–703.

Lipset, S. M., & Schneider, W. (1978). The Bakke case: How would it be decided at the bar of public opinion. *Public Opinion, 1*, 38–44.

McClendon, M. J. (1985). Racism, rational choices, and white opposition to racial change: A case study of busing. *Public Opinion Quarterly, 49*, 214–233.

McConahay, J. B. (1986). Modern racism, ambivalence, and the modern racism scale. In J. Dovidio & S. L. Gaertner (Eds.), *Prejudice, discrimination, and racism* (pp. 91–125). New York: Academic Press.

McConahay, J. B. (1982). Self-interest versus racial attitudes as correlates of anti-busing attitudes in Louisville: Is it the buses or the blacks? *Journal of Politics, 44*, 692–720.

McConahay, J. B. (1983). Modern racism and modern discrimination: The effects of race, racial attitudes, and context on simulated hiring decisions. *Personality and Social Psychology Bulletin, 9*, 551–558.

McConahay, J. B., Hardee, B. B., & Batts, V. (1981). Has racism declined in America? It depends on who is asking and what is asked. *Journal of Conflict Resolution, 25*, 563–579.

McConahay, J. B., & Hough, J. C., Jr. (1976). Symbolic racism. *Journal of Social Issues, 32*, 23–45.

Mezei, L. (1971). Perceived social pressure as an explanation of shifts in the relative influence of race and belief on prejudice across social interactions. *Journal of Personality and Social Psychology, 19*, 69–81.

Moe, J. L., Nacoste, R.W., & Insko, C. A. (1981). Belief versus race as determinants of discrimination: A study of southern adolescents in 1966 and 1979. *Journal of Personality and Social Psychology, 41*, 1031–1050.

Monteith, M. J., Devine, P. G., & Zuwerink, J. R. (1993). Self-directed versus other-directed affect as a consequence of prejudice-related discrepancies. *Journal of Personality and Social Psychology, 64*, 198–210.

Myrdal, G. (1944). *An American dilemma: The Negro problem and modern democracy.* New York: Harper.

Olson, J. M., & Zanna, M. P. (1993). Attitudes and attitude change. *Annual Review of Psychology, 44*, 117–154.

Precker, J. A. (1953). The automorphic process in the attribution of values. *Journal of Personality, 21*, 356–363.

Rogers, R. W., & Prentice-Dunn, S. (1981). Deindividuation and anger-mediated inter-racial aggression: Unmasking regressive racism. *Journal of Personality and Social Psychology, 41*, 63–73.

Rokeach, M. (1968). A theory of organization and change in value-attitude systems. *Journal of Social Issues, 24*, 13–33.

Rokeach, M. (1973). *The nature of human values.* New York: Free Press.

Rokeach, M., & Mezei, L. (1966). Race and shared belief as factors in social choice. *Science, 151*, 167–172.

Rokeach, M., & Rothman, G. (1965). The principle of belief congruence and the congruity principle as models of cognitive interaction. *Psychological Review, 72*, 128–142.

Rokeach, M., Smith, P. W., & Evans, R. I. (1960). Two kinds of prejudice or one? In M. Rokeach (Ed.), *The open and closed mind* (pp. 132–168). New York: Basic Books.

Rosenbaum, M. E. (1986a). Comment on a proposed two-stage theory of relationship formation: First, repulsion; then, attraction. *Journal of Personality and Social Psychology, 51*, 1171–1172.

Rosenbaum, M. E. (1986b). The repulsion hypothesis: On the nondevelopment of relationships. *Journal of Personality and Social Psychology, 51*, 1156–1166.

Scheier, M. F., Carver, C. S., Schulz, R., Glass, D. C., & Katz, I. (1978). Sympathy, self-consciousness, and reactions to the stigmatized. *Journal of Applied Social Psychology, 8,* 270–282.

Schuman, I., & Harding, J. (1964). Prejudice and the norm of rationality. *Sociometry, 27,* 353–371.

Schuman, H., Steeh, C., & Bobo, L. (1985). *Racist attitudes in America: Trends and interpretations.* Cambridge, MA: Harvard University Press.

Schwartz, S., & Bilsky, W. (1987). Toward a psychological structure of human values. *Journal of Personality and Social Psychology, 53,* 550–562.

Schwartz, S., & Struch, N. (1989). Values, stereotypes, and intergroup antagonism. In D. Bar-Tal, C. F. Graumann, A. W. Kruglanski, & W. Stroebe (Eds.), *Stereotyping and prejudice: Changing conceptions* (pp. 151–168). New York: Springer-Verlag.

Schwartz, S., Struch, N., & Bilsky, W. (1990). Values and intergroup social motives: A study of Israeli and German students. *Social Psychology Quarterly, 53,* 185–198.

Sears, D. O. (1988). Symbolic racism. In P. A. Katz & D. A. Taylor (Eds.), *Eliminating racism: Profiles in controversy.* New York: Plenum Press.

Sears, D. O., & Allen, H. M., Jr. (1984). The trajectory of local desegregation controversies and Whites' opposition to busing. In N. Miller & M. Brewer (Eds.), *Groups in contact: The psychology of desegregation* (pp. 123–151). New York: Academic Press.

Sears, D. O., & McConahay, J. (1973). *The politics of violence: The new urban blacks and the Watts riot.* Boston: Houghton-Mifflin.

Sheatsley, P. B. (1966). White attitudes toward the Negro. *Daedalus, 95,* 217–238.

Sidanius, J., Devereux, E., & Pratto, F. (1992). A comparison of symbolic racism theory and social dominance theory as explanations for racial policy attitudes. *Journal of Social Psychology, 132,* 377–395.

Silverman, B. I. (1974). Consequences, racial discrimination, and the principle of belief congruence. *Journal of Personality and Social Psychology, 29,* 497–508.

Skitka, L. J., & Tetlock, P. E. (1993). Providing public assistance: Cognitive and motivational processes underlying liberal and conservative policy preferences. *Journal of Personality and Social Psychology, 65,* 1205–1223.

Smeaton, G., Byrne, D., & Murnen, S. K. (1989). The repulsion hypothesis revisited: Similarity irrelevance or dissimilarity bias? *Journal of Personality and Social Psychology, 56,* 54–59.

Smith, C. R., Williams, L., & Willis, R. H. (1967). Race, sex, and belief as determinants of friendship acceptance. *Journal of Personality and Social Psychology, 5,* 127–137.

Sniderman, P. M., & Hagen, M. (1985). *Race and inequality.* New York: Chatham House.

Sniderman, P. M., Hagen, M., Tetlock, P. E., & Brady, H. (1986). Reasoning chains: Causal models of racial policy reasoning. *British Journal of Political Science, 16,* 405–430.

Sniderman, P. M., & Piazza, T. (1993). *The scar of race.* Cambridge, MA: The Belknap Press of Harvard University Press.

Sniderman, P. M., Piazza, T., Tetlock, P. E., & Kendrick, A. (1991). The new racism. *American Journal of Political Science, 35,* 423–447.

Sniderman, P. M., & Tetlock, P. E. (1986a). Symbolic racism: Problems of political motive attribution. *Journal of Social Issues, 42,* 129–150.

Sniderman, P. M., & Tetlock, P. E. (1986b). Reflections on American racism. *Journal of Social Issues, 42,* 173–188.

Stein, D. D., Hardyck, J. A., & Smith, M. B. (1965). Race and belief: An open and shut case, *Journal of Personality and Social Psychology, 1,* 281–289.

Struch, N., & Schwartz, S. H. (1989). Intergroup aggression: Its predictors and distinctness from ingroup bias. *Journal of Personality and Social Psychology, 56,* 364–373.

Taylor, D. G., Sheatsley, P. B., & Greeley, A. M. (1978). Attitudes toward racial integration. *Scientific American, 238,* 42–49.

Thompson, M., Zanna, M. P., & Griffin, D. W. (1995). Let's not be indifferent about (attitudinal) ambivalence. In R. E. Petty & J. A. Krosnick (Eds.), *Attitude strength: Antecedents and consequences.* Mahwah, NJ: Lawrence Erlbaum Associates.

Triandis, H. C. (1961). A note on Rokeach's theory of prejudice. *Journal of Abnormal and Social Psychology, 62,* 184–186.

Triandis, H. C., & Davis, E. (1965). Race and belief as determinants of behavioral intentions. *Journal of Personality and Social Psychology, 2,* 715–725.

Vescio, T. K., Biernat, M., & Theno, S. A. (1996). *Anti-homosexual attitudes and family values.* Unpublished manuscript, University of Kansas.

Weigel, R. H., & Howes, P. W. (1985). Conceptions of racial prejudice: Symbolic racism reconsidered. *Journal of Social Issues, 41,* 117–138.

Weiner, B. (1993). On sin versus sickness: A theory of perceived responsibility and social motivation. *American Psychologist, 48,* 957–965.

Woodmansee, J. J., & Cook, S. W. (1967). Dimensions of verbal racial attitudes: Their identification and measurement. *Journal of Personality and Social Psychology, 7,* 240–250.

Zanna, M. P., & Rempel, J. K. (1988). Attitudes: A new look at an old concept. In D. Bar-Tal & A. W. Kruglanski (Eds.), *The social psychology of knowledge* (pp. 315–334). New York: Cambridge University Press.

8 Toward a Theory of Commitment

John Lydon
McGill University

One day as a graduate student I entered the office of a faculty member known for his paternalistic style. As I entered the room, he called out, "So are you going to marry the girl or not?" After taking a moment or two to recover from the shock of the question, I responded that I did not know but that I was now making progress. I explained that I formerly thought that I could go home in the evening and just think long and hard and "figure out" what to do. I finally realized that this would be a decision of the heart (or if you prefer—the gut) and not just a decision of the head.

Ironically, at the time, I was trying to do a dissertation on the psychology of commitment. I had been reading drafts of chapters from the Brickman commitment book (1987) and as I related to the faculty member, I could now begin to understand what Brickman meant when he characterized commitment as a "nonrational" decision. This was not to say that commitment is necessarily irrational but that it somehow goes beyond rationality. The faculty member retorted, "If you want to talk about non-rational decisions, come back and see me when you're thinking of having kids. Now that is a non-rational decision! How many Saturday evening dinners, Porsches, trips to Europe is a child worth?" he asked rhetorically.

So here I am, married, with three kids, writing a chapter about commitment. Although I will make reference to many who have theorized and collected data about commitment, I will not present a comprehensive and detailed review of the literature. Instead I would like to present some ideas about an emergent theory of commitment that draws on my commitment forbearers, most especially Brickman. I will try to support these ideas not just with the previously published data I have on commitment, but also by presenting some new data on commitments that strike at the core of people's lives—romantic relationships and pregnancy decisions. These studies should refresh our appreciation of how commitments may influence people's lives.

What Do We Mean By Commitment

From a prototype perspective, Fehr (1988) found that lay conceptions of commitment in a free recall listing refer most frequently to perseverance, responsibility, living up to one's word, and devotion. Moreover, examining the centrality (or prototypicality) of commitment features revealed that loyalty, responsibility, living up to your word, faithfulness, trust, and being there for the other in good and bad times were most prototypical of subjects' conceptions of commitment.

In social psychology, possibly the broadest and most widely known definition of commitment is the one offered by Kiesler and Sakumura (1966), "the pledging or binding of an individual to behavioral acts" (p. 349). In the organizational behavior literature a variety of definitions of commitment have been offered but Mathieu and Zajac (1990) suggest that a "common theme" among them is that commitment is "a bond or linking of the individual to the organization" (p. 171).

From a sociological perspective, Kanter (1972) defined commitment as "the attachment of the self to the requirements of social relations that are seen as self-expressive . . . a person is committed to the extent that he sees it as expressing or fulfilling some fundamental part of himself" (p. 66). In the close relationships literature, Rusbult (1983) defined commitment as "the tendency to maintain a relationship and to feel psychologically 'attached' to it" (p. 102). And in the stress and coping literature, Kobasa (1982) defined commitment as "the ability to believe in the truth, importance, and interest value of what one is doing, and the willingness to exercise influence or control in the personal and social situations in which one is involved" (p. 708).

From these I gleaned a working definition of commitment as an internal psychological state in which a person feels tied to or connected to someone or something. But it may be apparent in reviewing some of these descriptions and definitions of commitment that commitment might be better conceptualized as a broad theoretical construct rather than a specific variable. An understanding of what researchers mean by commitment then requires one to examine some of the variables that have been related to commitment. For example, Kiesler (1971) identified the publicness of one's attitude as an antecedent of behavioral commitment. This is consistent with relationship phenomena such as engagements and marriage ceremonies. Rusbult (e.g., 1983), in studying close relationships, has emphasized the notion of investments or "sunken costs" (Becker, 1960) in creating feelings of commitment independent of relationship satisfaction. Staw (1976) found that personal responsibility for incurring costs increases commitment.

Our approach has been based on a relationship between commitment and the self. As seen in Fig. 8.1, we conceptualize core beliefs, values, and identities as specific indicators of a latent variable, the self.[1] People then feel especially committed to goals, projects and life tasks[2] that express their core beliefs, values, and identities.

By core beliefs, we refer to those overarching assumptive beliefs (Janoff-Bulman, 1989; Parkes, 1975) that I may have about myself and my world such as "I am a good person" (Steele, 1988) and "people get what they deserve" (Lerner, 1980). The literature suggests that people are highly motivated to reaffirm these beliefs when they are threatened (e.g., Lerner & Simmons, 1966; Steele & Liu, 1983). We would expect then that a person would be especially committed to a goal or project that maintains and expresses core, overarching, assumptive beliefs.

By values we refer to those "shared prescriptive or proscriptive beliefs about ideal modes of behavior and end-states of existence that are activated by, yet transcend object and situation" (Rokeach, 1980, p. 262; see also Schwartz, 1992). Whereas an assumptive belief may be characterized as more of a premise about oneself and one's world, values act as standards for the self and the world. A person may assess and judge a goal or project in terms of the importance and relevance it has for one's values. Thus, two people may differ in how highly they value freedom (or the sanctity of life) and as a result they may react differently to an unplanned pregnancy. Moreover, two people who value freedom (or sanctity of life) highly may differ in how relevant they believe the value is to the given situation (Seligman, this volume) and as a result they may react differently to the unplanned pregnancy. We would expect then that a person would feel most committed to goals and projects that are seen as relevant to important personal values.

Identities (Thoits, 1982; 1986) refer to specific roles or self-conceptions. Identities may vary in personal importance and centrality. Moreover, a specific life event may have different implications for different identities. A woman suing for divorce may see negative implications for an identity as a partner and a lover but she may see positive implications for an identity as an independent, autonomous person. From a commitment perspective, we suggest that a person is

---

[1]One may wonder which self I am referring to given that self theorists often refer to multiple selves. Even though one might choose to conceptualize the self as multiple selves, not all selves are equal. For example, William James of multiple-self fame was not an ethical relativist. James (1890/1950) stated: "So the seeker of his truest, strongest, deepest self must review the list carefully, and pick out the one on which to stake his salvation . . . the fortunes of this self are real. Its failures are real failures, its triumphs real triumphs, carrying shame and gladness with them" (p. 310).

[2]In recent years, personal goal systems have been conceptualized and labeled in a number of different ways (e.g., current concerns, personal projects, personal striving, life tasks). We use these terms for their general heuristic value (and rather interchangeably) but the reader interested in the nuances of these terms is referred to Pervin (1989) and Buss and Cantor (1989).

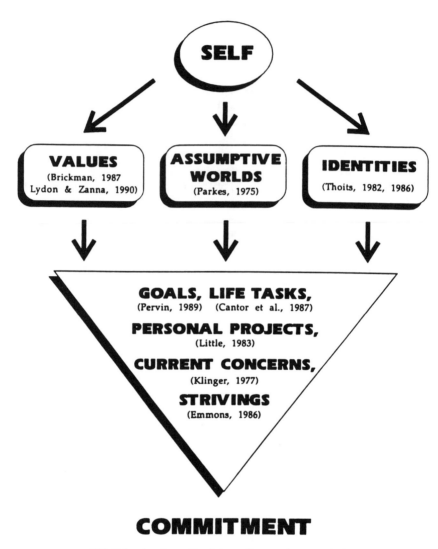

FIG. 8.1.   A schematic of the self-commitment relation.

committed to a goal or project to the extent that it has positive more than negative implications for important roles and identities.

Related to our thinking about identities is the notion of self-complexity (Linville, 1987). This refers to the interdependence of one's self-conceptions. Thus, two people may have a similar number of identities but they may differ in how interrelated the identities are. The structural configuration of one's identities may influence the relationship between an identity and commitment. So, for example, two boys may share a dislike of hockey but for one an identity as a hockey player is tied to important identities of son, brother, friend, and class leader. As a result, he may feel relatively more committed to hockey than the other boy for whom a hockey identity is not associated with other important identities.

In developing the link between the self and commitment, we drew on Steele's (1988) theory of self-affirmation as a framework (cf. Brickman, 1987; Burke & Reitzes, 1991). Steele proposed that we conceive of the self as a system that strives to explain one's own behavior and the behavior of others in a way that is "adaptively and morally adequate" (p. 266). Whenever events threaten the system (e.g., a person receives an insult) then a process of self-affirmation ensues whereby an individual seeks out other ways to reaffirm his or her overall sense that things are right in the world. For example, using the forced-choice paradigm, Steele and Liu (1983) replicated the standard dissonance effect: Subjects writing counterattitudinal essays under high choice shifted their attitudes about tuition increases as a way to reduce the dissonance between holding a certain attitude and yet writing an essay opposite to the attitude. However, according to self-affirmation theory, the concern that needed to be addressed was not the specific inconsistency between attitudes and behavior but the threat to one's sense of being a good, honest, reliable person. Importantly then, subjects did not shift their attitudes when given the opportunity to self-affirm in some other way—by completing a survey about personally important values. If the powerful effects of dissonance could be attributed, at least in part, to self-affirmation processes then what effect might self-affirmation have on goals or projects consonant with the self?

Whereas Steele and others (e.g., Gollwitzer & Wicklund, 1985; Steele, Spencer, & Lynch, 1993; Tesser & Cornell, 1991) have emphasized the ego-defensive function of self-affirmation processes, a commitment approach highlights the expressive as well as the defensive functions of self-affirmation (Brickman, 1987). Although threats to the self may heighten self-affirmation processes, we also expect that people seek out opportunities to express their true selves and then persist in the face of subsequent adversity (Brunstein, 1993). Moreover, when the self-threatening event involves a significant life event (e.g., loss of a loved one) in contrast to the self-threatening events of the laboratory, we expect that the fluidity of self-affirmation processes (i.e., affirming a feature of the self unrelated to the specific threat) will be tested more strongly (Taylor, 1983).

The notion of a self *system* and concerns about the *general* integrity of the self are a reminder that core beliefs, values, and identities are not completely independent of each other. In one respect, this may appear to lessen the importance of values (the theme of this volume) for the study of commitment. On the contrary, Rokeach (1980) in fact recognized that values act as an important interface between the self and behavior. Values then are a significant feature of self-affirmation processes that engender meaning which in turn promotes commitment.

In sum then, core beliefs, values, and identities define in an important way who we are. They serve as a bridge from the self to life experiences by informing us about the meaning that life experiences have for the self. Meaning may fulfill epistemic concerns about life experiences, but meaning then seeks expression in a "motivational process" of commitment that energizes the person to pursue a goal in the face of adversity (Novacek & Lazarus, 1990). Thus, we are most committed to goals that affirm who we are—that give meaning to our lives.

Testing Our Notion of Commitment

The question then is how do we test the notion that we are especially committed to goals and projects that express core beliefs, values, and identities. The easiest and most straightforward method may be to collect data on self-reported commitment—give people a few items to rate about their commitment. My concern with this is that I am not sure how reliable self-reports of commitment are. Just imagine having a sample of newlyweds rate their commitment on a 7-point scale. We may not be surprised if the mean is 6.7 with little variance. In order to strengthen a self-report measure of commitment, I reasoned that self-reported commitment under adversity would be a more reliable indicant of commitment than self-reported commitment under more favorable conditions because it would be tested (see also Brickman, 1987; Kelley, 1983). The notion then is that under adversity one will report relatively greater commitment to projects and goals expressive of the self than to those not expressive of the self.

The strategy for the first study was to test the hypothesis using the Personal Projects Analysis (PPA) developed by Brian Little (1983). A personal project is defined by Little as "a set of interrelated acts extending over time, which is intended to maintain or attain a state of affairs foreseen by the individual" (p. 276). By using Little's procedure, subjects respond to questions about projects that are particularly meaningful and relevant to them. Projects are as varied as "trying to clarify my religious beliefs" to "redecorating my room" to "losing ten pounds."

A computerized version of the PPA was presented via a network of PCs to small groups of subjects seated at separate work stations—42 subjects in total. They were prompted to list 8 personal projects of which the computer randomly selected 2 projects. In this study, one item from the PPA assessing value relevance served as a particular indicator of the degree to which the projects affirmed the self. Subjects were asked to rate the extent to which each project was "consistent with the values which guide your life." To assess adversity, subjects were asked to rate both how stressful and how difficult each project was. Finally, supposedly after the PPA was completed, subjects were asked to test out a questionnaire for an ostensible future study on personal projects. Embedded within the questionnaire were three items assessing commitment. Subjects were asked the face valid item about the extent to which they were committed to a project. They were also asked how attached they were to the project and how obligated they felt to the project.

Not surprisingly, stress and difficulty were correlated, $r(40) = .48$, and were averaged for a measure of adversity. Attachment and obligation correlated with commitment, $rs = .58$ and $.61$, respectively. Moreover, attachment and obligation were related, $r = .33$, and the three items were internally consistent, alpha $= .75$. As a result, the three items were averaged as a measure of commitment.

The strategy then was to enter the measures of values and adversity into a hierarchical regression analysis and see if the product of the two (the interaction term) could account for significant variance above and beyond the simple main effects. The interaction term would test the notion that values predict commitment in the face of adversity.

In the first step of the regression, value relevance and adversity accounted for 19.5% of the variance in commitment with both variables significantly related to commitment, $ps < .05$. Importantly though, in the second step of the regression, the product of values by adversity accounted for an additional 9.2% of the variance, $p < .05$. As seen in Fig. 8.2, under low adversity (one standard deviation below the mean for adversity), values did not discriminate between self-reports of commitment but under high adversity values did discriminate between self-reports of adversity. Moreover, this pattern was obtained for each of the three commitment items when analyzed separately.

In addition, we examined whether the interaction of values by adversity could account for significant variance above and beyond another explanatory model of commitment (Rusbult's Investment Model). This is a model derived from interdependence theory (Kelley & Thibaut, 1978) that emphasizes satisfaction (rewards minus costs) and investments (sunken costs—things that one puts into a relationship that are lost if the relationship ends) as predictors of commitment. In

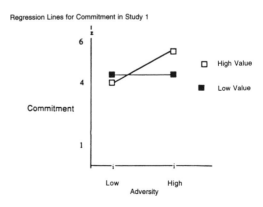

FIG. 8.2. Commitment to personal projects: A value by adversity interaction.
Note. Expected values are based on the equation using the b weights for values, adversity, and values by adversity. From J. Lydon and M. Zanna, 1990, *Journal of Personality and Social Psychology, 58,* pp. 1040–1047. Copyright 1990 by the American Psychological Association. Reprinted with permission.

this model, commitment tends to be a rational decision based on a cost-benefit analysis of how much one depends upon a relationship or job. Measures of the rewards, costs, and investment in the personal projects were entered first and accounted for significant variance in commitment, consistent with Rusbult's findings. In the second step, the simple effects of values and adversity were entered and did not account for additional variance. However, in the third step, the interaction of values and adversity accounted for significant variance in commitment independent of variables from the Investment Model.

Thus, across a variety of personal projects, the predicted set of relations was found: Values predicted commitment under adversity, independent of the investment model. But maybe a person first feels committed and then infers value relevance. Or adversity may create value relevance. This study did not uncouple temporally the interactive contributions of value relevance and adversity. Another study was designed to test the notion that value relevance at the outset of a project could predict commitment as one subsequently encountered adversity.

Students in a course on therapeutic recreation were required to do 8 weeks of volunteer work as part of a course requirement. The strategy was to measure value relevance at the outset of the projects and then assess adversity 6–8 weeks later to predict commitment and intentions to continue at the end of the course requirement. Ninety-seven students were tested in class at beginning of the project. Forty-eight of these students were then recruited 6 weeks later for a questionnaire study outside of class time.

This study also served as an opportunity to develop a measure of self-affirmation based on other data concerning correlates of value relevance and Steele's conceptualization of self-affirmation. Five items were embedded in the initial questionnaire:

1. To what extent is volunteer work a reflection of your value system?
2. To what extent is volunteer work a statement about your view of the world?
3. To what extent is the primary concern of volunteer work something or someone other than yourself?
4. To what extent does volunteer work reveal something about your identity? and
5. To what extent is doing volunteer work important to your self-worth?

Adversity and commitment were measured in the same way as the personal projects study described earlier.

The data analytic strategy used for this study involved entering first a measure of self-reported commitment at Time 1 to establish a baseline level of commitment. In the second step of the regression, simple effects for self-affirmation and

FIG. 8.3.   A longitudinal analysis of values (Time 1) predicting
commitment (Time 2) in the face
of subsequent adversity.
Note. Expected values are based
on the equation using the b
weights for values, adversity,
and the interaction term of values by adversity. From J. Lydon
and M. Zanna, 1990, *Journal of
Personality and Social Psychology, 58*, pp. 1040–1047. Copyright 1990 by the American Psychological Association. Reprinted with permission.

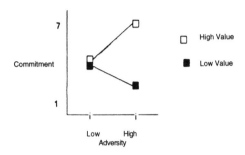

adversity were entered, and then in the third step the product term of self-affirmation by adversity was entered to test for an interaction.

Commitment at Time 1 accounted for 19.9% of the variance in commitment reported at Time 2. The simple effects for self-affirmation and adversity could not account for significant additional variance. Importantly though, the product term accounted for an additional 54% of the variance in Time 2 commitment. Thus, self-affirmation could account for a change in commitment when faced with adversity. As seen in Fig. 8.3, those who saw their projects as expressing their values and affirming the self came to feel more committed to their projects as they faced more adversity. In contrast, those who did not see their projects expressing their values and affirming the self came to feel less committed as they faced more adversity. This same pattern of data (self-affirmation by adversity interaction) was obtained in response to a question about students' intentions to continue their volunteer work beyond the requirements of the course ($p < .01$). In sum, this study provided somewhat stronger evidence for the direction of the value-commitment relation. (For a detailed report of the two studies described earlier, please see Lydon & Zanna, 1990.)

COMMITMENT AND PREGNANCY DECISIONS

An important limitation to the aforementioned studies is that the outcome measures are self-reports of felt commitment. The question then is, "Can self-reported commitment predict a subsequent and significant personal behavioral decision?" To examine this question, we (Lydon, Dunkel-Schetter, Cohan, & Pierce, in press) studied women making pregnancy decisions (to carry vs. abort). In addition to examining the relation between felt commitment and behavioral decisions, this population allowed us to study a number of other interesting questions about commitment.

If felt commitment predicts a behavioral commitment, might the behavioral commitment, in turn, increase felt commitment for those making the stressful decision to continue the pregnancy? Behavior may bolster attitudinal commitment as dissonance (Brehm & Cohen, 1962) and entrapment (Staw, 1976) researchers have suggested (cf. Lydon & Dunkel-Schetter, 1994; Lydon, Zanna, & Ross, 1988). Given the prior prediction that felt commitment will predict subsequent behavioral decisions, there could be a restricted range problem in making such a prediction. It may be difficult to see *increases* in attitudinal commitment among a group that is very high in attitudinal commitment prior to the behavioral decision.

If women who decide to continue rather than abort the pregnancy are generally high in commitment, we may then consider what impact such feelings of commitment have for other outcomes. We speculated that commitment to a pregnancy may influence health behaviors. In this study we predicted that women who decided to continue the pregnancy would report a decrease in smoking once they received confirmation that they were pregnant and they would report smoking fewer cigarettes than those who decided to abort the pregnancy.

Finally, we considered what impact feelings of commitment might have on the termination of a pregnancy. Might levels of commitment prior to a decision predict levels of distress following an abortion (the termination of a potential commitment)?

Adversity was an important moderating variable in the earlier studies because projects varied greatly in the degree of stress and difficulty incurred. However, some life events by their nature will challenge most everyone's commitment. In these cases, studying stressful life events, the prediction is a simple effect or correlation between self-affirmation (values) and commitment rather than an interaction with adversity. We have conceptualized the decision to carry versus abort an unplanned pregnancy as a stressful life event (see also, Adler, David, Major, Roth, Russo, & Wyatt, 1990) and therefore we expect that self-affirmation will predict commitment for our sample in general.

The study involved interviewing women at a clinic for a pregnancy test before they received their test results (Time 1), and then interviewing them within 9 days of receiving their test results (Time 2) and then again 4 to 7 weeks later (Time 3). Our sample consisted of 57 women who completed at least a partial Time 1 interview, received positive pregnancy test results, did not have a miscarriage, and then completed a Time 3 interview.

Self-affirmation was operationalized in terms of the meaning of the pregnancy. Meaning was assessed by asking women how much they agreed or disagreed with statements that: "Having a baby right now would (a) reflect my values, (b) make me feel good about myself, (c) reflect my concern for others, and (d) be a good and fair thing to do." In turn women were asked the same four statements with the stem "To not have a baby right now would . . . " The mean for the latter four items was subtracted from the mean of the first four items to create a meaning score (alpha = .81).

Commitment was assessed by asking women to what extent they felt committed, obligated, attached, enthusiastic, a sense of duty, a sense of enjoyment, a burden, and a relief if not pregnant (last two items reversed), alpha = .91. Smoking behavior was assessed by asking about smoking status (never, used to but not now, and currently smoke) and, if currently smoking, how many cigarettes per day were smoked.

Affective states were assessed using 16 items from the Affects Balance Scale (Derogatis, 1975). Negative affect was assessed with 12 items: nervous, tense, anxious, regretful, guilty, ashamed, sad, unhappy, worthless, hopeless, angry, and resentful. Positive affect was assessed with four items: pleased, contented, glad, and delighted. The average of the positive affects minus the average of the negative affects created an affect balance score, alpha = .91.

Consistent with earlier work we found that our measure of how value-laden and self-defining the pregnancy was (the meaning of pregnancy measure) correlated with how committed women reported being, although in this context the correlation was quite high, $r(50) = .76$. Moreover, the meaning measure predicted pregnancy decision, $r(54) = .76$,[3] but this was mediated, in part, by self-reported commitment, Beta = .27, $sr(54) = .17$, $p < .05$. Commitment correlated .84 with decision and remained robust after partialling out meaning, Beta = .64, $sr(54) = .40$, $p < .01$.

Because pregnancy decision was a dichotomous variable, it might be useful to look at commitment scores as a function of pregnancy decision (continue vs. abort). On a 5-point scale, the average commitment score for those who continued the pregnancy was 3.68 and the average for those who aborted was 1.55, $t(55) = 11.74$. In sum, it appears that the meaning of the pregnancy engendered feelings of commitment that predicted a significant behavioral decision—to carry versus abort the pregnancy.

We then considered whether the behavioral decision to continue the pregnancy might bolster feelings of commitment. In addition to making the decision to continue the pregnancy, women may begin to experience some stress and difficulties during the first trimester of the pregnancy that could create some dissonance and, in turn, increase commitment. As a colleague once suggested, morning sickness is nature's way of inducing commitment. Thus, the behavioral decision and adversity may promote increased feelings of commitment.

As a group, those who decided to continue the pregnancy were already high in commitment at Time 1 (M [24] = 3.66). A low commitment group was created from those in the bottom tertile of the Time 1 commitment scores (M [8] = 2.67),

---

[3]Fifty-six women who completed the affect balance scale at each time point were deemed eligible for analyses across time. Because meaning at Time 1 and Time 2 and commitment at Time 1 and Time 2 were highly correlated, scores on these measures were averaged. Four women did partial Time 1 interviews and three women did partial Time 2 interviews and they were utilized for analyses across time points using their meaning and commitment scores from either Time 1 or Time 2.

those in the second tertile (M [7] = 3.69) constituted a moderator commitment group, and those in the third tertile (M [9] = 4.53) constituted the high commitment group. Using a 3(Time 1 Commitment: Low-Moderate-High) × 2(Time 1 vs. Time 3) between-within ANOVA, we found an interaction, $F(1,21)$ = 5.36, $p < .02$, such that those low in Time 1 commitment ($M = 2.67$) reported increased commitment at Time 3 ($M = 3.40$), $t(21) = 3.54, p < .01$.

This increase in commitment might be attributed to regression to the mean. However, those high in commitment did not report a decrease in commitment, $t < 1$ (nor did the moderates report a change in commitment, $t < 1$). Moreover, the grand mean for the entire sample at Time 1 (including those who aborted) was 2.35. Thus, the low commitment carry group actually moved *away* from the Time 1 grand mean.

To test our prediction about health behavior, we examined changes in smoking among those who continued the pregnancy(all generally committed by Time 3), and we compared their Time 3 smoking with those who aborted. Those who continued the pregnancy reported a significant decrease in number of cigarettes smoked per day from Time 1 (M [6] = 6.50) to Time 3 (M [6] = 1.33), dependent $t(5) = 3.32, p < .03$. Moreover, those who continued the pregnancy reported less smoking at Time 3 than those who aborted ($M = 9.58$), $t(16) = 3.86, p < .01$. Thus, commitment to the pregnancy appeared to be reflected in behavior (decreased smoking) that would promote the commitment (a healthy baby).

Adjustment to Abortion.   Does commitment predict distress among those who terminated the pregnancy? Because commitment was such a strong predictor of pregnancy decision we found very few women with even moderate levels of commitment who decided to abort the pregnancy (as well, very few with low commitment decided to continue the pregnancy). As a group, those who aborted the pregnancy experienced an increase in distress from Time 1 to Time 2 but then a decrease from Time 2 to Time 3 (Cohan, Dunkel-Schetter, & Lydon, 1993). Essentially, these women were distressed while coping with an unplanned pregnancy (Time 2) but not while coping with an abortion (Time 3). We reasoned though that commitment would moderate responses to the abortion decision. We found that for those who aborted the pregnancy, commitment at the outset (an average of Time 1 and Time 2 reports of commitment) predicted level of distress (affect balance score) at Time 3 (controlling for Time 1 and Time 2 affect), Beta = .53, $sr(26) = .50, p < .01$. A median split of commitment scores among those who aborted (Median = 1.30 on a 1 to 5 scale) was used to conduct a 2(Time 1 Commitment: High vs. Low) x 3(Affect: Time 1, Time 2, Time 3) repeated measures ANOVA. The significant commitment group by time interaction, $F(2,52) = 6.21, p < .01$ revealed that those *relatively* high in commitment reported less positive and more negative emotions at Time 3(affect balance $M = +.77$) than those low in commitment ($M = 1.95$), $t(52) = 3.23, p < .01$.

Interestingly then, women who reported even slight feelings of commitment at Time 1 (group $M = 2.01$, $SD = .50$) did not experience the same degree of recovery postabortion decision as those with virtually no feelings of commitment at Time 1 (Range 1.0 to 1.30).

In sum, the meaning of the pregnancy was highly correlated with felt commitment. Women felt commitment to the pregnancy to the extent that it affirmed core beliefs, values, and identities. Commitment, in turn, mediated the relationship between meaning and behavioral decision. The decision to continue the pregnancy bolstered commitment for those relatively low in commitment. Those continuing the pregnancy also demonstrated their commitment by reporting a decrease in smoking. Finally, commitment moderated affective responses to the decision to terminate the pregnancy.[4]

COMMITMENT TO LONG-DISTANCE DATING RELATIONSHIPS

The dating study (Lydon, Pierce, & O'Regan, 1995) was designed in part to replicate the self-commitment relation in the interpersonal relationships domain—a context people typically associate with commitment. We chose to study students in long-distance dating relationships to test whether self-reported commitment the month prior to leaving home to come to McGill could predict behavioral persistence and resistance to the threat of distance and increased availability of attractive alternatives. Also, we wanted to extend our finding that commitment predicts distress among those who aborted their pregnancy by examining what effect the loss of a committed relationship might have on a student's emotional well being as well as other aspects of one's life like health and GPA.

Students were telephoned the month before leaving home to begin their first term at McGill. Eligibility criteria included living outside the province of Quebec and being in a dating relationship at the time. Those who agreed to participate were sent a questionnaire by mail. Fifty-nine of 62 questionnaires were returned and completed and another 27 were completed by students on campus for an orientation weekend. Students were then telephoned in November to come to the lab to complete a second questionnaire. Of the 69 students coming to the lab, 39 were still in the same dating relationship and 30 were no longer in the same relationship. A third assessment in March included 60 students, 27 of whom were still together.

The meaning of the relationship (self-affirmation measure adapted from the

---

[4]This study also examined pregnancy commitment in relation to the intentionality of the pregnancy, emotional responses to pregnancy test results, other life goals, and history of abortions. For a full report, please see Lydon, Dunkel-Schetter, Cohan, & Pierce (in press).

pregnancy study) was correlated with self-reported commitment at Time 1, r (84) = .53, $p < .001$. Moreover, commitment measured at Time 1 predicted relationship breakup by Time 2. Those who were still together in November had reported more commitment in August ($M = 3.51$) than those who broke up by November ($M = 3.02$), $t(67) = 2.70$, $p < .01$.

To test the hypothesis that commitment would predict distress for those whose relationship ended, we created standard scores for Time 2 measures of affect balance, physical symptoms and Fall GPA. Fall GPA ($N = 57$) correlated with affect balance and physical symptoms, both $rs(55) = .36$, $p < .01$, and affect balance correlated with physical symptoms, $r(55) = .40$, $p < .01$. An overall distress score was computed by subtracting the affect balance and GPA scores from physical symptoms and dividing by three. In this way, higher numbers reflect more distress. There was no difference between those who remained together versus those whose relationships ended on the Time 2 distress measure or the three indices contributing to the distress measure (affect, symptoms, GPA), $ts < 1$. Relationship termination per se did not predict distress. The question then was whether commitment to a relationship would predict distress following the termination of the relationship.

We first entered Time 1 affect balance as a control variable in a hierarchical regression and in the second step we entered commitment (Time 1) to predict distress for those whose relationships ended ($n = 30$).[5] Commitment accounted for 18% of the variance in distress, Beta $= .44$, $sr(25) = .42$, $p < .03$. Separate analyses for affect, GPA, and symptoms revealed that commitment was a reliable predictor of illness symptoms and affect at Time 2 but not GPA when controlling for affect at Time 1.[6]

Summary of Findings

So we can see then across four studies that the degree to which a goal, project, or decision affirmed core beliefs, values, and identities in turn predicted self-reported commitment: to personal projects; volunteer work; pregnancy decisions and long-distance dating relationships. Moreover, commitment prompted persistence with a goal or a project under adversity: intending to continue volunteer projects, continuing a pregnancy, and continuing a long-distance dating relationship. Such persistence, in turn, bolstered commitment as suggested by the low commitment women who continued the pregnancy. Finally, commitment predicted the distress created by the termination of a pregnancy and the ending of a romantic relationship.

---

[5]We were unable to obtain copies of academic transcripts for 2 of the 30 participants whose relationships ended. Analyses were performed on the 28 participants for whom we had complete data.

[6]Please see Lydon et al. (1995) for a more complete, detailed set of analyses.

COMMITMENT-ADVERSITY RELATION

Adversity may not only test commitment as I suggested earlier but it may also serve to increase commitment or create commitment, which is consistent with earlier commitment theory and research. For example, Staw (1976) demonstrated that as people incur costs they increase their commitment to a course of action. Brickman (1987) went further to suggest that costs or a negative element must be present in some way for commitment to even exist. The one apparent anomaly in the commitment literature is Rusbult's Investment Model in which costs are negatively related to commitment. However her data on costs and commitment have been inconsistent (e.g., Rusbult, 1983). Instead, investments have been consistently and positively related to commitment. Investments are in fact "sunken costs" to use the classic term of Becker (1960). They are those things that one puts into a relationship that one loses if the relationship ends.

There are a couple of important points then about adversity. First, in some quasi-objective sense we can say that there are different levels of adversity. In moving from low to moderate adversity we may encounter increased costs and challenges. This may create commitment, test commitment, and increase commitment. However, in moving from moderate to high adversity we may encounter severe threats to commitment or loss of commitments. Those committed may experience increased distress (Brown, Bifulco, & Harris, 1987; Oatley & Bolton, 1985) or disengage from their commitment as a coping mechanism. Alternatively, they may transform their self to accommodate the loss experience via changes to core beliefs, values, or identities. For example, a person may find meaning in the loss experience (Frankl, 1963; Silver & Wortman, 1980; Taylor, 1983) or come to a new understanding that some life events are uncontrollable. This underscores the point that commitment loss engenders distress, in part, because it threatens the self-system. Adjustment to a commitment loss may then be related to the ways in which one reaffirms the self.

Recently, we have begun exploring threats to relationship commitments. In a pilot study, male undergraduates in dating relationships came to the lab and had a 5 minute interaction with an ostensible female subject (confederate). Threat was operationalized by the availability (married vs. single) of the attractive female confederate. Subsequently, subjects responded to scenarios in which their current dating partner did something negative (stood them up, revealed to others something personally embarrassing). Rusbult and her colleagues (Rusbult, Verette, Whitney, Slovik, & Lipkus, 1991) found that subjects were more likely to report that the protagonist in a scenario would engage in accommodation behaviors (constructive responses that defuse conflict more than the destructive responses that escalate conflict) to the extent that the protagonist was more committed to the relationship. We found that subjects reported less accommodation toward *their* current dating partner after an interaction with an attractive available alternative than after an interaction with the same attractive but unavailable alternative, $F(1,10) = 7.21$, $p < .02$. Thus, commitment threat evoked a decrease in relationship enhancing behaviors.

When the potential threat of an attractive alternative is clear and the alternative is the focus of attention, one may respond by devaluing the attractiveness of the alternative as a coping response (Johnson & Rusbult, 1989). We suspect though that the devaluing effect is more likely with those early on in their relationships and who are moderately committed to their relationships. An attractive alternative may be threatening during a time of uncertainty about one's commitment. Those in more established relationships (e.g., marriage, living together) may not be as threatened and thus may not be as motivated to devalue. However, the threat may be heightened for those in established relationships by presenting an alternative who finds them attractive. This creates a conundrum though because by devaluing in this instance, one loses the personal benefits to self-esteem by being liked by a valued other. We are currently testing this situation in the lab.

An alternative source of threat to the relationship can be a change in the health status of a loved one. In a pilot study of 10 elderly couples in which one had advanced dementia but was still living at home, we conceptualized the situation as one in which a person cares for a spouse until the day the spouse dies. Instead, our caregivers described this as a situation in which they envisioned caring for their spouse until the day that they (the caregivers) would die. The stress and strain of caring was readily apparent in our pilot data. With these caregivers, stress was *negatively* related to commitment, $r(8) = -.59$, $p < .10$.

We speculate that during the early stages of dementia, a caregiver may experience increased commitment corresponding to the increased adversity. Subsequently, as adversity reaches extremely high levels commitment may decline. The question then is: Would a decline in commitment as adversity reaches high to extremely high levels reflect a disengagement (giving up) of commitment or would it reflect a return to the levels of commitment felt under the low to moderate level of stress that was subsequently eclipsed by an acute commitment response to moderately high stress?

The second point about adversity concerns its subjective quality and the appraisals we make about the costs and stressors creating adversity. We can appraise a cost as an investment, a sunken cost, if we stay with a goal or project. However, if an ongoing goal or project is terminated then we have a loss experience. Similarly, we can see a stressor as a challenge to maintain or increase commitment or we may appraise the stressor as a severe threat to the viability of the goal or project.

In the caregivers study, caregivers were presented with three representative scenarios of potentially stressful situations due to their spouse's dementia. For each scenario, two responses by the caregiver were presented, one reflecting an appraisal of challenge and the other reflecting an appraisal of threat. For example, one scenario concerned the dementia patient becoming extremely angry and remaining angry despite efforts by the caregiver to calm the patient. The caregiver fears that the patient could hurt him or herself or the caregiver. The challenge question asked participants to what extent they were "likely to accept the incident as a natural consequence of dementia, and attempt to treat outburst of anger as a challenge in living that one must overcome." The threat question asked participants to what extent they were "likely to feel uneasy or upset, and see dementia as a threat to the daily lives of you (caregiver) and (the patient)?"

Commitment to the relationship was correlated with the degree to which caregivers responded to the situations in terms of a challenge $r(8) = .69$, $p < .05$. Although this is a very small sample of data, it serves to remind us of the possible reciprocal relation between commitment and adversity. Not only may adversity influence felt commitment by testing commitment and increasing commitment, but commitment may also influence self-reports of adversity by prompting positive appraisals of stressful and difficult circumstances. In our current longitudinal study, assessments of the dementia patients are being used as our objective adversity measure and self-reported stress as our subjective appraisal measure. We expect a curvilinear relationship (inverted U) between objective stress and commitment such that commitment will increase while patient functioning decreases until patient functioning declines to a level that the caregiver cannot adequately meet. Moreover, we expect that commitment will predict lower subjective appraisals of stress, *controlling* for objective levels of stress.

By conceptualizing the commitment-adversity relation as reciprocal, we may integrate seemingly disparate commitment research, namely those from a dissonance tradition and those from an equity or interdependence tradition. From a dissonance perspective, there must be some equilibrium between adversity and commitment. This can be created by altering one's commitment or by altering appraisals of adversity. In some instances, adversity is fixed such as when costs are irretrievable investments. With adversity fixed then only commitment can be adjusted to reduce dissonance. In other instances, adversity may be more subjective (e.g., the attractiveness of the alternative) and one may reduce dissonance by appraising adversity as less severe.

The early work of Rusbult and her colleagues examining commitment from an interdependence perspective focused on satisfaction (rewards minus costs), attractiveness of alternatives and investment as predictors of commitment (e.g., Rusbult 1980; 1983). However, more recently, interdependence theory has explicated how factors examined as predictors of commitment may also be influenced by commitment (Rusbult & Buunk, 1993). Sunken costs (investments), satisfaction (rewards higher than costs), and unattractive alternatives may promote commitment. In turn, commitment may increase appraisals of rewards, alter appraisals of costs as investments, and decrease appraisals of the attractiveness of alternatives (e.g Johnson & Rusbult, 1989).

CONTENT OF COMMITMENT

In resolving the tensions between commitment and adversity, one might reconsider what we postulate to be the underlying bases of commitment—core beliefs, values, and identities. In conceptualizing these within a self that has an associative network (Linville, 1987), one might consider the specific elements that are at the core of one's self (dispositionally) or the specific elements related to a particular commitment. We are currently testing this notion by recruiting subjects for an experiment that appeals to one of two value orientations. One value orientation is relevant to half the subjects and irrelevant to the other half of the subjects whereas the second value orientation is relevant to the second half of subjects and irrelevant to the first. In this way each subject has an equal chance to be in either a value relevant or value irrelevant experiment. Moreover, the value relevance manipulation then is not confounded with a particular value domain. Will subjects be more likely to participate at 8:00 am when they are recruited for an experiment that expresses a value domain of particular importance to them? Pilot data reveal that for those who see their behavior as tied more to their attitudes, values, and dispositions, low self-monitors (Snyder, 1987), participation is greater at 8:00 am for a value relevant experiment (100%, $n = 4$) than for a value irrelevant experiment (0%, $n = 4$), overall value relevance by adversity by self-monitoring interaction, $F(1,24) = 4.69$, $p < .05$. Thus, when their commitment is tested (8:00 am), low self-monitors only reveal a commitment to experiments that are relevant to their particular values.

The specific beliefs, values, and identities expressed by a commitment may be particularly relevant in understanding adjustment to commitment loss (suggested by Costanzo at the symposium). For example, consider women who aborted their pregnancy but felt committed to the pregnancy because it was expressive of nurturance as a value. Would such women then seek other ways of expressing nurturance as a way to cope and adjust to the termination of the pregnancy? It may be that goals or projects that express the specific value or identity threatened are especially salient ways of coping and are therefore utilized most frequently and most readily. However, in theory, a goal or project that is of similar relevance to the self as a whole may restore a sense of well-being.

It is tempting then to propose that possessing many identities, values, and beliefs configured in a highly elaborate and complex way would be the key to buffering the distress of a lost commitment. An alternative middle level of analysis may be derived from Thoits (1992) work on identity configurations. She found that the importance and centrality of specific identities was not related to well-being. Instead, particular combinations of identities such as parent and worker (the "breadwinner" configuration) were related to well-being. For example, men who were employed but divorced were at higher risk for substance abuse and men who were married and had children but were unemployed were at risk for psychological distress. By considering the content underlying commitments, we may discover that people often have a couple of core beliefs, values, and identities that sustain them. When one identity (belief or value) is threatened, a person may be sustained by the other while the cognitive repair work of either restoring the threatened identity (belief, value) or discovering a new identity (belief, value) ensues.

DIMENSIONS OF COMMITMENT

Commitment has often been conceptualized as multidimensional (Brickman, 1987; Johnson, 1991; Lydon & Dunkel-Schetter, 1994; Mathieu & Zajac, 1990; Meyer & Allen, 1984; Novacek & Lazarus, 1990). In reviewing these, we find the approach taken by Johnson in the relationships literature and Meyer and Allen in the organizational behavior literature to be most appealing. Essentially, they conceptualized commitment in terms of "want to," "ought to," and "have to" dimensions. Johnson elaborated in describing the want to as a personal commitment that is based on one's attitude toward the relationship, one's attitude toward the partner, and a relational identity (the extent to which the relationship is incorporated into the self). Johnson labeled the ought to dimension as a moral commitment that is based on the value of consistency per se, the value one assigns to the stability of a particular type of relationship (e.g., marriage) and the personal sense of obligation one feels to the particular person. For Johnson, moral commitment reflects the values, obligations, and standards that one has *chosen* and internalized. This is in contrast to the have to commitment that Johnson labeled as structural commitment, which is based on irretrievable investments, social reaction, difficulty of termination procedures, and availability of alternatives.

Although intuitively appealing and theoretically interesting, it has been difficult to date to demonstrate empirically all three dimensions. Rusbult (1991) argued that personal commitment may be found in the satisfaction component of her investment model and structural commitment may be found in the investment and alternatives components. People want to be committed to highly satisfying relationships and people feel that they have to be committed to relationships in which they have invested a great deal and in cases where their alternatives are not very attractive. Johnson, as stated earlier, has other components within personal and structural commitment but clearly the most distinctive aspect of his approach is the notion of moral commitment.

Rusbult (1991) argued that the data do not support the concept. Her approach has been to operationalize moral commitment in terms of subjective norms and she has found that subjective norms do not contribute to investment model predictions of commitment. An alternative explanation may be that subjective norms assess structural commitment more than moral commitment and that students self-reported commitment to a dating relationship is not highly contingent on their parents, friends, and religion—the sources of subjective norms reported. Our finding that value relevance predicted commitment in the face of adversity above and beyond investment model variables (Lydon & Zanna, 1990, Study 1) suggests that the notion of moral commitment may be a viable one. Moreover, in the long-distance dating study, our measure of the meaning of the relationship (self-affirmation) did not correlate with relationship satisfaction even though it did correlate with relationship commitment. This suggests that not only may moral commitment be a distinct dimension of commitment, but it also may be one of particular importance and relevance as we explore the relationship between commitment and distress (Stein, 1992).

The challenge we see here is in identifying samples and situations that would tease apart moral commitment from structural and personal commitment. It is difficult to separate the moral force from within versus the moral force of one's social context. We suggest that close relationships in the gay community may be especially fruitful in examining moral commitment in a context where structural commitment may be reduced. Because society in general has tended to ostracize gays and lesbians, societal norms may be less relevant. In fact, structural forces such as marriage typically are not available to those in homosexual relationships. This may create more of an openness and freedom that challenges those in homosexual relationships to identify internal constraints (moral commitment) in the absence of strong external constraints regarding relationship commitment and fidelity.

The distinction between moral and personal commitment may be obscured in highly satisfying relationships in which what a person wants to do and what a person ought to do become inseparable. For example, in a parent child relationship, even though the ideal for a parent may be to provide unconditional love, the young child ultimately responds to this love with expressions of love and affection toward the parent. Thus, the parent receives positive feedback and validation during the first few years of the child's life for doing what a parent ought to do. It may be interesting to examine foster parents, step parents, or parents of autistic children who do not have a foundation of being validated by the young child. The value of unconditional love and commitment to the child may be put to a greater test in these parenting situations.

CLOSING

This is just a reminder that there are more hard issues to be faced and more hard thinking and more hard data to be acquired in order to advance a theory of commitment.

In closing, I would like to return to values, and commitment. Both of these concepts are frequently thought of as restrictive, primitive props that people rely upon out of weakness. I think that some of the contributors to this volume help stretch our thinking about values so that we may see values serving an expressive and not just a defensive function. So too, I would like us to stretch our thinking about commitment. The most predominant model of commitment today is based on a notion of commitment as dependency. I prefer to think of commitment more in Brickman's terms. I would not exclude the notion of commitment as dependency. But commitment also can be a way of fulfillment. Commitment, I suggest, bridges the self to the social world. Although the road that follows may be destructive, to not cross the bridge and take any road is to deny a fundamental part of the self as a social being. It is not in isolation but in our connectedness (to people, ideas, or goals) that we may realize and become our true selves.

ACKNOWLEDGMENTS

I gratefully acknowledge the financial support of the Social Sciences and Humanities Research Council of Canada (SSHRC) and Fonds pour la Formation de Chercheurs et l'Aide à la Recherche (Quebec). I also appreciate the comments made by Michael Johnson, Connie Kristiansen, and the editors on an earlier draft of the chapter.

REFERENCES

Adler, N. E., David, H. P., Major, B. N., Roth, S. H., Russo, N. F., & Wyatt, G. E. (1990). Psychological responses after abortion. *Science, 248,* 41–44.

Becker, H. S. (1960). Notes on the concept of commitment. *American Journal of Sociology, 66,* 32–40.

Brehm, J. W., & Cohen, A. R. (1962). *Explorations in cognitive dissonance.* New York: Wiley.

Brickman, P. (1987). Commitment. In C. B. Wortman & R. Sorrentino (Eds.), *Commitment, conflict, and caring,* (pp. 1–18). Englewood Cliffs, NJ: Prentice-Hall.

Brown, G. W., Bifulco, A., & Harris, T. O. (1987). Life events, vulnerability, and onset of depression: Some refinements. *British Journal of Psychiatry, 150,* 30–40.

Brunstein, J. C. (1993). Personal goals and subjective well-being: A longitudinal study. *Journal of Personality and Social Psychology, 65,* 1061–1070.

Burke, P. J., & Reitzes, D. C. (1991). An identity theory approach to commitment. *Social Psychology Quarterly, 54,* 239–251.

Buss, D. M., & Cantor, N. (Eds.) (1989). *Personality psychology: Recent trends and emerging directions.* New York: Springer.

Cantor, N., Norem, J. K., Niedenthal, P. M., Langston, C. A., & Brower, A. M. (1987). Life tasks, self-concept ideals, and cognitive strategies in a life transition. *Journal of Personality and Social Psychology, 53,* 1178–1191.

Cohan, C. L., & Dunkel-Schetter, C., & Lydon, J. (1993). Pregnancy decision making. *Psychology of Women Quarterly, 17,* 223–239.

Derogatis, R. L. (1975). *Affects balance scale.* Baltimore, MD: Clinical Psychometrics Research.

Emmons, R. A. (1986). Personal strivings: An approach to personality and subjective well-being. *Journal of Personality and Social Psychology. 51,* 1058–1068.

Fehr, B. (1988). Prototype analysis of the concepts of love and commitment. *Journal of Personality and Social Psychology, 55,* 557–579.

Frankl, V. E. (1963). *Man's search for meaning.* New York: Pocket Books.

Gollwitzer, P., & Wicklund, R. (1985). Self-symbolizing and the neglect of others' perspectives. *Journal of Personality and Social Psychology, 48,* 702–715.

James, W. (1890/1950). *Principles of psychology* (Vol 1). New York: Dover.

Janoff-Bulman, R. (1989). Assumptive worlds and the stress of traumatic events: Applications of the schema construct. *Social Cognition, 7,* 113–136.

Johnson, M. P. (1991). Commitment to personal relationships. *Advances in Personal Relationships, 3,* 117–143.

Johnson, D. J., & Rusbult, C. E. (1989). Resisting temptation: Devaluation of alternative partners as a means of maintaining commitment in close relationships. *Journal of Personality and Social Psychology, 57,* 967–980.

Kanter, R. M. (1972). *Commitment and community: Communes and utopias in social perspectives.* Cambridge, MA: Harvard Press.

Kelley, H. H. (1983). Love and commitment. In H. H. Kelley, E. Berscheid, A. Christensen, J. H. Harvey, T. L. Huston, G. Levinger, E. McClintock, L. A. Peplau, & D. R. Peterson (Eds.), *Close relationships* (pp. 265–314). New York: Freeman.

Kelley, H. H., & Thibaut, J. W. (1978). *Interpersonal relations: A theory of interdependence.* New York: Wiley.

Kiesler, C. (1971). *The psychology of commitment.* New York: Academic Press.

Kiesler, C., & Sakumura, J. (1966). A test of a model for commitment. *Journal of Personality and Social Psychology, 3,* 349–353.

Klinger, E. (1977). *Meaning and void: Inner experience and the incentives in people's lives.* Minneapolis: University of Minnesota Press.

Kobasa, S. (1982). Commitment and coping in stress resistance among lawyers. *Journal of Personality and Social Psychology, 42,* 707–717.

Lerner, M. J. (1980). *The belief in a just world: A fundamental delusion.* New York: Plenum.

Lerner, M. J., & Simmons, C. H. (1966). Observer's reaction to the "innocent victim": Compassion or rejection? *Journal of Personality and Social Psychology, 4,* 203–210.

Linville, P. W. (1987). Self-complexity as a cognitive buffer against stress-related illness and depression. *Journal of Personality and Social Psychology, 52,* 663–676.

Little, B. (1983). Personal projects: A rationale and method for investigation. *Environment and Behavior, 15,* 273–309.

Lydon, J., & Dunkel-Schetter, C. (1994). Seeing is committing: A longitudinal study of bolstering commitment in amniocentesis patients. *Personality and Social Psychology Bulletin, 20,* 218–227.

Lydon, J., Dunkel-Schetter, C., Cohan, C., & Pierce, T. (in press). Pregnancy decision making as a significant life event: A commitment approach. *Journal of Personality and Social Psychology.*

Lydon, J., Pierce, T., & O'Regan, S. (1995). Coping with (moral) commitment to long-distance relationships. Manuscript submitted for publication.

Lydon, J., & Zanna, M. (1990). Commitment in the face of adversity: A value-affirmation approach. *Journal of Personality and Social Psychology, 58,* 1040–1047.

Lydon, J., Zanna, M., & Ross, M. (1988). Bolstering attitudes by autobiographical recall: Attitude persistence and selective memory. *Personality and Social Psychology Bulletin, 14,* 78–86.

Mathieu, J., & Zajac, D. (1990). A review and meta-analysis of the antecedents, correlates, and consequences of organizational commitment. *Psychological Bulletin, 108,* 171–194.

Meyer, J., & Allen, N. (1984). Testing the "side-bet theory" of organizational commitment: Some methodological considerations. *Journal of Applied Psychology, 69,* 372–378.

Novacek, J., & Lazarus, R. S. (1990). The structure of personal commitments. *Journal of Personality, 58,* 693–715.

Oatley, K., & Bolton, W. (1985). A social-cognitive theory of depression in reaction to life events. *Psychological Review, 92,* 372–388.

Parkes, C. M. (1975). What becomes of redundant world models? A contribution to the study of adaptation to change. *British Journal of Medical Psychology, 48,* 131–137.

Pervin, L. A. (Ed.). (1989). *Goal concepts in personality and social psychology.* Hillsdale, NJ: Erlbaum.

Rokeach, M. (1980). Some unresolved issues in theories of beliefs, attitudes, and values. In H. E. Howe, Jr. & M. M. Page (Eds.), *1979 Nebraska Symposium on Motivation.* Lincoln: University of Nebraska Press.

Rusbult, C. E. (1980). Commitment and satisfaction in romantic associations: A test of the investment model. *Journal of Experimental Social Psychology, 16,* 172–186.

Rusbult, C.E. (1983). A longitudinal test of the investment model: The development (and deterioration) of satisfaction and commitment in heterosexual involvement. *Journal of Personality and Social Psychology, 45,* 101–117.

Rusbult, C. E. (1991). Commentary on Johnson's commitment to personal relationships: What's interesting, and what's new? *Advances in Personal Relationships, 3,* 151–169.

Rusbult, C. E., & Buunk, B. P. (1993). Commitment processes in close relationships: An interdependence analysis. *Journal of Social and Personal Relationships, 10,* 175–204.

Rusbult, C. E., Verette, J., Whitney, G. A., Slovik, L. F., & Lipkus, I. (1991). Accommodation processes in close relationships: Theory and preliminary empirical evidence. *Journal of Personality and Social Psychology, 60,* 53–78.

Schwartz, S. H. (1992). Universals in the content and structure of values: Theoretical advances and empirical tests in 20 countries. *Advances in Experimental Social Psychology, 25,* 1–65.

Silver, R. L., & Wortman, C. B. (1980). Coping with undesirable life events. In J. E. Garber & M. E. P. Seligman (Eds.), *Human helplessness: Theory and applications* (pp 279–340). London: Academic Press.

Snyder, M. (1987). *Public appearances/private realities: The psychology of self-monitoring.* New York: Freeman.

Staw, B. (1976). Knee-deep in the big muddy: A study of escalating commitment to a chosen course of action. *Organizational Behavior and Human Performance, 16,* 27–44.

Steele, C. (1988). The psychology of self-affirmation: Sustaining the integrity of the self. In L. Berkowitz (Ed.), *Advances in experimental social psychology* (Vol. 21, pp. 261–302). New York: Academic Press.

Steele, C., & Liu, T. (1983). Dissonance processes as self-affirmation. *Journal of Personality and Social Psychology, 45,* 5–19.

Steele, C., Spencer, S., & Lynch, M. (1993). Self-image resilience and dissonance: The role of affirmational resources. *Journal of Personality and Social Psychology, 64,* 885–896.

Stein, C. (1992). Ties that bind: Three studies of obligation in adult relationships with family. *Journal of Social and Personal Relationships, 9,* 525–547.

Taylor, S. E. (1983). Adjustment to threatening events: A theory of cognitive adaptation. *American Psychologist, 38,* 1161–1173.

Tesser, A., & Cornell, D. P. (1991). On the confluence of self processes. *Journal of Experimental Social Psychology, 27,* 501–526.

Thoits, P. A. (1982). Conceptual, methodological, and theoretical problems in studying social support as a buffer against life stress. *Journal of Health and Social Behavior, 23,* 145–159.

Thoits, P. A. (1986). Multiple identities: Examining gender and marital status differences in distress. *American Sociological Review, 51,* 259–272.

Thoits, P. (1992). Identity structures and psychological well-being: Gender and marital status comparisons. *Social Psychology Quarterly, 55,* 236–256.

9

Values, Deservingness, and Attitudes Toward High Achievers: Research on Tall Poppies

Norman T. Feather
Flinders University of South Australia

My interest in the study of values goes back for many years but it was especially stimulated by Milton Rokeach's Presidential address to the Society for the Psychological Study of Social Issues (SPSSI) in the late 1960s (Rokeach, 1968), and by the subsequent publication of his book *The Nature of Human Values* (Rokeach, 1973) in which he presented his ideas about values and his research findings. I found Rokeach's contributions both challenging and insightful. He argued that, although the study of values was a central concern of the social sciences, it had been neglected by social psychologists when compared with the amount of attention they had given to the study of attitudes and attitude change. He provided a careful conceptual analysis of the nature of values and distinguished values from related concepts such as attitudes, needs, and norms. He developed a measurement procedure, the Value Survey, that could be applied to a range of interesting problems. He showed how different political ideologies could be related to the relative importance of values concerned with freedom and equality. And he presented a theory of cognitive and behavioral change that gave a prominent role to those kinds of contradictions that involved discrepancies between values that were central to self-conceptions and other types of beliefs that were less central to self-maintenance and self-enhancement.

Rokeach's contributions helped to revitalize the study of values. Over the past 25 years social psychologists have given more attention to values in areas such as cross-cultural psychology, attitude theory, and political psychology. It is still the case, however, that more could be done, especially in relation to basic questions such as the relations between the general values that people hold and their more specific attitudes, and between these values and their behavior.

I have tried to address these questions in a research program that began over

20 years ago. My analysis of the values and action link has drawn on ideas from expectancy-value theory. This general approach has been a long interest of mine, especially as it relates to those important aspects of human motivation that concern choice, performance, and persistence in achievement situations (Feather, 1959, 1982). The application of the expectancy-value approach to bridging the gap between values and actions has been discussed in other publications (Feather, 1975, 1990, 1992b) and I do not propose to cover the same ground again. The main concern of the present chapter is to describe research that examines the values–attitude link in the context of our attitudes toward people who occupy positions of high status and how we react when they fall from those high positions.

I review some studies from my research program that investigated high profile public figures who were either at the top of the ladder or who had fallen from it, some studies that manipulated status experimentally by using hypothetical vignettes, and some studies that assessed the importance of a wide range of values and then related value importance to general attitudes toward high achievers. In some of these studies the role of values was inferred; in the studies that were concerned with general attitudes the values were directly measured.

I also present some theoretical ideas about relations between values and attitudes. The basic proposition is that values function to confer valence on objects and events (Feather, 1990, 1992b, 1995). That is, general values, once activated, are assumed to influence our subjective evaluations of objects and events in specific situations so that, for example, some possible actions and outcomes are seen to be attractive while others are seen to be aversive. This proposition is elaborated in more detail in a subsequent section. It plays an important part in a theoretical analysis of deservingness, also described subsequently. I focus on deservingness because the evidence from my research program shows that attitudes toward high achievers and toward their fall are linked to the degree to which they are seen to deserve their high positions and any fall from them that may occur.

TALL POPPY RESEARCH

The research program on high status achievers is an extensive one and the main studies have been described in a recent review (Feather, 1994). The program was stimulated by a commonly held belief in my country that Australians like to cut "tall poppies" down to size, where a tall poppy is defined as "a person who is conspicuously successful" and (frequently) as "one whose distinction, rank, or wealth attracts envious notice or hostility" (Ramson, 1988).

However, the significance of the topic extends beyond national boundaries. A lot of research has been conducted on achievement needs and the effects of these needs on thought and action (e.g., Atkinson & Feather, 1966; McClelland, 1985; Spence, 1983) but, by comparison, there is not a large literature on the attitudes that people hold toward those who occupy high positions, whether their status be achieved or ascribed. The status variable has not had the attention that it deserves. Yet the vertical dimension is an ever-present structural aspect of social life. A close examination of variables that affect our attitudes to those in high places and our reactions to their fall is a step in the direction of opening up the status variable to closer scrutiny.

The research on tall poppies was not guided by a single formalized theory. That would have been premature. Instead I began by drawing on ideas from different theoretical perspectives, depending on the context of each investigation and the questions that were asked. Of particular interest were Heider's (1958) discussion of how a person reacts to the lot of another person, attribution theory as it relates to the analysis of motivation and emotion, the conceptual analysis of personal and cultural values, theoretical approaches to the analysis of justice and deservingness, and social comparison approaches to the analysis of envy (Feather, 1994). The relevance of these approaches becomes evident as I describe studies from the program.

The research program was not concerned with competitive situations where a person seeks to surpass a rival and where the defeat of the rival serves self-interest. One would expect these close encounters to result in a certain amount of pleasure when a competitor or enemy is brought down or defeated. The winner takes the spoils and improves his or her position. In contrast, my research has been concerned with tall poppies who are not involved in some interpersonal struggle but are viewed at a distance. They may be public figures who hold high political office, megastars in the world of entertainment, leaders in sport, or high status people in literature, science, or the arts, whose achievements are publicized usually through the mass media. They may be persons who are not known to the general public but who have performed very well in a particular context (e.g., a straight A student at school or university, or a business leader or manager in an organization). In all cases they have high status, standing above others by virtue of their position.

The program involved both experimental and correlational studies. In this chapter I focus on a selection of studies from the program that provide information about the role of values in regard to attitudes toward high achievers and reactions to their fall. The general question to be answered is how do our values influence these attitudes and reactions. For example, do power and achievement values influence our attitudes toward high achievers, leading a person to favor their reward? Do egalitarian values influence these attitudes, leading a person to favor the fall of tall poppies from their high positions to a level where they become equal with others? To what extent are our attitudes toward high achievers and their fall governed by considerations of deservingness? Do values combine with other variables such as perceived responsibility to influence judgments of deservingness? These are some of the questions that I attempt to answer in subsequent sections.

STUDIES OF PUBLIC FIGURES

I begin by describing studies that used real-life tall poppies or high achievers. These studies came later in my research program but presenting them first will help to introduce some of the key variables that I have investigated. These studies also have the advantage of ecological validity when compared with studies described subsequently that used hypothetical scenarios involving stimulus persons. The people who were being judged by subjects were prominent public figures who had a lot of exposure in the mass media and who were very successful in their chosen pursuits. They were people who would be known at a distance by virtually every Australian.

The first study (Feather, Volkmer, & McKee, 1991) involved a large sample of 377 male and female students from Flinders University. They answered questions that related to three Australian tall poppies who came from either politics, sport, or entertainment. There were three versions of the questionnaire corresponding to these three domains, and three tall poppies for each domain.[1] Subjects first answered questions about the causes of each person's success that referred to ability or talent, hard work or effort, outside or external assistance, and opportunity or luck. They then rated the degree to which they considered that each tall poppy deserved to be in his or her high position and whether the tall poppy deserved to maintain his or her high position in the future. They also rated how pleased they were that the tall poppy held his or her present high position and how pleased they would be if the tall poppy were to rise even further or to fall from his or her present high position. In addition, they rated each tall poppy on a set of semantic differential, bipolar adjective scales. A factor analysis of the intercorrelations between these ratings enabled the derivation of two personality dimensions, self-centered personality and good mixer, in terms of which each tall poppy could be described. Finally, subjects responded to a hypothetical situation where each tall poppy fell from his or her high position and was described as either responsible for the fall or not responsible for the fall. They rated how sorry, pleased, or disturbed they would feel about the fall in each case.

Table 9.1 presents a sample of the results for the responsible and not responsible hypothetical conditions, averaging subjects' responses across the three tall poppies that they rated. The pattern of correlations was generally similar for both

---

[1]The three political leaders were Robert Hawke, Andrew Peacock, and Janine Haines; the three sports leaders were Alan Border, Pat Cash, and Lisa Curry-Kenny; the three star entertainers were Paul Hogan, John Farnham, and Kylie Minogue. All were public figures in Australia.

TABLE 9.1

Correlations Between Feelings About the Fall and Causal Attributions and Personality Characteristics

				Feelings About Fall				
	Responsible Condition				Not Responsible Condition			
Variable	Sorry	Pleased	Disturbed		Sorry	Pleased	Disturbed
Causal attributions							
Ability	0.21***	-0.29***	0.10		0.28***	-0.29***	0.15**
Effort	0.21***	-0.32***	0.07		0.29***	-0.29***	0.13*
Assistance	-0.15**	0.08	-0.20***		-0.14**	0.05	-0.14**
Luck	-0.07	-0.09	-0.16**		-0.03	-0.10	-0.11*
Deserve							
Present position	0.35***	-0.37***	0.12*		0.43***	-0.29***	0.15**
Maintain position	0.34***	-0.33***	0.16**		0.39***	-0.28***	0.14**
Personality							
Self-centered	-0.34***	0.31***	-0.14**		-0.43***	0.23***	-0.15**
Good mixer	0.38***	-0.33***	0.16**		0.49***	-0.30***	0.22***

Note. Ns ranged from 337 to 357 due to some missing cases. Tests of significance are two-tailed. Reprinted from Feather et al. (1991) with the permission of the authors and the Australian Psychological Society.
*p < .05. **p < .01. ***p < .001.

conditions. It is clear from the correlations in Table 9.1 that those subjects who reported feeling more pleased about the fall of tall poppies were those who were less likely to attribute the success of the tall poppies to ability and effort, less likely to indicate that the tall poppies both deserved their high positions and deserved to maintain them, more likely to perceive the tall poppies as self-centered, and less likely to perceive them as good mixers (a variable that included items concerned with friendliness, integrity, and being in touch with the average person). The correlations tended to be in the reverse direction when subjects' ratings concerned how sorry or disturbed they felt about the fall of the tall poppies or high achievers. These ratings tended to be positively related to causal beliefs that the tall poppies rose to their high positions because of ability and effort, negatively related to causal beliefs that the high status was a result of external assistance and good luck, positively related to judgments that the tall poppies deserved their high positions and also deserved to maintain them, positively related to perceptions that the tall poppies were good mixers, and negatively related to perceptions that the tall poppies were self-centered.

A further analysis showed that subjects also reported feeling more sorry, less pleased, and more disturbed about the fall of the tall poppies when the tall poppies were described as not responsible for the fall when compared with the condition where they were described as responsible for it.

Other results from the study are presented in Table 9.2, again averaging responses across the three tall poppies that each subject rated (Feather et al., 1991). In this case the ratings of feeling pleased about each tall poppy's present position, about a hypothetical rise or improvement in that position, and about a hypothetical fall, were those that were obtained earlier in the questionnaire. The results in Table 9.2 that concern feeling pleased about the fall are consistent with those reported in Table 9.1. In addition, however, Table 9.2 provides information about those variables that related to reported positive affect and deservingness. These results show that subjects' ratings of how pleased they felt about both the tall poppies' current success and about any possible further rise were positively related to causal attributions concerning ability and effort, negatively related to attributions concerning external assistance, positively related to ratings of deservingness, negatively related to the perceived self-centeredness of the tall poppies, and positively related to the degree to which the tall poppies were perceived to be good mixers. In addition to its links with affect, the deservingness variable was positively related to ability and effort attributions for the tall poppies' success, negatively related to causal attributions that referred to external assistance, negatively related to the perceived self-centeredness of the tall poppies, and positively related to the good mixer variable.

The results also showed that subjects were generally more favorable in various ways toward tall poppies in the sports domain when compared with tall poppies in the politics and entertainment domains. Rising to eminence in sport is clearly a matter of effort and skill and less attributable to external assistance and luck than

TABLE 9.2
Correlations Between Deserve and Pleased Measures and Causal Attributions and Personality
Characteristics

	Deserve		Pleased		
Variable	Present Position	Maintain Position	Present Position	Rise Further	Fall
Causal attributions					
Ability	0.61***	0.54***	0.49***	0.49***	-0.40***
Effort	0.64***	0.53***	0.52***	0.50***	-0.42***
Assistance	-0.21*	-0.23***	-0.23***	-0.22***	0.30**
Luck	0.01	-0.03	-0.01	0.03	0.10
Deserve					
Present position	--	0.83***	0.69***	0.69***	-0.56***
Maintain position	0.83***	--	0.67***	0.70***	-0.61***
Personality					
Self-centered	-0.56***	-0.55***	-0.59***	-0.58***	0.53***
Good mixer	0.55***	0.51***	0.57***	0.56***	-0.50***

Note. Ns ranged from 345 to 367 due to some missing cases. Tests of significance are two-tailed. Reprinted from Feather et al. (1991) with the permission of the authors and the Australian Psychological Society.
*$p < .05$; **$p < .01$; ***$p < .001$.

might be the case in the other two domains (see Feather et al., 1991, Table 9.1). Future research could use larger samples of public figures selected from a variety of domains that vary in their relevance for the subjects who make the judgments. High profile tall poppies could also be interviewed for their own opinions about how they are perceived by others and about how others might react to their fall.

Similar results to those from the Feather et al. (1991) study were obtained in a subsequent study (Feather, 1993a, 1993b) that involved only political leaders, one of whom (Robert Hawke) had recently lost his position as Prime Minister of Australia, suffering a dramatic fall from the top of the political ladder. Thus, in his case we were dealing with an actual fall rather than with a hypothetical fall. Again subjects' reported affective reactions to the success or failure of the tall poppies were related to how they attributed causality for the success or failure, the degree to which the success or failure was seen to be deserved, and the degree to which the subjects perceived the tall poppies as having positive or negative personality characteristics.

In this study I also obtained ratings of the degree to which each political figure was seen as responsible for a fall should it occur. For Hawke, who had already been displaced from the top political position in Australia, these responsibility ratings were positively related to causal attributions to lack of ability and lack of effort, negatively related to causal attributions to external forces and bad luck, positively related to judgments that Hawke deserved his present fallen status and also deserved to maintain it, positively related to the degree to which Hawke was perceived to be arrogant, and negatively related to the degree to which he was seen to possess integrity (Feather, 1994, Table 15).

VALUE STRUCTURES

How do values enter into these relations? They may enter in a number of different ways. How we react to the personality of a high achiever may depend on our own value priorities. For example, if a tall poppy is seen to be unscrupulous and to lack integrity, then we would be more likely to want to see the tall poppy fall if we place a high value on honesty and responsibility. We may be more supportive of a tall poppy who is friendly and has good interpersonal relations if we hold strong communal values. We may endorse the entrepreneurial and competitive actions of a tall poppy if we assign a lot of importance to individualistic values, such as those that are concerned with self-direction and personal achievement. In general, how we judge the moral character of any person will depend on the values that we hold. Moreover, our judgments concerning whether a tall poppy deserves the high status or deserves to fall are likely to depend in part on our dominant values. There would be general agreement that questions of justice and deservingness are closely related to value priorities.

Before addressing these possibilities, however, I should be clear about what I mean by values. I regard values as beliefs about desirable or undesirable ways of behaving or about the desirability or otherwise of general goals. For example, a person might find honesty preferable to dishonesty and freedom preferable to lack of freedom. Values are more abstract than attitudes in the sense that they transcend specific objects, events, and situations. They are closely linked to the self-concept and they function as evaluative criteria that people use when judging outcomes and events, when deciding between courses of action, and when setting plans in motion that are directed toward goals. The values that people hold are fewer in number than the much larger set of specific attitudes and beliefs that they express and endorse. Values are not equal in importance but they form a hierarchy of importance for each individual, group, or culture, with some values being more important than others. Values have some stability about them but they may change in relative importance depending on changing circumstances. They are not cold cognitions but are linked to the affective system. People feel happy when their important values are fulfilled; angry when these values are frustrated. These ideas obviously owe a lot to Rokeach (1973).

In addition, however, I have proposed that values can be conceived as abstract structures or schemas that can be represented as associative networks, with each central value linked to a set of attitudes and beliefs (Feather, 1971, 1975, 1990). The networks for a particular value may vary from person to person and from group to group in their content and structural organization. These differences would reflect differences in the meaning of the value despite a common core of meaning (Feather, 1975, p.16). For example, freedom as a value may have a different structure of relations for different persons and groups, depending on the set of attitudes and beliefs that surround it and to which it is linked. In some cases the structure may be complex and finely differentiated; in other cases it may be simple and not elaborated in any detailed way. Yet the value still concerns freedom even though it is articulated in different ways.

The network of relations that involves the value is a learned network based on each person's own experience. Moreover, one would expect that the network would involve consistent sets of relations that may nevertheless be modified in the light of new experience as a person deals with discrepant information (Feather, 1971). It may be the case that more strongly held values are centers or hubs in more complex and more differentiated networks of attitudes and beliefs (cf. Lusk & Judd, 1988; Tesser & Leone, 1977), and that resolution of discrepancies may involve a lot of cognitive work when strongly held values are in conflict (cf. Tetlock, 1986). Alternatively, it might be argued that more strongly held values are hubs in simply defined structures and exert their influence rapidly, enabling a quick and definite response to situations and events under conditions where there is no value conflict. Research is needed to resolve these alternative possibilities, taking situational and personality differences into account.

The associative network for a particular value would also include links to other values and their networks. Figure 9.1 presents an example for two values, value X and value Y, that are assumed to be associated. Value X is linked to attitudes 1, 2, and 3 and value Y to attitudes 1, 3, and 4. Each of these attitudes is in turn linked to wider sets of specific beliefs not represented in the diagram. Attitudes 1 and 2 would be related because they are both linked to value X. Attitudes 3 and 4 would be related because they are both linked to value Y. Note that attitudes 1 and 3 each share common values (value X and value Y) but attitudes 2 and 4 do not have any values in common. Thus, this form of representation allows for the fact that attitudes may be multidetermined in the sense that

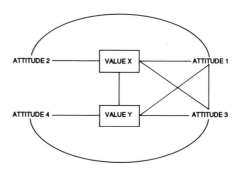

FIG. 9.1.   Structures relating attitudes to underlying values.

they may express the influence of more than one underlying value. One implication of this arrangement is that one would expect that attitudes 1 and 3 would be associated because of their common value base, whereas attitudes 2 and 4 may be unrelated.

Value X may also be more important to the person than value Y. This possibility is represented in Fig. 9.1 by the vertical arrangement of the values, with value X placed above value Y. It is not implied by this arrangement that value X derives from value Y or vice versa, but only that value X is judged to be more important by an individual in his or her value system. A very important value would be more central to the self than a less important value, having more influence on a person's attitudes and beliefs.

Values are activated or primed depending on their strength and the presence of situational cues. For example, a person who values equality strongly would be sensitive to many different forms of equalities and inequalities within situations, even when situational cues are minimal. The value is activated with relative ease because it is a strong value. Situational cues may also prime a value. For example, freedom as a value would be activated when a situation poses the possibility that basic freedoms might be restricted. Pleasure would be activated in a situation that poses the possibility of hedonic fulfillment. The value is activated because there are relevant cues in the situation that elicit it, even though it may be less important than other values that remain latent.

Once activated a value may also prime attitudes and beliefs that are part of its associative network and that are relevant to the particular situation. For example, when equality as a value is aroused within the context of a situation that condones discrimination against women, attitudes and beliefs that are connected to equality and women's rights may also be activated. The activation of the value spreads to other relevant attitudes and beliefs that are part of the associative network. The activation of a value may also have the effect of inducing new attitudes and beliefs when novel situations are encountered and dealt with in a cognitive way. These new attitudes and beliefs would then be recruited to the associative network that defines the value.

This rather abstract discussion summarizes how I conceive of values. It is consistent with the assumption that I have proposed previously that values, once activated, may induce valences or subjective values on objects and events, influencing the way a person construes an immediate situation in relation to its affective and motivational properties (Feather, 1975, 1990, 1992b, 1995). It is also consistent with the assumption in functional theories of attitudes that attitudes may serve value-expressive functions (Katz, 1960; Maio & Olson, 1994). Thus, I assume that we relate possible actions and outcomes within particular situations to our value systems, testing them against our general conceptions about what we believe is desirable or undesirable in terms of our own value priorities. A major function of the values that people hold is to influence the subjective values that they assign to possible actions and outcomes within a situation so that some actions and outcomes are seen as attractive (or positively valent) and some as aversive (or negatively valent). For example, outcomes that are expected to lead to personal influence would be seen as attractive by a person who values power; ways of behaving that involve bending the rules would be seen as aversive by a person who values honesty. I therefore distinguish between the general values that people hold and the subjective evaluations that they assign to possible actions and outcomes. In an important sense, our general values influence our affective appraisal or evaluation of the different actions and outcomes that are possible within specific situations.

How can this conceptual analysis be related to the results concerning public figures that I reported? First, knowledge about the personality characteristics of a tall poppy and about the tall poppy's behavior may activate values that prime associated attitudes relating to the tall poppy and his or her behavior. For example, knowledge that a person has consistently displayed a lack of integrity over a number of situations and continues to do so in a current situation may activate values concerned with honesty and responsibility and induce negative attitudes toward the person and his or her behavior. Prosocial values may be activated in the case of a person who is known to be kind and considerate toward others, and these values may prime positive attitudes toward the person and his or her behavior. Over time, attributions may be made about the tall poppy's moral character on the basis of the consistent positively or negatively valued behavior that has been observed. For example, the tall poppy may be seen as lacking integrity or as a person with positive moral values. Second, values and induced attitudes are important components of an analysis of deservingness that I have described previously (Feather, 1992a, 1993b) and which I now elaborate further. Whether a tall poppy is seen to deserve to hold his or her high position or deserves to fall depends on the values of the person who is judging the tall poppy and on how these values function to induce positive or negative evaluations of the tall poppy's actions and outcomes.

VALUES, RESPONSIBILITY, AND DESERVINGNESS

The results from the studies with public figures and from other studies in my research program have shown that deservingness is a key variable in regard both to attitudes toward tall poppies and reactions to their fall (Feather, 1994). These results consistently indicated that subjects were more positive toward tall poppies when their success was seen to be deserved rather than undeserved. Similarly, their reactions to the fall of tall poppies were more sympathetic when the fall was seen to be undeserved rather than deserved. These relations between affect and deservingness were not restricted to tall poppies. They applied more generally to successful or unsuccessful other persons (e.g., Feather, 1992a).

But how can we analyze deservingness, taking values into account? I have developed a model of deservingness that combines ideas from attribution theory, balance theory, and value theory. One important variable that is assumed to influence whether or not a person is seen to deserve an outcome is the degree to which the person is perceived to be personally responsible for it. The concept of responsibility is a complex one and it can be linked both to a person's actions and intentions and to a person's defined role. Thus Hamilton and Hagiwara (1992) asserted that "there are two fundamental considerations in a responsibility judgment. The actor's *deeds,* including the mental state with which they were performed; and the actor's *role,* including the obligations for which the role occupant would normally be considered accountable" (p.159).

The first consideration assumes that a person is responsible for an event or outcome when the cause of an action or outcome has its locus in the person and when it is under the control of the person and can be related to the person's intentions. This general definition of personal responsibility is consistent with usage in the legal and psychological literature. For example, both Heider's (1958) definition of different levels of responsibility and Piaget's (1932) analysis of moral judgment included intentionality as an important determinant of responsibility. Legal definitions of responsibility also refer to intentionality as a key component (e.g., Fincham & Jaspars, 1980; Hart, 1968). So do discussions concerning the attribution of blame (Shaver, 1985) and the experience of injustice (Mikula, 1993). Responsibility was linked to volition in my structural balance model of communication effects (Feather, 1964, 1967). Weiner's (1986) attributional theory of motivation and emotion included controllability as one of the attributional dimensions. He has discussed responsibility in relation to the attributional dimension of perceived controllability and has included it as a key variable in the analysis of social motivation (Weiner, 1993, 1995, in press; see also, Feather, in press).

The second aspect of responsibility takes account of role obligations and the obligations for which the occupant of the role is normally accountable. For example, parents are responsible for the welfare of their children; a goal-keeper is responsible for defending the goal area in a soccer match; military commanders are responsible for sending soldiers into battle. In these cases responsibility is tied to the role and the duties and obligations that the role entails. When these role obligations are present, responsibility may be allocated for an outcome (e.g., a negative event) despite the fact that it was unintended (e.g., as when parents violate a duty of care, are negligent, and their child is injured). This aspect of responsibility that pertains to roles is also basic to the legal process but, as Hamilton and Hagiwara (1992) indicated, it has been somewhat neglected by psychologists. In the present context, tall poppies who have risen to positions of high status may be seen to have a responsibility or obligation to occupy their role so as not to violate the high expectations that others might have of them in regard to role-appropriate behavior. They are trusted to behave in a way that fits their privileged position and they are accountable if they fail to fulfil their obligations.

The high status brings with it the responsibility of behaving in a way that conforms to the superior role. In this sense responsibility is linked to trust and obligation.

These different aspects of responsibility have also been discussed by Hamilton (1978, 1992) and by Schlenker, Britt, Pennington, Murphy, and Doherty (1994). The latter authors proposed that, "people are held responsible in a situation to the extent that (a) a clear, well-defined set of prescriptions is applicable to the event (prescription–event link), (b) the actor is perceived to be bound by the prescriptions by virtue of his or her identity (prescription–identity link), and (c) the actor seems to be connected to the event, especially by seeming to have (or to have had) personal control over the event, such as intentionally producing the consequences (identity–event) link" (p. 635). In their terms, "responsibility is the adhesive that connects an actor to an event and to relevant prescriptions that should govern conduct; thus responsibility provides a basis for judgment and sanctioning" (p. 635).

People may be responsible for both positive and negative events and outcomes and in social situations they may respond in various ways to a judgment that they are responsible (e.g., Bies, 1987; Hamilton, 1992; Hamilton & Hagiwara, 1992; Kelman & Hamilton, 1989; Schlenker et al., 1994; Snyder & Higgins, 1988; Tedeschi & Reiss, 1981; Weiner, 1992). For example, they may deny responsibility for a negative event, make excuses that are internal or external in their attribution, plead mitigating circumstances, justify the event, apologize for it, convey the impression that it is normal practice, or provide other sorts of accounts as they negotiate the question of responsibility. In role situations these responses may vary depending on whether the role involves a hierarchical or equal relationship or a close or distant relationship, and they may also vary across cultures (Hamilton & Hagiwara, 1992).

The different meanings of responsibility have in common the idea that a person or other who is responsible for an event and its consequences is linked to the event or owns it by virtue of his or her intention or role. This representation of responsibility as involving a unit relation between an individual and his or her action is an important part of the subsequent analysis.

I begin this analysis by asking how does responsibility relate to deservingness? It can be assumed that deservingness for an outcome depends in part on the degree to which a person is seen to be responsible for it. For example, if a tall poppy rose to high status because of a lucky event (e.g., being born into a wealthy family), he or she may be seen to deserve the high status less than when the high status was achieved because of skillful application and hard work. The lucky tall poppy would be perceived as less responsible for the outcome than the hard-working tall poppy and therefore less deserving of it. Similarly, a student who obtained a low grade in an examination because of sickness would be seen as less responsible for the poor performance and as less deserving of the low grade when compared with a student whose low grade was the result of lack of effort (Feather, 1992a). In general, therefore, a person cannot be held to deserve an outcome for which he or she is not responsible.

However, although perceived responsibility for an outcome is a key variable that affects judgments of deservingness, it is not the only variable. The analysis of deservingness also has to consider other variables, especially those that relate to values. I have proposed that deservingness may be analyzed in relation to the conjunction of positively or negatively valued behaviors and positively or negatively valued outcomes (Feather, 1992a, 1994). Outcomes would be perceived to be deserved if a positively valued outcome followed positively valued instrumental behavior, or if a negatively valued outcome followed negatively valued instrumental behavior.In contrast, outcomes would be perceived to be undeserved if a positively valued outcome followed negatively valued instrumental behavior, or if a negatively valued outcome followed positively valued instrumental behavior.

These different possibilities are illustrated in the four structures in Fig. 9.2. Each of these structures involves a person in the role of a judge, evaluating actions and outcomes as they relate to some actor who could be self or other, and judging the degree to which the actor deserves or does not deserve the outcome. In these structures a positive sentiment or attitudinal relation is represented by a solid line and a negative sentiment or attitudinal relation by a dashed line. For example, in Fig. 9.2a both action and outcome are positively valued by the person; in Fig. 9.2d the action is negatively valued but the outcome is positively valued. In all of the structures action and outcome are bound together by a positive unit relation represented by a solid bracket, that is, the outcome is associated with or belongs to the action.

The top two structures in Fig. 9.2 are balanced according to Heider's (1958) principle. The cycles involve either three positive relations as in Fig. 9.2a or two negative relations and one positive relation as in Fig. 9.2b. The relations fit together in a consistent manner and there would be no pressure to change them. In contrast, the bottom two structures in Fig. 9.2 are unbalanced according to Heider's (1958) principle. For both Fig. 9.2c and Fig. 9.2d the cycle involves two positive relations and one negative relation. These relations form an inconsistent or unbalanced set and they would be associated with a certain amount of tension or pressure to change that may or may not be easy to resolve.

This kind of analysis recognizes that an actor may be seen to be responsible for an outcome that he or she does not deserve. For example, a positively valued action (e.g., hard work on the part of a student) may be associated with a negatively valued outcome (e.g., a low grade in the exam); a negatively valued action (e.g., dishonest business practices) may be associated with a positively valued outcome (e.g., rising to a high level in the management structure of a firm). These two cases that involve attitudinal relations of opposite sign are represented in Fig. 9.2c and Fig. 9.2d respectively. They are cases where controllable actions for which an actor is perceived to be responsible are associated with outcomes that are likely to be seen as undeserved. The other two structures

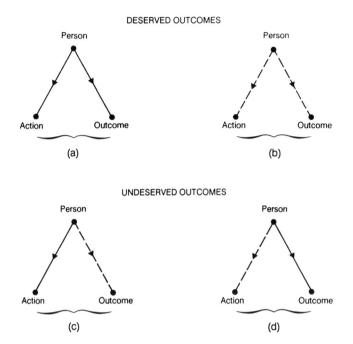

FIG. 9.2.   Balanced and unbalanced structures representing deserved and undeserved outcomes.

in Fig. 9.2 involve attitudinal relations of the same sign. They represent situations where outcomes are seen to be deserved, as when a high achiever achieves success by diligence and hard work, Fig. 9.2a, or when a high achiever suffers a fall because of unethical behavior, Fig. 9.2b. Note that this analysis of deservingness has general application and is not restricted to the rise or fall of tall poppies.

Following the earlier discussion (pp. 223–225, Fig. 9.1), it is assumed that the positively or negatively valued actions and outcomes in Fig. 9.2 can be related to the underlying general values that are held by the person or judge. That is, the general values that the person holds (e.g., honesty, achievement) would influence the subjective values or positive and negative valences that are assigned to the specific instrumental actions and their outcomes. They would affect the strength and sign of the person's immediate attitudes toward these actions and outcomes via an associative network. For example, a person for whom honesty and achievement are important general values would positively evaluate both honest actions and the success that followed these actions in a specific situation. The success would be seen to be deserved. Dishonest actions would be negatively evaluated and the positive outcome (success) that followed these actions would then be seen to be undeserved. Whether an outcome is seen to be deserved or not deserved therefore depends on the values of the person who makes the judgment, but the effects of these values are assumed to be mediated via their effects on the way specific actions and outcomes are evaluated (Feather, 1990, 1995).

EXTENDED STRUCTURES

The model in Fig. 9.2 can be extended in a number of ways. There is not space to discuss these possible extensions in detail but two such extensions are presented in Figs. 9.3 and 9.4 where, in each case, the actor being judged is another person. In these structures the other person is included as an entity, in addition to the person who takes the role of judge. This extension enables the representation of different kinds of relations between person and other and between other and action. All of the relations in Figs. 9.3 and 9.4 are from the point of view of the person or judge.

In Figs. 9.3 and 9.4 a positive unit relation is used to link other and action. This unit relation is represented by a solid bracket and it denotes that other is perceived to own the action, that is, is seen to be responsible for it. A negative unit relation between other and action, represented by a dashed bracket, could be used to represent cases where other is seen as not responsible for the action, that is, is perceived in some sense as disowning it.

In Fig. 9.3 the other new relations are positive or negative unit relations that connect person and other and these relations are also represented by solid or dashed brackets respectively. These positive and negative unit relations can be used to model cases where other belongs to the person's ingroup (positive unit relation) or to a perceived outgroup (negative unit relation).

The relations that connect person and other in Fig. 9.4 are positive or negative sentiment or attitudinal relations and they are represented by solid or dashed lines respectively. These positive and negative attitudinal relations can be used to model cases where the person likes the other (positive attitudinal relation) or dislikes the other (negative attitudinal relation).

All of the other relations in Figs. 9.3 and 9.4 have the same meaning as before, and, as in Fig. 9.2, the structures are partitioned into those relating to deserved outcomes and those relating to undeserved outcomes.

The structures in Figs. 9.3 and 9.4 enable one to frame hypotheses about the effects of ingroup versus outgroup membership and interpersonal liking or disliking on judgments of deservingness. Note that in each of these extended figures only two structures are completely balanced in all cycles. These are the structures in Figs. 9.3a and 9.4a respectively, where a member of a person's ingroup or a liked other is seen to engage in positively valued behavior that leads to a positively valued outcome, and in Figs. 9.3d and 9.4d respectively, where a member of a person's outgroup, or a disliked other, is seen to engage in negatively valued

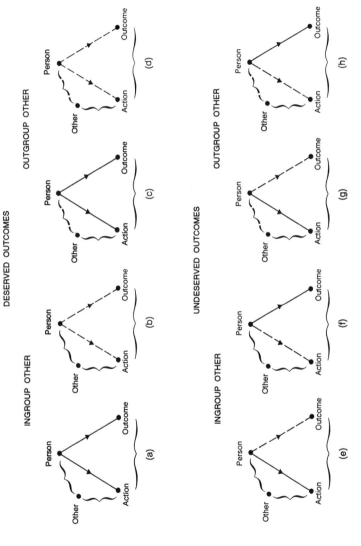

FIG. 9.3. Balanced and unbalanced structures representing deserved and undeserved outcomes for ingroup other and outgroup other.

231

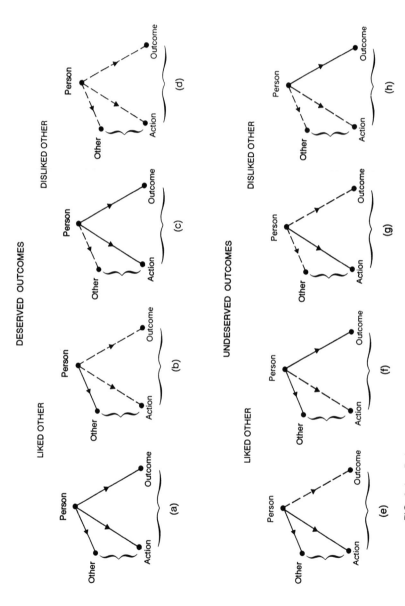

FIG. 9.4. Balanced and unbalanced structures representing deserved and undeserved outcomes for liked other and disliked other.

behavior that leads to a negatively valued outcome. In each of these cases the outcome would be perceived to be deserved.

All of the other structures in Figs. 9.3 and 9.4 are unbalanced to the degree that only one cycle out of the three cycles in each structure is balanced according to Heider's (1958) principle. These unbalanced structures may vary in the ease with which the inconsistencies can be resolved. Balance could be restored if one or more of the relations were to change in sign. Which relations change would depend upon their strength or resistance.

It is probably the case that the person's positive or negative evaluation of other's action and other's outcome are both fairly resistant to change when these relations are grounded in the stable and important values that the person holds. Relations in the person–action–outcome triad that define whether an outcome is deserved or undeserved may then retain their formal structure. That means that the bottom four structures in Figs. 9.3 and 9.4 that relate to undeserved outcomes would remain unbalanced even if changes in other relations were possible. However, the attitudinal relations in the person-action-outcome triad may change in the direction of balancing the triad if they are weak relations based on values that are not strongly held.

Changes in the person–action–outcome triad would not be necessary in structures (b) and (c) in Figs. 9.3 and 9.4 that both relate to deserved outcomes. It would be possible to achieve complete balance in these structures by changing either the person-to-other relation or the other-to-action relation. For example, to resolve the imbalance in Fig. 9.3b, person may either relegate other to the outgroup (the positive unit relation changes to negative) or person may see other as not responsible for the negatively valued action (the positive unit relation changes to negative). As another example, in Fig. 9.4c, person may develop a positive attitude toward other (the negative attitudinal relation changes to positive) or perceive other as not responsible for the positively valued action (the positive unit relation changes to negative). Either change in each structure would resolve the imbalance.

In general, judgments that relate to the balanced structures in Figs. 9.3 and 9.4 should occur more automatically than those that relate to the unbalanced structures. This prediction follows from the assumption that it is the balanced or consistent structures that are laid down in memory (Feather, 1971) and responses relating to these kinds of structures are more likely to occur quickly and without much cognitive effort. On the other hand, unbalanced structures would require that a person engage in cognitive work to resolve inconsistencies. Responses relating to unbalanced structures should therefore take longer to process and they would be both less automatic and less predictable.

It is clear that the structures in Figs. 9.3 and 9.4 extend the analysis of deservingness and enable predictions to be made about the effects of social identity (ingroup vs. outgroup) and interpersonal relations (positive vs. negative liking), thus connecting with two important areas in social psychology. Whether relations in the person–action–outcome triad are balanced or unbalanced remains as an important criterion for judging whether outcomes are deserved or undeserved. But judgments about deservingness or undeservingness are also assumed to be modified by the nature of the unit and attitudinal relations between person and other and by whether or not other is seen to own or be responsible for the action. A jury decision concerning guilt and whether a defendant deserves to be punished, for example, may be influenced by whether or not some of the jury members share a common social identity with the defendant (e.g., in terms of gender, class, or ethnic background), by attitudes of like or dislike for the defendant that may have developed in the course of the trial, and by judgments about the defendant's responsibility for the alleged offense.

The detailed working-out of the extended model presented in Figs. 9.3 and 9.4 depends on assumptions about the strength of relations within each structure and their resistance to change. As I have emphasized in previous discussions (Feather, 1971), applications of balance theory need to consider not only the sign of relations (positive or negative) but also their strength so that the precise mode of resolving imbalance can be determined.

It is interesting to note that Heider (1958) made the connection between balance and deservingness when discussing reactions to the lot of another person (Feather, 1994). Thus he stated that "the situation is balanced if the experiences of another are in accord with what he deserves" (p. 284). The present analysis takes this idea a lot further and relates perceptions of deservingness (and undeservingness) not only to balanced or unbalanced structures but also to other variables that centrally include perceptions of personal responsibility and underlying values that influence a person's evaluative reactions to actions and their outcomes. The analysis also implies that there may be a tendency for people to process information in the direction of moving toward the balanced deservingness structures. Perhaps this tendency underlies the belief in a just world where people get what they deserve, a belief that has been discussed by Lerner (1980, 1991).

EXPERIMENTAL STUDIES OF TALL POPPIES

The studies of public figures to which I referred previously had the advantage of involving real-life tall poppies who were conspicuously successful but the disadvantage of not permitting experimental manipulation and control over important variables. One cannot intervene to manipulate the status of a prime minister, or a leading sportsperson or a megastar in the entertainment world. One has to deal with events as they are, drawing comfort from the fact that the results have a high level of ecological validity and are interesting in their own right.

The early studies in my research program on tall poppies involved the experimental manipulation of status (Feather, 1989). The theoretical analysis of deservingness that I have just presented came later, prompted in part by the research on public figures and by the results of these earlier experimental studies. Status was varied by using hypothetical scenarios or vignettes. In the first of these investigations scenarios were presented to subjects about a stimulus person who either had a consistently high level of performance at high school (the tall poppy) or had a level of performance that was consistently about average (Feather, 1989). I manipulated the extent to which the stimulus person fell from his or her original position in the final important examination that qualified the student for entry into university. Would subjects experience some degree of satisfaction or *Schadenfreude* when the stimulus person fell or would subjects report sympathy or unhappiness about the fall? Would these affective reactions be more pronounced for the high achiever than for the average achiever? Would reactions to the stimulus person's fall depend upon the extent of the fall and on how attractive the stimulus person was seen to be?

There were 531 male and female students who participated in this study. They came from high schools in metropolitan Adelaide and they were all in Grade 11, the penultimate grade before completing high school. These subjects answered a questionnaire in which they were presented with a scenario that described a male or female stimulus person who was either a high or average achiever at school. Subsequently the stimulus person was described as suffering a fall in academic performance in the final important public examination that qualifies students for tertiary studies. The fall could take one of three forms: from high performance to middle performance, from high performance to low performance, from middle performance to low performance.

Subjects rated the high and average achiever on a variety of scales before information about the fall was provided. These scales concerned causal attributions for the stimulus person's performance, personality characteristics, and attraction to the stimulus person. After they received information about the fall, they rated the stimulus person again with respect to causal attributions for the fall, whether they would feel privately pleased about the stimulus person's fall, how they thought the stimulus person would feel about the fall, and whether they would feel more friendly toward the stimulus person, about the same as before, or less friendly.

Some of the main results are presented in the top half of Table 9.3. Table 9.3 shows that subjects were generally displeased about the stimulus person's fall. They did not report *Schadenfreude* or satisfaction about the stimulus person's diminished performance. Table 9.3 also shows that they expressed least displeasure about the fall when the stimulus person fell from high to middle and most displeasure when the fall was from middle to low. Similarly, they reported feeling more friendly toward the stimulus person when the fall was from high to middle and least friendly when it was from middle to bottom.

More specific comparisons showed that subjects reported that they would feel less displeasure when the stimulus person fell from the high to the middle

TABLE 9.3
Mean Scores for Post-Fall Variables in Relation to Status for Study 1 and Study 2

		Mean Scores for Study 1			
		Type of Fall			
Variable	Midpoint of Scale	High to Middle Status	High to Low Status	Middle to Low Status	df	F
Deserve to fall	4	4.34	4.05	4.31	2,509	1.91
Respondent pleasure about fall	4	3.57	3.16	2.78	2,511	11.38***
Stimulus person pleasure about fall	4	1.72	1.33	1.66	2,513	6.49**
More friendly attitude	2	2.16	2.12	2.04	2,506	3.40*

| | Mean Scores for Study 2 | | | |
Variable	Midpoint of Scale	High Achiever	Average Achiever	df	F
Report to authorities	4	2.86	2.09	1,351	16.06***
Discuss with others	4	4.64	4.42	1,353	1.20
Pleased about discovery	4	4.81	4.33	1,353	7.96**
Penalty for cheating	3.5	3.32	3.04	1,352	9.41**
Deserve penalty	4	4.17	3.46	1,352	15.98***
Pleased about expulsion	4	3.52	2.93	1,351	19.40***

Note. In Study 1, $N = 175$ for high to middle fall; $N = 173$ for high to low fall; $N = 183$ for middle to low fall. In study 2, $N = 361$. Minor variations from those Ns occurred because of missing cases. Reprinted from Feather (1989) with the permission of the author and the Australian Psychological Society.
*$p < .05$. **$p < .01$. ***$p < .001$.

position than from the high to low position, less displeasure when the fall was from high to low than from middle to low, and less displeasure when the fall was from high to middle than from middle to low. All of these differences between means were statistically significant. Subjects also reported that they would feel more friendly toward the stimulus person who fell from the high status position to the middle status position than when the fall was from middle to low, but the other comparisons that involved the more friendly attitude variable were not statistically significant. Note that a fall below the average position would denote a failure on the scale of performance. It is not surprising that subjects, who were students themselves, would report feeling especially displeased about this outcome and that they would also report that the stimulus person would be more displeased (see Table 9.3).

How do these results relate to underlying values? One interpretation is that subjects showed a preference for the average position in the classroom, a preference that may reflect the influence of egalitarian values. The high achieving student or tall poppy who fell to the middle of the class would become more similar and equal to others. The average achiever who fell away from the middle of the class would be removed from the collectivity defined by the middle or normal range of accomplishment. Thus a fall to the average position in the middle of the class was the least aversive outcome and a fall away from the middle of the class was the most aversive outcome. The middle of the class may be seen to define the collectivity and a preference for that position would express collectivist, egalitarian values. There is evidence from research described in a subsequent section that favoring the fall of tall poppies in general is positively related to the strength of egalitarian values.

The results also showed that, although the high achiever and the average achiever were initially perceived differently in regard to their personalities and the causes of their performance, there was no evidence that subjects found the high achiever less attractive. Thus, ability, effort, and friendly teachers were seen as more important causes of the high achiever's initial success when compared with the success of the average achiever; good luck was rated as a more important cause for the average achiever; the high achiever was seen as more achievement-oriented and assertive, and as more introverted and less sociable than the average achiever; but both stimulus persons were similar as far as their attraction to subjects was concerned, where attraction was measured in terms of whether subjects would interact closely with the stimulus person, would like the stimulus person, and so on. The results did show, however, that there were negative correlations between initial attraction toward the stimulus person and subjects' reports about how pleased they felt about the stimulus person's fall, that is, the less they liked the stimulus person, the more pleased they were about the fall.

A previously unpublished analysis of data from this first study also showed that subjects' ratings of how much they believed the stimulus person deserved to fall was positively related to the importance assigned to lack of ability as a cause of the fall, $r(522) = .16, p < .001$; positively related to the importance assigned to lack of effort or hard work, $r(523) = .16, p < .001$; negatively related to the importance assigned to the difficulty of the exam, $r(523) = -.10, p < .05$; and negatively related to the importance assigned to bad luck, $r(522) = -.12, p < .01$. So, as was the case in the studies involving public figures (Feather, 1993b; Feather et al., 1991), causal attributions predicted deservingness (see pp. 220–222). Deservingness ratings for the fall were also positively correlated with how pleased subjects reported they would feel about the fall, $r(519) = .12, p < .01$, and negatively correlated with subjects' reports that they would feel more friendly toward the stimulus person, $r(514) = -.13, p < .01$.

A second study (Feather, 1989) investigated a different kind of fall and it provided information about the cause of the fall, information that was absent in the first study. The fall in the second study occurred because of a misdemeanor (cheating at an examination). There were 361 male and female subjects in the second study. These subjects were sampled from the introductory psychology class at Flinders University. They completed a questionnaire that presented a hypothetical scenario that described either a male or female person who was either a high or average achiever on university examinations. As in the first study, subjects first rated the stimulus person on personality characteristics and on items designed to measure attraction.

Subsequently, subjects were presented with information that asked them to suppose that, while they were sitting a major examination with the high or average achiever, they became aware that the stimulus person was cheating. Subjects then answered questions about the actions they would take and how they would privately feel. These questions concerned whether they would report the stimulus person to the authorities, whether they would discuss the cheating with their fellow students, how they would privately feel if the stimulus person was caught cheating by someone in authority, what level of penalty should be exacted by a disciplinary committee, to what extent the stimulus person deserved to be expelled from the university, and how pleased they would be if the stimulus person were to be expelled.

The main results are presented in the bottom part of Table 9.3. The results show that subjects were more pleased when the high achiever was caught cheating than when the average achiever was caught. They were also more pleased when the high achiever was expelled from the university than when the average achiever was expelled. They also indicated that they would be more likely to report the high achiever to the authorities, that they would award a harsher penalty to the high achiever for cheating, and that they considered that the high achiever deserved the penalty more when compared with the average achiever. As was the case in the first study, subjects perceived the high achiever and the average achiever differently in regard to their personality characteristics. They saw the high achiever as more achievement-oriented and assertive than the average achiever and less sociable and less of a good mixer when compared with the average achiever. Whether the stimulus person was a high achiever or an average achiever made no difference to the attraction that subjects initially reported for either stimulus person. Initial attraction to each stimulus person was again negatively correlated with reported feelings of pleasure that related to the fall.

A further previously unpublished analysis of data from this second study showed that subjects' ratings of how much they believed the stimulus person deserved to be expelled from the university for cheating was positively related to their ratings of how pleased they would feel that the offender had been caught, $r(358) = .27$, $p < .001$, and how pleased they would feel about the stimulus person's expulsion, $r(357) = .57$, $p < .001$; positively related to the level of severity of the penalty that subjects believed should be assigned to the stimulus person for the offence, $r(358) = .34$, $p < .001$; and positively related to the subjects' ratings of whether it would be likely that they would report the offender to the authorities, $r(356) = .31$, $p < .001$.

In what ways do these results reflect the effects of underlying values and perceived responsibility? Consistent with the theoretical analysis of deservingness that I presented in an earlier section, values would enter as influences on subjects' judgments of deservingness because a negatively valued behavior (cheating) was followed by a negatively valued outcome (punishment) that the transgressor was seen to deserve, especially if he or she was a tall poppy. Subjects may also have viewed the high achiever's cheating as more serious because it would call into question his or her previous success at examinations and whether that success was achieved by honest means. They may also have condemned the high achiever more because of a belief that high status is a privilege that carries with it a responsibility to behave properly and to set a good example to others. That is, their reactions may have related to the responsibilities and obligations that were seen to be attached to the high achiever's superior position. This interpretation is consistent with the earlier discussion (pp. 226–227) of responsibility that relates to a person's role.

On the other side of the coin, the results showed that subjects reported feeling less pleased when the average achiever was punished, consistent with the low ratings of pleasure that were reported in the first study when the average achiever suffered a fall. Thus, in both studies there was suggestive evidence that the fall of the average achiever was viewed more sympathetically, at least as far as subjects' ratings of pleasure about the fall were concerned, perhaps reflecting the influence of collectivist values.

Other experimental studies that also involved hypothetical vignettes have been conducted in the research program on tall poppies (Feather, 1994). One study was specifically related to testing aspects of the deservingness model and provided support for it (Feather, 1992a). Another study compared reactions to hypothetical tall poppies in two different cultures, Australia and Japan (Feather & McKee, 1992). These studies were more complex in form than the two that I have reported, and I do not describe them here (see Feather, 1994, for a summary). The results showed, however, that, as more details about the context were included in the vignettes and as new variables were added, the effects of status differences were diminished and some of the effects that were observed in the two earlier studies were not obtained. The exception to this statement is the study involving the student who cheated (Feather, 1989) where strong status differences were obtained when information about the cause of a negative outcome was provided, that is, when a misdemeanor was followed by a penalty.

I have concluded on the basis of the experimental studies that attitudes toward tall poppies and reactions to their fall "depend upon a range of variables that include the perceived causes of their success and failure, judgments about the extent of their deservingness, the domain in which the success and failure occurs, and whether the fall is an extreme one or results in the tall poppy being more like others. Many of these variables exert their influence independent of status" (Feather, 1994, p. 40).

The results also showed that attitudes toward tall poppies and reactions to their fall were related to subjects' perceptions of the personalities of the tall poppies (e.g., whether the high achievers were seen as arrogant or whether they were seen to possess integrity). These kinds of personality attributes are probably inferred from observations of a tall poppy's behavior. They would involve a value dimension, some personality attributes (e.g., integrity) being positively valued and some (e.g., arrogance) being negatively valued, based on the positively or negatively valued behaviors from which the personality attributes are inferred (Feather, 1994, p. 67). As noted previously, observations of another's positively or negatively valued behaviors over situations, over time, and in relation to what is normative for the group or culture, may result in attributions of high or low moral character. At this general level of analysis, tall poppies who are perceived to be of high moral character may then be reacted to in positive ways, and they would be seen to deserve their high status and to be less deserving of a fall in status should it occur. In contrast, tall poppies who are perceived to be of low moral character may be reacted to more negatively, and they would be seen as less deserving of their high status and to deserve a fall in status should it occur.

Thus "attitudes toward the high achiever when compared with the average achiever are not necessarily more or less favorable but depend upon the information given and the context of achievement" (Feather, 1994, p. 20). So do reactions to the fall of a high achiever. One cannot generalize and say that people are negative toward all high achievers and like to see them fall. That would be the case for "bad" tall poppies who are seen not to deserve their high position but it is not likely to be the case for "good" tall poppies who are perceived to deserve their high status. Thus, an important variable that influences our attitudes toward specific tall poppies and how we react to their fall is the degree to which we construe their rise or fall as justly deserved. As I have argued, these judgments of deservingness are influenced by the degree to which the other person is seen to be responsible for his or her actions and outcomes, by the values of the person who is making the judgments, and by relations between person and other that reflect shared or nonshared social identity (ingroup vs. outgroup) or interpersonal attitudes of like or dislike.

GENERAL ATTITUDES TOWARD HIGH ACHIEVERS

A final set of studies to which I now turn were concerned with examining the value correlates of general attitudes toward high achievers (Feather, 1989, 1994). These studies used a specially constructed scale called the Tall Poppy Scale consisting of 20 items. Half of the items in the scale express positive attitudes toward tall poppies and half express negative attitudes. The full scale is presented in Table 9.4.

TABLE 9.4
The Tall Poppy Scale

Items

1. People who are very successful deserve all the rewards they get for their achievements.
2. It's good to see very successful people fail occasionally.
3. Very successful people often get too big for their boots.
4. People who are very successful in what they do are usually friendly and helpful to others.
5. At school it's probably better for students to be near the middle of the class than the very top student.
6. People shouldn't criticize or knock the very successful.
7. Very successful people who fall from the top usually deserve their fall from grace.
8. Those who are very successful ought to come down off their pedestals and be like other people.
9. The very successful person should receive public recognition for his/her accomplishments.
10. People who are "tall poppies" should be cut down to size.
11. One should always respect the person at the top.
12. One ought to be sympathetic to very successful people when they experience failure and fall from their very high positions.
13. Very successful people sometimes need to be brought back a peg or two, even if they have done nothing wrong.
14. Society needs a lot of very high achievers.
15. People who always do a lot better than others need to learn what it's like to fail.
16. People who are right at the top usually deserve their high position.
17. It's very important for society to support and encourage people who are very successful.
18. People who are very successful get too full of their own importance.
19. Very successful people usually succeed at the expense of other people.
20. Very successful people who are at the top of their field are usually fun to be with.

Note. Items 1, 4, 6, 9, 11, 12, 14, 16, 17, and 20 comprise the Favor Reward subscale; items 2, 3, 5, 7, 8, 10, 13, 15, 18, and 19 comprise the Favor Fall subscale. Adapted from Feather (1989) with the permission of the author and the Australian Psychological Society.

The results of factor analyses justify considering the two sets of positive and negative items separately (Feather, 1989). Thus the data analyses have involved two subscales. The first subscale contains the 10 items that express negative attitudes toward tall poppies and that favor the tall poppy's fall (e.g., "People who are very successful get too full of their own importance"; "Those who are very successful ought to come down off their pedestals and be like other people"; "People who always do a lot better than others need to learn what it's like to fail"). I call this variable *Favor Fall*. The second subscale contains the 10 items that express positive attitudes toward tall poppies and that favor rewarding them (e.g., "It's important for society to support and encourage people who are very successful"; "People who are right at the top usually deserve their high position"; "Society needs a lot of very high achievers"). I call this variable *Favor Reward*.

These two tall poppy variables have been correlated with a number of other variables that include global self-esteem, perceived competence in the classroom, right-wing authoritarianism, voting preference, and value priorities (Feather, 1989, 1991, 1993a, 1993b, 1994; Feather & McKee, 1993; Feather et al., 1991). The focus in this section is on the value correlates of favor fall and favor reward. I expected that favoring the reward of tall poppies would be positively related to the importance that individuals assigned to values concerned with achievement and power and that favoring the fall of tall poppies would be negatively related to the importance assigned to these value types. An emphasis on achievement and power is consistent with support for high achievers who have risen to high status positions and it is also consistent with not favoring their fall.

In contrast, I expected that there would be a negative correlation between favoring the reward of tall poppies and the importance assigned to egalitarian values and a positive correlation between egalitarianism and favoring the fall of tall poppies. An emphasis on equality would imply a preference for reducing status differences and for creating a society where opportunities are equal for all.

These hypotheses have been tested by relating the favor fall and favor reward variables to the value types from the Schwartz Value Survey (Schwartz, 1992), to egalitarianism as measured by a scale that I developed (Feather, 1994), and to the measure of Protestant Ethic (PE) values devised by Mirels and Garrett (1971). The results of the relevant studies have been summarized previously (Feather, 1994).

Table 9.5 presents a sample of these results from a study that involved 205 male and female subjects from the general population of metropolitan Adelaide (Feather, 1989). These subjects completed a questionnaire that involved the Tall Poppy Scale, the Schwartz Value Survey (Schwartz, 1992), and the Rosenberg Self-Esteem Scale (Rosenberg, 1965), as modified by Bachman, O'Malley, and Johnston (1978). The value types listed in Table 9.5 are an earlier version of those reported by Schwartz (1992).

The results in Table 9.5 show that favoring the reward of tall poppies was positively related to scores on Schwartz's power, achievement, stimulation, and conformity value types. Schwartz (1992) viewed the central goal of power values as the "attainment of social status and prestige, and control or dominance over people and resources" (p. 9), the defining goal of achievement values as "personal success through demonstrating competence according to social standards" (p. 8), the defining goal of stimulation values as "excitement, novelty, and challenge in life" (p. 8), and the defining goal of conformity values as the "restraint of actions, inclinations, and impulses likely to upset or harm others and violate social expectations or norms" (p. 9). Examples of power values in the Schwartz Value Survey are authority, wealth, social power, preserving my public image, and social recognition; examples of achievement values are ambitious, successful, capable, and influential; examples of stimulation values are an exciting life, a varied life, and daring; examples of conformity values are obedient, self-discipline, politeness, and honoring parents and elders. These kinds of values were rated as more important by those who were more in favor of rewarding tall poppies.

The results in Table 9.5 also show that subjects who were more in favor of the fall of tall poppies assigned less importance to achievement values when com-

TABLE 9.5

Mean Scores, Standard Deviations, and Correlations for Value Subscales, Favor Fall, Favor Reward, Global Self-Esteem, Gender, and Left-Wing Political Preference

| | | | Correlations | | | | |
Variable	Mean	SD	Favor Fall	Favor Reward	Gender	Left-Wing Political Preference	Global Self-Esteem
Value subscale							
Hedonism	4.36	1.55	.16*	.09	.03	.04	-.02
Achievement	4.22	1.10	-.19**	.40***	-.04	-.21*	.14*
Social Power	2.38	1.38	.02	.33***	-.08	-.32***	-.07
Self-direction	4.55	1.06	-.07	.03	.03	.15	.11
Stimulation	3.55	1.51	.12	.18*	.03	-.08	-.03
Maturity	4.33	1.14	-.05	.04	.15*	.20*	.00
Prosocial	4.83	.94	-.05	.00	.21**	.25**	-.02
Security	4.12	1.03	.06	.11	.09	-.05	-.10
Restrictive conformity	4.07	1.25	.10	.22**	.16*	-.15	-.17*
Tradition maintenance	2.52	1.31	.19**	.08	.10	.01	-.25***
Spiritual	4.08	1.64	-.11	.02	.21**	.22*	.07
Tall poppy variables							
Favor fall	38.02	11.95	--	-.36***	-.06	.21*	-.31***
Favor reward	44.82	10.52	-.36***	--	.04	-.32***	.06
Gender	1.49	.50	-.06	.04	--	.04	-.16*
Political preference	1.54	.50	.21*	-.32***	.04	--	-.01
Global self-esteem	41.19	5.26	-.31***	.06	-.16*	-.01	--

Note. $N = 205$ except for correlations involving political preference where $N = 122$. There were minor variations from these Ns due to missing cases. Means for value subscales have been converted to the -1 to 7 scale. Political preference was coded as follows: Liberal Party = 1, Labor Party = 2. Gender was coded as follows: Male = 1, Female = 2. Tests of significance are two-tailed. Adapted from Feather (1989) with the permission of the author and the Australian Psychological Society.

*$p < .05$. **$p < .01$. ***$p < .001$.

pared with subjects who were less in favor of the fall of tall poppies. The former subjects also saw hedonistic and tradition-maintenance values as more important. The hedonistic value type includes pleasure and enjoying life as defining values and Schwartz (1992) proposed that this value type is "derived from organismic needs and the pleasure associated with satisfying them" (p. 8). The tradition-maintenance value type includes respect for tradition, being humble, accepting my portion in life, and devout as defining values. Schwartz proposed that the motivational goal of this value type is "respect, commitment, and acceptance of the customs and ideas that one's culture or religion impose on the individual" (p. 10).

The results of a further study (Feather, 1994, pp. 49–53) that involved 281 male and female students from the introductory psychology class at Flinders University showed that the favor reward variable was positively related to scores on the Mirels and Garrett (1971) measure of PE values, $r(105) = .26, p < .01$. This scale was designed to assess the main components of the "protestant ethic" as described by Weber (1976), namely individual activism, self-discipline, hard work, and the denial of pleasure for its own sake (Feather, 1984). One would expect that individuals who supported the Protestant work ethic would also favor rewarding tall poppies.

A previously unpublished analysis of data from this study showed that favoring the reward of tall poppies was also related to the importance assigned by subjects to the following Schwartz (1992) value types: power, $r(211) = .17, p <$ .05; achievement, $r(214) = .29, p < .001$; stimulation, $r(215) = .14, p < .05$; conformity, $r(212) = .18, p < .01$; and security, $r(211) = .24, p < .001$. Thus these correlations replicated the results in Table 9.5, at least in regard to power, achievement, stimulation, and conformity values. However, favor reward was unrelated to egalitarianism, $r(113) = -.02$, ns, as measured by the scale presented in Table 9.6. Thus, the prediction of a negative relation between these variables was not confirmed by the results from this sample.

TABLE 9.6
The Egalitarianism Scale

Items

1. There is too large a gap between the rich and the poor in our society.
2. Society functions better when everyone has an equal share of the profits.
3. It is wrong for top executives to be paid very high salaries when other workers receive a much lower wage.
4. Everyone should have an equal chance and an equal say in most things.
5. We should try to level out the differences that exist in our society so that people can become more equal.
6. People should be treated equally because we are all human beings.

Note. Reprinted from Feather (1994) with the permission of the author and the publisher.

The results also showed that favoring the fall of tall poppies was positively related to scores on Schwartz's (1992) conformity value type, $r(208) = .18$, $p < .01$, but that was the only statistically significant correlation between favor fall and the Schwartz value types (Feather, 1994). However, the favor fall variable was positively related to egalitarianism for this sample, $r(112) = .24$, $p < .01$. One would expect that those who hold egalitarian values would favor bringing down tall poppies to a level where status differences are reduced. Favoring the fall of tall poppies was also positively related to the Mirels and Garrett (1971) measure of PE values for this sample, $r(104) = .23$, $p < .05$ (Feather, 1994).

The favor fall variable was again positively related to egalitarianism, $r(332) = .25$, $p < .001$, in another study that involved 339 male and female subjects who were sampled from the general population of metropolitan Adelaide (Feather, 1994, pp. 49–53). Moreover, the expected negative correlation between favor reward and egalitarianism was obtained for this sample, $r(332) = -.11$, $p < .05$. Both the favor reward and favor fall variables were positively related to the Mirels and Garrett (1971) measure of PE values, thus replicating the results of the study with the Flinders University students (Feather, 1994). The respective correlations were as follows; favor reward and PE values, $r(328) = .26$, $p < .001$; favor fall and PE values, $r(328) = .14$, $p < .01$.

The positive correlations that were obtained between PE scores and the favor reward and favor fall variables in both of these studies may reflect the effects of values such as conformity that the PE scale may also measure in addition to individualistic achievement and ascetic values. There is evidence that scores on the PE scale are positively related to the importance assigned by individuals to conformity values, such as being obedient (Feather, 1984, 1994).

The results of another recent study (Feather, 1993a) showed that the favor fall and the favor reward variables were related in different ways to aspects of right-wing authoritarianism (respectful submission, punitive aggression, conventionality, and rule-following) that were derived from a factor analysis of the 24-item version of Altemeyer's (1981, pp. 305–306) Right-Wing Authoritarianism Scale. The correlational evidence from this study indicated that favoring the reward of high achievers was positively related to respectful submission, positively related to conventionality, and positively related to rule-following, all of which imply some adherence to values concerned with conformity and tradition. Favoring the fall of high achievers was positively related to punitive aggression, positively related to respectful submission, and negatively related to rule-following. Wanting to see tall poppies fall was therefore linked to aggression and nonconformity. The positive correlation between the favor fall variable and respectful submission is hard to explain, though it is consistent with the respect for humility and tradition noted previously (Table 9.5). A multiple-regression analysis showed that it was the less punitively aggressive rule-follower with high global self-esteem who was more likely to favor rewarding tall poppies; the more punitively aggressive rebel with low self-esteem was more likely to favor the fall of high achievers. Higher global self-esteem probably reflects the degree to which individuals have had a successful record of obtaining outcomes in the past that they value themselves and that their culture also values (Feather, 1985, 1991). Differences in global self-esteem may also reflect differences in the importance that individuals assign to achievement values (see Table 9.5 for some supporting evidence).

Other results from my research program showed differences between more to the right Liberal Party voters and more to the left Labor Party voters with respect to the favor reward and favor fall variables. In Australia the Liberal Party tends to be more conservative in its political orientation than the Labor Party, favoring individual enterprise and achievement and respect for authority. The Labor Party tends to be more concerned with social welfare and with reducing inequalities between people. The two parties may therefore be contrasted in regard to their political platforms and ideologies, consistent with the conservative–liberal distinction found in studies of political ideology and personality (see Skitka & Tetlock, 1993).

My results have shown that Liberal Party voters in Australia were more likely to favor rewarding tall poppies when compared with Labor Party voters (Feather, 1989, 1993b; Feather et al., 1991). Less consistently, Labor Party voters were more likely to favor the fall of tall poppies when compared with Liberal Party voters (Feather, 1989). These differences would partly reflect differences in the underlying value priorities of the voters that influenced their endorsement or nonendorsement of the policies of each political party. Indeed the results in Table 9.5 show that there were clear differences in the value priorities of Liberal and Labor Party voters. Those subjects who expressed a preference for the more to the left Labor Party assigned higher importance to maturity (or universalist) values, prosocial (or benevolence) values, and spiritualist values when compared with those who preferred the more conservative Liberal Party. Labor Party supporters saw achievement values and power values as less important for themselves when compared with Liberal Party supporters. Thus Liberal Party voters tended to be more conservative, more respectful of authority, and more achievement-oriented than Labor Party voters in their value priorities and somewhat less likely to emphasize social, communal values. Other evidence showed that Liberal Party voters also tended to be higher in right-wing authoritarianism (especially in regard to conventionality and rule-following) when compared with Labor Party voters (Feather, 1993a).

Finally, there is also evidence of cultural differences in general attitudes toward high achievers that probably reflect value differences. Feather and McKee (1993) found that Japanese students had significantly higher mean scores on the favor fall variable when compared with Australian students but the mean scores from the two samples for the favor reward variable were similar. They interpreted the former difference as consistent with cultural differences in the construal of self that may be taken to reflect differences in cultural norms and values. The Japanese culture is commonly assumed to emphasize the interpersonal context, ingroup solidarity, harmony, and self-effacement (e.g., Markus & Kitayama, 1991), whereas the Australian culture may be assumed to place more emphasis on independence and autonomy (Feather, 1986, 1994; Feather & McKee, 1992, 1993). The tall poppy who asserts independence and individuality would be seen in Japan as violating norms and values concerned with ingroup loyalty, harmony, and humility, and there would be a tendency to level the tall poppy. In fact, in Japan there is a proverb that states that the nail that sticks up should be pounded down. In Australia individualistic achievement may be more acceptable in a cultural sense even though it may also conflict with collectivist, egalitarian values that are also important (Feather, 1975, 1986, 1993c, 1994).

CONCLUDING COMMENTS

The research that has been described in the present chapter does not exhaust the range of studies that I have conducted. My aim was to consider only that part of the research program that related to values. To this end I have focused on some theoretical ideas about values, how values might be integrated into the analysis of deservingness, and how they might influence attitudes toward high achievers and reactions to their fall.

Other parts of my research program that have investigated tall poppy attitudes in relation to variables such as global self-esteem, perceived competence, and envy have drawn upon theoretical approaches mainly concerned with social comparison and the psychology of envy (e.g., Salovey, 1991; Tesser, 1988). For example, the results have shown that subjects with high global self-esteem and high perceived competence were more likely to favor the reward of tall poppies; those with low global self-esteem and low perceived personal competence were more likely to favor their fall (Feather, 1989, 1991; Feather et al., 1991; see Table 9.5). Conversely, support and sympathy for a fallen tall poppy tended to be stronger among those subjects who were lower in global self-esteem (Feather, 1991, 1994). These findings would reflect the effects of a person's own comparative position on how he or she reacts to the rise or fall of tall poppies, as well as the possible effects of achievement values that are associated with global self-esteem (Feather, 1994, p. 44).

We also found that reported feelings of envy were related to the level of another person's achievement and to the relevance of that high achievement for the individual (Feather & McKee, 1992). These results are consistent with findings from related research on social comparison envy (e.g., Salovey & Rodin, 1984; Tesser, 1988). However, research on social comparison envy has been mainly restricted to situations where the comparison other is close to the person who makes the comparison. In contrast, my research has studied tall poppies who are not close or personally known to subjects but who are judged at a distance.

The research on tall poppies draws attention to questions that concern status, values, and deservingness. These questions are relevant to many areas of our everyday life, including how we react to leaders in various pursuits who rise to prominence, maintain their high positions, or fall. As noted previously social psychologists have tended to neglect these issues. In recent years they have shown more interest in studies of close relationships than in studies that examine the effects of status. But we live in a social world that is structured along vertical as well as along horizontal lines. Studies of status, values, and justice should help to restore the balance, opening up new areas of enquiry that have both theoretical and applied importance.

ACKNOWLEDGMENTS

I am indebted to the Australian Research Council for financial support for the studies described in this Chapter.

REFERENCES

Altemeyer, B. (1981). *Right-wing authoritarianism.* Winnipeg, Canada: University of Manitoba Press.

Atkinson, J. W., & Feather, N. T. (Eds.). (1966). *A theory of achievement motivation.* New York: Wiley.

Bachman, J. G., O'Malley, P. M., & Johnston, J. (1978). *Adolescence to adulthood.* Ann Arbor, MI: Institute for Social Research.

Bies, R. J. (1987). The predicament of injustice: The management of moral outrage. In B. Staw & L. Cummings (Eds.), *Research in organizational behavior* (Vol. 9, pp. 289–319). Greenwich, CT: JAI.

Feather, N. T. (1959). Subjective probability and decision under uncertainty. *Psychological Review, 66,* 150–164.

Feather, N. T. (1964). A structural balance model of communication effects. *Psychological Review, 71,* 291–313.

Feather, N. T. (1967). A structural balance approach to the analysis of communication effects. In L. Berkowitz (Ed.), *Advances in experimental social psychology* (Vol. 3, pp. 99–164). New York: Academic Press.

Feather, N. T. (1971). Organization and discrepancy in cognitive structures. Psychological Review, *78,* 355–379.

Feather, N. T. (1975). *Values in education and society,* New York: Free Press.

Feather, N. T. (Ed.). (1982). *Expectations and actions: Expectancy-value models in psychology.* Hillsdale, NJ: Lawrence Erlbaum Associates.

Feather, N. T. (1984). Protestant ethic, conservatism, and values. *Journal of Personality and Social Psychology, 46,* 1132–1141.

Feather, N. T. (1985). Masculinity, femininity, self-esteem, and subclinical depression. *Sex Roles, 12,* 491–500.

Feather, N. T. (1986). Cross-cultural studies with the Rokeach Value Survey: The Flinders program of research on values. *Australian Journal of Psychology, 38,* 269–283.

Feather, N. T. (1989). Attitudes towards the high achiever: The fall of the tall poppy. *Australian Journal of Psychology, 41,* 239–267.

Feather, N. T. (1990). Bridging the gap between values and actions. In E. T. Higgins & R. M. Sorrentino (Eds.), *Handbook of motivation and cognition: Foundations of social behavior* (Vol. 2, pp. 151–192). New York: Guilford.

Feather, N. T. (1991). Attitudes towards the high achiever: Effects of perceiver's own level of competence. *Australian Journal of Psychology, 43,* 121–124.

Feather, N. T. (1992a). An attributional and value analysis of deservingness in success and failure situations. *British Journal of Social Psychology, 31,* 125–145.

Feather, N. T. (1992b). Values, valences, expectations, and actions. *Journal of Social Issues, 48,* 109–124.

Feather, N. T. (1993a). Authoritarianism and attitudes toward high achievers. *Journal of Personality and Social Psychology, 65,* 152–164.

Feather, N. T. (1993b). The rise and fall of political leaders: Attributions, deservingness, personality, and affect. *Australian Journal of Psychology, 45,* 61–68.

Feather, N. T. (1993c). Values and culture. In W. J. Lonner & R. Malpass (Eds.), *Psychology and culture* (pp. 183–189). Boston: Allyn & Bacon.

Feather, N. T. (1994). Attitudes toward high achievers and reactions to their fall: Theory and research concerning tall poppies. In M. Zanna (Ed.), *Advances in experimental social psychology* (Vol. 26, pp. 1–73). San Diego, CA: Academic Press.

Feather, N. T. (1995). Values, valences, and choice: The influence of values on the perceived attractiveness and choice of alternatives. *Journal of Personality and Social Psychology, 68,* 1135–1151.

Feather, N. T. (in press). Extending the search for order in social motivation. *Psychological Inquiry.*

Feather, N. T., & McKee, I. R. (1992). Australian and Japanese attitudes towards the fall of high achievers. *Australian Journal of Psychology, 44,* 87–93.

Feather, N. T., & McKee, I. R. (1993). Global self-esteem and attitudes toward the high achiever for Australian and Japanese students. *Social Psychology Quarterly, 56,* 65–76.

Feather, N. T., Volkmer, R. E., & McKee, I. R. (1991). Attitudes towards high achievers in public life: Attributions, deservingness, personality, and affect. *Australian Journal of Psychology, 43,* 85–91.

Fincham, F., & Jaspars, J. (1980). Attribution of responsibility: From man the scientist to man as lawyer. In L. Berkowitz (Ed.), *Advances in experimental social psychology* (Vol.13, pp. 81–138). New York: Academic Press.

Hamilton, V. L. (1978). Who is responsible? Toward a social psychology of responsibility attribution. *Social Psychology, 41,* 316–328.

Hamilton, V. L. (1992). *Everyday justice: Responsibility and the individual in Japan and the United States.* New Haven, CT: Yale University Press.

Hamilton, V. L., & Hagiwara, S. (1992). Roles, responsibility, and accounts across cultures. *International Journal of Psychology, 27,* 157–179.

Hart, H. L. A. (1968). *Punishment and responsibility.* New York: Oxford University Press.

Heider, F. (1958). *The psychology of interpersonal relations.* New York: Wiley.

Katz, D. (1960). The functional approach to the study of attitudes. *Public Opinion Quarterly, 24,* 163–204.

Kelman, H. C., & Hamilton, V. L. (1989). *Crimes of obedience: Toward a social psychology of authority and responsibility.* New Haven, CT: Yale University Press.

Lerner, M. J. (1980). *The belief in a just world: A fundamental delusion.* New York: Plenum.

Lerner, M. J. (1991). Integrating societal and psychological rules of entitlement: The basic task of each social actor and fundamental problem for the social sciences. In R. Vermunt & H. Steensma (Eds.), *Social justice in human relations* (Vol. 1, pp. 13–32). New York: Plenum.

Lusk, C. M., & Judd, C. M. (1988). Political expertise and the structural mediators of candidate evaluations. *Journal of Experimental Social Psychology, 24,* 105–126.

McClelland, D. C. (1985). *Human motivation.* Glenview, IL: Scott, Foresman.

Maio, G., & Olson, J. M. (1994). Value-attitude-relations: The moderating role of attitude functions. *British Journal of Social Psychology, 33,* 301–312.

Markus, H. R., & Kitayama, S. (1991). Culture and the self: Implications for cognition, emotion and motivation. *Psychological Review, 98,* 224–253.

Mikula, G. (1993). On the experience of injustice. *European Review of Social Psychology, 4,* 223–244.

Mirels, H. L., & Garrett, J. B. (1971). The Protestant ethic as a personality variable. *Journal of Consulting and Clinical Psychology, 36,* 40–44.

Piaget, J. (1932). *The moral judgment of the child.* New York: Harcourt Brace.

Ramson, W. S. (1988). *Australian national dictionary.* Melbourne: Oxford University Press.

Rokeach, M. (1968). A theory of organization and change within value-attitude systems. *Journal of Social Issues, 24,* 13–33.

Rokeach, M. (1973). *The nature of human values.* New York: Free Press.

Rosenberg, M. (1965). *Society and the adolescent self-image.* Princeton, NJ: Princeton University Press.

Salovey, P. (1991). Social comparison processes in envy and jealousy. In J. Suls & T. A. Wills (Eds.), *Social comparison: Contemporary theory and research* (pp. 261–286). Hillsdale, NJ: Lawrence Erlbaum Associates.

Salovey, P., & Rodin, J. (1984). Some antecedents and consequences of social-comparison jealousy. *Journal of Personality and Social Psychology, 47,* 780–792.

Schlenker, B. R., Britt, T. W., Pennington, J., Murphy, R., & Doherty, K. (1994). The triangle model of responsibility. *Psychological Review, 101,* 632–652.

Schwartz, S. H. (1992). Universals in the content and structure of values: Theoretical advances and empirical tests in 20 countries. In M. Zanna (Ed.), *Advances in experimental social psychology* (Vol. 25, pp. 1–65). New York: Academic Press.

Shaver, K. G. (1985). *The attribution of blame: Causality, responsibility, and blameworthiness.* New York: Springer-Verlag.

Skitka, L. J., & Tetlock, P. E. (1993). Providing public assistance: Cognitive and motivational processes underlying liberal and conservative policy preferences. *Journal of Personality and Social Psychology, 65,* 1205–1223.

Snyder, C. R., & Higgins, R. L. (1988). Excuses: Their effective role in the negotiation of reality. *Psychological Bulletin, 104,* 23–35.

Spence, J. T. (Ed.). (1983). *Achievement and achievement motives: Psychological and sociological approaches.* San Francisco: Freeman.

Tedeschi, J. T., & Reiss, M. (1981). Verbal strategies in impression management. In C. Antaki (Ed.), *The psychology of ordinary language explanations of social behavior* (pp. 271–309). Orlando, FL: Academic Press.

Tesser, A. (1988). Toward a self-evaluation maintenance model of social behavior. In L. Berkowitz (Ed.), *Advances in experimental social psychology* (Vol. 21, pp. 181–227). New York: Academic Press.

Tesser, A., & Leone, C. (1977). Cognitive schemas and thought as determinants of attitude change. *Journal of Experimental Social Psychology, 13,* 340–356.

Tetlock, P. E. (1986). A value pluralism model of ideological reasoning. *Journal of Personality and Social Psychology, 50,* 365–375.

Weber, M. (1976). *The Protestant Ethic and the spirit of capitalism* (T. Parsons, Trans.). London: George Allen & Unwin (Original work published 1904–1905).

Weiner, B. (1986). *An attributional theory of motivation and emotion.* New York: Springer-Verlag.

Weiner, B. (1992). *Human motivation: Metaphors, theories, and research.* Newbury Park, CA: Sage.

Weiner, B. (1993). On sin and sickness: A theory of perceived responsibility and social motivation. *American Psychologist, 48,* 957–965.

Weiner, B. (1995). *Judgments of responsibility: A foundation for a theory of social conduct.* New York: Guilford Publications.

Weiner, B. (in press). Searching for order in social motivation. *Psychological Inquiry.*

10

Value Transmission in Families

Meg J. Rohan
Mark P. Zanna
University of Waterloo

Folk wisdom preaches the inevitability of children growing up to resemble their parents. When we consider socially undesirable behaviors, such as prejudice ("prejudice begets prejudice") the disadvantages of the possible replication process are clear. Thus, insofar as we are interested in either encouraging or disrupting this process, there is a need to examine the reality of the folk wisdom.

In this chapter, we look at some of the evidence that supports the folk wisdom "The apple never falls far from the tree." We discuss the usefulness of the examination and comparison of value systems as a comprehensive way to conceptualize similarities and differences between parents and their children, and we discuss the techniques used to measure values. We report the results of a study conducted to answer two fundamental questions: "How much like their parents do adult children become?" and "What influences this similarity?" Finally, we discuss the implications of our findings and suggest some directions for future research.

PARENT–CHILD SIMILARITY

Early research into parent–child similarity seemed to presume a strong relation between the values, attitudes, and behaviors of parents and those of their children, and focused instead on the *relative* influence of mothers and fathers in the socialization of particular attitudes and values. For example, Newcomb and Svehla (1937) reported that although daughters were more influenced by their mothers in their attitudes towards religion, they were more influenced by their fathers in their attitudes towards communism. During the 1960s, however, the assumption of parent–child concordance was left behind in the flurry of research that investigated the "Generation Gap" (for a review of research before 1979, see Troll & Bengtson, 1979). The focus of more recent research has been the search for possible predictors of children's values, attitudes, and behavior (e.g., Doumit Sparks, Thornburg, Ispa, & McPhail Gray, 1984; Eisenberg, Wolchik, Goldberg, & Engel, 1992; Hoge, Petrillo, & Smith, 1982). In addition, based on the assumption that accurate perception precedes the acceptance or rejection of parental attitudes and values, more attention has been paid to the similarity between children's values, attitudes, or behaviors and children's *perceptions* of their parents' values, attitudes, or behaviors (e.g., Cashmore & Goodnow, 1985; McBroom, Reed, Burns, Hargreaves, & Trankel, 1985; Smith, 1982). Thus, a great deal of research evidence relating to child–parent similarity exists. But what conclusions, if any, can be reached?

First, age of the child makes a difference. For example, after reviewing research concerning the similarity between parents' and children's attitudes towards outgroups, Aboud (1988) concluded that the influence of parents is particularly weak when children are young, and that children must reach a certain level of development before they can understand and internalize their parents' attitudes. However, in research with older children and their parents, generally—although not always—more concordance is reported. For example, Altemeyer (1988) found correlations that ranged from .27 to .51 between the right-wing authoritarian attitudes of university-aged children and those attitudes of their parents; Romero (1994) found a .65 correlation between parents' liberalism–conservatism scores and those of their college-aged children.

Second, the degree of parent–child similarity depends on the issue, the attitude, the behavior, or the value being investigated. For example, Troll, Neugarten, and Kraines (1969) found that whereas there were strong correlations between parents' and children's dedication to causes, there were very weak correlations between the emphasis parents and their children placed on materialist values. Furthermore, because research has generally focused on particular attitudes or behaviors or narrow set of values, an overall picture of parent–child similarities and differences cannot be drawn clearly. For this reason, we decided to focus our attention on the value systems—not isolated sets of values, but value *systems*—of parents and their children as a way of understanding similarity at a more comprehensive level.

USE OF VALUE SYSTEM COMPARISONS AS A COMPREHENSIVE INDEX OF PARENT–CHILD SIMILARITY

One of the primary assumptions made about values is that all people possess value systems in which a relatively small number of values are organized in a coherent framework. In addition, the values people hold are assumed to have cognitive, affective, and behavioral consequences (see Kluckhohn, 1951; Rokeach, 1973; Schwartz, 1992; Williams, 1968). Values are thought to function as "the criteria people use to select and justify actions and to evaluate people (including the self) and events" (Schwartz, 1992, p. 1). Thus, the measurement and comparison of the value systems of parents and their children accomplishes our purpose that was to find a broad, yet tractable way to conceptualize general similarities and differences between parents and their children.

Values also are relevant to our motivating research interest—the study of the development and transmission of prejudice. The role of values in prejudice and discrimination has been emphasized by research which suggested that prejudice towards members of other ethnic, racial, and social groups is influenced primarily by the perceived dissimilarity of values and beliefs (e.g., Rokeach, Smith, & Evans, 1960). When the concepts of "symbolic racism" (McConahay & Hough, 1976; Sears & Kinder, 1971) and "racial ambivalence" (Gaertner, 1976; Kovel, 1970) were introduced during the 1970s, the idea that values served as justifications or as underlying motivations for attitudes and behavior gained precedence. More recently, Zanna, Haddock, and Esses (1990) examined the role of "symbolic beliefs" (beliefs about the relation between social groups and basic values and norms) as one of the components of attitudes towards racial, ethnic, and social groups; their findings highlight the importance of values, and suggest that negative attitudes towards other groups are related to the perception that cherished values are threatened. Sagiv and Schwartz (1995) also have demonstrated a relation between value priorities and willingness for social contact with minority group members.

VALUE MEASUREMENT

Various procedures have been developed to measure value systems. One of the earliest examples is the Study of Values test developed by Allport, Vernon, and Lindzey (1960) in which the relative strength of six basic values was measured (see Braithwaite & Scott, 1991 for a review of this and other value questionnaires). One of the most popular measures has been the Value Survey developed by Rokeach (1973). In this survey, 18 terminal (i.e., end state) values and 18 instrumental (i.e., modes of behavior) values are ranked for their importance. However, these and other value measurement instruments suffer from a serious flaw—though the underlying assumption is that values are organized into a coherent system, none of the instruments attempt an exhaustive description of that system.

Recently, Schwartz (e.g., 1992) has addressed this limitation. He proposed an integrated system that is structured by 10 value types.[1] He has strong evidence

---

[1]The 10 value types are made up of 56 individual values. Recently, Schwartz (e.g., this volume) has suggested the omission of values which were originally included to measure a Spirituality value

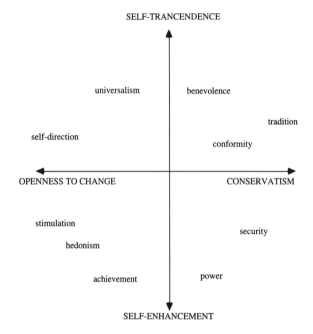

FIG. 10.1.   Location of the 10 value types along two dimensions.

for the structure across very diverse cultural, linguistic, geographic, religious, and racial groups. Thus, although people may differ widely in their endorsement of the values that comprise the 10 value types, the structure of the value system using the 10 value types seems universal.

Two dimensions structure the value system, and the 10 value types are located along these two dimensions. Figure 10.1 shows the two dimensions—a self-transcendence/self-enhancement dimension and an openness to change/conservatism dimension—and the location of the 10 value types along these two dimensions. The two dimensions can be understood as underlying motivations.

The value types Universalism and Benevolence both involve concern for others whereas Achievement and Power both emphasize concern for the self. Self-Direction and Stimulation both involve an openness to change, whereas Tradition, Conformity, and Security emphasize order and resistance to change. Hedonism shares elements of both Openness and Self-Enhancement.

type but which were then subsumed under other value types (Spiritual life, Meaning in Life, Inner Harmony, and Detachment). In the study we later report, analyses were based on 56 values (although analyses using 52 values were virtually identical). To complete the inventory, respondents are instructed to first identify those values that are "of supreme importance" and those values to which they are opposed, thereby providing anchors for rating the remaining values, for which a scale ranging from 0 to 6 is used.

Because an integrated system is proposed, clear hypotheses about the associations and conflicts among the 10 value types can be made: Adjacent values should be related, and value types that do not share an underlying motivation will be in conflict. So, for example, to the extent a person values Conformity he or she also can be expected to place importance upon Tradition and Security, and is unlikely to place a high priority on Self-Direction or Stimulation.

Hypotheses concerning the relation between the value types and other variables also can be generated (Schwartz, this volume). First, other variables will be associated similarly with value types that are adjacent in the value structure because they will have the same motivational goal. So, for example, if variable X is related to the value type Security, then it also will be related to value types Power and Conformity, because all three value types have the underlying goal of Conservatism. Second, associations with other variables should decrease monotonically as one moves around the circular structure of value types in both directions from the value that correlates most highly with the variable in question.

PARENT-OFFSPRING VALUE SIMILARITY

If values serve as underlying motivations for attitudes and behavior, then measurements of integrated systems of values can be useful as comprehensive descriptions of individuals. Such descriptions then can be used as the basis of investigations into general similarities and differences between people. With this in mind, we used the Schwartz value inventory in a study designed to provide us with information about parent–child similarity. Male university students[2] and their parents were invited to complete a questionnaire package; 71 students and 96 parents (50 mothers, 46 fathers) returned the packages. For all analyses reported here, we used the 56 values aggregated into the 10 value types. Because the 10 value types form an integrated system in which there are predictable relations among values, we looked at the similarity between parents' and their adult children's *value profiles* rather than at the similarity of individual value types—we therefore focused on similarity at the level of the value system, and we examined the way parents and children differentiated and evaluated the 10 value types.

First, how similar were the value profiles of husbands and wives? We examined value similarity by correlating the value profiles of husbands and wives *within each family*. For each couple we calculated the correlation between the husband's and wife's priority ratings on the 10 value types; for each couple, then, we had a correlation coefficient that described the degree of similarity between

---

[2]Because this was a preliminary exploration, we decided to look only at sons' similarity to their parents. We also have begun collecting similar data from daughters and their parents.

their value profiles.[3] We found that couples' value profiles were very similar in terms of the relative importance husbands and wives placed on the 10 value types. The average correlation between husbands' and wives' value profiles within each family was high: .68.

Because mothers and fathers held such similar value profiles, patterns that emerged in analyses using aggregates of mothers' and fathers' values were very similar to patterns found in analyses using mothers' and fathers' values separately. For ease of presentation, therefore, we report the results of analyses of data at the level of parents rather than at the level of mothers and fathers.

We found that mothers and fathers held highly similar value profiles. The next question, then, was whether adult children were similar to their parents in terms of *their* value profiles. Again, to examine similarity, we correlated the value profiles of parents and adult children within each family. The distribution of these profile similarity correlations (displayed in Fig. 10.2) shows that the average similarity correlation between adult children and their parents, *within* each family, was high (average correlation = .54).

However, our sample was relatively homogeneous—almost all of the students and their parents lived in the area surrounding the University. We therefore needed to understand the contribution of the culturally shared aspect of values. Although it may be crucial to interpretation, the problem of accounting for cultural agreement in indices of similarity between children and their parents has received little or no attention.

We chose to use a method of accounting for cultural similarity that allowed us to compute a baseline against which to assess the significance of observed similarity correlations (although there are other approaches, see Kenny & Acitelli, 1994, for a discussion). We created "pseudo-couples" by randomly matching husbands and wives, and "pseudo-families" by randomly matching parents and adult children. We then correlated the value profiles within each pseudo-couple and within each pseudo-family.

Given our homogeneous sample, we expected the contribution of the culturally shared aspect of values to be strong. Thus, it was not surprising that the average profile similarity correlation between randomly matched husbands and wives was high (average correlation over 1,000 separate matchings = .57) and that the average profile similarity correlation between randomly matched parents and adult children was also high (average correlation over 1,000 separate matchings = .44).

For husbands and wives, the average profile similarity correlation of properly matched couples was significantly greater than the average profile similarity correlation between husbands and wives who had been *randomly* paired with

---

[3]For use as data points, in these and subsequent analyses, value profile similarity correlations were transformed using Fisher's z transformation. In these analyses, slight discrepancies in degrees of freedom reflect missing data.

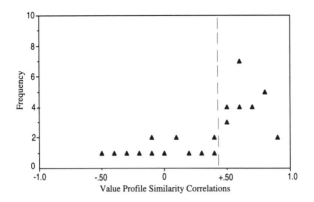

FIG. 10.2.   Distribution of value profile similarity correlations.

each other (.68 vs. .57; $t(44) = 4.18$, $p < .001$), showing that husbands and wives did, indeed, hold similar value profiles.

For parents and adult children, the difference between the average profile similarity correlation for properly matched parents and their adult children and the average profile similarity correlation for randomly matched parents and children approached significance (.54 vs. .44; $t(48) = 1.86$, $p = .07$). It seems the folk wisdom that children grow up to be like their parents received some, but not overwhelming, support.

WHAT MIGHT INFLUENCE PARENT–CHILD VALUE PROFILE SIMILARITY?

Although *on average* the value profile similarity correlations between parents and their adult children were high, there was a considerable range—similarity correlations ranged from $-.47$ to $+.90$. What factors might result in greater parent–child value similarity?

In our consideration of potential moderators of parent–adult child value similarity, we looked for measurable properties or characteristics of parents that would affect their behavior towards their children. We assumed parents' behavior towards their children would either assist in the transmission of parental values, or would lead children to rebel and develop value profiles that differed from their parents'. We also wanted the parental property or characteristic to be related to our primary research interest of prejudice; one of our associated research goals is to identify characteristics of parents that could be used as indicators of children's "at risk for bigotry" status.

For two reasons, then, we decided to examine the effect of parents' authoritarian beliefs. First, because of the nature of authoritarianism—authoritarianism is often conceptualized as a personality variable, thus affecting most, if not all, aspects of individuals' lives—we expected that parents' authoritarian beliefs would influence their behavior generally, and especially towards their children. We therefore expected that the differences in behavior that result from possessing an authoritarian worldview would be related to relative success or failure in the transmission of parental values. Second, authoritarianism previously has been implicated in prejudice (e.g., Adorno, Frenkel-Brunswik, Levinson, & Sanford, 1950). More recently, Altemeyer (e.g., 1988) has collected data that suggest a strong link between scores on his measure of right-wing authoritarian beliefs and measures of prejudice.

To measure parental authoritarianism, we used Altemeyer's scale (Altemeyer & Hunsberger, 1992) of right-wing authoritarianism (RWA).[4] Using 9-point scales, participants rated their endorsement of 30 items that were designed to tap the three components Altemeyer believes underlie right-wing authoritarianism.

The first component is *conventionalism*—a high degree of adherence to social conventions: for example, "There is no 'one right way' to live your life. Everybody has to create his or her *own* way." (This item is, of course, reversed scored.) The second component is *submission* to authorities perceived as legitimate: for example, "Authorities, such as parents and our national leaders, generally turn out to be right about things, and the radicals and protestors are almost always wrong." The third component is *aggression* towards people perceived as violating respected authorities: for example, "Once our government leaders and the authorities condemn the dangerous elements in our society, it will be the duty of every patriotic citizen to help stomp out the rot that is poisoning our country from within." It is not surprising that Altemeyer has found high correlations between his scale and prejudice (see Altemeyer, 1988, 1994).

We also were able to look at the relation between RWA and prejudice in our sample of parents and adult children—in the questionnaire packages we included a 6-item scale (see Appendix A) that can be understood as a rough index of supportiveness towards minority groups.[5] In both our sample of parents and our sample of adult children the right-wing authoritarian scale was significantly related to this measure of attitudes towards minority groups (parent sample: $r(49)$ = .51, $p < .001$; adult child sample: $r(68) = .40, p < .001$): the more right-wing authoritarian the individual, the more negative the attitude towards minority groups.

Incidentally, another reason we included our rough index of attitudes towards

---

[4]Internal consistency of the scale was high in both parent and adult child samples: parents α = .94; adult children α = .92.

[5]Parents and adult children rated their endorsement of the six statements, using 9-point scales. Most of the items were very similar to items in the Modern Racism Scale (McConahay, 1986; items 3, 4, 5, & 6), which is a scale widely used by American researchers to measure attitudes towards Black people. The internal consistency of the scale was high: parents α = .83; adult children α = .80.

minority groups in questionnaire packages was to have some indication of whether any of the 10 value types were related to prejudice. The value type we were particularly interested in was Universalism, in view of its emphasis on "understanding, accepting, and showing concern for the welfare of *all* human beings" (Schwartz, this volume). Indeed, Universalism was strongly associated with the prejudice (as measured by our rough index) of parents ($r(49) = -.39, p < .005$) and adult children ($r(69) = -.44, p < .001$): to the extent that parents and adult children placed a high degree of importance on Universalism, they were more likely to report supportive attitudes towards minority groups.[6]

RIGHT-WING AUTHORITARIANISM AND THE VALUE SYSTEM

How does right-wing authoritarianism relate to the value system? As discussed earlier, Schwartz hypothesized that associations between the 10 value types and other variables should decrease monotonically as one moves around the circular structure of value types in both directions from the value that correlates most highly with the variable in question. Indeed, this is the pattern of associations we found.[7]

As can be seen in Figure 10.3, people who held right-wing authoritarian beliefs were significantly more likely than people who did not hold these beliefs to place emphasis on Conformity ($r(162) = .48, p < .001$), Tradition ($r(162) = .41, p < .001$), Security ($r(163) = .34, p < .001$), Power ($r(163) = .23, p = .003$), and Benevolence ($r(163) = .18, p = .02$). People who held right-wing authoritarian beliefs were *less* likely than people who did not hold these beliefs to place emphasis on Self-Direction ($r(163) = -.32, p < .001$), Stimulation ($r(163) = -.31, p < .001$) and Universalism ($r(164) = -.25, p < .001$).

Recall that the Schwartz value theory proposes that underlying the 10 value types are two dimensions (an openness to change versus conservatism dimension and a self-transcendence versus self-enhancement dimension; see Fig. 10.1) that

---

[6]Parents' scores on our rough index of prejudice were significantly related to their adult children's scores ($r(49) = .37, p = .008$). However, parents' endorsement of Universalism in part mediated this relation. In a regression analysis where parents' prejudice scores and parents' priorities on Universalism were entered to predict adult children's prejudice scores, the relation between parents' prejudice and adult children's prejudice was attenuated: The Beta for parental racism was reduced from .37 ($p = .008$) to .27 ($p = .06$) and the Beta for parental Universalism was $-.23$ ($p < .10$).

[7]Schwartz (e.g., 1992, p. 56) suggests that average ratings of the value types should be partialled out of the correlation between an outside variable and value types to control for response tendencies. However, because there was no relation between RWA scores and average ratings of the value types, this was not considered necessary. For these analyses, we treated all participants (mothers, fathers, and sons) as independent observations, which gave us a sample size of 167. Variations in degrees of freedom again reflect missing data.

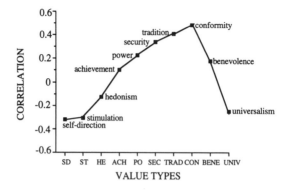

FIG. 10.3. Correlations between the 10 value types and right-wing authoritarianism.

function as motivations. As previously mentioned, Schwartz conceptualizes values as the criteria people use to select and justify their actions; if we consider the motivations underlying those value types that are significantly related to right-wing authoritarianism, we may be able to understand more clearly the criteria right-wing authoritarians use.

Conformity, Tradition, and Security are value types compatible with the underlying motivation of conservatism, and, as mentioned earlier, these value types emphasize order and resistance to change. Underlying Self-Direction and Stimulation is a intrinsic motivation for mastery and an openness to change, and these value types lie in direct opposition to Conformity, Tradition, and Security. Underlying Power is the motivation of self-enhancement, which results in an emphasis on the "attainment or preservation of a dominant position within the more general social system" (Schwartz, 1992, p. 9). That Benevolence is positively related to RWA supports the suggestion made by Schwartz that although Benevolence and Universalism both are motivated by a concern for others and the transcendence of selfish interests, underlying Benevolence is a motivation to promote the interests of the *ingroup,* whereas underlying Universalism is a motivation towards the welfare of *all* people. This explains the strong negative correlation of Universalism with RWA.

These findings strongly support Altemeyer's definition of right-wing authoritarianism, and also allowed us to feel more confident about our choice of right-wing authoritarianism as a factor that may moderate parent–child value profile similarity: Parents who strongly supported right-wing authoritarian beliefs are likely to have distinctly different value profiles from parents who do not endorse such beliefs, and these beliefs are likely to be associated with distinct patterns of behaviors or characteristics.

RIGHT-WING AUTHORITARIANISM AND OTHER
PARENTAL CHARACTERISTICS

We did not expect that on their own, particular parental behaviors or characteristics would be associated with success or failure in the transmission of parental values. Rather, the *cluster* of behaviors and characteristics that are related to right-wing authoritarianism, we proposed, would result in differing types of parent–child interactions, and would be related to success or failure of transmission. To get at least some sense of the distinct behavioral patterns or characteristics that may be exhibited by parents who possessed right-wing authoritarian worldviews, we explored the relation between parental RWA and parents' style of relating to others.

In the questionnaire packages we included Bartholomew's Relationship Style Questionnaire (RSQ), which measures social and emotional attachments to others (Griffin & Bartholomew, 1994). The RSQ has two underlying dimensions (image of self as worthy or unworthy of love and support, and image of other as trustworthy and available or unreliable and rejecting), and scores on each dimension are combined to give totals on four styles of relating: Fearful, Dismissing, Secure, and Preoccupied. As expected, styles of relating were not directly related to value profile similarity. However, whereas right-wing authoritarianism was unrelated to Secure and Dismissing patterns of relating, parents who endorsed right-wing authoritarian beliefs were more likely to exhibit two patterns of relating to other people: a Fearful pattern ($r(49) = .33$, $p = .02$), in which intimate contact with others is avoided, and a Preoccupied pattern ($r(49) = .37$, $p = .007$), in which self-acceptance is dependent on acceptance by valued others. Underlying both of these styles is a negative image of self, and whereas the Preoccupied pattern is motivated by a positive image of others, the Fearful pattern is motivated by a negative image of others.

Do right-wing authoritarian parents have specific goals in the socialization of their children? To answer this question, we also included Kohn's Parenting Values Survey, which investigates the goals parents have in socializing their children (Kohn, 1977). In Kohn's survey, parents are given a list of 13 qualities, and are asked to say which three they most wanted and which three qualities they least wanted to foster in their children. These 13 qualities, we proposed, could be understood as either serving "instrumental," means–end goals or "expressive," relationship-related goals. For example, "that he is neat and clean" serves an instrumental goal, whereas "that he is considerate of others" serves an expressive goal (see Appendix B for the complete list). Compared with parents who did *not* endorse right-wing authoritarian beliefs, right-wing authoritarian parents were more likely to choose a greater number of qualities that served instrumental goals ($r(49) = .45$, $p < .001$) and less likely to choose qualities that served expressive goals ($r(49) = -.45$, $p < .001$).

We found that parental right-wing authoritarianism not only was related to distinct value profiles, but also was related to at least one parental characteristic that may relate directly to parents' interactions with their children. Furthermore, right-wing authoritarianism was related to particular kinds of goals parents have in the socialization of their children, which is also likely to have effects on the way parents interact with their children. So, if parental right-wing authoritarianism is related to distinct behavior patterns and parenting goals, then it is also likely to be useful in our investigation of value transmission: right-wing authoritarian parents are likely to use different methods in the socialization of their children than non right-wing authoritarian parents, and these differences may relate to the success or failure of the transmission of parental values.

INFLUENCE OF PARENTAL RIGHT-WING AUTHORITARIANISM

The question we addressed, then, was whether parental right-wing authoritarianism influenced the magnitude of the parent–adult child value relation. Can parental right-wing authoritarianism account for the variation in parent–adult child value profile similarity?

The relation between parental right-wing authoritarianism[8] and similarity of value profiles was, indeed, significant ($r(47) = -.32, p = .03$). Compared with highly right-wing authoritarian parents, non right-wing authoritarian parents were *more likely* to have children who grew up to have similar value profiles. So, parental right-wing authoritarianism *does* seem to have a moderating effect.

To look more closely at the moderating effect of right-wing authoritarianism, parents were categorized as either "High Right-Wing Authoritarian" or "Low Right-Wing Authoritarian" on the basis of a median split, and within-family value profile similarity correlations again were used as data points. When parents were categorized as either High or Low in their right-wing authoritarian beliefs, there was a significant difference between the average parent–child value profile similarity correlations of the two groups. The average profile similarity correlation among High RWA parents and their offspring was .42, whereas the average profile similarity correlation among Low RWA parents was .62.

Recall that we created pseudo-families as a way of understanding the contribution of the culturally shared aspect of values. We therefore used the average correlation of these randomly matched pairs of parents and adult children as a

---

[8]The correlation between mothers' RWA and fathers' RWA was high: $r(43) = .65, p < .001$. Mothers' and fathers' RWA scores were aggregated by averaging.

baseline against which to evaluate the significance of the finding that the average value profile similarity correlation differed as a function of parental RWA.[9]

The adult children of Low RWA parents were significantly more likely to hold value profiles that were similar to their parents' value profiles than the *randomly* matched parents and children (.62 vs. .44; $t(25) = 3.32, p < .005$). In contrast, the adult children of High RWA parents were no more likely to hold value profiles that were similar to their parents than randomly matched parents and children (.42 vs. .44; $t(22) < 1$, ns). The folk wisdom therefore received some qualified support: if parents are *not* right-wing authoritarians, their children are more likely to grow up to hold similar value profiles.

HOW DO ADULT CHILDREN VIEW THEIR PARENTS?

In our sample of male university students and their parents, we found that parental right-wing authoritarianism moderated the degree of parent–adult child value profile similarity. Earlier we discussed the differing relationship styles and socialization goals that were associated with parents' right-wing authoritarian beliefs; it seems likely that factors such as parents' relationship style and parents' goals for the socialization of their children will influence the interactions they have with their children. In what ways do the interactions of High right-wing authoritarian parents and their children differ from the interactions of Low right-wing authoritarian parents and their children? To capture important aspects of the differing ways High and Low right-wing authoritarian parents interacted with their children, we focused on parents' parenting style. In the same way that right-wing authoritarianism is associated with a *general* cluster of behaviors and characteristics, we expected that parents' parenting style would relate to a number of parental behaviors and characteristics that are *specifically* associated to the way parents interact with their children.

A substantial research literature exists concerning the impact of parents' parenting style on the socialization of children. There is wide acceptance of the notion that particular styles of parenting promote "effective" socialization. For example, firm control when coupled with parental warmth should promote the

---

[9]We calculated the random-match baseline on the assumption that there was just one overall culture. However, because it was possible that there existed two subcultures (i.e., a High RWA culture and a Low RWA culture), we calculated baselines for the subcultures two ways: First, we randomly matched all children with High RWA parents and all children with Low RWA parents; second, we randomly matched High RWA parents with their children, and Low RWA parents with their children. The baselines calculated ranged from .43 to .47. Because these correlations did not differ significantly from the random match baseline which was calculated using *all* parents and *all* children, and for ease of presentation, to test significance we used the baseline calculated using all children and all parents.

development of such qualities as social responsibility and self-control (e.g., see Maccoby & Martin, 1983). However, this notion has been criticized (e.g., Lewis, 1981), and whether this style of parenting is appropriate at all stages of children's life is not clear. Balswick and Macrides (1975), for example, suggested that a very restrictive parenting style may lead to frustration and rebellion in adolescents. Recently, Grusec and Goodnow (1994) proposed that the effective transmission of parental attitudes and values through parental discipline strategies largely depended upon whether children accurately perceive their parents' message.

For the purposes of understanding the effect of parents' parenting style on the transmission of parental values, we therefore first looked at adult children's accuracy in their perception of their parents' values, and then looked at whether particular aspects of parents' parenting style (both as reported by parents and as perceived by adult children) related to value transmission.

First, in general, how accurately did the adult children perceive their parents' values? As part of their questionnaire package, student participants were instructed to complete the Schwartz Value Inventory in the way they expected their parents would complete the Inventory. Students, on average, were very accurate—the average correlation between parents' value profiles and their profiles as perceived by *their* adult children (i.e., the correlation between actual and perceived parents' values within each family) was high ($r(47) = .67$). This accuracy was significantly greater than a baseline calculated by randomly matching parents' actual value profiles with students' perceptions of parental value profiles (.67 vs. .52; $t(48) = 3.42$, $p < .001$). This accuracy was unrelated to parental right-wing authoritarianism.

To understand important aspects of parents' parenting style, we relied on the work of Maccoby and Martin (1983) who, in following up Baumrind's classic work in the area (e.g., Baumrind, 1971), proposed that parenting style can be characterized by two dimensions—responsiveness and demandingness. These dimensions also can be understood as representing warmth and control.

From these two dimensions, four types of parenting styles can be identified: Authoritarian, Authoritative, Permissive–Indulgent, and Permissive–Neglectful (see Fig. 10.4).

Authoritarian parents are very demanding. They expect their children to live up to their rigid standards, but they are not very responsive, and do not encourage verbal give and take. Authoritative parents are *also* demanding, and *also* have firm standards, but unlike the authoritarian parents, they *are* responsive. They will explain the reasons behind their requests, and encourage discussion. Permissive-Indulgent parents are very responsive, just as the Authoritative parents, but they are not demanding, and do not have clear standards for they way they expect their children to behave. Finally, Permissive–Neglectful parents are neither responsive nor demanding, and they pay their children very little attention.

No adequate measures existed to measure adults' retrospective ratings of the

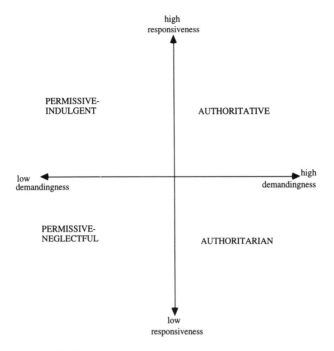

FIG. 10.4.   Four category model of parenting style.

their parents on these four parenting styles, so we designed a new measure. We constructed descriptions of each of the four types of parenting styles (see Appendix C for descriptions of mothers' parenting styles). Student participants read the four descriptions and then reported which prototype best described first their mothers, and then their fathers when the students were growing up. Using 5-point scales, student participants also rated the extent to which their parents' parenting style resembled *each* of the four prototypical parenting styles. Parent participants also read the four descriptions (which were corrected to read "I" instead of "my mother" or "my father"), reported which prototype best described them as parents, and rated the extent to which their parenting style resembled each prototype. It is highly likely that although parents predominantly exhibited one particular style, they also used other styles to a greater or lesser extent. Having the ratings of each of the styles measured these tendencies.

Each sentence in the descriptions was designed to capture important aspects of parenting styles. For example, "My mother has a strict and unchanging set of standards by which she tries to shape, control, and judge my behavior and attitudes," captured Authoritarian parents' demandingness. Lack of responsiveness is reflected in "My mother does not encourage discussion because she believes that children should accept their parents' word for what is right." Although Authoritative parents are demanding, they keep their demands to a minimum, and explain the reasons behind their requests: "My mother believes in having firm control, but does not overload me with rules and restrictions"; "She expects me to do what she says, and she explains the reasoning behind her requests and decisions." Authoritative parents' responsiveness sets them apart from Authoritarian parents: "My mother listens to my opinions and will give me what I ask for or want if she thinks it is reasonable." Permissive–Indulgent parents are not demanding: "Whenever possible my mother avoids asserting her authority, and she also avoids imposing controls or restrictions." But Indulgent parents *are* responsive: "My mother allows me to make my own decisions, and gives me whatever I ask for." Permissive–Neglectful parents are *neither* responsive nor demanding: "My mother does not pay much attention to me, but also makes few demands of me"; "My mother does not have the time or motivation to think about my needs."

We computed scores on the dimensions of Responsiveness and Demandingness. The Responsiveness score was computed by adding together the ratings of the two styles that are *high* in responsiveness (Indulgent and Authoritative) and subtracting ratings of the two styles that are *low* in responsiveness (Neglectful and Authoritarian). The Demandingness score was computed by adding together ratings of the two styles that are *high* in demandingness (Authoritarian and Authoritative) and subtracting ratings of the two styles that are *low* in demandingness (Indulgent and Neglectful). Although we had parents' reports of their parenting style, we decided that because we were interested in the effects of parents' parenting styles, it was more important to examine adult children's *perceptions* of their parents' parenting styles.[10]

MEDIATING EFFECTS OF PERCEPTIONS
OF PARENTING STYLE

Parental right-wing authoritarianism moderated the parent–adult child value profile similarity relation: Greater parent–adult child value profile similarity was observed between low right-wing authoritarian parents and their children compared with high right-wing authoritarian parents and their children. Whether the moderating effect of parental right-wing authoritarianism was *mediated* by adult children's perceptions of their parents' parenting style was our next question. Do adult children's perceptions of their parents' parenting style make a difference to whether or not parents' endorsement (or non endorsement) of right-wing authori-

---

[10]There were, however, significant correlations between parents' reports and adult children's perceptions of parents' parenting styles: The correlation between reported responsiveness and perceived parental responsiveness was .46 ($p < .001$), and the correlation between reported demandingness and perceived parental demandingness was .31 ($p = .03$).

tarian beliefs influences the transmission of parental values? If adult children's perceptions mediate the effect of parental authoritarianism, then three things needed to be verified.

First, is parental right-wing authoritarianism related to adult children's perceptions of parenting style? Are right-wing authoritarian parents perceived to use different parenting styles than non right-wing authoritarian parents? For example, are non right-wing authoritarian parents more *responsive* and less *demanding* than highly right-wing authoritarian parents? Second, are perceptions of parenting style related to the value profile similarity between parents and their adult children? For example, are parents who are more responsive *more* likely to have adult children with similar value profiles than parents who are not so responsive? And third, when we take adult children's perceptions of their parents' style of parenting into account, is the relation between parental right-wing authoritarianism and the parent–child value profile similarity relation attenuated?

First, parents' endorsement of right-wing authoritarian beliefs was negatively related to adult children's perceptions of parental responsiveness ($r(49) = -.36$, $p < .01$) and positively related to their adult children's perceptions of parental demandingness ($r(49) = .38, p < .005$). The less right-wing authoritarian parents were, the more likely their adult children were to perceive them as being responsive and not demanding. The first condition for mediation was satisfied: Parental right-wing authoritarianism *was* related to adult children's perceptions of parenting style.

The second condition for mediation was also satisfied: Perceptions of parenting style were related to the value profile similarity between parents and their adult children. Perceived parental responsiveness was significantly positively related to parent–child similarity ($r(49) = .36, p < .01$). To the extent that they perceived their parents as responsive in their parenting style, adult children were more likely to have value profiles that resembled their parents' value profiles. Perceived parental demandingness was negatively related to parent–child profile similarity, though not significantly ($r(49) = -.18$, ns). It seemed as though parents' responsiveness played the more important role in whether or not parental values are passed on to children, and we therefore concentrated on examining its role in all following analyses.[11]

Finally, if we take adult children's perceptions of parents' responsive parenting style into account, is the relation between parental right-wing authoritarianism and parent–child value profile similarity reduced? Recall that the correlation between parental right-wing authoritarianism and parent–adult child value profile similarity was significant ($r(47) = -.32, p = .03$). The more right-wing authoritarian parents were in their beliefs, the *less* likely their children were to

---

[11]Because adult children's perceptions of mothers' and fathers' responsiveness was significantly related ($r(65) = .49, p < .001$), it again made sense to talk about *parents* rather than mothers and fathers separately.

grow up to hold similar value profiles. Indeed, recall that when we grouped parents into either a "High" or "Low" right-wing authoritarian category, the profile similarity correlations were significantly different (average profile similarity correlations of .42 vs. .62).

To satisfy the third condition of mediation, when parenting style is taken into account, the relation between parental right-wing authoritarianism and parent–adult child value profile similarity should be reduced. For example, to show that parenting style *perfectly* mediated the relation, the predictive power of parental right-wing authoritarianism would drop to zero in a regression analysis when parenting style and parental right-wing authoritarianism were both entered to predict parent–child value similarity. In addition, parenting style would be a significant predictor of parent–child value profile similarity.

We found that the predictive power of parental right-wing authoritarianism was reduced to a non-significant level, and that responsive parenting style was a significant predictor of parent–adult child value profile similarity (see Fig. 10.5): The Beta for parental right-wing authoritarianism was reduced from −.32 to −.22 when perceptions of responsive parenting style were taken into account, and the Beta for perceived responsive parenting style was .28, which was signifi-

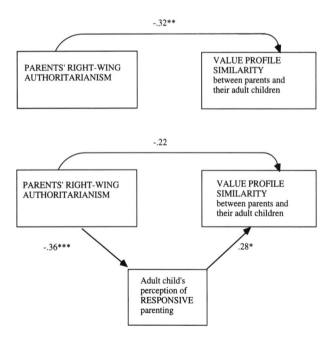

$^*p < .05.$ $^{**}p < .01.$ $^{***}p < .001.$

FIG. 10.5.   Mediating effects of parenting style perceptions.

cant ($p < .05$). So, the relation between parental right-wing authoritarianism and parent–adult child value profile similarity seems to be mediated, at least in part, by adult children's perceptions of their parents' responsive parenting style.

IMPLICATIONS

The folk wisdom that "the apple never falls far from the tree" therefore received qualified support, and we have preliminary answers to our two questions "How much like their parents do adult children become?" and "What influences their similarity?" Our search for a parental characteristic that influences the parent–child relationship seemed successful: Parental right-wing authoritarianism moderated the degree to which adult children's value profiles resembled their parents' value profiles. Further, we found that parental responsiveness mediated the effect of parental authoritarianism. But why does parental responsiveness lead to more successful value transmission?

To get some insight into the way parental responsiveness might influence value transmission, we looked at adult children's evaluations of their parents on three specific dimensions. Perceptions of parental responsiveness were linked to positive evaluations of parental trustworthiness ($r(69) = .57, p < .001$), fairness ($r(69) = .44, p < .001$), and lack of hypocrisy ($r(68) = .51, p < .001$). Furthermore, a composite index of these evaluations was significantly negatively related to parental RWA: Non right-wing authoritarian parents were more likely to be positively evaluated on the three dimensions ($r(49) = -.31, p = .03$). Perhaps, therefore, it is not surprising that the adult children of non right-wing authoritarian, responsive parents would be more likely to take on similar values as their parents—it seems the adult children had positive opinions of their parents, were therefore more likely to use them as models and were less likely to rebel.[12]

It is interesting to note that although *on average* the adult children of highly authoritarian parents did not replicate their parents value profiles, there seemed to be two fairly distinct subgroups: Adult children of highly right-wing authoritarian parents were either not at all like their parents, or were quite similar. In comparison, the adult children of low right-wing authoritarian parents were all *generally* similar to their parents—no distinct subgroups existed.[13] Further examination showed that adult children's perceptions of their highly authoritarian

---

[12]Although it is conceptually possible that these evaluations mediated the parental RWA–value profile similarity relation, mediation analyses showed that this was not the case, primarily because these evaluations were not significantly related to value profile similarity.

[13]Though it was not significantly different, there also was more variability in the value profile similarity correlations for High RWA parents and their adult children ($SD = .52$) than for Low RWA parents and their adult children ($SD = .40$).

parents' responsiveness differentiated between those who belonged to each of the two subgroups. Although we need to explore this finding in more detail, and replicate it with a larger sample, it seems likely that those children most at risk for growing up to resemble their highly right-wing authoritarian parents are those who perceive their parents to be responsive. Indeed, in our sample, these adult children held more right-wing authoritarian beliefs than either the other adult children of highly right-wing authoritarian parents or the adult children of non right-wing authoritarian parents.

The study we have reported was our first exploration—with male university students and their parents—of the question "What is it that makes some children, and not others, grow up to be like their parents?" The results from this study suggest it may be important and highly informative to do a longitudinal study in which we identify high and low right-wing authoritarian parents and focus on their children through adolescence—a time when values and attitudes are being developed.

We have shown the usefulness of values in conceptualizing general similarities and differences between parents and their adult children. We plan in future research to begin, not only to map the development of values related to prejudice, but also to delineate and evaluate the usefulness of various indicators—beginning with parental authoritarianism—in parent–child relationships for predicting who will develop or *carry on* the prejudice of their parents. Perhaps with a clear understanding of the mechanisms of transmission, we will be in a better position to suggest ways to encourage the transmission of those values and attitudes that will promote mutually rewarding relationships among people.

ACKNOWLEDGMENTS

Preparation of this chapter was supported in part by a Social Sciences and Humanities Research Council of Canada (SSHRC) Doctoral Fellowship to the first author and a SSHRC grant to the second author. We would like to thank David Kenny and Shalom Schwartz for alerting us to the issue of cultural similarity, and also thank Ziva Kunda and James Olson for their comments on earlier drafts.

REFERENCES

Aboud, F. (1988). *Children and prejudice*. Cambridge, MA: Basil Blackwell.
Adorno, T. W., Frenkel-Brunswik, E., Levinson, D. J., & Sanford, R. N. (1950). *The authoritarian personality*. New York: Harper.
Allport, G. W., Vernon, P. E., & Lindzey, G. (1960). *Study of values. Manual and test booklet* (3rd ed.) Boston, MA: Houghton Mifflin.

Altemeyer, B. (1988). *Enemies of freedom: Understanding right-wing authoritarianism.* San Francisco: Jossey-Bass.

Altemeyer, B. (1994). Reducing prejudice in right-wing authoritarians. In M. P. Zanna & J. M. Olson (Eds.), *The psychology of prejudice* (pp. 131–148). Hillsdale, NJ: Lawrence Erlbaum Associates.

Altemeyer, B., & Hunsberger, B. (1992). Authoritarianism, religious fundamentalism, quest, and prejudice. *International Journal for the Psychology of Religion, 2,* 113–133.

Balswick, J. O., & Macrides, C. (1975). Parental stimulation for adolescent rebellion. *Adolescence, 10,* 253–266.

Baumrind, D. (1971). Current patterns of parental authority. *Developmental Psychology Monograph, 4.*

Braithwaite, V. A., & Scott, W. A. (1991). Values. In J. P. Robinson, P. R. Shaver, & L. S. Wrightsman (Eds.), *Measures of personality and social psychological attitudes* (pp. 661–753). New York: Academic Press.

Cashmore, J. A., & Goodnow, J. J. (1985). Agreement between generations: A two-process approach. *Child development, 56,* 493–501.

Doumit Sparks, A., Thornburg, K. R., Ispa, J. M., & McPhail Gray, M. (1984). Prosocial behaviors of young children related to parental childrearing attitudes. *Early Child Development and Care, 15,* 291–298.

Eisenberg, N., Wolchik, S. A., Goldberg, L., & Engel, I. (1992). Parental values, reinforcement, and young children's prosocial behavior: A longitudinal study. *The Journal of Genetic Psychology, 153,* 19–36.

Gaertner, S. L. (1976). Non-reactive measures in racial attitude research: A focus on "Liberals." In P. A. Katz (Ed.), *Toward the elimination of racism* (pp. 183–211). New York: Pergamon.

Griffin, D. W., & Bartholomew, K. (1994). The metaphysics of measurement: The case of adult attachment. *Advances in Personal Relationships, 5,* 17–52.

Grusec, J. E., & Goodnow, J. J. (1994). Impact of parental discipline methods on the child's internalization of values: A reconceptualization of current points of view. *Developmental Psychology, 30,* 4–19.

Hoge, D. R., Petrillo, G. H., & Smith, E. I. (1982). Transmission of religious and social values from parents to teenage children. *Journal of Marriage and the Family, 44,* 569–580.

Kenny, D. A., & Acitelli, L. K. (1994). *Measuring similarity in couples.* Unpublished manuscript. University of Connecticut.

Kluckhohn, C. K. M. (1951). Values and value orientations in the theory of action. In T. Parsons & E. Sils (Eds.), *Towards a general theory of action* (pp. 388–433). Cambridge, MA: Harvard University Press.

Kohn, M. (1977). *Class and conformity: A study in values* (2nd ed.). Chicago, IL: University of Chicago Press.

Kovel, J. (1970). *White racism: A psychohistory.* New York: Pantheon.

Lewis, C. C. (1981). The effects of parental firm control: A reinterpretation of findings. *Psychological Bulletin, 90,* 547–563.

Maccoby, E. E., & Martin, J. A. (1983). Socialization in the context of the family: parent-child interaction. In E. M. Hetherington (Ed.), *Socialization, personality, and social development* (pp. 1–101). New York: Wiley.

McBroom, W. H., Reed, F. W., Burns, C. E., Hargreaves, J. L., & Trankel, M. A. (1985). Intergenerational transmission of values: A data-based reassessment. *Social Psychology Quarterly, 48,* 150–163.

McConahay, J. B. (1986). Modern racism, ambivalence, and the modern racism scale. In J. F. Dovidio & S. L. Gaertner (Eds.), *Prejudice, discrimination, and racism* (pp. 91–125). New York: Academic Press.

McConahay, J. B., & Hough, J. C., Jr. (1976). Symbolic racism. *Journal of Social Issues, 32,* 23–45.

Newcomb, T., & Svehla, G. (1937). Intra-family relationships in attitudes. *Sociometry, 1,* 180–205.

Rokeach, M. (1973). *The nature of human values.* New York: Free Press.

Rokeach, M., Smith, P. W., & Evans, R. I. (1960). Two kinds of prejudice or one? In M. Rokeach (Ed.), *The open and closed mind* (pp. 132–168). New York: Basic Books.

Romero, M. (1994, August). *Parental influence on college students' attitudes about peace and justice.* Poster presented at the Annual convention of the American Psychological Association, Los Angeles.

Sagiv, L., & Schwartz, S. H. (1995). Value priorities and readiness for out-group social contact. *Journal of Personality and Social Psychology, 69,* 437–448.

Schwartz, S. H. (1992). Universals in the content and structure of values: Theoretical advances and empirical tests in 20 countries. In M. P. Zanna (Ed.), *Advances in experimental social psychology* (Vol. 24, pp. 1–65). San Diego: Academic Press.

Sears, D. O., & Kinder, D. R. (1971). Racial tensions and voting in Los Angeles. In W. Z. Hirsch (Ed.), *Los Angeles: Viability and prospects for metropolitan leadership* (pp. 51–88). New York: Praeger.

Smith, T. E. (1982). The case of parental transmission of educational goals: The importance of accurate offspring perceptions. *Journal of Marriage and the Family, 44,* 661–674.

Troll, L., & Bengtson, V. (1979). Generations in the family. In W. R. Burr, R. Hill, F. I. Nye, & I. L. Reiss (Eds.), *Contemporary theories about the family: Research-based theories* (pp. 127–161). New York: Free Press.

Troll, L., Neugarten, B. L., & Kraines, R. J. (1969). Similarities in values and other personality characteristics in college students and their parents. *Merrill-Palmer Quarterly, 15,* 323–336.

Williams, R. M.. (1968). Values. In E. Sils (Ed.), *International encyclopedia of the social sciences* (pp. 283–287). New York: Macmillan.

Zanna, M. P., Haddock, G., & Esses, V. M. (1990, June). *On the nature of prejudice.* Paper presented at the Nags Head Conference on Stereotypes and Intergroup Relations, Kill Devil Hill, NC.

APPENDIX A
Measure of Attitudes Toward Minority Groups

1. It's good to live in a country where there are so many different ethnic and racial groups.
2. Some races or ethnic groups are, by their nature, more violent than others.
3. The government should not make any special effort to help minority groups because they should help themselves.
4. Over the past few years, the government and the news media have given more attention to minorities than they deserve.
5. Minorities are getting too demanding in their push for special rights.
6. Discrimination against racial and ethnic minorities is no longer a problem in Canada.

Note. Items 3, 4, 5, and 6 are very similar to items in the Modern Racism Scale (McConahay, 1986).

APPENDIX B
Kohn's List of Parenting Goals Categorized as Either Instrumental or Expressive

Instrument Goals

that he have good manners
that he tries hard to succeed
that he is neat and clean
that he acts like a male should
that he obeys his parents well
that he is a good student

Expressive Goals

that he is honest
that he has good sense and sound judgment
that he has self-control
that he get along with other people
that he is responsible
that he is considerate of others
that he is interested in how and why things happen

Authoritarian Parent Prototype

My mother has a strict and unchanging set of standards by which she tries to shape, control, and judge my behavior and attitudes. She places great importance on obedience, and she favors forceful measures when my actions or beliefs conflict with her standards of acceptable conduct. She has tried to teach me conventional values such as work, tradition, respect for authority, and preservation of order. She does not encourage verbal give and take, because she believes that children should accept parents' word for what is right.

Authoritative Parent Prototype

My mother sets clear standards for me. She expects me to do what she says, and she explains the reasoning behind her requests and decisions. She listens to my opinions, and she will give me what I ask for or want if she thinks it is reasonable. She believes in having form control, but she does not overload me with rules and restrictions. She will admit to her mistakes and she is loving and supportive. She thinks it is important for me to be both happy and productive. She wants me to be independent and assertive as well as respectful, and be able to fit in with others.

Permissive-Indulgent Parent Prototype

My mother is tolerant and accepting. She makes few demands of me. Whenever possible she avoids asserting her authority, and she also avoids imposing controls or restrictions. She does not try to structure or influence what I say or do. She does not insist that I conform to standards made by other people, and allows me to decide for myself what is right and wrong. My mother allows me to make my own decisions, and gives me whatever I ask for.

Permissive-Neglectful Parent Prototype

My mother is heavily involved in other activities, and has little time to spare me. She does not pay much attention to me, but also makes few demands of me. She responds to my immediate demands in a way that quickly resolves the problem. My mother does not have clear standards for the way she wants me to behave, and she intervenes only when it is absolutely necessary. My mother does not have the time or motivation to think about my needs.

11 Making Choices: Media Roles in the Construction of Value-Choices

Sandra J. Ball-Rokeach
University of Southern California

William E. Loges
Baylor University

> *In their hearts, most journalists know . . . that politics while it can be enjoyed for its own sake, is fundamentally about choices and values and the direction a society takes.*
> —Rosen (1993, p. 9)

It seems that any time human societies face the pervasive ambiguities that accompany massive social change, the discussion inevitably turns to values. One reason why is that old structures and ways of doing things come into conflict with emerging structures and patterns of behavior. A profound problematic ensues. Its essential element is legitimacy (Habermas, 1975). Under the shifting sands of change and resistance to change, under the pervasive ambiguity (Ball-Rokeach, 1973) of not feeling certain that one understands fundamental questions of what is going on and why? who am I? and who are we? people must not only construct artificially stable social realities, they must also legitimate them. In traditional societies, this communication work took place in interpersonal networks. In contemporary societies, interpersonal discourse takes place in the context of a communication environment dominated by media discourse.

One of the ways that we know that no one social reality has exclusive claim to legitimacy in contemporary society is the awesome number of social issues found in any day's dose of media news. The central arguments put forth in this chapter concern the construction of one type of social issue: What is the most legitimate way to allocate scarce and prized resources? The concept of a value-choice frame is introduced as an efficient conceptual tool for analysis of issue construction, and media system dependency (MSD) theory is suggested as a theoretical tool for analysis of media roles in this process.

277

FROM FRAMES TO VALUE-FRAMES TO VALUE-CHOICE FRAMES

A *frame* is the linguistic window through which we see or interpret. For example, interpersonal conflict frequently entails a "talking past one another" problem arising from very different frames. When parents frame their disciplinary actions vis à vis their children in terms of responsible socialization, children often frame such actions as threats to their in-group status with peers. The framing concept has been applied widely in analyses of media texts (Entman, 1993; Gamson, Croteau, Hoynes, & Sasson, 1992; Gitlin, 1980; Kellner, 1990). According to Gamson et al., the concept of "Frame plays the same role in analyzing media discourse that schema does in cognitive psychology—a central organizing principle that holds together and gives coherence and meaning to a wide array of symbols. . . . Media frames, largely unspoken and unacknowledged, organize the world for both journalists who report it and, in some important degree, for us who rely on their reports" (p. 384).

Ball-Rokeach and Rokeach (1987) have suggested that the essential frame employed in media discourse is a *value-frame*. As the term insists, a value frame consists of one or more values as the linguistic window or interpretive schema. Employing Rokeach's (1973) definitions, there are two types of values; terminal values or desired end states of existence (e.g., freedom, equality, family security), and instrumental values or preferred modes of conduct (e.g., behaving honestly, lovingly, or independently). Values are *evaluative* heuristics applied to self, other, and situation. Unlike other heuristics (e.g., statistical probabilities), values are accessible to most, if not all, members of a society; they are windows through which the everyday person can see as well as the most sophisticated analyst. Whether child or old person, people are able to articulate their own and others' value systems (Rokeach, 1973; Rokeach & Ball-Rokeach, 1989), including the value priorities associated with major political figures and their issues (Alexander, 1986; Loges & Ball-Rokeach, 1995). The need to connect with the masses of people is a major reason why media discourse, whether it be in the form of "news" or "entertainment" or advertising, is coded or framed in value terms. For reasons similar to those of the media, competing interest groups also tend to frame their respective positions in value terms (Ball-Rokeach, Power, Guthrie, & Waring, 1990). Value-frames, then, are the most common currency of justification, for constructing and communicating to self and others an evaluative heuristic for why a group's interests are legitimate (i.e., moral and competent). In discussing the importance of the media's role in the process of value-framing an issue, Ball-Rokeach and Rokeach (1987) state:

> [T]he value-framing concept points to the criteria that determine what is relevant with regard to issue formation and resolution. It is, we suggest, the ability to control those criteria that gives the power to create the meaning (or acceptable

range of meaning) of an issue. The question, then, goes beyond public and policy agenda-setting to the researchable question of the media system's power to control the meaning of events. (p. 184)

Whereas a value-frame is a certain type of frame, a value-choice frame is a certain type of value-frame. A *value-choice frame* is a frame consisting of two or more values in a state of tension or conflict. It is the choice feature and the tension it produces that distinguishes a value-choice frame from the more general value-frame. For example, in the allocation of any scarce material or nonmaterial resource, there are competing bases of legitimacy. If a job can only be given to one person out of many applicants, several value-frames may be salient—for example, being capable, equality, friendship, or being loyal—and these often stand in a state of tension with each other. Ideally, one could simultaneously satisfy all of these evaluative heuristics; however, the allocation decision usually does not permit this. Decision makers must choose to place one of these values over the others and they must justify their choice to themselves and to others. The product is a value-choice frame, such as the employer who says: The requirements of the job are such that being capable must outweigh all other value considerations.

When it comes to societal or community resource allocation issues, such as the allocation of wealth, opportunity, or status, value-choice frames necessarily become the discourse heuristic. A social issue, by definition, involves two or more conflicting views of the "proper" choice. With "properness" of choice problematic, popular and media discourses focus on the value-choices seen to be at issue. Proponents on each side of an issue construct value-choice frames to legitimate to themselves and to communicate to others why their choice is more moral or competent than their opponents'. Competition for control over scarce and prized resources thrusts political decision makers, interest groups, and the public into symbolic conflict waged in one language they share, the language of values, and the nature of the conflict forces them to move beyond value-frames to value-choice frames. In contrast to the hiring situation earlier, contests to control which value-choice frame will dominate discourse and decision-making about a social issue must be waged in and through the mass media.

AMBIGUITY, UNSTABLE SOCIAL WORLDS, AND VALUES

The experience of ambiguity is a chronic condition of people's lives in contemporary societies. Pervasive ambiguity (Ball-Rokeach, 1973) is the inability to establish stable relational links between events (e.g., self, social situations, and other actor individuals or groups). Pervasive ambiguity is a logical outcome of rapid social change. Change is manifested in massive disjunctures between "what is" and "what was" or between "what ought to be" and "what is" (Kluegel & Smith, 1986). People living under these structurally ambiguous conditions seem doomed to an endless pursuit of ways to understand the what, why, and how of their social environs. Put another way, social reality is unstable, requiring constant reconstruction. Demands on cognitive and affective resources are many and intense. Due to their shared experiences of pervasive ambiguity, individuals *and* their interpersonal networks face two basic and chronic problems. The first is stress management. Due to the centrality of the media system in personal and social life, people frequently go beyond the stress reduction resources available to them through interpersonal network associations to choose media play over other ways to reduce stress.

The second problem is information, the information required to remodel or rebuild established definitions of one's social world. This problem cannot be managed within the resources available to individuals *and* their interpersonal networks (Hirschburg, Dillman, & Ball-Rokeach, 1986). The very nature of complex and changing societies lowers the premium that once was placed upon the knowledge of elders, parents, and local neighborhood leaders. In fact, Meyrowitz (1985) argues that electronic media contribute directly to the loss of faith in and respect for traditional authority figures because the "backstage" information about our idols available on television diminishes the sense of mystery and distance that once surrounded them. When it comes to understanding the social world, experience-based knowledge or expertise has become an ephemeral resource. The work of forming attitude preferences about every new object, situation, or issue choice has only transitory payoff. The world and its assumptions about "what is" and "what ought to be" simply change too fast for our repertoire of attitudes to have lasting utility for understanding our social world, and, thus, at least parts of our personal worlds.

This phenomenological reality has stimulated lay searches for values to anchor reality and renewed academic interest in value theory and research. Trans-object and trans-situational values are more resistant to being superannuated or to having their salience and utility undermined by rapidly changing social environs. Values also afford travel through the multiple levels of social organization that impinge on individual and interpersonal network life (Rokeach, 1979). The "globalism" of contemporary life may be better understood as the loss of localism. Classical sociological theorists spoke to this phenomenon long ago in the massive social transformation known as modern society. In so many words, they (e.g., Durkheim, Weber, and Tonnies) noted the pervasive ambiguity of life for those experiencing the tumultuous transition from traditional to modern society. In parallel fashion, another massive social transformation is underway, one that is sensed better than it is articulated. Numerous "post-something" descriptors—postindustrial, postmodern, postmaterialist, and so on—reveal a fundamental inability to define what kind of society is coming; the definition is reduced to what kind of society we are leaving. Nonetheless, it is fair to say that social worlds have become even more complexly organized, and individual and interpersonal network worlds have lost their traditional geographic and social boundaries. However ambiguously, individuals and their networks are connected to increasingly large units of societal reorganization, for example, to regions that know no national borders. In vain, reactionary movements promote ethnic identity as a cultural form to ward off the entropy effects of economic and political movements that cross and confuse structural categories of class, caste, race, gender, age, and sexual orientation.

Under such profoundly ambiguous and psychicly threatening conditions, values remain as one of the few ways of encoding and decoding self and other. It is meaningful to speak of personal values, family values, group values, social movement values, community values, subcultural values, organizational values, institutional values, regional values, and societal values. Values travel well across the multiple (micro/macro) social worlds. Individuals and their interpersonal networks may employ values as codes to define even pervasively ambiguous worlds. For example, in perhaps the most chaotic of social environments—South Africa in the turmoil preceding its first nonracially segregated presidential election in April, 1994—white President F. W. de Klerk addressed an audience of Black and White citizens during a debate with his opponent Nelson Mandela. In response to charges that he represents only the interests of White people, de Klerk responded that he no longer represents a "White party," but a set of values to which, presumably, any person could subscribe (heard on "All Things Considered" on April 14, 1994). Clearly, de Klerk recognized that appeals to values could transcend race even in, or especially in, South Africa. A similar use of values as transcendental political rhetoric is found in Ronald Reagan's acceptance of the 1980 Republican presidential nomination (Loges & Ball-Rokeach, 1995). Speaking in Detroit on July 17, 1980, he said "I want to carry our message to every American, regardless of party affiliation, who is a member of this community of shared values" ("Text of Reagan's Speech," 1980).

Under the ambiguity conditions described earlier, the salient information resources of the media system make it central to the lives of individuals, interpersonal networks, communities, organizations, social movements, and society at large. It is for this and other reasons that the media system is conceived as an information system (Ball-Rokeach, 1985). In the concrete, the media system is made up of interrelated and interdependent broadcast, print, and interactive-electronic media organizations that tend to share values, goals, norms, and the like. In the abstract, the media system controls access to its information resources—to gather, create, process, and disseminate information. The media system's power to affect thoughts, feelings, and behavior rests fundamentally on the implications of these information resources in people's attempts to attain their understanding, orientation, and play goals. With increasing frequency, these resources are exclusive in the sense that no other information system (e.g., personal, interpersonal, network, community, even the state's) has control over equally rich resources. What other information system, for example, specializes in the production of understandings and interpretations of the past, present, and future, and has the resources to connect citizens to government, consumers to producers, and residents to their communities?

THE PROCESS OF CONSTRUCTING THE AMERICAN
HEALTH CARE ISSUE AS A VALUE-CHOICE

In *The Social Transformation of American Medicine,* Starr (1982) discusses the history of the struggle to control the allocation of a central resource, the practice and delivery of health care. This issue has emerged again in the U.S. context where it holds a high position on media, public, and policymaker agendas. Historical and contemporary struggles center on a prerequisite to victory in sociopolitical contests, the mobilization of legitimacy. In the early 1990s, this struggle took form in several competing health reform plans with proponents seeking to construct, and opponents seeking to destruct, legitimacy. Legitimacy contests are waged in the language of values (Ball-Rokeach, 1971; Rokeach, 1973). Values are the preferred ends (terminal values) and desired means of achieving those ends (instrumental values) that proponents employ to justify, and opponents employ to attack, the morality or competence of competing plans (Ball-Rokeach, Rokeach, & Grube, 1984; Rokeach, 1973). Health is a terminal value that is not contested; it is uniformly extolled by all sides. Many values enter the discourse, but at the heart of this, as with any other, political debate are the terminal values equality and freedom (Ball-Rokeach, 1976; Ball-Rokeach & Tallman, 1979; Rokeach, 1973; Rokeach & Ball-Rokeach, 1989).

Specifically, the equality–freedom value choice takes a central position in the symbolic logics of contestants' attempts to mobilize legitimacy to their side on resource allocation issues. It is this value-choice that constitutes the logic of Rokeach's (1973) two-value model of politics. Other values enter into the rhetorical contest, but they are peripheral to the central equality–freedom choice. In political issues that do *not* concern resource allocation per se, the contest to control the value-choice frame may not reduce to an equality–freedom choice. In Watergate (Ball-Rokeach & Rokeach, 1987), for example, the contest was between the Nixon value-choice (loyalty over honesty) and the Ervin Senate Committee value-choice (honesty over loyalty). Nonetheless, every *resource allocation* decision that requires a priori legitimation or post hoc justification must deal with certain issues that implicate equality and freedom end states.

At some level, all such decisions necessarily involve either (a) choices between allocating resources according to concerns for the welfare of the whole or the part, of this part or that part, of the group or the individual, or (b) choices designed to simultaneously serve the welfare of the whole and the part, this part and that part, and the group and the individual. The four general ideologies—communism, capitalism, socialism, and fascism—legitimate different answers to these resource allocation decisions (Rokeach, 1973). Communist ideology clearly opts for collective welfare over individual welfare and employs a high equality–low freedom mode of legitimization. Capitalists clearly opt for the welfare of the individual over the group and the part over the whole (e.g., what's good for the part may benefit the whole, but not the other way around), and employ a high freedom–low equality mode of legitimization. Fascists restrict any collective welfare conception to the state, and restrict individual level conceptions to winners. To legitimate resource allocation decisions, they must deprecate both equality and freedom as immoral and incompetent. Socialists opt for the simultaneous benefiting of collective and individual welfare, justifying their choices with a high equality–high freedom stance. Socialist ideology, in contrast to capitalist ideology, endorses the assumption that serving the collective welfare can simultaneously serve individual welfare, but not the other way around. Thus, the socialist's resource allocation problem is to benefit the collective welfare without infringing upon individual freedom.

With regard to health delivery and practice, different resource allocation decisions or preferences should be based on different equality–freedom value-choices. Barbara Starfield (1994) demonstrates the strong connection between decisions regarding health-care resource allocation and the value-choices that underlie the general distribution of resources in a society. In the context of the United States in the 1990s, the legitimation contest should be limited to capitalist and socialist value-choice frames. This is because, at this point in time, only a small percentage of Americans advocate or hold low freedom positions (Ball-Rokeach & Rokeach, 1987). For instance, in May of 1989 a survey of 411 randomly selected residents of San Bernardino, California showed that only 48 people ranked freedom in the bottom third of a list of 18 terminal values. Over 50% placed it in the top third (Loges & Ball-Rokeach, 1995).

The Major Plans and Their Value-Frames

Proponents of two of the three major health reform positions frame their arguments as a value-choice between equality and freedom. "Single Payer" plan advocates are fairly explicit in their equality–freedom value choice; they place greater priority on equality than on freedom. For example, they explicitly extol the morality of providing equal or universal access and condemn as immoral the failure to do so. Single Payer proponents also, but less explicitly, suggest that allowing market forces to operate unchecked in the name of freedom has led to both incompetent and immoral outcomes (with regard to the former, high cost, and the latter, denial of health services to millions of Americans).

Proponents of Republican alternatives implicitly, and sometimes explicitly, frame the legitimacy of their plan in a value-choice that gives priority to freedom over equality. Despite variations in the several plans offered by Republicans, they all endorse a mechanism for free market competition and, at least, short-term acceptance of unequal access. Various other values are called upon to justify their giving greater priority to freedom than to equality; for example, these proponents argue that it is the individual's "responsibility" to save money to purchase health insurance.

Whereas Single Payer proponents tend to emphasize morality over competence dimensions, proponents of one or another Republican free market plan tend to emphasize competence over morality. This is particularly evident in Republican attacks on other plans. A frequent attack is that government-operated Single Payer plans are necessarily incompetent because they lack the efficiency of market-run plans, and that the government is by nature incompetent (Republican Senator Phil Gramm of Texas threatens that a government health service would be as efficient as the Postal Service). The focus in this attack suggests that it is worse to allow the incompetence of inefficiency than it is to allow the immorality of more than 37 million Americans being uninsured and, therefore, denied equal access to health-care resources.

The third and most visible plan in 1994 was advocated by the Clinton Administration. It was justified in a way that obfuscates the tension between equality and freedom and, thus, the tension between morality and competence. Clinton plan proponents seemingly wished to avoid making a value-choice. They suggested that both equality and freedom—criteria of morality and competence that constitute legitimacy—can be given the same high priority. The attempt to deny the inherent tension in a capitalist society between equality and freedom is evident in the way that President Clinton (1993) value-framed his plan in a speech to Congress in 1993. He proposed six principles according to which his and any other health plan should be evaluated. They are, in the order presented, (1) security (guaranteed universal and nonrevocable health coverage); (2) simplicity (getting rid of costly and wasteful paperwork); (3) savings (reduce the 14% of GNP spent on health care); (4) choice (individuals' right to choose plans and doctors); (5) quality (maintain and publicly evaluate hospital and doctor performance); and (6) responsibility (both social, as in companies that make profit from health services, and personal, as in reduction of health risks).

Clinton led with the most controversial political value in American society, equality (Ball-Rokeach et al., 1984), but he camouflaged it as security. This practice accords with a more general flight from the "L" word or "Liberal" in post-1960s American politics; liberal being a code word for those who place high priority on equality as a value that should, along with freedom, guide resource allocation decisions (Ball-Rokeach, 1992). The principles of simplicity, savings, choice, and quality combine explicit and implicit appeals to freedom and competence. The last principle, responsibility, is interesting for its emphasis upon both corporate and personal dimensions. As previously indicated, it is not uncommon for more conservative plan advocates to call for personal responsibility, but Clinton calls for both social and personal morality. Social morality is, as we have previously implied, a more central concern of Single Payer advocates who emphasize morality over competence and equality over freedom.

From the present analytical perspective, the Clinton speech is fundamentally coded in terms of both equality and freedom, but its apparent logic is not to frame the health-care plan as a value-choice. Rather, the values or principles employed to establish its legitimacy are presented in such a way as to appeal across the American ideological spectrum, akin to the more general thrust of "new Democrat" politics. A difficulty with this strategy is that the refusal to prioritize equality and freedom creates ambiguity with respect to resource allocation decisions. Which way, for example, would administrators of the Clinton plan go when a choice must be made between security and savings or security and choice? What would be preserved at all costs and what would be sacrificed if necessary?

Looking at these three plans from the perspective of the two-value model of politics, Single Payer proponents represent the clear socialist position. Their choice of equality over freedom does not entail a deprecation of freedom (as with communist frames). Rather it rests on the assumption that serving the collective welfare is moral and competent, because it can competently provide for individual welfare. Republican plan proponents clearly disagree with this assumption. They propose a classical capitalist value-choice of maximizing individual freedom over collective equality with respect to health-care resources. The assumption is that putting freedom of the individual first will lead to moral and competent outcomes, because doing so will insure quality and savings that benefit everyone. In a lengthy review of the Clinton health plan, Elizabeth McCaughey (1994) made frequent mention of the interference in the market that the president's proposal represented, and emphasized as well the limitations of personal freedom of choice (of physicians, health plans, and treatments) she saw in the Clinton plan. (McCaughey was elected Lieutenant Governor of New York as a Republican in 1994.) William Kristol, chairman of the Project for the Republican Future (and former chief of staff to Vice President Quayle) advised Republicans in early April, 1994, not to fear opposing the principle of universal coverage (Meyerson, 1994). This, Clinton's first principle, is the proposal that most clearly implicates the value of equality.

The Clinton plan represented a backing away from both socialist and capitalist value-choices. Specifically, Clinton did not take a side (or took both sides) vis à vis key questions that divide socialist and capitalist resource allocation justifications—can serving collective welfare (equality) also serve individual welfare (freedom), and is the morality of serving collective welfare compatible with competence considerations?

Health Plans and Ambiguity

This is not to say that the present decoding of health plans is clear to the vast majority of Americans or to the media organizations that bring the issue to them. Instead, public opinion poll data and media discourse would suggest that most people experience ambiguity with regard to what is being proposed and how it will affect the various segments of American society (Jamieson & Capella,

1995). As with so many policy issues, specific resource allocation plans are not usually understood in their massive detail, but in terms of the values—the value-choices—they present.

It may be hypothesized that ambiguity results not only from the multiplicity of plans (multiple definitions of the moral and competent thing to do), but also from obfuscation of the equality–freedom choice by proponents of the Clinton plan. Obfuscation prevented people used to decoding capitalist rhetoric as an equality–freedom value-choice from decoding the meaning of the Clinton plan. If this speculation is correct, then it affords an account of why people, in general, and media commentators, in particular, expressed felt ambiguity toward the Clinton plan (e.g., it's hard to understand, complicated, or confusing). The process of constructing the health reform issue could not be complete until proponents (or opponents) of the Clinton plan succeeded in framing it in more understandable choice terms. Similarly, despite defeat of the Clinton plan in 1994, the long-term legitimacy struggle to control how this resource allocation issue is framed as a value-choice has no clear winner at this point. Attention has turned to reform of Medicare and Medicaid, but the debate remains contested along the same rhetorical axes. Liberals in Congress (now in a Democrat minority) argue for equality; Republicans argue for market-oriented reforms (e.g., encouraging use of health maintenance organizations by Medicare patients); and Clinton attempts to carve out a middle ground that remains vague as to the value-choices he favors. One prediction that can be made is that the Clinton no-choice frame will not work and its proponents will adopt the capitalist high freedom–low equality frame. This is because that is where the majority of Americans are vis à vis the freedom–equality value choice. As the 1996 general election approaches, the need to appeal to majorities will become more intensely felt.

A general hypothesis that returns the discussion to the media's role in value-framing resource allocation issues may be stated: The eventual winner of the legitimacy contest will be the contesting group that succeeds in having its value-choice frame adopted by the mass media. When the media system adopts one of the contending parties' ways of framing the health-care issue, public discourse of the issue will be bounded by that frame. Winners of the media frame attain "restrictive power" (Bachrach & Baratz, 1962), the power to enforce their value-choice and its criteria of morality and competence as the point of departure for public, and most private, discussion of the issue.

ACCOUNTING FOR MEDIA ROLES IN SOCIAL
ISSUE CONSTRUCTION

Woven into the previous analysis of the contest to control the value-choice frame of social issues are a number of assumptions and concepts drawn from media system dependency (MSD) theory (Ball-Rokeach, 1985, 1994; Ball-Rokeach et al., 1984; Colman, 1990; Grant, Guthrie, & Ball-Rokeach, 1991; Loges, 1994; Waring, 1995). This theory of media power is neither a weak effects, nor a powerful effects model. Rather its major aim is to identify the complex of micro and macro conditions that determine whether or not the media system will affect the course of events in personal and social life. The clear assumption in the present analysis of the construction of value-choice frames of social issues is that the media do play powerful roles.

Two types of effects have been emphasized. The first concerns individuals' understandings of the meaning of resource allocation issues (what value-choices are at stake?) and their consequences for formation of attitude preferences vis à vis those issues. The second concerns media effects upon the interest groups that struggle to control the value-choice frames of resource allocations issues. Both of these effects processes are complex.

Complexity can be reduced somewhat with the introduction and application of the central organizing concept of MSD theory, the media system dependency relation. The essential hypothesis is that asymmetric and intense media system dependency relations create the conditions for powerful media effects.[1] This hypothesis holds at both micro and macro levels of analysis. The question thus becomes: What is a MSD relation and why is it hypothesized to be asymmetric and intense in this case of the construction of value-choice frames of the health care allocation issue?

The Media System Dependency Relation

Definition: the extent to which attainment of an individual's, group's, organization's, or system's goals is contingent upon access to the information resources of the media system, relative to the extent to which attainment of media system goals is contingent upon the resources controlled by individuals, groups, organizations or other social systems, respectively. (Ball-Rokeach et al., 1990, p. 250)

The MSD relation is a variation of Emerson's (1962, 1964) power-dependence relation wherein each actor's power lies not in resources per se, but in relationships with others who require access to those resources. As such, media system power is conceived to derive from the implication of the system's information resources in others' goal attainment. Media system power is constrained by the extent to which others' resources are implicated in its goal attainment, and the extent to which alternative resources outside the media system's control will help others attain their goals.

A scale for the measurement of individuals' MSD relations has been devel-

---

[1]Scope is another characteristic of the relation. It is not fully discussed in this paper because it bears no simple linear relationship to effects expectations (see: Ball-Rokeach & Grant, 1990 and Loges, 1994 for a discussion of scope).

oped and employed in research (Aydin, Ball-Rokeach, & Reardon, 1991; Ball-Rokeach et al., 1984; Colman, 1990; Grant et al., 1991; Halpern, 1994; Loges, 1994; Loges & Ball-Rokeach, 1993; Power & Ball-Rokeach, 1988; Waring, 1995). In its most recent form (see Ball-Rokeach & Grant, 1990), the scale has 18 items, with six 3-item subscales designed to measure conceptual types of dependency relations (social understanding, self understanding, interaction orientation, action orientation, social play, and solitary play). The most thorough analysis of its characteristics is based on a two-city survey data base. Adult respondents were asked "how helpful is _____ (television, newspapers, radio, and movies) in your daily life to _____?" (achieve one or another understanding, orientation, or play goal). The response format is a Likert-type scale varying from extremely helpful to not at all helpful. No empirical scale to measure supraindividual MSD relations has been developed yet, but this is the next step in the development of the research program.

Why is the Individual MSD Relation Asymmetric and Intense?

The MSD relation is asymmetric because individuals per se do not control resources to which media organizations must have access to achieve their goals (e.g., profit, legitimacy, or technological advances), while individual understanding, orientation, and play goals frequently require access to media resources. Social and self-understanding goals have been emphasized in the foregoing discussion. The most immediate and obvious media resource implicated in individuals' attempts to understand the health-care issue and its implications for their lives is information dissemination (i.e., the capacity to deliver the story on health care). However, behind this resource are two others; information gathering (e.g., reporters to gather facts about the competing proposals) and information processing (e.g., value-choice framing of the health-care issue).

Many of the reasons why the individual MSD relation is intense have been suggested previously. The most important of these are personal goal salience, threat, and ambiguity. Unlike other personal goals that vary widely in salience (e.g., understanding foreign relations), adequate health care is a salient personal goal for Americans across the socioeconomic spectrum. The major exception would be young people lacking a conception of their own mortality. A primary reason why it is such a salient concern is that access to adequate health care is under a condition of threat. Threat is one of the key conditions that is said to intensify MSD relations generally (Loges, 1994).[2]

Part of the motivation of political strategists on all sides of the debate to

---

[2]A perceived threat scale has been developed and employed in empirical analyses (Ball-Rokeach & Grant, 1990; Loges, 1994; Waring, 1995).

control use of the term *crisis* to refer to the state of affairs in American health care may be to control the possibility of activating people's perceptions of threat. Kristol, the Republican strategist, advocated in January of 1994 that Republicans in Congress take issue with the term "crisis" as it was applied to health care (Meyerson, 1994). After trying out such advice in his response to the State of the Union address later that month, Senate Minority Leader Bob Dole of Kansas was forced by press criticism to retreat slightly from the "no crisis" position to avoid appearing uncaring and out of touch (Clymer, 1994a, 1994b; "Yes, there is . . . ," 1994). If resource (mis)allocation has reached *crisis* proportions, as it does during economic depressions and as many believe it has in health care, then a more equal distribution is called for. If concerns about allocation are not severe enough to merit the term *crisis,* then it is more acceptable to argue publicly that protecting freedom is of greater importance than solving relatively mild allocation problems.

Pervasive ambiguity is another reason for the salience of the health-care issue. In this case, it is assumed that a condition of pervasive ambiguity is experienced by most Americans. Ambiguity has been described with respect to the meaning of the competing health-care proposals and their personal implications. It has been argued that interest groups and the media generally seek to control the way people resolve their ambiguity vis à vis resource allocation issues by constructing value-choice frames. This condition of pervasive ambiguity has emerged for two basic reasons: one is the value-choice obfuscation present in the Clinton proposal, and the other is the virtual exclusion of interest groups with more clear value-choice frames (e.g., Single Payer) from access to media resources (Jamieson & Capella, 1995).

Effects on Individuals: Meaning and Attitude Preferences

Once the media value-choice frame of a resource allocation issue is established in a stable way, individuals can position themselves with respect to it according to their value priorities and the personal interests they signify. However, in the case of health-care allocation, such stability awaits resolution of interest group conflict to win the media value-choice frame. The winner will be the one that succeeds in getting the media to frame the issue in their, and not their opponents', value-choice frame. Accordingly, no clear effects of media value-choice frames on individuals can yet be discerned. They are in process. When and if they do occur, they should be manifested in individuals' resolutions of ambiguity—the extent to which they define the issue in terms of the dominant media value-choice frame—and in the consequent attitude preferences they exhibit vis à vis the allocation of health-care resources. Reduction of ambiguity should also reduce the intensity of individuals' MSD relations.

Thus, at the individual level, media power is evidenced in the extent to which individuals adopt the dominant media value-choice frame. Adoption of that frame sets into motion a process of value and attitude activation wherein individuals form specific cognitive and affective responses to the health care reform plan as it is framed in the media. If, for example, the Republican value-choice (freedom over equality) is the dominant evaluative heuristic adopted by the media, then people who rank freedom very high and equality very low in their personal value systems will form quite different attitude preferences and feelings than people who rank both equality and freedom high in their personal value systems.

Whereas these individual differences will effect different attitude preferences and different affective responses, a more basic structural determinant is the nature of the MSD relation. All individuals are conceived to have asymmetric media dependency relations, but the intensity of that relation varies. Intensity is conceived to directly affect the probability that individuals will invest sufficient attention and involvement in processing media messages to set into motion the activation of their cognitive and affective responses (Colman, 1990). Thus, under conditions of low intensity asymmetric relations, individuals may not expose themselves to, much less attend to, health-care media content. These persons would be empirically indicated by "don't know" or other responses that signify the absence of attitude preference formation vis à vis the health-care issue. Of course, for reasons of salience stated earlier, we would expect most people to exhibit relatively intense MSD relations vis à vis the goal of understanding health reform proposals and their personal implications.

A Brief Comment on the Role of Interpersonal Networks

Interpersonal networks might be conceived as an alternative information system that individuals may employ to attain their goals. However, in this and many other situations, interpersonal networks do not control comparable information resources. They may process media messages, but they cannot affect the message production process or the criteria by which some aspects of an issue are covered and framed, while others are ignored. Moreover, dynamic social environments marked by ambiguity (e.g., what does this health-care plan mean?) and change (e.g., what's the latest compromise plan?) put even the most knowledgeable of opinion leaders in an information deficit situation. The media system is the generic information production system; interpersonal networks enter late in the production process at the point of interpretive consumption when social issues have already been framed. Put another way, the media system is the proactive constructor of social issue value-choice frames, and the interpersonal network is a reactive interpreter.

Characteristics of the Interest Group–Media Dependency Relation

The interest group-media dependency relation in the case of the health-care issue is conceived to be asymmetric and intense. It is asymmetric because the media control resources that are implicated in interest group goal attainment to a far greater extent than the reverse. It is intense because those media resources are critical to interest group success. The asymmetry of the interest group–media relation, however, is neither as invariant nor as extreme as the asymmetry of the individual MSD relation. Interest groups do control resources that they may employ to enhance or threaten media profits; for example, they may provide advertising revenues or they may employ boycotts and protest to endanger media economic interests. Moreover, interest groups may make themselves resources to the extent that they become the "news" that media seek to cover. The context of most social issue debates, however, is not one that usually permits an interest group to parlay those resources in such a way as to create a symmetric MSD relation. The playing field is made uneven by the plethora of competing groups with the shared goal of being the news. Some interest groups have more financial and communication resources than others in the struggle to be the "news," but even the most wealthy has to gain access to media information resources to attain its goals.

In contrast to individuals' MSD relations, interest group dependency relations directly implicate all three media information resources. For example, many interest groups involved in the health-care issue seek to affect how media deploy all of their information resources, how they gather, create, process, and disseminate news about the issue. Interest groups allocate time, money, and effort to get their position not only covered, but also covered favorably. Part and parcel of this effort is the goal of establishing their value-choice frame as the one that the media employ in telling the story of the health debate. As a result, interest groups not only have intense and asymmetric MSD relations, but also have relations characterized by broad resource scope.

Effects on the Conduct and Outcome of Interest Group Conflict

The central interest group goal that we have focused on in this analysis is control of the value-choice frame of resource allocation issues, generally, and the health issue in particular. As previously suggested, achievement of this goal is essential to the overriding interest group goal of maintaining or acquiring control over scarce and prized resources. Interest groups representing hospitals, insurance companies, medical professions, and their clients cannot win the health-care resource allocation struggle through interpersonal channels alone. They operate in an ecology where the most profound fact of life is that all of the players must gain access to media information resources to attain their respective goals. This includes politicians and voters. For better or worse, the media system has become the strongest link between the politician and her or his constituents. The politician's overriding goal of re-election magnifies the effect of the media as the key structural links between politicians and voters. Knowing the intense dependency relation between politicians and the media and between voters and the media, interest groups must pressure politicians indirectly by winning over voters or public opinion to their position. The most basic effect is that the contest for legitimacy (e.g., control over the health-care value-choice frame) must be waged according to media rules of discourse or definitions of what is newsworthy.

The dilemma posed by the concrete realities of the media's centrality to waging and winning interest group struggles has a number of more specific effects on interest groups. It obviously affects how interest groups allocate their resources; they must allocate resources to gain media coverage and to attempt to control the nature of that coverage. It also affects how they phrase their position; they must use media savvy rhetorical strategies of argument (e.g., value-laden language). In addition, the mode of such argument must satisfy the requirements of a "good" news media story (dramatic, conflict-ridden, and communicable in seconds). A good argument as judged by academic or scholarly criteria (e.g., logical structure of argument) will not be processed, much less gathered up as news. Many observers have noted the distortion effects of the requirement to conform to media system definitions of the good story (e.g., Gitlin, 1980; Singer & Endrenny, 1986). Central among these is the distortion of group goals, particularly the confusion of means with ends (e.g., the means goal of attaining media coverage becomes the end goal).

Value-choice frames, whether visually or verbally communicated, do satisfy the criteria of a good media story. They are lay language terms, they are efficient, they speak to conflict, and they may be communicated in dramatic terms likely to generate cognitive and affective responses. The "Harry and Louise" commercials created by health insurance interest groups are an example; they pit individual freedom (the right to choose one's doctor, ordinary people faced with impersonal government) against social equality (government insured universal access).

Media As Referees, Players, or Rule-Makers?

One way to answer the question of just how much power is being attributed to the media system in the struggle to control the value-choice frame of resource allocation issues is to return to the relational notion of power that lies at the heart of MSD theory. When dependency relations are hypothesized to be intense and asymmetric in the media's favor, the conditions exist for the media to be relatively powerful. Media power is of a certain kind, however. It is the power to control not only access to knowledge construction, but also the rules of discourse that operate in the knowledge construction process. In the present instance, the media system is hypothesized to be both player and rule-maker in the construction of value-choice frames of the health-care issue. Its roles go well beyond those of a neutral referee. The observations required to empirically observe media power cannot be limited to analysis of the faithfulness of media coverage of a press conference. The exercise of media rule-making power begins with the other players' knowledge of the rules of political conflict in contemporary society; specifically, knowledge of the requirement to wage conflict through the media and according to their criteria of access to their information resources (e.g., making oneself newsworthy). The specific manifestations of this power do not usually involve the media independently imposing a value-choice frame on an issue. Rather, interest groups construct media savvy frames and seek to sell them to the media in a buyer's market.

Media power, however, is neither absolute nor unconstrained. Individuals can limit media power with indifference to the health-care issue (i.e., lower their motivation investment in the goal of understanding the issue). Interest groups can allocate their resources to seek to bypass the media-based knowledge construction process by buying air time or using direct mail. Interest groups can also seek to limit media power by effectively protesting the way the media are employing their resources to construct the meaning of an issue. Interest groups also may seek to constrain media power by using their knowledge of the media system's more symmetric relations with economic and political systems. They may, for example, seek to undermine the advertising base of media operations through boycott strategies, or they may seek to threaten the media's freedom to act by getting regulatory policies enacted. Although these counterbalancing strategies to constrain media power are theoretically possible, practical realities of time and limited resources undermine their viability for all but the most well-heeled interest groups. Hospital and health insurance groups have evidenced, through their ad campaigns against the Clinton proposal, far more capacity to constrain media power vis à vis the value-choice framing of the health-care issue than have other interest groups supporting the Clinton or Single Payer plans (e.g., labor or consumer groups). Even here, however, there is some rule-making power on the part of the media system. It controls the rules of interest group access through its ability to demand payment for air time or space.

Macro to Micro Effects

The effects of interest group–media dependency relations upon the construction of the value-choice frame of the health issue are conceived to be indirect upon individuals and their interpersonal networks. This macro to micro effects process is but one example of a more general effects conception in MSD theory. There are at least two specific effects that have been alluded to in the previous analysis.

One is that the individual's ability to gain and maintain a stable understanding of the health-care issue is fundamentally contingent upon a stable resolution of the contest to control the media value-choice frame. Individuals should experience ambiguity or unstable understandings of the issue until the issue is clearly framed in value-choice terms.

The other macro-to-micro effect follows when and if a stable media value-choice frame emerges from the play of media-interest group dependency relations. When a value-choice frame consistently dominates media discourse on the health care issue, most individuals' attitude preferences will be formed within that frame. Their attitude preferences are not directly controlled; rather, it is the contrasts that individuals will make that are controlled. Specifically, individuals will contrast their value priorities with the value-choice suggested in the frame, and form attitude preferences accordingly. The primary and important exception is the rare individual whose understanding of the issue comes from an alternative information system. For example, health-care activists have their own interest group value-choice frame to operate from, even when it is not the frame that dominates media discourse.

If an interest group is successful in reducing the ambiguity surrounding health care—in part by successfully controlling the value-choice frame—then one may expect the MSD relations of people sympathetic to that group to become less intense. If that group can also reduce the perception of threat or crisis—as Republicans did in early 1994—they may further reduce the intensity of people's MSD relations. Finally, if a group can deploy alternative information resources, such as direct mail and group meetings, they can maintain a core of support among people who are, in a sense, weaned away from the media system for this issue.

In fact, the success of the Republican Party in the presidential campaigns of the 1980s, as well as Senate races in 1980, Congressional races in 1994, and gains in state and local elections, has been partly attributed to their development and use of direct mail (through such innovators as Richard Wirthlin) and evangelical Christian grassroots organizers. Thus, the conservative position on health reform, which features a high freedom–low equality value-choice frame, may benefit from less intense MSD relations on this issue because conservatives have successfully mobilized and utilized non-mass media resources either to supplant or to supplement media system resources.

DISCUSSION

The specific example of media value-choice framing effects upon individuals' attitude preferences toward health-care reform suggests at least two more general observations. The first is that "choice" conceptions and measures of values, attitudes, and behavior ground value-attitude or value-behavior analyses in the everyday realities of people who have to selectively allocate their resources. The present conception differs from a rational choice model. People's underlying value-choices are conceived to account for their attitude preferences and behavioral choices. This choice process may or may not be conscious and may or may not be rational (e.g., maximization of personal outcomes). The phenomenological reality of having to make choices is most clear in the case of social issues, because social issue formation and resolution forces explicit discourse to legitimate one mode of allocation over others. The symbolic, as opposed to material, utility of value-choices derives not only from the fact that legitimacy is constructed in these terms, but also from their efficiency as central signifiers of meaning employed to encode and decode an ambiguous world. In the present example, people's attitude preferences for the Single Payer, Republican, or Clinton health care reform proposals are conceived to reflect underlying value choices or preferences for equality vis à vis freedom. Research is underway to test the hypothesis that follows from this line of thought; namely, that equality–freedom value-choices will predict attitude preferences toward health-care and other resource allocation issues. Over and above the issue of whether it is the equality–freedom or some other value-choice that is predictive, the more general issue addressed is whether choice-based conceptions and measures afford more predictive power than nonchoice conceptions or measures (e.g., the more conventional isolated or independent ratings of values and attitudes).

The second conclusion drawn from the foregoing analysis is that many of the choices individuals make cannot be understood without sensitive incorporation of the way the media pose those choices. This is particularly the case with social issues, which, by definition, emerge and take the form of legitimacy contests waged in the public sector. Most social issues, including the health-care issue analyzed here, involve a macro knowledge construction process in which the media system's information resources are of paramount importance. Relevant aspects of media system dependency theory have been brought to bear upon the illustrative case of the formation of value-choice frames that proponents of different health care plans have constructed to legitimate their plan over their competitors' plans. In the formative stages of social issues, individuals and their interpersonal networks have little information other than that disseminated by the media to construct their understandings of the competing resource allocation plans. Especially when the debate has personal salience, as the health-care debate certainly has for most Americans, people will experience pervasive ambiguity. Under such conditions, they cannot have stable attitude preferences. Stable attitude preferences require efficient ways of coding the meaning of alternatives. We have suggested that such constructions are in terms of the value-choices that competing plans present. These value-choices, however, cannot be presented directly to individuals by plan proponents; they must be mediated by the one information system that is designed to stand at the junction of macro and micro levels of discourse. Specifically, the media system employs its information resources to construct the value-choice frame of the debate. That frame not only codes the meaning of the victorious proponent's position or plan, but also centers the meaning of competing issue positions. This process of macro discourse negotiation—the struggle to win the media value-choice frame—is not voluntary. It, like the individuals' media behavior to resolve ambiguity, is a product of media system dependency relations.

The last few decades of media theory and research have cohered around a rejection of the notion of passive individuals who simply get bombarded by media exposure. This has led to the development of the present media system dependency theory and many other perspectives that take into account the motivational dynamics of individuals' media behavior. The unique aspect of MSD theory is the idea that individuals, interpersonal networks, and larger macro groupings develop dependency relations with the media; more to the point, with relatively unique media information resources to which they must have access in order to attain goals. Media power lies in these dependency relations. No quantity-based measure of media exposure time can get at these or other motivational dynamics suggested in active conceptions of media audiences. Yet such measures still dominate in much of the research that portends to inform about media effects. Alternative measures, such as those developed to measure MSD relations, are generally more time consuming to administer, but they offer much more explanatory potential.

REFERENCES

Alexander, J. (1986). The "form" of substance: The Senate Watergate Hearings. In S. J. Ball-Rokeach & M. G. Cantor (Eds.), *Media, audience, and social structure* (pp. 243–251). Newbury Park, CA: Sage.

Aydin, C. E., Ball-Rokeach, S. J., & Reardon, K. K. (1991, May). *Mass media resources for social comparison among breast cancer patients.* Paper presented to the 41st Annual Conference of the International Communication Association, Chicago, IL.

Bachrach, P., & Baratz, M. S. (1962). Two faces of power. *American Political Science Review, 51,* 947–952.

Ball-Rokeach, S. J. (1971). The legitimation of violence. In J. F. Short, Jr. & M. E. Wolfgang (Eds.), *Collective violence* (pp. 100–111). Chicago: Aldine.

Ball-Rokeach, S. J. (1973). From pervasive ambiguity to a definition of the situation. *Sociometry, 36,* 378–389.

Ball-Rokeach, S. J. (1976). Receptivity to sexual equality. *Pacific Sociological Review, 19,* 519–540.

Ball-Rokeach, S. J. (1985). The origins of individual media system dependency: A sociological framework. *Communication Research, 12,* 485–510.

Ball-Rokeach, S. J. (1992). So what's happening and why don't we know it? Newsletter of the Sociology of Culture Section, *American Sociological Association, 6,* 3–5.

Ball-Rokeach, S. J. (1994, July). *A theory of media power and a theory of media use: Different stories, questions, and ways of thinking.* Paper presented to the 44th Annual Conference of the International Communication Association, Sydney, Australia.

Ball-Rokeach, S. J. & Grant, A. E. (1990, August). *A scale for the measurement of individuals' media dependency relations.* Paper presented to the Annual Meetings of the American Sociological Association, Washington, DC.

Ball-Rokeach, S. J., Power, G. J., Guthrie, K. K., & Waring, H. R. (1990). Value-framing abortion in the United States: An application of media system dependency theory. *International Journal of Public Opinion, 2,* 249–273.

Ball-Rokeach, S. J. & Rokeach, M. (1987). The future study of public opinion: A symposium. *Public Opinion Quarterly, 51,* 184–185.

Ball-Rokeach, S. J., Rokeach, M., & Grube, J. (1984). *The great American values test: Influencing behavior and belief through television.* New York: The Free Press.

Ball-Rokeach, S. J., & Tallman, I. (1979). Social movements as moral confrontations: With special reference to civil rights. In M. Rokeach (Ed.), *Understanding human values* (pp. 82–94). New York: Free Press.

Clinton, W. J. (1993). *Address to the joint session of Congress on health care reform.* Weekly Compilation of Presidential Documents, 29, 1836–1846.

Clymer, A. (1994a, January 26). Dole, in G.O.P. response to Clinton, asserts there is "no health care crisis." *The New York Times,* p. A8.

Clymer, A. (1994b, January 27). G.O.P. line gels on idea of no real health crisis. *The New York Times,* p. A12.

Colman, W. (1990). *Health moves to prime time: Evaluating the impact of a prime-time television movie of the week on viewers' content relevant health beliefs.* Unpublished doctoral dissertation, University of California, Los Angeles.

Emerson, R. M. (1962). Power-dependence relations. *American Sociological Review, 27,* 31–40.

Emerson, R. M. (1964). Power-dependence relations: Two experiments. *Sociometry, 27,* 282–298.

Entman, R. (1993). Framing: Toward Clarification of a fractured paradigm. *Journal of Communication, 43*(4), 51–58.

Gamson, W. A., Croteau, D., Hoynes, W., & Sasson, T. (1992). Media images and the social construction of reality. *Annual Review of Sociology, 18,* 373–393.

Gerbner, G., Gross, L., Morgan, M., & Signorielli, N. (1993). Growing up with television: The cultivation perspective. In J. Bryant & D. Zillman (Eds.), *Media effects: Advances in theory and research* (pp. 17–40). Hillsdale, NJ: Lawrence Erlbaum Associates.

Gitlin, T. (1980). *The whole world is watching.* Berkeley, CA: University of California Press.

Grant, A. E., Guthrie, K. K., & Ball-Rokeach, S. J. (1991). Television shopping: A media system dependency perspective. *Communication Research, 18,* 773–798.

Habermas, J. (1975). *Legitimation crisis.* Boston: Beacon.

Halpern, P. (1994). Media dependency and political perceptions in an authoritarian political system. *Journal of Communication, 44*(4), 39–52.

Hirschburg, P. L., Dillman, D. A., & Ball-Rokeach, S. J. (1986). Media system dependency theory: Responses to the eruption of Mount St. Helens. In Ball-Rokeach, S.J. & M.G. Cantor (Eds.), *Media, audience, and social structure* (pp. 117–126). Newbury Park, CA: Sage.

Jamieson, K. H. & Capella, J. N. (1995). *Media in the middle: Fairness and accuracy in the 1994 health care reform debate.* A report by the Annenberg Public Policy Center of The University of Pennsylvania.

Kellner, D. (1990). *Television and the crisis of democracy.* Boulder, CO: Westview.

Kluegel, J. R. & Smith, E. R. (1986). *Beliefs about inequality: Americans' views of what is and what ought to be.* New York: Aldine de Gruyter.

Loges, W. E. (1994). Canaries in the coal mine: Perceptions of threat and media system dependency relations. *Communication Research, 21*(1), 5–23.

Loges, W. E. & Ball-Rokeach, S. J. (1993). Dependency relations and newspaper readership. *Journalism Quarterly, 70*(3), 602–614.

Loges, W. E. & Ball-Rokeach, S. J. (1995, May). *Making sense of values in political rhetoric.*

Presented at the 45th Annual Conference of the International Communication Association, Albuquerque, NM.

McCaughey, E. (1994, February 7). No exit: Under the Clinton health care plan, how exactly will your coverage and treatment change? Here's everything you wanted to know about the 1,364 page bill, but were afraid to ask. *The New Republic,* pp. 21–25.

Meyerson, A. (1994, Winter). Kristol ball: William Kristol looks at the future of the GOP. *Policy Review,* pp. 14–15.

Meyrowitz, J. (1985). *No sense of place: The impact of electronic media on social behavior.* New York: Oxford University Press.

Power, J. G. & Ball-Rokeach, S. J. (1988). *A media system dependency approach to the AIDS epidemic.* A report to the Student Senate, University of Southern California.

Rokeach, M. (1973). *The nature of human values.* New York: Free Press.

Rokeach, M. (Ed.) (1979). *Understanding human values.* New York: Free Press.

Rokeach, M., & Ball-Rokeach, S. J. (1989). Stability and change in American value priorities, 1968–1981. *American Psychologist, 44,* 775–784.

Rosen, J. (1993). Who won the week? *Tikkun, 8,* 7–10, 94.

Singer, E., & Endrenny, P. (1986). The reporting of social science research in the mass media. In S. J. Ball-Rokeach & M. G. Cantor (Eds.), *Media, audience, and social structure* (pp. 293–313). Newbury Park, CA: Sage.

Starfield, B. (1994, November). *Health care systems and services research and development.* Paper presented to the Forum on Meeting the Challenge: Health, Safety, and Food for America. National Academy of Sciences, Washington, DC.

Starr, P. (1982). *The social transformation of American medicine.* New York: Basic Books.

"Text of Reagan's Speech Accepting GOP Nomination." (July 18, 1980). *Los Angeles Times,* Part 1, p. 16.

Waring, H. R. (1995). *Media system dependency and identity: The development of America's gay and lesbian alternative media and the transformation of homosexuality.* Unpublished doctoral dissertation, University of Southern California, Los Angeles, CA.

12

What Values Do People Prefer in Children? A Comparative Analysis of Survey Evidence From Fifteen Countries*

Douglas Baer
University of Western Ontario

James Curtis
University of Waterloo

Edward Grabb
University of Western Ontario

William Johnston
University of Alberta

S. M. Lipset's analyses of the value differences between Canadians and Americans provide the best-known examples of comparative research on values involving these two countries (Lipset, 1963a, 1963b, 1964, 1966, 1968, 1985, 1986, 1990). Lipset's work on this topic has enjoyed a longstanding prominence, in part because of his thought-provoking claims about the nature of value differences between the United States and Canada, as well as his rather controversial "origins" explanation for these alleged differences.[1] This chapter tests some of the implications of Lipset's research, by placing data from the United States and Canada in a broader international context. We begin with a brief review of Lipset's argument concerning Canadian-American value differences, and then discuss how his argument is part of a more general "first new nation" thesis of American exceptionalism. The more general thesis, which is most clearly stated in Lipset's early writings, is that, in terms of predominant values, the United

---

*The order of authors is alphabetical.

[1]Although not explicitly stated, Lipset's treatment of values is consistent with the definitions used by most of his leading contemporaries (e.g., Parsons, 1951, pp. 12–13; Williams, 1960, pp. 24–25). That is, to Lipset values are standards of what is considered to be desirable within a collectivity, reflecting shared cultural traditions that are instilled in individuals, to varying degrees, by the major institutions of socialization operating in the collectivity (see, for example, Lipset, 1963a, p. 517).

States is the most "modern" nation relative to the other countries of the world. We then test this argument using evidence on child-rearing values from 15 nations.[2]

LIPSET'S THESIS: THE UNITED STATES AS "THE FIRST NEW NATION"

Briefly stated, the central argument in Lipset's comparison of Canada and the United States is that, primarily because of being on opposing sides during the American Revolution, the people of these two countries developed substantial differences in value systems, most of which have endured to the present day. In Lipset's view, the revolt of the thirteen colonies against British rule in 1776 ultimately led to the creation of the modern American nation, a liberal democratic society in which primary emphasis is placed on such ideas as personal independence, equal opportunity for all individuals, and the freedom of each citizen to pursue his or her own path to achievement and happiness. In contrast, it is argued, the rejection of the ideals of the American Revolution by the Canadian colonies led to a more "British"-style value system in the northern nation. Even today, it is said, Canada's value system resembles the British system in putting relatively greater stress on such goals as deference to established authority, the priority of collective over individual rights, and the restriction of personal liberty to preserve social order.

Lipset's thesis of Canadian-American value differences has stimulated a large body of research and discussion, some of it supportive and much of it critical of his arguments (e.g., Archibald, 1978; Arnold & Tigert, 1974; Baer, Curtis, Grabb, & Johnston, 1995; Baer, Grabb, & Johnston, 1990a, 1990b, 1993; Bell & Tepperman, 1979; Clark, 1975; Crawford & Curtis, 1979; Curtis, 1971; Curtis, Grabb, & Baer, 1992; Grabb & Curtis, 1988, 1992; Hagan & Leon, 1977; Merelman, 1991; Nevitte & Gibbins, 1990; Rokeach, 1973; Truman, 1971). With a few exceptions, these subsequent analyses have concentrated largely on the comparison of Canada and the United States, which has also been the focus of Lipset's most recent research. However, Lipset's early comparative writings place his work on Canada and the United States in a larger analysis that includes two other English-speaking democracies—Australia and Great Britain—and, in some instances, subsumes a variety of other countries, as well (e.g., Lipset, 1963a, 1967; Lipset & Solari, 1967).

In virtually all of this early work, Lipset stresses one consistent theme: Within

---

[2]We should note that child-rearing values are not the specific concern of Lipset's writings on national differences. As will be clarified below, Lipset's thesis is far more general and pervasive, in that it appears to encompass virtually all forms or types of values in the different countries. The present paper can in part be seen as a test of his thesis for a particular category of values, one that has received relatively limited attention in his more general argument.

the broad international spectrum, the American system of values occupies an exceptional, almost a unique, location. His views are underscored in the title of his book, *The First New Nation* (1963a). In this book, Lipset states his conviction that, among Britain's former possessions, the United States is truly "the first new nation . . . the first major colony successfully to break away from colonial rule through revolution" (p. 16). He sees the exceptional nature of American culture as rooted in the complete and fundamental break between the United States and Britain, which can be contrasted with the much later, more gradual, and, in some respects, only partial breaks that occurred in Canada and Australia (Lipset, 1963a, p. 521, 1963b, chap. 7).

Interestingly, though, Lipset takes the "first new nation" perspective on the United States still further in some of his discussions, going beyond the context of the English-speaking democracies alone. For example, he contrasts the United States with "the Spanish colonies in Central and South America," noting that "while the United States exemplifies a new nation which successfully developed an industrial economy, a relatively integrated social structure (the race issue apart) and a stable democratic polity, most of the nations of Latin America do not" (Lipset, 1963a, p. 16). Lipset also argues that Latin America, in contrast to the United States, "has been dominated for long centuries by ruling elites who created a social structure congruent with feudal social values" (Lipset, 1967, p. 4). Using a variant of Talcott Parsons's "pattern variables" conception, Lipset portrays the Latin American value system as more particularistic and ascriptive than the American system, with a relatively weaker commitment to such values as individualism, achievement, and universalism (Lipset, 1967, p. 7; Parsons, 1951).

More generally, Lipset's (1967) view is that the value systems of "the more economically developed countries," especially the United States and certain northern European nations, are significantly different from the value systems found in the underdeveloped countries of Latin America, and also from those found in certain "European Latin countries," such as Spain, France, and Italy (p. 33).

While Lipset (1967) notes that values have changed over time in some of these nations, especially where countries have become more developed economically, in his view the value systems of these other nations remain different from the United States in key respects (p. 32). Even for comparisons of the United States to the other developed nations, Lipset believes there are significant value differences. Thus, for example, he cites various studies of parents, college students, and children, all of which lead him to conclude that Americans learn to believe more strongly in ideas like individuality and personal achievement, while their counterparts in Germany, Britain, Japan, and elsewhere are brought up to place relatively greater stress on ascriptive values and on such ideas as obedience to authority and obligation to the group or society (Lipset, 1963a, pp. 274–278).

It is noteworthy that, in referring to the United States as the first new or modern nation, Lipset essentially concurs with many other leading social scientists writing in the 1950s and 1960s, including Parsons (1951; see also Robertson, 1982) in sociology, McClelland (1961) in social psychology, and Almond and Verba (1963) in political science. His use of the word, "modern," to characterize American society or American values (e.g., 1967, pp. 33, 35, 38) is also significant, for it reveals the close parallels between his discussion of values and that provided by so-called "modernization theory."

While there are different versions of modernization theory, they all share in common an argument for the primacy of culture as a force for social change. Thus, writers working from this perspective generally agree that certain kinds of values are essential prerequisites for economic and social development to occur in societies (see, for example, Inkeles, 1966, 1973; Inkeles & Smith, 1974; Lerner, 1965; McClelland, 1961; Triandis, 1973; Weiner, 1966; for reviews, see Allahar, 1989, chap. 3; Hofstede, 1980, pp. 216–218; Yang, 1988).[3]

The question of what constitutes a genuinely modern set of values does not have a simple answer, because not all modernization theorists agree. However, the literature suggests a range of interconnected values, most of which can be tentatively grouped into two broadly defined clusters. These clusters may be labeled "individualism" and "future orientation."

First, modern value systems involve a strong belief in individualism. Individualism here subsumes a large number of related value preferences, most notably achievement, freedom of choice, personal ambition, hard work, self-directedness or autonomy, active individual participation or involvement in public affairs, and universalism. We should also note that individualism in this sense is not to be confused with an excessive preoccupation with the "self," the kind of self-interest that Triandis has called "narcissistic individualism" (Triandis, McCusker, & Hui, 1990), or that Durkheim called "egoism" (Durkheim, 1965, pp. 172–173). On the contrary, modern or developed countries, it is suggested, require citizens who freely pursue their individual goals, but within the constraints imposed by their ties to the collectivity. This means, for example, greater tolerance of diversity and respect for the rights of other people. Individualism thus entails a fundamental "group" or "collective" orientation.[4]

---

[3]We should note that, in recent years, modernization theory has lost much of its currency in social science. Undoubtedly, this is partly the result of subsequent criticisms levelled by various Marxist writers, dependency theorists, and others, who have usually stressed structural factors, especially economic dominance or subordination, as the key reasons for cross-national differences. It is interesting to note, however, that Lipset, at least, continues to embrace the modernization school's fundamental emphasis on the role of culture in explaining social change. For example, in his presidential address to the American Sociological Association, Lipset recently maintained that "cultural factors appear even more important than economic ones" when attempting to explain the historical development of democratic political systems (Lipset, 1994, p. 5)

[4]It is notable that Lipset does not acknowledge this connection between individualism and group or collective orientation in his discussion of these values, nor does he draw the distinction between

The second broad category of value preferences that is emphasized by most modernization theorists may be loosely labeled "future orientation." This set of values reflects, in particular, the importance to be placed on progress and "looking forward" in modern societies. Included here are such ideas as optimism about the future, openness to new experiences and change, a belief in science and the capacity of humans to master nature, the efficacy of rationality and human planning, and so forth.

Although Lipset does not refer explicitly to all of these ideas when discussing the United States in comparative perspective, there is a close fit between many of the values in this list and those Lipset sees as characteristic of the American value system. It is also of interest, particularly because of the measures we use in this chapter, that in some of the research he cites, differences in parental values play a key role in demonstrating the distinctiveness of the United States from other nations (see also Lipset, 1967, pp. 39–40; 1990, p. 127).

The purpose of this chapter is to assess the extent to which Americans subscribe to an exceptionally modern system of values compared to other peoples, using cross-national evidence on child-rearing values. Of course, an analysis of the values that people would like to see inculcated in children is just one way of examining cross-national differences. Such an analysis might even seem limited in scope, because the values people choose as important for children may not be identical to those that they believe are important for adults. Nevertheless, recent cross-cultural research on values suggests that, because of the complexity of the values question, it is advisable to study values within specific contexts or situations rather than at a more general or abstract level of analysis (e.g., Schwartz & Bilsky, 1990). Moreover, an assessment of child-rearing values should be a particularly informative way of comparing national cultures. It reveals, in particular, what values are stressed in the context of the family, and so may provide insights into the cultural legacy that people would most like to see retained by future generations.

For a variety of reasons, it is important to re-assess Lipset's argument on American exceptionalism using more evidence. First, because Lipset's discussion and empirical support are, in some cases, more than 25 years old, it is quite possible that the pattern of cross-national value differences he perceived for the 1950s and 1960s has changed substantially. Second, using other data, there already is considerable evidence to suggest that Lipset has overstated or incorrectly characterized the differences between the United States and other nations, most notably Canada. Studies have shown, for example, that Americans are: less likely than Canadians, as well as people from several other nations, to participate

---

individualism and egoism (see Baer, Grabb, & Johnston, 1990b). We also note some differences among social psychologists on whether or not individualism and collectivism are polar opposites (see, for example, Triandis, 1973; Triandis, McCusker, & Hui, 1990; see also the comparison of work by Triandis & Moghaddam in Schwartz & Bilsky, 1990, p. 879).

actively in voluntary associations (Curtis, Grabb, & Baer, 1992; Grabb & Curtis, 1992); less in favor of gender equality and more in favor of strict family discipline than are Canadians (Baer, Grabb, & Johnston, 1990a); and less likely than Canadians to question established authority or engage in various forms of civil dissent and disobedience (Baer, Curtis, Grabb, & Johnston, 1995).[5]

All of these findings appear to run counter to the view of the American value system as exceptionally modern, particularly in regard to the cluster of values referred to here as individualism. Finally, there is evidence in the social psychological literature that Americans are not clearly distinguishable from several other countries, especially Canada and the English-speaking democracies, but also various western European nations, in terms of their emphasis on individualism, autonomy, hard work, achievement, tolerance of ambiguity, and so forth (e.g., Hofstede, 1980; Lambert, Hamers, & Frasure-Smith, 1979).

We proceed now to a description of the data source and the measures and methods used in the present analysis.

DATA SOURCE AND METHODS

Our data source, the World Values Survey, is a cross-national study of representative samples of adults from 22 countries conducted by Inglehart and associates in the period from 1981 to 1983 (Inglehart et al., 1990). Because information on the dependent measures and on the eight control variables was not collected for all nations, our investigation is limited to 15 of the original 22 countries. The 15 countries include the four English-speaking nations compared in Lipset's *The First New Nation*: Australia, Canada, Great Britain, and the United States; the Canadian sample is also divided into English and French Canadians, because of more recent work by Lipset and others suggesting important differences in values between these two subgroups.[6] The other 11 countries are Belgium, France, Iceland, Ireland, Italy, Japan, the Netherlands, Northern Ireland, Norway, Spain, and West Germany.[7] Sample sizes ranged from 287 (in Northern Ireland) to

---

[5]The latter study revealed, for example, that Americans were significantly more likely than English or French Canadians to believe that employees in the workplace should follow their superiors' instructions without question. Americans were also significantly less likely than both Canadian groups to engage in such activities as boycotts or lawful demonstrations. These and other differences occurred both before and after controls on a range of background variables.

[6]Ideally, we would have been interested to look at sub-groups within the American sample, as well. The most notable distinction in the American case would probably involve that between people from the American south and those residing in the rest of the country. Other research has suggested important differences in values and behaviors between people in these two regions (e.g., Baer, Grabb, and Johnston, 1993; see also Nisbett, 1993). Unfortunately, our data source made no provision for such a breakdown within nations, so that neither the American sample nor any of the other samples could be subdivided along regional lines.

[7]The seven excluded countries were Denmark, Finland, Hungary, Mexico, South Africa, the Soviet Union, and Sweden.

1,797 (in the U.S.). Except for Northern Ireland, French Canada ($N = 407$), and Iceland ($N = 383$), all countries had samples of at least 1,000, even after cases with missing data were deleted.[8]

To measure child-rearing values, we relied on a question in which respondents were presented with a list of 17 "qualities which children can be encouraged to learn at home," and then asked "which, if any, do you consider to be especially important?" The 17 qualities included: (1) "good manners," (2) "politeness and neatness," (3) "independence," (4) "hard work," (5) "honesty," (6) "feeling of responsibility," (7) "patience," (8) "imagination," (9) "tolerance and respect for other people," (10) "leadership," (11) "self-control," (12) "thrift, sparing money and things," (13) "determination, perseverance," (14) "religious faith," (15) "unselfishness," (16) "obedience," and (17) "loyalty."

Rather than being asked to rate the importance of all 17 qualities, respondents in each nation were told to "choose up to five" that were "especially important." Therefore, each respondent could choose less than five qualities. Because the vast majority (84%) in fact chose five qualities, the analyses presented here are based on the full set of respondents.[9]

Not all of the 17 qualities involve the set of modern values specified in the literature. None of the qualities deals explicitly with questions of "future orientation." Nevertheless, eight of the items were chosen as possible measures of the "individualism" cluster of values outlined in the introduction. These include: independence, hard work, feeling of responsibility, imagination, tolerance and respect for other people, leadership, determination and perseverance, and unselfishness. In addition, two more items that could be viewed as "nonmodern"

---

[8]Original samples were actually somewhat larger for all countries, but were reduced because of missing data involving some of our control variables.

[9]A number of respondents ($N = 884$; 5.1% of the sample) actually chose more than five qualities. These cases were eliminated from the analysis. Most of these respondents gave six ($N = 281$), seven ($N = 96$) or eight ($N = 92$) responses, but a few answered "yes" to almost all of the items. Only in the case of Canada did no respondent answer with more than five items; otherwise, responses of this sort were located across the countries (in the U.S., the percentage was 6.1). We included respondents who answered less than five items; in preliminary work, we also conducted parallel analyses including only respondents who mentioned exactly five qualities as well as analyses including all respondents. No major differences in interpretation arose from these analyses. It should also be noted that the procedure used in the World Values Survey, whereby a limited number of qualities is chosen from a larger list, pertains to recent methodological debates about the use of rankings versus ratings in the measurement of values (e.g., Alwin & Krosnick, 1985; Krosnick & Alwin, 1988). Some leading researchers in the field, such as Kohn (1969) and Rokeach (1973), have tended to favour measures that require respondents to rank values in terms of the importance of each value relative to all the others. Other researchers prefer measures in which each value is rated individually as highly important or unimportant (on separate Likert scales, for example), and not ranked relative to all the others. Research suggests that there are advantages and disadvantages to either method. In this regard, the procedure used here may best be seen as a hybrid of the rating and ranking methods. All 17 qualities are rated in the same way, on a dichotomous (mentioned versus not mentioned) "scale;" however, at least some relative ranking of the qualities is also present, because of the requirement that only 5 of the 17 can be chosen.

were also identified: obedience and religious faith. The remaining seven qualities—good manners, politeness and neatness, honesty, patience, self-control, thrift, and loyalty—seemed to us to be more difficult to classify in this way. For that reason, we did not include them in the full analysis. However, we do report cross-national differences on these seven qualities, at least in the preliminary analyses, both for general interest and to provide a sense of the alternative choices that were made instead of the other 10 values.

Lipset's analyses generally do not involve controls for the effects of factors associated with both country of residence and the dependent measures. In contrast, other researchers working in this area do employ multivariate controls for different background factors (e.g., Baer, Grabb, & Johnston, 1990a; Curtis, Grabb, & Baer, 1992; Grabb & Curtis, 1992). Zero-order analyses would be most appropriate if differences in values were perceived to be solely the result of differences in national institutions or historical events. On the other hand, any significant individual-level effects of social status differences upon values would make it necessary to control for such effects, if we wish to make a precise assessment of the independent influences of institutions and historical events across the societies. Because there is disagreement on whether zero-order or controlled comparisons are more appropriate, we conduct both types of analyses.

Eight background variables were used as controls in the multivariate analyses. *Education* was measured as respondent's age at completion of schooling, because of wide variation in educational systems across the countries. The categories were: less than age 16, 16 to 19, and 20 or older. *Occupational status* was categorized into professional/managerial, white collar, skilled manual, unskilled manual, unemployed, retired, and housewife. *Community size* was coded into three groupings: rural area or village, small to midsized town, and large urban area. *Marital status* was divided into married (or common law) versus all others. *Children* simply distinguished between those respondents who had a child and those who were childless. *Gender* was male versus female. *Age* was respondent's exact age, in years. Finally, *religious attendance* was categorized into six groupings: more than once a week, once a week, once a month, specific holy days (e.g., Christmas and Easter), once a year, and less than once a year.

RESULTS

Which Qualities Are Mentioned Most Often Across Nations?

Table 12.1 shows the proportion of mentions made of the 17 qualities, for all 16 samples. It is interesting to note some general patterns in the pooled sample (all 17,214 respondents). First, we see that the quality mentioned most often is honesty: almost three quarters of the pooled sample list honesty as one of the five

TABLE 12.1
Between-Country Differences in Proportions, Without Controls

Country	N	Independent	Hard Work	Responsi-bility	Imagina-tion	Leader-ship	Determina-tion	Unself-ish	Tolerance	Obedience
Overall		.294	.193	.444	.106	.061	.161	.166	.498	.235
U.S.	2325	.296	.239	.418	.079	.079	.126	.155	.522	.239
E. Canada	921	.273	.213	.387	.107*	.043**	.191**	.210**	.547	.219
F. Canada	333	.143**	.181*	.488*	.088	.035*	.276**	.186	.494	.170*
Britain	1231	.228***	.130**	.224**	.113*	.027**	.169*	.396**	.619**	.347**
Australia	1228	.228***	.099**	.274**	.110*	.032**	.159*	.355**	.663**	.385**
N. Ireland	312	.169**	.189	.094**	.085	.028*	.100	.290**	.605**	.504**
Ireland	1217	.287	.232	.216**	.073	.065	.086*	.223**	.563*	.335**
Belgium	1145	.178**	.294*	.343**	.066	.031**	.165*	.107**	.424**	.243
France	1200	.171**	.335**	.383	.126**	.014**	.168*	.209**	.576**	.169**
Germany	1305	.470***	.179**	.599**	.125**	.296**	.242**	.033**	.403**	.127**
Italy	1348	.227**	.121**	.469*	.072	.032**	.166*	.018**	.428**	.249
Netherlands	1221	.252*	.099**	.520**	.097	.024**	.135	.065**	.567*	.194*
Spain	2303	.239*	.408**	.629**	.240**	.077	.123	.040**	.437**	.292*
Japan	1204	.448***	.137**	.668**	.092	.054*	.215**	.249**	.384**	.047**
Norway	1246	.533***	.034**	.625**	.124**	.008**	.118	.055**	.306**	.257
Iceland	927	.387**	.232	.488*	.058	.014**	.120	.209*	.577	.145**

TABLE 12.1
(Continued)

Country	N	Religious Faith	Thrift	Good Manners	Polite Neat	Honest	Patience	Self-Control	Loyalty
Overall	2325	.191	.167	.536	.340	.724	.152	.269	.246
U.S.	921	.378	.071	.588	.332	.786	.111	.295	.143
E. Canada	333	.260**	.120**	.570	.379*	.754*	.138*	.279	.191**
F. Canada	1231	.212**	.214**	.421**	.506**	.809	.158*	.333	.264**
Britain	1228	.118**	.068	.648*	.244**	.783	.131	.325	.321**
Australia	312	.215**	.133**	.504***	.292*	.694**	.121	.338*	.299**
N. Ireland	1217	.335	.077	.788***	.305	.838*	.107	.194**	.217*
Ireland	1145	.422*	.140**	.656**	.209**	.736*	.121	.313	.181*
Belgium	1200	.138**	.320**	.433***	.444***	.680**	.089	.265	.188*
France	1305	.096**	.297**	.203***	.493***	.745*	.087*	.300	.356**
Germany	1348	.152**	.270**	.389***	.249***	.723**	.123	.263*	.189***
Italy	1221	.199**	.177**	.536*	.363	.756*	.141*	.189**	.445***
Netherlands	2303	.108**	.129**	.563	.383*	.789	.115	.310	.203***
Spain	1204	.216**	.104*	.531*	.199***	.462***	.147*	.366**	.289***
Japan	1246	.049**	.287**	.666**	.180**	.558***	.493**	.145**	.175*
Norway	927	.105*	.105*	.595	.578**	.846	.110	.154**	.284**
Iceland		.084**	.125**	.599	.520**	.812	.147	.202**	.115

* Significantly different from U.S. at $p < .05$.
** Significantly different from U.S. at $p < .001$.
Global tests for between-country differences significant for all variables at $p < .001$.

important qualities to instill in children. Moreover, except for Spain (at 46.2%) and Japan (55.8%), over 70% of respondents in all countries mention honesty as important. Only three other qualities receive a majority or near-majority of mentions in the total sample: Good manners (53.6%), tolerance and respect for other people (49.8%), and feeling of responsibility (44.4%). Support for these values was fairly consistent, but there were some anomalies: good manners are not highly valued in France (20.3%), tolerance and respect is not quite as highly valued in Norway (30.6%) and there is a bit more variability in the case of responsibility (only 9.4% of the respondents in Northern Ireland mention this value, and the percentage in Ireland is 21.6%). Of these four values, only the latter two might be represented in the category of modern values, suggesting that such values may not be the highest priority among respondents generally.

The relatively low priority of modern values is perhaps more apparent if we look at the qualities that are least likely to be mentioned by the combined samples. Four of the five least-mentioned qualities are modern by our classification: leadership (with only a 6.1% response), imagination (10.6%), determination and perseverance (16.1%), and unselfishness (16.6%) (with patience, at 15.2%, being the fifth). For the full set of nations, then, it appears that modern/individualist values, at least as defined here, are of some importance but are not the most salient qualities to emphasize in children.

Cross-National Comparisons Without Controls

The central concern of this chapter is to examine the relative differences in child-rearing values across all countries, especially as they relate to the question of American exceptionalism. The evidence in Table 12.1 indicates, first of all, that there is almost no support for the suggestion that the United States has the most modern set of values when it comes to child-rearing. In no cases are the Americans the most likely of the 16 samples to mention any one of the eight modern qualities as we have categorized them. Americans do rank among the top few samples for three of the eight: leadership (7.9%, which is the 2nd highest mention but just 1.8% above the pooled average), hard work (23.9%, 4th highest, 4.5% above the pooled average), and independence (32%, 5th highest, 0.2% above the pooled average); however, the American response rates are below the middle rank on the other five: responsibility (41.8%, 9th highest, 2.6% below the pooled average), tolerance and respect (52.2%, 9th highest, 2.4% above the pooled average), unselfishness (15.5%, 10th highest, 1.1% below the pooled average), determination and perseverance (12.6%, 11th highest, 3.5% below the pooled average), and imagination (7.9%, 12th highest, 2.7% below the pooled average). Among the English democracies, residents of the United States rate independence, hard work, responsibility, and leadership more highly than residents of English Canada, Britain, Australia, and Northern Ireland. Only in the case of determination and imagination do the other English countries yield higher proportions, and even here the differences are small. Generally, English Canada is very close to the United States; aside from leadership, the only significant differences are those in which English Canada rates the modern value more highly (imagination, determination, unselfishness). Across most of these items, Britain, Australia, and Northern Ireland display lower proportions than English Canada and the United States.

If Lipset's characterization of the United States as more strongly oriented towards modern values is correct, we should find that the American sample mentions the two nonmodern or "antimodern" values less often than the other respondents. However, the Americans rank close to the average on obedience (23.9%, 0.4% above the pooled average) and are second only to the Irish sample as the group most likely to mention religious faith as an important quality for children: 37.8% of American respondents mention religious faith, which is 18.9% above the pooled average for this item.

On the residual set of seven items in our list, the American sample is relatively high on good manners (58.8%, or 5.2% above average), and honesty (78.6%, or 6.2% above average), and relatively low on thrift (7.1%, or 9.6% below average) and loyalty (14.3%, or 10.3% below average). The Americans are very close to average on politeness and neatness (0.8% below the average of 34.0%), on patience (4.1% below the average of 15.2%), and on self-control (2.6% above the average of 26.9%).

As to which groups are most likely to mention modern values, with a few exceptions, respondents from Germany, Japan, and Spain show a much higher probability of choosing these values than do people from the other nations. The hard work item is an exception to this pattern: The proportions for Germany and Japan are fairly low for this item, although the proportion for Spain is considerably higher than any other country. The non-English European countries do not stand out against the English countries as having particularly low probabilities associated with modern values. However, Italy has lower scores for independence, hard work, leadership, unselfishness, and, to some extent, imagination and tolerance/respect. Norway is somewhat anomalous, with high scores on independence and responsibility, but low scores on hard work, leadership, and, to some degree, tolerance, determination, and unselfishness.

In summary, then, there is little or no support for the argument that Americans espouse an exceptionally modern value system, based on the measures of child-rearing values considered here, and looking at the full range of nations. The only example of an unusual pattern for the United States is the high rating of religious faith, and this appears to run counter to the argument.

Comparing the Anglo-Democracies Without Controls

Although the United States seems not to stand as the most modern or individualist among the 16 groups considered in the analysis, it is possible that, if we confine the argument only to the other English-speaking democracies, the case for Lipset's first new nation thesis may find more support. If we look at Table 12.1 in this light and, following Lipset, compare the United States only with English Canada, Britain, Australia, and French Canada, we do see greater support for Lipset's view, at least on certain items. Americans are significantly more likely than all four to mention leadership, and are significantly more likely than all but English Canadians to mention independence and hard work; even here, the proportions for English Canadians are lower, but not significantly different from the American proportions. Americans are more likely to mention responsibility (44.4%) than those from English Canada, Britain, or Australia, but not respondents from French Canada (48.8%). What is intriguing about these results is that almost all of the items, except perhaps "feeling of responsibility," can be linked to the less collective-oriented elements of the individualism value cluster suggested in our introduction. It is interesting that, on these measures, Americans seem to stand out from the other Anglo nations.[10]

Results are a bit less clear when it comes to imagination or determination, which Americans mention less than English Canadians, French Canadians, Britains, or Australians. Still, the overall pattern seems to be one in which Americans are more disposed to mention "individualist" modern values.

In contrast, on the other modern qualities in our list, including the more collectivity-oriented items, such as tolerance/respect for other people and unselfishness, the Americans tend to rank towards the middle or the bottom in the Anglo samples. Instead, it is the British and Australians who mention tolerance/respect for others and unselfishness the most, with the English and French Canadians falling in the middle.

If we examine the two values that we have characterized as antimodern— obedience and religious faith—Americans rank fairly highly. They rank highest by far on religious faith (37.8% as opposed to 26.0% for English Canadians and even less for Britain, Australia, and French Canada). Their ranking for obedience is close to the middle, with French Canadians choosing this value significantly less often, but Britains and Australians choosing it considerably more often.

To summarize, if we confine our test for American exceptionalism to a comparison involving just the English countries used by Lipset (1963b) in *The First New Nation,* we find more consistent support for his argument. Even here, though, the support is limited to those modern values that seem to emphasize individualism in the less collective sense, as reflected in such ideas as independence, hard work, and leadership. The overall pattern still suggests a fair amount of similarity among the English democracies on modern values, with one marked departure: Americans are considerably more likely to choose the nonmodern value, religious faith, as an important quality in children.

---

[10]The same observations generally hold if we include Ireland and Northern Ireland as English-speaking nations, something which Lipset, however, did not do in his original comparisons of the Anglo-democracies.

Cross-National Comparisons With Controls

Tables 12.2 presents the results of a logistic regression analysis for between-country differences, with controls on the eight background variables. For the multivariate analyses, we chose to focus our attention on the eight modern and two nonmodern qualities counterposed to them, rather than deal with the entire set of 17 dependent variables. The logistic regression coefficients were calculated using indicator/dummy coding for the country variable to facilitate comparisons with the United States, the reference category. The antilogs of these coefficients represent a multiplicative effect on the odds ratio, that is, the ratio of individuals who chose the value in question to those who did not.

To make these data more intuitively interpretable, a set of reproduced probabilities is also presented in Table 12.3. This table shows expected probabilities at the average values of all of the independent variables in the logit equation. For multiple-category independent variables, the unweighted average of categories is employed, because these are easy to construct from effects-coded coefficients. All variables except the country variable are effects-coded. Thus, the expected probabilities are not quite equivalent to the proportions without controls shown in Table 12.1. Between-country comparisons within a table are appropriate, but between-table comparisons should be undertaken with caution.[11]

Overall, the patterns with controls are similar to those found in the bivariate results. The American respondents do not rank at the top on any of the modern values, although they do rank second on leadership (after Germany) and fourth on hard work. Americans are also relatively high on independence (6th). In contrast, the Americans are below the median rank on the other modern values, including the "collective" qualities of tolerance/respect and unselfishness, but also responsibility and imagination. Finally, the American sample, even with controls on the eight background variables, ranks clearly at the top on the nonmodern value, religious faith.

As for the other samples, people in Germany and Japan continue to be more likely to choose modern values than those in other countries in many cases. For example, both Germany and Japan are among the top three or four nations on independence, determination, and feeling of responsibility, while they are the bottom two on obedience. The Japanese also rank relatively highly on unselfishness and the Germans are somewhat above average on imagination. The differences between Spain and other countries become somewhat more pronounced with controls: Spain shows very high expected proportions for the hard work, responsibility, and imagination items.

Within the English-speaking nations, once again, there is some support for the

---

[11]Unlike ordinary least squares (OLS) or weighted least squares (WLS) linear probability models, logit models produce differences of proportions that will vary, depending on the level of the independent variables at which the function is evaluated. For some variables, the overall proportions across countries might appear to be slightly higher or lower than those shown in Table 12.1.

TABLE 12.2
Logistic Regression Coefficients for Between-Country Differences, With Controls

Country	Independence	Hard Work	Responsibility	Imagination	Leadership	Determination
U.S.	(ref.)	(ref.)	(ref.)	(ref.)	(ref.)	(ref.)
E. Canada	-.1702	-.1648	-.1173	+.2391	-.6993**	+.4781**
F. Canada	-.8660**	-.3632*	+.3590**	+.2142	-.8645*	+1.0977**
Britain	-.3859**	-.7902**	-.8119**	+.4205*	-1.2206**	+.4484**
Australia	-.4500**	-1.1031**	-.6355**	+.2586	-1.0965**	+.3364*
N. Ireland	-.4332*	-.4052*	-1.7786**	+.5172*	-1.0601*	+.0130
Ireland	+.3350**	-.1027	-.7728**	+.3953*	-.1377	-.0278
Belgium	-.6538**	+.2649*	-.2005*	-.1176	-1.0153**	+.3928*
France	-.8709**	+.4741**	-.0712	+.3759*	-1.9311**	+.3595*
Germany	+.6803**	-.3257**	+.7475**	+.3488*	+1.6164**	+.7681**
Italy	-.1810	-.9056**	+.3696**	+.0794	-.9547**	+.5093**
Netherlands	-.2717*	-1.0038**	+.5113**	+.1599	-1.2332**	+.0903
Spain	-.1037	+.7164**	+1.0355**	+1.6383**	-.0322	+.1841
Japan	+.5581**	-.6433**	+1.0504**	-.0052	-.3889*	+.6259**
Norway	+.8193**	-2.3206**	+.8600**	+.1898	-2.7499**	-.2969*
Iceland	+.0913	-.0067	+.2081	-.8557**	-1.8718**	-.2092

313

TABLE 12.2
(Continued)

Country	Tolerance & Respect Others	Unselfishness	Religious Faith	Obedience
U.S.	(ref.)	(ref.)	(ref.)	(ref.)
E. Canada	+.1375	+.3466**	-.3551**	-.1295
F. Canada	+.0010	+.2613	-.8549**	-.5946**
Britain	+.5217**	+1.3342**	-.9418**	+.4402**
Australia	+.6982**	+1.1083**	-.2283*	+.6537**
N. Ireland	+.5501**	+.9125**	-.4893**	+.9135**
Ireland	+.3984**	+.5399**	-.3992**	+.1398
Belgium	-.2876**	-.3914*	-1.1422**	-.1264
France	+.3009**	+.3857**	-1.0055**	-.5103**
Germany	-.5342**	-1.7323**	-.8952**	-.7366**
Italy	-.1409	-2.3124**	-.9375**	-.2486*
Netherlands	+.2506*	-.9603**	-1.3764**	-.3940**
Spain	-.1518	-1.3903**	-.9453**	+.0016
Japan	-.5729**	+.5474**	-1.8948**	-1.8309**
Norway	-.9561**	-1.1671**	-.9748**	+.1859
Iceland	+.1686	+.2957*	-1.0162**	-.4681*

* Significantly different from U.S. at $p < .05$.
** Significantly different from U.S. at $p < .001$.
Controls: sex, education, age, children (yes/no), marital status (married/not), community size, occupation, religious attendance.

TABLE 12.3
Expected Probabilities, Adjusting for Effects of Other Variables

Country	Independent	Hard Work	Responsibility	Imagina-tion	Leader-ship	Determina-tion	Tolerance	Unselfish	Religious Faith	Obedience
U.S.	.219	.349	.336	.077	.145	.139	.395	.142	.201	.282
E. Canada	.191	.313	.310	.096	.078	.206	.429	.190	.150	.256
F. Canada	.105	.272	.420	.094	.067	.325	.395	.177	.097	.178
Britain	.160	.196	.183	.113	.048	.201	.524	.386	.089	.379
Australia	.151	.151	.211	.098	.054	.184	.568	.344	.167	.430
N. Ireland	.154	.263	.079	.123	.056	.140	.531	.292	.134	.495
Ireland	.281	.326	.189	.111	.129	.135	.493	.221	.144	.311
Belgium	.127	.411	.292	.069	.058	.192	.329	.101	.074	.257
France	.105	.463	.320	.109	.024	.187	.469	.196	.084	.191
Germany	.356	.279	.517	.106	.461	.258	.277	.028	.093	.158
Italy	.189	.178	.423	.083	.061	.211	.362	.016	.090	.234
Netherlands	.176	.164	.458	.090	.047	.150	.456	.060	.060	.209
Spain	.201	.523	.588	.301	.141	.162	.360	.040	.089	.282
Japan	.328	.220	.591	.077	.103	.231	.269	.222	.036	.059
Norway	.388	.050	.545	.092	.011	.107	.201	.049	.087	.321
Iceland	.235	.348	.384	.034	.026	.115	.436	.182	.083	.197

Note. See Table 12.2 for tests of statistical significance.

argument of American exceptionalism for several of those items that seem to tap the less "collective" modern values. With controls, Americans rank the highest among the Anglo nations on leadership, hard work, independence, and, with the exception of French Canadians, feeling of responsibility. In contrast, it is the British and Australians who are most likely among the English countries to stress tolerance/respect and unselfishness, as well as imagination. All the other samples are also more likely than the Americans to stress determination/perseverance as a quality.

Latent Class Analysis

To what extent can it be said that the values that we have labeled modern fit together? That is, is there a consistent response pattern such that the choice of one tends to imply the choice of others? If the World Values survey had asked respondents, for example, to provide a 1 to 10 rating of each value, or if it had otherwise provided us with measurement that even approximated continuous variable distributions, we could have constructed a scale by adding together the scores of those individual indicators that correlated highly, providing some assessment of the reliability of this scale with a criterion measure such as Cronbach's alpha. Moreover, we could have subjected the entire set of items to confirmatory factor analytic methods to verify assumptions regarding response patterns. Dichotomous indicators are not, however, readily testable using conventional methods based on Pearson correlation coefficients. We, therefore, employed a method that constructs latent categorical variables using categorical indicators, much like factor analysis constructs latent continous variables using continuous indicators. This method is called *latent class analysis* (see Hagenaars, 1990, 1993; McCutcheon, 1987). Its major limitation is in the number of variables that can be handled at one time.[12]

In the latent class analysis presented next, we used five qualities that we have earlier characterized as modern in this analysis: independence, hard work, imagination, leadership, and determination. We also employed responsibility, tolerance, and unselfishness on the assumption that these might form a class similar to the idea of collective individualism discussed earlier. Finally, we added the two items that we have been treating as antimodern qualities: religious faith and obedience.

The results of this analysis, performed on the pooled sample of 16 countries, are shown in Table 12.4. This procedure constructs latent classes with the assumption that each respondent belongs to one and only one class. The numbers in

---

[12]As with log-linear models based on contingency tables, it is important to avoid extremely sparse cell structures, and also to avoid a model with an average cell size below 5. With 10 dichotomous variables, the contingency table would have 2^{10} (1,024) cells, thus requiring a sample size of over 5,000 to meet this criterion.

TABLE 12.4
Latent Class Model Parameters (Conditional Probabilities)

Indicator	Class 1 Achievement	Class 2 Respl/ Achieve	Class 3 Hard Work	Class 4 Obedience	Class 5 Relig	Class 6 Toler/ Unself	(All)
Independence	.5248	.4863	.2875	.0874	.1400	.2031	.294
Hard Work	.0883	.0001	.9866	.1412	.1681	.1375	.193
Responsibility	.0039	.9909	.5112	.2271	.3672	.3796	.444
Imagination	.2730	.1670	.0717	.0371	.0252	.0462	.106
Tolerance	.4629	.4944	.3125	.4027	.5654	.6953	.498
Leadership	.1309	.0939	.0983	.0252	.0405	.0001	.061
Determination	.3034	.2123	.1520	.0642	.0660	.1501	.161
Religious Faith	.0713	.0472	.0625	.2797	.9896	.0081	.191
Unselfishness	.1668	.0643	.0226	.1700	.1475	.3639	.166
Obedience	.0538	.0416	.0457	.9890	.0003	.0136	.235
Latent Class Probability	.1492	.2291	.1070	.2126	.1030	.1990	

Table 12.4 are conditional probabilities. Consider the first row in the table. If an individual is in latent Class 1, he or she has a .5248 probability of picking the "independence" item as an important value.[13] This proportion is considerably higher than it is for other entries in this row, except for latent Class 2 (at .4863). It is also considerably higher than the overall average probability that respondents will choose independence (.294). We can say, therefore, that independence can be considered to be one of the items that helps define latent Class 1 (for that matter, it also helps define latent Class 2). The same, generally, applies to the row associated with the indicator "imagination." Note here that the probabilities are all lower than the probabilities for independence. This is because respondents were generally less likely to choose this indicator. Given this fact, though, the probability of choosing imagination is much higher for people in latent Class 1 (and, to a lesser extent, latent Class 2). In a similar fashion, we can see that individuals in latent Class 1 are more likely to choose determination and leadership than are people in other classes.

The conditional probabilities shown in Table 12.4 suggest, then, that positive responses on the independence, imagination, and determination items combine to form what might be termed an "achievement orientation." This comes closest to the modern value orientation that we discussed earlier. This analysis suggests, however, that two distinct achievement patterns emerge, represented by latent Class 1 and latent Class 2 in Table 12.5. These two patterns are fairly similar, except that respondents in Class 2 also tend to choose the responsibility item (.9909), while while those in Class 1 do not (.0039). We have thus labeled Class 1 and Class 2 as "achievement" and "responsible achievement," respectively. An estimated 14.92% of the combined sample (.1492) is classified in the individualist achievement class, whereas 22.91% of the combined sample is classified in the responsible achievement class.[14]

Contrary to expectations, the hard work item did not fit together with the "achievement" items. Individuals in the two achievement classes (Class 1 and Class 2) had a lower than average probability of choosing the hard work item (.0883 for Class 1 and .0001 for Class 2). A third distinct class (10.7% of respondents) fits those respondents who tend to mention the hard work item. This class of respondents also has a somewhat lower than average likelihood of mentioning the tolerance item, .313 as opposed to an overall average of .498.

A fourth class fits those respondents (21.3%) who emphasize obedience as an important value in children; the probability that individuals in this class will

---

[13]Normally, for dichotomous indicators, there would be two conditional probabilities summing to 1.0: the probability of answering "yes" to a given value, given that the respondent is in Class 1, and the probability of answering "no"; for simplicity, we present only the former.

[14]The high proportions of respondents in both classes answering "yes" to tolerance does not imply that tolerance helps to define these classes, because respondents in virtually all classes tend to answer "yes" to this item.

TABLE 12.5
Latent Class Probabilities

Country	Class 1 Achievement	Class 2 Resp/ Achieve	Class 3 Hard Work	Class 4 Obedience	Class 5 Relig	Class 6 Toler/ Unself	N
Overall	.1492	.2291	.1070	.2126	.1030	.1990	
U.S.	.1328	.1420	.1369	.2234	.2396	.1252	2159
E. Canada	.1535	.1228	.1243	.2023	.1507	.2466	896
F. Canada	.0912	.2099	.1221	.1556	.1350	.2863	328
Britain	.1539	.0250	.0222	.3309	.0465	.4216	1146
Australia	.1319	.0600	.0182	.3744	.1033	.3122	1079
N. Ireland	.1020	.0000	.0411	.4925	.1529	.2115	308
Ireland	.1544	.0518	.0761	.3211	.2498	.1468	1158
Belgium	.1142	.1198	.1800	.2313	.0709	.2838	972
France	.0584	.1086	.1887	.1476	.0587	.4380	1146
Germany	.2413	.4781	.1352	.0869	.0584	.0001	1200
Italy	.1750	.2899	.0638	.2256	.1177	.1280	1076
Netherlands	.1211	.3218	.0387	.1785	.0547	.2853	1062
Spain	.1149	.2613	.2937	.2353	.0940	.0009	2249
Japan	.1322	.4645	.1022	.0191	.0029	.2791	1106
Norway	.2080	.5268	.0185	.2128	.0334	.0005	1198
Iceland	.0567	.1933	.1334	.1297	.0439	.4400	797

include obedience in their selections is .9890. In addition, this group is characterized as having a slightly higher than average probability of including religious faith (.2797, as opposed to an overall probability of .191) and a slightly lower than average probability of including tolerance or responsibility.

A fifth class (10.3%) represents individuals who mention religious faith as an important value. Interestingly, these individuals do not tend to include unselfishness among their choices (probability of .148, as opposed to an overall average probability of .166). Finally, a sixth class involves a higher than average probability of including unselfishness (.364, as opposed to .166 across all classes) and tolerance (.695 versus .498 for all classes).

As with factor analysis, the issue of how well the model fits needs to be assessed. Just as factor analysts concern themselves with the appropriateness of the number of factors chosen in an initial factor extraction, so too must latent class modelers concern themselves with the appropriateness of the number of classes (and, to a lesser extent, the exact form of the model). A six class model fits the model well, with a fairly low chi-square to degrees of freedom ratio given the large sample size (LR chi-square = 1780.61, df = 958). The estimated correct classification proportion is .896, which is reasonable given that these six classes are fitted to a table that has 1,024 cells.

The pattern shown in Table 12.4 replicates fairly well across each of the countries, although there are, as might be expected, some small country-to-country variations. Not shown in the tables is the fact that, in the United States, the distinction between individualist achievers (Class 1) and responsible achievers (Class 2) is heightened by the higher than average probability that American Class 1 respondents will choose hard work (.4505); in contrast, American Class 2 respondents do not choose this item at all. This slight variation does not appear in the case of any of the other countries, except for Spain (.5044). In the United States, there is also a greater tendency for those in the obedience class (Class 4) to include religious faith in the set of chosen values; in contrast to the .2797 conditional probability in Table 12.5, for the United States this parameter is estimated at .6497. This variation does not appear elsewhere, except perhaps to a lesser extent in English Canada (.454). In Germany, the hard work and obedience classes (Classes 3 and 4) are associated with very low probabilities of mentioning tolerance (.0010 and .0729). In France and Northern Ireland, this low probability of mentioning tolerance applies, but only for Class 4 (obedience), whereas for Spain, Norway, and the Netherlands, it applies only for Class 3 (hard work).

Table 12.5 shows the between-country differences in latent class proportions when an identical model is applied to each of the 16 samples. In this model, the conditional probabilities are constrained so that the construction of classes is identical in each country. If anything, Americans are less likely than average to fit into Class 1 or Class 2, the two achievement classes, although they are more likely than average to fit into Class 3, the hard work class. Americans are, as might be expected, considerably more likely than average to fit into the religious faith class (Class 5). Canadians fit a similar pattern but actually are slightly more likely than Americans to fall into the individualist achievement class and slightly less likely than Americans to fall into the responsible achievement class; this pattern is the exact opposite to that which might have been predicted by Lipset's characterization of Canadians as more collectivist and less individualist.

As with the earlier analyses, the Germans, Japanese, and Norwegians stand out as having very high proportions of individuals in the achievement classes, with a tendency to fall into the responsible achievement as opposed to the individualist achievement class. In contrast, very few individuals in Britain, Australia, Northern Ireland, or Ireland fit into the responsible achievement class. France and Iceland also have fairly low proportions of their populations in the achievement classes. Spain shows about average proportions in the two achievement classes together, but it must be noted that Tables 12.4 and 12.5 do not incorporate statistical controls as was the case with Tables 12.2 and 12.3. Finally, the proportion of individuals in the two achievement classes is fairly high in Italy, especially in relation to the United States, and the proportion of individuals in the responsible achievement class (but not the individualist achievement class) is quite high in the Netherlands.

Regression Analysis

Table 12.6 presents the results of an analysis in which the number of modern values selected by the respondent is summed to form an index, which is then evaluated using conventional ordinary least squares (O.L.S.). regression, with controls as discussed earlier.[15] The values used to create this dependent variable are: independence, imagination, leadership, and determination. Hard work was not included because it did not fit with the other four values in tests that were conducted and reported earlier (see the discussion surrounding Table 12.4). Although we could not employ a rigorous test of the scalability of the four items given the dichotomous nature of the indicators, the latent class analysis presented earlier provides some justification for treating them as a single unit. The major advantage of the regression model shown in Table 12.6 lies in its ease of interpretation and the fact that the inclusion of statistical controls is fairly straightforward. On the other hand, the formal model assumptions (continuously distributed dependent variable, continuously distributed indicators in scale construction) have not been fully met, so the findings should be treated as heuristic rather than as the results of a formal test.

---

[15]For the analyses in Table 12.6, as well as for those presented in Tables 12.4 and 12.5, it would have been interesting to aggregate our value measures in a manner more consistent with that used by other researchers, especially Schwartz (e.g., Schwartz & Bilsky, 1990). Unfortunately, there was insufficient overlap between our measures and the items used by Schwartz for us to attempt such a procedure.

TABLE 12.6
Between-Country Differences in Number of "Modern" Values Selected, With and Without
Controls

Country	Without Controls	With Controls	Regression Coefficient	N
U.S.	.5814	.5858	(ref)	2159
E. Canada	.6148	.5980	+.0122	896
F. Canada	.5438	.5895	+.0037	328
Britain	.5388	.5374	-.0484	1146
Australia	.5264	.5247	-.0610*	1079
N. Ireland	.3822	.5145	-.0712	308
Ireland	.5110	.6800	+.0942**	1158
Belgium	.4371	.4568	-.1290**	972
France	.4782	.5374	-.0484	1146
Germany	1.3275	1.0853	+.4995**	1200
Italy	.4188	.5867	+.0009	1076
Netherlands	.5055	.4935	-.0923	1062
Spain	.6800	.7799	+.1921**	2249
Japan	.8128	.7595	+.1737**	1106
Norway	.7771	.6659	+.0801*	1198
Iceland	.5734	.4685	-.1173*	797

Note. Values included: independence, leadership, determination/perseverence, imagination
*Significantly different from U. S. at $p < .05$.
**Significantly different from U. S. at $p < .001$.

In Table 12.6, the "without controls" column represents the within-country means, while the "with controls" column refers to least squares means, that is, adjusted for the effects of the independent variables. Finally, the regression coefficients provide some indication of the differences between various countries and the United States. Overall, Germany stands out as rating modern values very highly, considerably more than Japan, which is the country with the second highest score. Spain and Norway also score highly, especially with controls. Among the English democracies, only Australia is significantly different from the United States (.525 with controls, as opposed to .586 for the United States). Aside from Australia, Belgium, the Netherlands, and Iceland stand out as having significantly lower scores (with controls), whereas Ireland, Germany, Spain, Japan, and Norway score significantly higher. In the regression model reported in Table 12.6, education was positively related to the number of modern values chosen, whereas age and religious attendance were negatively related to the dependent variable. Marital status, number of children, and gender were not significantly related. The expected difference between someone who attends church weekly and someone who attends church once a year is approximately .20, whereas the expected difference between someone who has university education and someone who has some high school education would also be approximately .20.[16] These might be compared with magnitudes of the between country-differences shown in Table 12.6; generally, between country effects were stronger than the effects attributable to the control variables.[17]

DISCUSSION AND CONCLUSIONS

The findings from this set of cross-national comparisons, then, are not consistent with Lipset's thesis, and the ideas of other modernization theorists, that Americans should be highest in subscription to so-called modern values and lowest on nonmodern values. In fact, with controls, Americans are highest in endorsing the nonmodern value, religious faith. If the comparisons are limited to the four English-speaking democracies considered in *The First New Nation,* there is some limited support for Lipset's thesis of American exceptionalism. That is, Americans rank highest among these samples when we confine the comparisons to the more "self-oriented" modern values, such as independence, hard work, and leadership, while Britain and Australia tend to rank lowest. However, our latent class analysis suggests that some of the differences between Americans and other countries could be attributed to the higher American response on "hard work," which unexpectedly does not fall into the same class as the other modern values. It is clearly the case that Britons and Australians have a very low probability of being in the "responsible achievers" category identified in this analysis. In contrast, the American and English Canadian probabilities, while slightly below the average across all countries, are considerably higher than those for the British and Australians.

On what we have termed the collective modern values, such as unselfishness and tolerance and respect for other people, the Americans tend to give the lowest and the British and Australians the highest mentions, with the English Canadians and French Canadians generally in between. This pattern suggests that American socialization preferences may indeed be the most individualist in the English-speaking countries, in the self-oriented sense that Lipset typically emphasizes

---

[16]The regression coefficient for education was .0417; the regression coefficient for age was −.0046; the regression coefficient for religious attendance was −.0509. For the occupation variable, the most pronounced differences were between managers and professionals on the one hand (+.149) and most other occupations, on the other hand, which scored close to the reference category (.000). White collar workers scored between the other occupations and professional and managerial workers (+.090). The effects of these variables were all significant at $p < .0001$.

[17]The sum of squares associated with between-country differences ($SS = 428$, $df = 15$) was considerably higher than education ($SS = 134.2$, $df = 1$), age ($SS = 49.5$, $df = 1$), or occupation ($SS = 40.0$, $df = 7$), although there were more degrees of freedom associated with country in the model we employed.

when he raises the question, while British and Australian socialization priorities tend toward the collective orientation that Lipset would see as "British."

How do we explain these patterns of American exceptionalism? This question is difficult to answer from our results. What we can say with confidence is that the patterns do not occur because of the way the nations differ in socio-demographic profiles. We thought, in particular, that differences in educational attainment could be important to take into account, because the United States ranks quite highly compared to the other nations on this variable. However, the results are very similar with or without controls on education and the other background variables.

It is tempting to say that Lipset's theory of differences among the Anglo-democracies provides the appropriate explanation for the patterns of American exceptionalism within this category of nations. Perhaps, as Lipset argues, the differences are rooted in the lasting impact of formative events reinforced by subsequent laws and institutions. In some of his latest work, Lipset (1990) has added that these formative events led to the current patterns of comparatively high religiosity and strong moral conservatism in the United States. In short, he emphasizes that church and state were separated early in the United States and, as a result, Protestant fundamentalism of various types was allowed to flourish. This development affected the moral climate, according to Lipset. Bibby (1987) has put forward a variant of this view to explain the far higher levels of church attendance in the United States compared with Canada and Great Britain (see also Curtis, Grabb, & Baer, 1992). He indicates that there is comparatively more aggressive "marketing" of religion to the American population by the large number of sectarian competitors there (Bibby, 1987, pp. 218–219). These factors may help account for the Americans' relatively strong endorsement of "religious faith" in our analyses.

The theory of unique formative events is much less useful, though, when we set it against the wider international comparisons provided in our analyses. Americans are comparatively high on some modern values, but are by no means highest. This assessment includes the values on which the Americans stand out among the Anglo-democracies. In addition, the Americans are behind various nations on other modern values. Either we must now devise similar theories of formative events for these other nations, or this type of explanation is not partic-ularly useful. We are inclined to the latter conclusion.

There seems not to be very much support in our analyses for the other prevailing interpretations in the modernization literature either. In our analysis of individual items, the following national samples tended to be higher than the American sample on modern values: Germany, Japan, and Spain. In our latent class analysis, each of these countries showed extremely high proportions in the "responsible achievers" category. Norway, Italy, and the Netherlands also showed proportions that were considerably higher than those found in the United States. Three of these countries also had proportions in the "individualist achievers" class that were considerably higher than the United States (Germany, Norway, Italy) and all other countries were fairly similar to those of the United States. These countries are not highly Protestant, or more Anglo in origin, or more urban, or more industrialized, or more democratic than either the United States or various other nations that ranked lower on modern values. These are the predictions or explanations of modernity offered in the literature. Perhaps the reason the results depart from these views is that there has been much globalization of modern views through cultural diffusion. National interconnections through economic and media links may have promoted considerable diffusion of such ideas. In any case, the standard theories do not find much support in our results.

Focusing on national differences may, in fact, be the wrong approach, given our findings. On the contrary, the comparative results show a great deal of similarity across the nations in regard to the qualities people value in children. Perhaps here is where we should focus our attention. There was considerable similarity in the values mentioned most often in the nations: honesty, good manners, tolerance and respect for other people, and feeling of responsibility, in particular. It occurs to us that these are four of a set of qualities (along with obedience, politeness and neatness, self-control, and loyalty) that were ranked highly in several nations and that characterize what might be termed "the non-conflictual, predictable person." It appears that these may be a common set of high-priority traits that are desired in children across the national samples. This pattern may be telling us that the goals of the socialization process are very similar, regardless of the society in which we reside. The goals are to control conflict and to create predictable, helpful children. Because of the similar problems and goals of socialization across societies, there may also be strong cross-national consensus on what the ideal *adult* citizen should be like: trustworthy, well-mannered, good to other people, and responsible.

Our biggest reservation about making the latter suggestion, of course, is that our data deal only with qualities to be instilled in children. It is unclear whether the patterns of results would have been the same if qualities in adults had been examined in the World Values Survey. We suspect the results would have been similar, because the "social control" and "predictability" imperatives are omnipresent across societies. Nevertheless, it is conceivable that the pattern of national differences is different for adults. It will require further research before more conclusive evidence can be provided to address this possibility. It should also be noted that our data do not encompass all the possible elements of a modern value system; for example, we were not able in our analyses to consider national differences in future orientation, which, as noted in the introduction, appears to be integral to most conceptions of modernity. For that reason, the findings presented here represent one part of a much larger array of analyses that are necessary for a comprehensive assessment, both of Lipset's thesis on national value differences and of modernization theory in general.

ACKNOWLEDGMENTS

We gratefully acknowledge that our data source was made available by Ronald Inglehart and Neil Nevitte through the Inter-university Consortium for Political and Social Research. We also thank the Donner Canadian Foundation for its contributions in making the data available. Neither the original investigators nor the disseminating archive bears any responsibility for the analyses and interpretations presented here.

REFERENCES

Allahar, A. L. (1989). *Sociology and the periphery.* Toronto: Garamond.

Almond, G., & Verba, S. (1963). *The civic culture.* Princeton, NJ: Princeton University Press.

Alwin, D. F., & Krosnick, J. A. (1985). The measurement of values in surveys: A comparison of ratings and rankings. *Public Opinion Quarterly, 49,* 535–552.

Archibald, W. P. (1978). *Social psychology as political economy.* Toronto: McGraw-Hill Ryerson.

Arnold, S. J., & Tigert, D. J. (1974). Canadians and Americans: A comparative analysis. *International Journal of Comparative Sociology, 15,* 68–83.

Baer, D., Curtis, J., Grabb, E., & Johnston, W. (1995). *Respect for authority in Canada, the United States, Great Britain, and Australia. Sociological Focus, 28* (forthcoming).

Baer, D., Grabb, E., & Johnston, W. (1990a). The values of Canadians and Americans: A critical analysis and reassessment. *Social Forces, 68,* 693–713.

Baer, D., Grabb, E., & Johnston, W. (1990b). Reassessing differences in Canadian and American values. In J. E. Curtis & L. Tepperman (Eds.), *Images of Canada: The sociological tradition* (pp. 86–97). Scarborough, Canada: Prentice-Hall.

Baer, D., Grabb, E., & Johnston, W. (1993). National character, regional culture, and the values of Canadians and Americans. *Canadian Review of Sociology and Anthropology, 30,* 13–36.

Bell, D., & Tepperman, L. (1979). *The roots of disunity.* Toronto: McClelland and Stewart.

Bibby, R. (1987). *Fragmented gods.* Toronto: Stoddart.

Clark, S. D. (1975). The post Second World War Canadian society. *Canadian Review of Sociology and Anthropology, 12,* 25–32.

Crawford, C., & Curtis, J. (1979). English Canadian-American differences in value orientations. *Studies in Comparative International Development, 14,* 23–44.

Curtis, J. (1971). Voluntary association joining: A cross-national comparative note. *American Sociological Review, 36,* 872–880.

Curtis, J., Grabb, E., & Baer, D. (1992). Voluntary association membership in fifteen developed countries: A comparative analysis. *American Sociological Review, 57,* 139–152.

Durkheim, E. (1965). *The division of labour in society.* New York: Free Press.

Grabb, E., & Curtis, J. (1988). English Canadian-American differences in orientation toward social control and individual rights. *Sociological Focus, 21,* 127–141.

Grabb, E., & Curtis, J. (1992). Voluntary association membership in English Canada, French Canada, and the United States: A multivariate analysis. *Canadian Journal of Sociology, 17,* 371–388.

Hagan, J., & Leon, J. (1977). Philosophy and sociology of crime control: Canadian-American comparisons. *Sociological Inquiry, 47,* 181–208.

Hagenaars, J. (1990). *Categorical longitudinal data.* Beverly Hills, CA: Sage.

Hagenaars, J. (1993). *Loglinear models with latent variables.* Beverly Hills, CA: Sage.

Hofstede, G. (1980). *Culture's consequences: International differences in work-related values.* Beverly Hills, CA: Sage.

Inglehart, R. et al. (1990). *World values survey, 1981–1983. Computer file and codebook* (2nd ed.). Ann Arbor, MI: University of Michigan, Inter-University Consortium for Political and Social Research.

Inkeles, A. (1966). The modernization of man. In M. Weiner (Ed.), *Modernization: The dynamics of growth* (pp. 151–163). New York: Basic Books.

Inkeles, A. (1973). Making men modern. In A. Etzioni (Ed.), *Social change: Sources, patterns, and consequences.* New York: Basic Books.

Inkeles, A., & Smith, D. H. (1974). *Becoming modern.* Cambridge, MA: Harvard University Press.

Kohn, M. L. (1969). *Class and conformity.* Homewood, IL: Dorsey.

Krosnick, J. A., & Alwin, D. F. (1988). A test of the form-resistant correlation hypothesis. *Public Opinion Quarterly, 52,* 526–538.

Lambert, W. E., Hamers, J. F., & Frasure-Smith, N. (1979). *Child-rearing values: A cross-national study.* New York: Praeger.

Lerner, D. (1965). *The passing of traditional society.* New York: Free Press.

Lipset, S. M. (1963a). The value patterns of democracy: A case study in comparative analysis. *American Sociological Review, 28,* 515–531.

Lipset, S. M. (1963b). *The first new nation.* New York: Basic Books.

Lipset, S. M. (1964). Canada and the United States: A comparative view. *Canadian Review of Sociology and Anthropology, 1,* 173–185.

Lipset, S. M. (1966). Value patterns, class and the democratic polity: The United States and Great Britain. In R. Bendix & S. M. Lipset (Eds.), *Class, status, and power* (pp. 161–171). New York: Free Press.

Lipset, S. M. (1967). Values, education, and entrepreneurship. In S. M. Lipset & A. Solari (Eds.), *Elites in Latin America* (pp. 3–60). New York: Oxford University Press.

Lipset, S. M. (1968). *Revolution and counterrevolution.* New York: Basic Books.

Lipset, S. M. (1985). Canada and the United States: The cultural dimension. In C. F. Doran & J. H. Sigler (Eds.), *Canada and the United States* (pp. 109–160). Englewood Cliffs, NJ: Prentice-Hall.

Lipset, S. M. (1986). Historical conditions and national characteristics. *Canadian Journal of Sociology, 11,* 113–155.

Lipset, S. M. (1990). *Continental divide.* New York: Routledge.

Lipset, S. M. (1994). The social requisites of democracy. *American Sociological Review, 59,* 1–22.

Lipset, S. M., & Solari, A. (Eds.). (1967). *Elites in Latin America.* New York: Oxford University Press.

McClelland, D. C. (1961). *The achieving society.* Princeton, NJ: Van Nostrand.

McCutcheon, A. (1987). *Latent class analysis.* Beverly Hills, CA: Sage.

Merelman, R. M. (1991). *Partial visions: Culture and politics in Britain, Canada and the United States.* Madison, WI: University of Wisconsin Press.

Nevitte, N., & Gibbins, R. (1990). *New elites in old states. Ideologies in the Anglo-American democracies.* Toronto, Canada: Oxford University Press.

Nisbett, R. E. (1993). Violence and U.S. regional culture. *American Psychologist, 48,* 441–449.

Parsons, T. (1951). *The social system.* New York: Free Press.

Robertson, R. (1982). Parsons on the evolutionary significance of American religion. *Sociological Analysis, 43,* 307–326.

Rokeach, M. (1973). *The nature of human values.* New York: Free Press.

Schwartz, S. H., & Bilsky, W. (1990). Toward a theory of the universal content and structure of values: Extensions and cross-cultural replications. *Journal of Personality and Social Psychology, 58,* 878–891.

Triandis, H. C. (1973). Subjective culture and economic development. *International Journal of Psychology, 8,* 163–180.

Triandis, H. C., McCusker, C., & Hui, C. H. (1990). Multimethod probes of individualism and collectivism. *Journal of Personality and Social Psychology, 59,* 1006–1020.

Truman, T. (1971). A critique of Seymour Martin Lipset's article, 'Value Differences, Absolute or Relative: The English-Speaking Democracies.' *Canadian Journal of Political Science, 4,* 497–525.

Weiner, M. (Ed.). (1966). *Modernization: The dynamics of growth.* New York: Basic Books.

Williams, R. (1960). *American society.* New York: Knopf.

Yang, K. (1988). Will societal modernization eventually eliminate cross-cultural psychological differences? In M. H. Bond (Ed.), *The cross-cultural challenge to social psychology* (pp. 67–85). Beverly Hills, CA: Sage.

Author Index

A

Abelson, R. P., 27, 48
Aboud, F., 154, 172
Acitelli, L. K., 258, 273
Adler, N. E., 200, 211
Adorno, T. W., 29, 48, 260, 272
Ajzen, I., 71, 74, 77, 84, 92, 93, 94, 97, 100, 101
Alexander, J., 278, 296
Allahar, A. L., 302, 326
Allen, H. M., Jr., 157, 188
Allen, N., 209, 212
Allon, N., 155, 184
Allport, G. W., 255, 272
Almond, G., 302, 326
Altemeyer, R., 29, 48, 67, 74, 82, 100, 179, 184, 245, 248, 254, 260, 273
Alwin, D. F., 1, 23, 305, 326, 327
Anderberg, M. R., 140, 149
Archibald, W. P., 300, 326
Arian, A., 10, 23
Armor, D., 33, 50
Arnold, S. J., 300, 326
Asher, H. B., 142, 149
Atkinson, J. W., 217, 248
Attanucci, J., 91, 101
Atwoos, L. E., 80, 88, 104
Aydin, C. E., 288, 296

B

Bachman, J. G., 142, 248
Bachrach, P., 286, 296
Baer, D., 300, 304, 306, 324, 326
Bailey, J., 172, 173, 174, 186
Bailey, S., 85,104
Ball-Rokeach, S. J., 55, 67, 69, 74, 75, 78, 79, 80, 81, 88, 89, 100, 277, 278, 279, 280, 281, 282, 283, 284, 286, 287, 288, 296, 297, 298
Balswick, J. O., 266, 273
Baratz, M. S., 286, 296
Barnette, W. L., 80, 100
Baron, J., 41 48
Bartholomew, K., 263, 273
Batra, R., 136, 147, 148, 149, 151
Batts, V., 156, 180, 187
Baumrind, D., 266, 273
Beattie, J., 41, 48
Beatty, S. E., 137, 138, 141, 142, 145, 146, 147, 148, 149, 150
Beck, L., 93, 100
Becker, G., 46, 48
Becker, H. S., 192, 205, 211
Beech, R. P., 80, 82, 88, 104
Bell, D., 324, 326
Bengtson, V., 254, 274
Berlin, I., 44, 48
Best, R. J., 136, 143, 148, 149, 150
Bettman, J. R., 27, 49
Bibby, R., 324, 326
Biernat, M., 159, 161, 164, 167, 179, 184, 185, 189
Bies, R. J., 227, 248
Bifulco, A., 205, 211
Bilsky, W., 22, 24, 88, 104, 154, 171, 188, 303, 321, 327
Blackwood, P., 63, 74
Blasi, A., 85, 100
Bluck, S., 33, 50
Bobbitt, P., 37, 38, 48

Bobo, L., 156, 188
Boettger, R., 31, 35, 40, 41, 42, 45, 50
Bolton, W., 205, 213
Borgida, E., 131, 132
Bousch, D. M., 136, 146, 147, 148, 149, 150
Brady, H., 157, 188
Braithwaite, V. A., 84, 100, 255, 273
Breckler, S. J., 93, 104
Brehm, J. W., 200, 211
Brewer, M. B., 171, 182, 184
Brickman, P., 123, 132, 191, 195, 196, 205, 209, 211
Brock, T. C., 109, 110, 133
Bromley, S., 156, 185
Brown, G. W., 205, 211
Bruner, J. S., 109, 133
Brunstein, J. C., 195, 211
Burke, P. J., 195, 211
Burns, C. E., 254, 273
Burris, C. T., 155, 186
Buss, A. H., 89, 90, 101
Buss, D. M., 193, 211
Buunk, B. P., 207, 213
Byrne, D., 60, 74, 168, 180, 184, 188

C

Cacioppo, J. T., 60, 74
Calabresi, G., 37, 38, 48
Campbell, A., 10, 23, 156, 185
Campbell, J., 90, 100
Candee, D., 97, 100
Cantor, N., 89, 90, 105, 193, 211
Capella, J. N., 285, 289, 297
Carson, R. T., 38, 49
Carver, C. S., 90, 100, 173, 185, 187, 188
Cashmore, J. A., 254, 273
Chaiken, S., 33, 39, 159, 185
Chemansky, D., 17, 23
Chéron, E. J., 145, 147, 148, 151
Cherry, F., 60, 74
Chonka, L. B., 143, 148, 151
Clark, S. D., 300, 326
Clarke-Stewart, A., 84, 100

Clinton, W. J., 284, 297
Clore, G. L., 168, 184
Clymer, W. J., 284, 289, 297
Coffman, T., 156, 186
Cohan, C. L., 199, 202, 203, 211, 212
Cohen, A. R., 200, 211
Cohen, J., 79, 100
Cohen, S., 171, 172, 186
Colby, A., 90, 100
Coleman, L. M., 169, 173, 186
Colman, W., 287, 288, 290, 297
Coney, K. A., 136, 149
Conroy, W. J., 80, 100
Converse, P. E., 10, 23
Conway, M., 109, 110, 133
Cook, S. W., 172, 189
Cornell, D. P., 195, 213
Cosmides, L., 36, 48
Crandall, C. S., 159, 180, 179, 185
Crawford, C., 300, 326
Crittendon, P., 87, 93, 96, 99, 101
Crosby, F., 156, 185
Croteau, D., 278, 297
Crowne, D. P., 116, 132
Cuerrier, J. P., 93, 105
Curtis, J., 300, 304, 306, 324, 326

D

David, H. P., 200, 211
Davis, E., 167, 189
Davison, M. L., 85, 105
de Vries, B., 85, 97, 101, 105
DeBono, K. G., 89, 105, 108, 117, 121, 122, 123, 131, 132
DeCourville, N. H., 80, 82, 103
Derogatis, R. L., 201, 211
DeSeve, K. L., 80, 101
Deshaies, P., 93, 105
Devereux, E., 172, 188
Devine, P. G., 93, 94, 97, 101, 174, 176, 183, 185, 187
Dillman, D. A., 280, 297
DiRenzo, G. J., 37, 48
Don-Yehiya, E., 11, 23
Doumit Sparks, A., 254, 273

Douvan, E., 138, 139, 151
Dovidio, J. F., 153, 154, 171, 176, 177, 178, 185
Dunkel-Schetter, C., 199, 200, 202, 203, 209, 211, 212
Durkheim, E., 36, 37, 48, 302, 326
Durkin, K., 54, 75
Dutton, D. G., 153, 154, 177, 185

E

Eagly, A. H., 123, 132, 159, 185
Eisenberg, N., 94, 97, 101, 254, 273
Eiser, J. R., 47, 48
Eisert, D. C., 147, 150
Elkins, D., 33, 50
Elster, J., 37, 48
Emerson, R. M., 287, 297
Endrenny, P., 292, 298
Engel, I., 254, 273
Entman, R., 278, 297
Esses, V. M., 155, 171, 179, 183, 185, 186, 255, 274
Evans, R. I., 154, 163, 187, 255, 274

F

Faludi, S., 79, 83, 101
Farber, J., 173, 186
Fazio, R. H., 73, 74, 98, 100
Feather, N. T., 85, 86, 101, 216, 217, 218, 219, 220, 221, 222, 223, 224, 225, 226, 227, 228, 230, 233, 234, 235, 236, 237, 239, 240, 241, 242, 243, 244, 245, 246, 247, 248, 249
Feldman, S., 154, 158, 185
Fenigstein, 89, 90, 101
Festinger, L., 26, 27, 48, 123, 132
Fincham, F., 226, 249
Fishbein, M. N., 71, 74, 77, 84, 92, 93, 94, 97, 100, 101
Fiske, S. T., 47, 50, 72, 74, 92, 101
Flanagan, O., 87, 99, 101
Flay, B. R., 88, 102
Ford, M. R., 88, 97, 101
Frager, R., 123, 124, 133

Frankl, V. E., 205, 212
Frasure-Smith, N., 304, 327
Freank, R. H., 99, 101
Freiden, J. B., 147, 149
Frenkel-Brunswick, E., 29, 48, 260, 272
Friedman, B. L., 87, 88, 97, 101
Friedman, M., 87, 88, 93, 97, 99, 101
Friedman, S., 84, 100
Furnham, A., 1, 23

G

Gaertner, S. L., 153, 154, 171, 172, 176, 177, 178, 185, 255, 273
Gamson, W. A., 278, 297
Gangestad, S., 90, 105
Gareau, C., 80, 82, 103
Garreau, J., 144, 149
Gergen, K. J., 100, 101, 172, 185
Gibbins, R., 300, 327
Gibbons, F. X., 173, 174, 176, 185
Gibbs, J., 97, 100
Gilchrist, R. S., 61, 73, 74, 75
Gilligan, C., 86, 87, 91, 93, 96, 99, 101
Gitlin, T., 278, 292, 297
Glass, D. C., 171, 172, 173, 185, 186, 187, 188
Goldberg, L., 254, 273
Golding, G., 97, 104
Goldsmith, R. E., 147, 149
Gollwitzer, P., 195, 212
Goodnow, J. J., 254, 266, 273
Gorsuch, R. L., 92, 101
Grabb, E., 300, 304, 306, 326
Graham-Brown, S., 17, 23
Grant, A. E., 287, 288, 297
Greeley, A. M., 156, 185, 188
Green, P. E., 143, 149
Greene, D., 94, 104
Greenstein, T. N., 1, 23, 67, 74, 78, 80, 102, 104
Greenwald, A. G., 93, 104
Griffin, D. W., 175, 188, 263, 273
Grube, J. W., 55, 67, 74, 78, 79, 80, 81, 88, 89, 100, 102, 282, 284, 286, 287, 288, 297

Gruenfeld, D. H., 41, 48
Grunert, K. G., 22, 23, 145, 149
Grunert, S. C., 21, 22, 23, 144, 149
Grusec, J. E., 266, 273
Guthrie, K. K., 278, 283, 287, 288, 297
Gutman, J., 137, 151
Guttman, L., 13, 23
Guvran, R., 17, 23

H

Habermas, J., 277, 297
Haddock, G., 82, 102, 155, 171, 179,
    183, 185, 186, 255, 274
Hagan, J., 300, 326
Hagen, M., 157, 188
Hagenaars, J., 316, 326
Hagiwara, S., 226, 227, 249
Hall, D. B., 137, 150
Halpern, P., 288, 297
Hamers, J. F., 304, 327
Hamid, P. N., 88, 102
Hamilton, V. L., 227, 249
Hannum, K., 29, 30, 41, 50
Hardee, B. B., 156, 180, 187
Harding, J., 172, 188
Hardyck, J. A., 154, 163, 168, 188
Hargreaves, J. L., 254, 273
Harris, T. O., 205, 211
Hart, H. L. A., 226, 249
Hass, R. G., 153, 154, 155, 158, 159,
    171, 172, 173, 174, 175, 180, 186
Hawkins, D. I., 136, 149
Heider, F., 226, 228, 233, 234, 249
Heitmeyer, J. R., 147, 149
Helmreich, R., 82, 105
Herman, C. P., 71, 75
Hershey, J. C., 41, 48
Hewer, A., 84, 96, 97, 100, 102
Hewer, R., 84, 103
Higgins, E. T., 66, 67, 71, 74, 75, 99,
    102, 174, 186
Himmelweit, H. T., 10, 23
Hirschburg, P. L., 280, 297
Hmaisi, R., 17, 23
Hodge, C., 153, 186

Hoffman, S., 161, 180, 186
Hofstede, G., 302, 304, 327
Hoge, D. R., 254, 273
Homer, P. M., 136, 137, 138, 141, 142,
    144, 145, 146, 147, 148, 149, 150
Hopkins, S. W., Jr., 80, 102
Hotte, A. M., 86, 87, 102, 103
Hough, J. C., Jr., 153, 154, 156, 157,
    164, 187, 255, 273
House, P., 94, 104
Howes, P. W., 179, 189
Hoynes. W., 278, 297
Hui, C. H., 302, 303, 328
Huismans, S., 16, 24
Humphreys, P., 10, 23
Hunsberger, B., 260, 273
Hunter, W., 97, 104
Hyland, M., 168, 186

I

Inbar-Saban, N., 67, 75
Ineles, A., 302, 327
Inglehart, R., 304, 327
Insko, C. A., 154, 163, 167, 168, 186,
    187
Ispa, J. M., 254, 273

J

Jackson, L. A., 153, 155, 186
Jaeger, M., 10, 23
James, W., 193, 212
Jamieson, K. H., 285, 289, 297
Janda, J., 10, 23
Janis, I. L., 40, 49
Janoff-Bulman, R., 193, 212
Jaspars, J., 226, 249
Johnson, B. T., 109, 123, 131, 132
Johnson, D. J., 206, 207, 212
Johnson, E. J., 27, 49
Johnson, M. P., 209, 212
Johnston, J., 242, 248
Johnston, W., 300, 303, 304, 306, 324,
    326
Jones, E. E., 172, 173, 185, 187

Juhl, H. J., 21, 22, 23
Jussim, L., 169, 173, 186

K

Kahle, L. R., 22, 23, 136, 137, 138,
  139, 140, 141, 142, 143, 144, 145,
  146, 147, 148, 149, 150, 151
Kahn, A. R., 109, 131, 132
Kahneman, D., 27, 39, 41, 49
Kamakura, W. A., 140, 150
Kanter, R. M., 192, 212
Kappes, B. M., 85, 86, 103
Karlins, M., 156, 186
Katkin, E. S., 80, 100
Kato, K., 90, 102
Katz, D., 109, 132, 224, 249
Katz, I., 153, 154, 155, 158, 159, 171,
  172, 173, 174, 175, 180, 185, 186,
  187, 188
Katz, M., 10, 23
Kearney, K. A., 67, 74
Kearney, K. Z., 78, 102
Kelley, H. H., 196, 197, 212
Kellner, D., 278, 297
Kelman, H. C., 227, 249
Kendrick, A., 157, 168, 169, 179, 188
Kennedy, P., 138, 143, 148, 150
Kenny, D. A., 258, 273
Keown, C., 145, 147, 148, 149
Kernberg, O. F., 89, 102
Kiesler, C., 192, 212
Kim, C. H., 147, 148, 149
Kinder D. R., 10, 23, 153, 154, 156,
  157, 186, 255, 274
King, G., 174, 176
Kitayama, S., 90, 91, 97, 98, 99, 102,103
Kittay, E. F., 86, 103
Kitwood, T., 84, 93, 102
Klecka, W. R., 13, 23
Klingel, D. M., 135, 146, 150
Kluckhohn, C. K. M., 2, 23, 255, 273
Klugel, J. R., 157, 158, 185
Knetsch, J. L., 39, 39
Kobasa, S., 192, 212
Koch, J., 84, 100

Kohlberg, L., 84, 85, 91, 93, 94, 96,
  97, 100, 102, 103
Kohn, M. L., 263, 273, 305, 327
Kosinski, M. J., 137, 150
Kovel, J., 156, 186, 255, 273
Kraines, R. J., 254, 274
Kristensen, K., 22, 23, 145, 149
Kristiansen, C. M., 47, 49, 54, 58, 74,
  77, 78, 79, 80, 82, 87, 89, 94, 102, 103
Kropp, F. G., 147, 148, 150
Krosnick, J. A., 305, 326, 327
Krulewitz, J. E., 155, 186
Kulka, R. A., 135, 138, 139, 146, 150,
  151
Kurokawa, M., 90, 102

L

Lake, R. A., 177, 185
Lambert, W. E., 304, 327
Lane, R., 26, 49
Langer, E., 47, 49
Larrabee, M. J., 91, 92, 103
Larsen, K. S., 161, 180, 186
Lasch, C., 90, 103
Lavine, H., 131, 132
Lazarus, R. S., 196, 209, 212
Lennon, R., 94, 97, 101
Leon, J., 300, 326
Lepper, M. R., 60, 74
Lerch, L., 169, 173, 186
Lerner, D., 302, 327
Lerner, M. J., 193, 212
Levine, C., 84, 96, 102, 103
Levinson, D. J., 29, 48, 260, 272
Lewis, C. C., 266, 273
Li, K., 91, 105
Lieberman, A., 33, 49
Liebman, C. S., 11, 23
Lindzey, G., 255, 272
Linville, P. W., 173, 187, 194, 208, 212
Lipkus, I., 205, 213
Lipset, S. M., 10, 23, 154, 187, 299,
  300, 301, 302, 303, 304, 311, 327
Little, B., 196, 212
Liu, R., 137, 144, 145, 147, 148, 150

Liu, T., 89, 105, 193, 195, 213
Loewen, L., 33, 50
Loftus, E., 81, 103
Loges, W. E., 278, 281, 283, 288, 297, 298
Lowery, C. R., 88, 97, 101
Lubin, B., 68, 75
Luce, R. D., 143, 150
Lucindo, D. J., 173, 186
Lukes, S., 37, 49
Lyden, J. E., 89, 103, 109, 124, 130, 131, 132, 199, 200, 202, 203, 209, 210, 211, 212
Lynch, M., 195, 213
Lyons, N. P., 88, 91, 97, 98, 103

M

Maccoby, E. E., 266, 273
Macrides, C., 266, 273
Madrigal, R., 136, 140, 145, 147, 148, 150
Mager, J., 144, 145, 146, 147, 150, 151
Maio, G. R., 131, 132
Major, B. N., 200, 211
Malkiel, G. B., 47, 49
Mann, L., 40, 49
Markus, H. R., 66, 74, 90, 91, 97, 98, 99, 102, 103
Marlowe, D., 116, 123, 124, 132
Martin, J. A., 266, 273
Maslow, A. H., 138, 151
Matheson, K., 82, 87, 103
Mathieu, J., 192, 209, 212
Mayton, D. M., 1, 23
McBroom, W. H., 254, 273
McCarty, J. A., 89, 104
McCaughey, E., 285, 298
McClelland, D. C., 302, 327
McClendon, M. J., 157, 187
McClintock, C. G., 7, 23
McConahay, J. B., 153, 154, 156, 157, 164, 172, 177, 180, 187, 188, 255, 273
McCusker, C., 302, 303, 328
McCutcheon, A., 316, 327
McGuire, W. J., 47, 49

McKee, I. R., 218, 219, 220, 221, 237, 239, 241, 246, 247, 249
McLaughlin, J. P., 171, 185
McLellan, D. D., 80, 104
McPhail Gray, M., 254, 273
Mellers, B., 28, 49
Merelman, R. M., 300, 327
Messick, D. M., 7, 23
Meyer, J., 209, 212
Meyers, D. T., 86, 103
Meyerson, A., 285, 289, 298
Meyrowtiz, J., 280, 298
Mezei, L., 154, 163, 168, 187
Micheletti, P., 29, 30, 41, 50
Miller, A., 82, 103
Miller, J. B., 92, 103
Miller, N., 108, 133
Miller, W. E., 10, 23
Misra, S., 137, 138, 141, 142, 148, 149
Mitchell, P. G., 28, 49
Mitchell, R. C., 38, 49
Moe, J. L., 154, 163, 167, 168, 186, 187
Mongeau, C., 93, 105
Monteith, M. J., 93, 94, 97, 101, 183, 185, 187
Moore, L., 172, 173, 174, 186
Mosion, N., 86, 87, 103
Mueller, T. E., 145, 147, 148, 151
Murnen, S. K., 168, 188
Murray, T. H., 87, 99, 103
Myrdal, G., 154, 187

N

Nacoste, R., 154, 163, 167, 168, 186, 187
Nasby, W., 90, 103
Nash, J. E., 155, 186
Natan, L., 6, 24
Neugarten, B. L., 254, 274
Nevitte, N., 300, 327
Newcomb, T., 253, 274
Nisbett, R. E., 304, 327
Noddings, N., 86, 103
Novacek, J., 196, 209, 212
Novak, 140, 150
Nutall, R. L., 123, 124, 133

O

O'Brien, R. M., 136, 146, 150
O'Malley, P. M., 242, 248
O'Regan, S., 203, 204, 212
Oakley, J., 99, 103
Oatley, K., 205, 213
Olson, J. M., 131, 132, 178, 179, 187
Ordonez, L., 28, 49
Ortberg, J., 92, 101
Ostrom, T. M., 109, 110, 133
Oyserman, D., 91, 98, 103

P

Parish, T. S., 85, 86, 103
Parkes, C. M., 193, 213
Parsons, T., 299, 301, 302, 327
Pasternack, J. F., 94, 97, 101
Payne, J. W., 27, 49
Pelletier, L. G., 93, 105
Penner, L. A., 80, 82, 104
Pervin, L. A., 193, 213
Peterson, R. s., 33, 50
Petrillo, G. H., 254, 273
Petty, C. R., 173, 174, 176, 185
Petty, R. E., 60, 74
Piazza, T., 157, 159, 168, 169, 179, 188
Pierce, T., 199, 203, 204, 212
Polak, R. L., 60, 74
Poulos, B., 146, 147, 148, 150
Power, J. G., 278, 287, 288, 297, 298
Pratkanis, A. R., 93, 104
Pratt, M. W., 97, 104
Pratto, F., 172, 188
Precker, J. A., 168, 187
Prentice-Dunn, S., 173, 187
Pruitt, D. G., 7, 24

R

Rankin, W. L., 67, 74, 78, 102
Rao, V. R., 143, 149
Rapacchi, B., 137, 145, 151
Raskin, R., 90, 104
Raz, J., 37, 49

Razio, R. H., 77, 105
Reardon, K. K., 288, 296
Reed, F. W., 254, 273
Reed, M., 161, 180, 186
Reitzes, D. C., 195, 211
Rempel, J. K., 92, 105, 159, 189
Rest, J. R., 85, 97, 105
Reynolds, T. J., 137, 151
Rholes, W. S., 85, 104
Rizzo, N., 172, 173, 174, 186
Robertson, R., 131, 132, 302, 327
Robinson, A. B., 87, 88, 97, 101
Rogers, A. G., 97, 104
Rogers, C. R., 66, 74
Rogers, R. W., 173, 187
Rokeach, M. N., 1, 2, 16, 17, 22, 24, 26,
  29, 49, 54, 55, 57, 66, 67, 69, 74, 75,
  78, 79, 80, 81, 82, 86, 88, 89, 97, 100,
  104, 107, 133, 138, 151, 153, 154,
  163, 187, 193, 195, 213, 255, 274,
  278, 283, 297, 300, 305, 327
Rokkan, S., 10, 23
Romero, M., 254, 274
Ros, L., 94, 104
Rose, G. M., 136, 147, 148, 150, 151
Rosen, J., 277, 298
Rosenbaum, M. E., 168, 187
Rosenblatt, R. R., 85, 86, 103
Ross, M., 200, 212
Roth, S. H., 200, 211
Rothman, G., 154, 163, 187
Rusbult, C. E., 192, 205, 206, 207,
  209, 212, 213
Russo, N. F., 200, 211

S

Sagiv, L., 3, 4, 13, 16, 21, 22, 24, 255, 274
Sakumura, J., 192, 212
Salancik, G. R., 109, 110, 133
Sampson, R., 97, 104
Sanders, K. R., 80, 88, 104
Sanford, R. N., 29, 48, 260, 272
Sasson, T., 278, 297
Sawa, G. H., 67, 75
Sawa, S., 67, 75

Saxe, 156, 185
Scheier, M. F., 89, 90, 100, 101, 173, 187, 188
Schneider, W., 154, 187
Schrum, L. J., 89, 104
Schulz, R., 173, 187, 188
Schuman, H., 156, 188
Schuman, I., 172, 188
Schwalbe, M. L., 92, 104
Schwartz, S. H., 3, 4, 13, 16, 21, 22, 24, 67, 71, 72, 75, 88, 92, 97, 104, 154, 171, 180, 188, 193, 213, 255, 261, 262, 274, 303, 321, 327
Scott, W. A., 84, 100, 255, 273
Sears, D. O., 10, 23, 24, 153, 154, 155, 156, 157, 158, 159, 186, 188, 255, 274
Seliger, M., 10, 24
Seligman, C., 61, 75
Shamir, M., 10, 23
Sheatsley, P. B., 156, 185, 188
Sherrid, S. D., 80, 82, 88, 104
Shils, E. E., 29, 49
Shoham, A., 136, 147, 148, 150, 151
Sidanius, J., 172, 188
Silver, R. L., 205, 213
Silverman, B. I., 168, 188
Simmons, C. H., 193, 212
Singer, E., 292, 298
Skitka, L. J., 42, 50, 179, 188
Slovik, L. F., 205, 213
Smeaton, G., 168, 188
Smith, C. R., 167, 188
Smith, D. H., 302, 327
Smith, E. I., 254, 273
Smith, E. R., 157, 158, 186
Smith, M. B., 85, 88, 89, 90, 91, 104, 109, 133, 154, 163, 168, 188
Smith, M. C., 147, 148, 50
Smith, P. W., 154, 163, 187, 255, 274
Smith, T. E., 254, 274
Smooha, S., 20, 24
Sniderman, P. M., 157, 158, 159, 168, 169, 179, 188
Snyder, M., 60, 75, 89, 90, 105, 108, 116, 133, 208, 213
Solari, A., 300, 327

Solomon, R. C., 96, 105
Sparks, P., 54, 75
Speicher, B., 97, 100
Spence, J. T., 82, 105
Spencer, S., 195, 213
Spranca, M., 41, 48
Stapp, J., 82, 105
Starfield, B., 283, 298
Staw, B., 192, 200, 205, 213
Steeh, C., 156, 188
Steele, C. M., 89, 105, 193, 195, 213
Stein, C., 210, 213
Stein, D. D., 154, 163, 168, 188
Stephan, W. G., 173, 174, 176, 185
Stephenson, B., 173, 174, 176, 185
Stipek, D., 91, 105
Stokes, D. E., 10, 23
Struch, N., 154, 171, 188
Suedfeld, P., 33, 45, 50
Sukhdial, A., 146, 147, 148, 150
Sullivan, L. A., 153, 186
Svehla, G., 253, 274
Syme, G. J., 61, 75

T

Tallman, I., 282, 297
Tanke, E. D., 89, 105
Tavris, C., 82, 105
Taylor, D. G., 156, 188
Taylor, J. M., 86, 101
Taylor, S. E., 47, 50, 72, 74, 195, 205, 213
Tepperman, L., 324, 326
Terr, L., 91, 105
Terry, H., 90, 104
Tesser, A., 33, 50, 195, 213
Tessler, R. C., 92, 104
Tetlock, P. E., 2, 22, 26, 27, 28, 29, 30, 31, 32, 33, 35, 36, 38, 40, 41, 42, 45, 47, 49, 50, 51, 54, 75, 157, 168, 169, 179, 188
Thaler, R., 39, 49
Theno, S. A., 154, 161, 164, 167, 184, 189
Thibaut, J. W., 197, 212

Thoits, P. A., 193, 208, 213
Thoma, S. J., 85, 91, 92, 105
Thompson, M., 175, 188
Thornburg, K. R., 254, 273
Tigert, D. J., 300, 326
Trankel, M. A., 254, 273
Treadway, C. M., 109, 131, 132
Trevethan, S. D., 97, 105
Triandis, H. C., 167, 189, 302, 303, 328
Troll, 254, 274
Tronto, J. C., 86, 87, 93, 96, 99, 105
Truman, T., 300, 328
Tukey, J. W., 143, 150
Tummula, P., 90, 102
Tversky, A., 27, 41, 51
Tyler, A., 47, 51

U-V

Utsey, M., 145, 147, 148, 149
Valette-Florence, P., 137, 145, 151
Vallerand, R. J., 93, 105
Verba, S., 302, 326
Verette, J., 205, 213
Veroff, J., 138, 139, 151
Vescio, T. K., 159, 161, 164, 167, 184, 189
Volkmer, R. E., 218, 219, 220, 221, 237, 241, 246, 247, 249

W

Wackenhut, J., 153, 154, 171, 172, 186
Walbaum, A. B. C., 33, 50
Walker, L. J., 85, 91, 92, 97, 101, 105
Walters, G., 156, 186
Ward J. V., 86, 101
Waring, H. R., 278, 287, 288, 297, 298
Watkins, H., 137, 144, 145, 147, 148, 150
Weeks, W. A., 136, 137, 147, 143, 148, 151
Weigel, J., 61, 75
Weigel, R. H., 61, 75, 179, 189
Weiner, B., 91, 105, 179, 189
Weiner, M., 299, 328

Wernon, P. E., 255, 272
White, R. W., 109, 133
Whitney, G. A., 205, 213
Wicklund, R., 195, 212
Wildavsky, A., 41, 51
Williams, B., 37, 51
Williams, L., 167, 188
Williams, R. M., 255, 274, 299, 328
Willis, R. H., 167, 188
Wilson, J. P., 86, 105
Wolchik, S. A., 254, 273
Wong, T. J., 168, 180
Woodmansee, J. J., 172, 189
Wortman, C. B., 205, 213
Wulff, D. W., 16, 24
Wyatt, G. E., 200, 211

Y

Yang, K., 302, 328
Young, R. A., 80, 105

Z

Zajac, D., 192, 209, 212
Zaller, J., 47, 51
Zanna, M. P., 47, 49, 54, 58, 71, 74, 75, 77, 78, 79, 82, 89, 92, 94, 102, 103, 105, 124, 130, 131, 132, 155, 159, 171, 175, 178, 179, 183, 185, 186, 187, 188, 189, 199, 200, 210, 212, 255, 274
Ziman, J., 141, 151
Zukerman, M., 68, 75
Zuwerink, J. R., 183, 187

Subject Index

A

Accountability, 40-43
  blame, 35
  demands, trade-offs and, 35, 36
  decision making and, 40-42
  demagoguery, 35
  see Values
Achievement values, 7
Accountability
  FDA and, 40-42, 45
Adversity, *see* Commitment
Ambiguity, 304
Ambivalence, 172-176, *see* Prejudice

B

Belief Congruence theory, 154, 163,
  164, 167-169
Blacks
  blend construct, 158-160
  race study, 165, 166
  see Prejudice
Blame
  decision making and, 40, 41
Blend construct, *see* Prejudice
Buckpassing, 41-43

C

Child abuse, *see* False memory
  syndrome
Commitment
  Affects Balance scale, 201
  attachment/obligation, 197
  attitudinal, 200
  behavioral, 199-201
  core beliefs and, 193
  defined, 192
  dependency and, 211
  dimensions of, 209, 210
  ego defensive function of, 195
  forced choice paradigm, 195
  health and, 200
  identity and, 193
  Interdependence model, 197, 198
  interrelated, 194, 195
  long-distance dating study, 203, 204
  Personal Projects Analysis (PPA),
    196, 197
  pregnancy/abortion decisions and,
    199-203
  prototypes of, 192
  Rusbult's Investment Model, 197,
    198
  self-affirmation theory, 195
  self-complexity, 194
  self-report and, 196, 199
  sexual orientation and, 210
  smoking and, 201
  testing notion of, 196
  value relevance/adversity, 197-200
  values as standards, 193, 195
  volunteerism, 198, 199
Commitment-adversity relation
  accommodation behavior, 205, 206
  caregiver study, 206, 207
  content/loss of commitment, 208
  costs and challenges of, 205
  identity configurations, 208, 209
  moral/personal, 210
  reciprocal nature of, 207

Rusbult's Investment Model, 205, 209
stress and negativity, 206, 207
threat to self-esteem, 205, 206
value relevance, 209, 210
Competence, 247, *see* Tall poppies research
Conflicting values
cross-issues variation, 36
identifying, 36
Cooperation, as variable, 6-8
Cross-cultural, view of values, 289-325

D

Decision making
accountability and, 40-42
avoidance and, 40-43
blame and, 40, 41
buckpassing and, 41-43
delayed, 40, 41
monetary, 39
morality/immorality and, 38, 39
obstacles and, 40
self-esteem and, 40
trade-offs and, 37
Decision-making experiment, 6, 7

E

Envy, 247, 248, *see* Tall poppy research

F

False memory syndrome (FMS), 79-83
Family values
Rokeach Value Survey (RVS), 161-163
sexual orientation and, 161-163
see Values, Value transmission

H

Hedonism, 5, 8, 17

Homosexual relationships
commitment, 210
family values and, 155, 161
see Sexual orientation

I

Identity
cognitive repair and, 208, 209
threatened, 208, 209
Individualism, 304
Interdependence Theory (Rusbult's Investment Model), 197, 198
Interpersonal cooperation, 6-10

L

List of Values rating scale (LOV), 22
attitude research, 135, 137, 138
behavior prediction, 136
conformity and, 136
consumer behavior and, 136-139, 147, 148
consumption and social values and, 139, 140
cross-cultural comparisons, 145, 146
data analysis approaches, 142-144
geographic variability, 144, 145
internal-level rating scales, 142
internal/external forces, 136
Maslow's hierarchy and, 146, 147
natural foods and, 136
Rokeach Value Survey (RVS) and, 141, 142
Values and Lifestyle Segmentation program (VALS), 141
values, as systems, 140

M

Media system dependency theory (MSD), 277, 286-294
value-frame, 278, 279, 283-286, 289
decoding values, 281
effect of, 281

health care issue, 282-289
information ambiguity, 279-286,
  289
interest groups/media dependency
  relation, 291-293
interpersonal networks, 290
macro/micro effects, 293, 294
media as referee/rulemaker, 292,
  293
terminal vs. instrumental values,
  278
value-choice frame, 279
Media
  roll of, 277-296
  see Value-choices
Memory
  distortion of, 69, 70
  effect of trauma on, 81
  False memory syndrome (FMS), 79-
  83
  recovered memories, 81
  short term, and Rokeach Value
  Survey, 141, 142
  see false memory syndrome
Minority groups
  attitude toward, 260, 261
  see Prejudice
Moral/personal commitment, 210
  see Commitment
Morality, 84
  abortion and, 85, 96
  capital punishment and, 85
  care orientation and, 86, 87, 91, 96
  cognitive development and, 93
  decision making and, 38, 39
  Defining Issues Test (DIT), 85-87
  justice orientation and, 87, 96
  model for, 97-99
  moral dilemma, 92-94
  moral orientation, 97-99
  moral orientation-value distinction,
  86-88
  moral reasoning stages, 84, 85, 93
  personal norms, 92, 93
  process-content distinction, 85, 87
  self-concept, 89, 90

self-dissatisfaction, 88, 89
self-identity, 88, 89
self-respect, 89
self-schemas, 90, 91
value-attitude-behavior relations,
  77, 83, 85-87
values and, 94

O

Outgroups, 155, 156, 158, 184
  ambivalence, 173
  antagonistic responses to, 179, 180
  Jewish/Arab conflict and, 16-21
  political conservatism and, 179
  prejudice and, 163, 164, 182-184
  readiness for social contact, 16, 18
  social contact with, 16-21
  tolerance vs. intolerance, 18
  universalism and tradition, 18, 19
  violating values, 180-182
  see Prejudice, Sexual orientation,
  Individualism

P

Personal Project Analysis (PPA) for
  commitment, 196, 197
Political ideology, see Voting behavior
Power values, 7, 9
Pregnancy
  abortion and, 202-203
  adversity and, 200
  commitment decisions, 199-203
  health and, 200
  smoking and, 201
Prejudice, 16
  ambivalence-amplification model,
  172-174, 177, 178
  ambivalent racism perspective, 153,
  154
  Anti-Fat Attitudes Questionnaire,
  180
  aversive racism and, 176-82
  Aversive Racism theory, 153, 154

belief congruence theory, 154, 163, 164, 167-169

Blacks and, 154, 156-158, 165, 166, 169, 171-184

blend construct, 158-162

duality of attitudes, 172

egalitarian/humanitarian ideal, 153, 154, 158, 178, 179

homosexuals and, 155, 161

individualism, 155, 158, 172

learned, 253, 255, 260, 272

Modern Racism Scale, 154, 156, 172, 173

National Election Study (1984), 158

promoting/suppressing, 179

Protestant work ethic and, 153, 154, 157, 158, 172, 180

race study (employee), 165, 166, 174, 175

race/sexual orientation studies, 159-164

racial ambivalence, 171-176

rejection of outgroup and, 155

Symbolic Racism, 154, 169-171

symbolic/modern racism, 156, 157, 161, 164, 172, 182

value blocking, 183, 184

value congruence, 164

values and, 153

R

Racial ambivalence, 171-176

Racism, aversive

ambivalence, 171-176

dominative, 176, 177

justification theory, 177

literature, 156-158

manipulating for egalitarian self-image, 178, 179

racial ambiguity, 177

stigmatized groups, 173, 182

see Prejudice

Religion, 253, 306, 311, 320, 323

Religiosity/ethnocentrism, 16

Rokeach value survey, 22, 33

S

Security, 9

Self, concept of, 88-91

guilt, 91

in China, 91

in Japan, 90, 91

Self-esteem, 247

decision making and, 40

see Tall poppies research

Self-identity, see Morality, Values

Sexual orientation, 159-164, 167

family values and, 161-163

Heterosexuals' Attitudes Toward Homosexuals scale (HATH), 161,180

see also Homosexuals

Single-value approaches, 1, 2, 21

as idiosyncratic, 21

Social adaption theory, see List of Values

Social-content postulate, 36-40

cross-domain trade-offs, 36

defining conflicting values, 36

monetary value, 39

motivational obstacles, 40

resisting decision making, 37, 38

value conflict responses, 37

Status, effects of, see Tall poppies research

Symbolic Racism theory, 169-171

Sympathetic identification with underdog, 172, 173

T

Tall poppies research (Australia)

attribution theory, 217, 226

cultural view, 246, 247

defined, 216, 217

deservingness, 217, 220, 225, 226, 234, 235

ingroup/outgroup membership, 230-232

noncompetitive nature of, 217

person-action-outcome triad, 233, 234

political views and, 245, 246
positive/negative attitudes toward, 240-247
Protestant work ethic and, 244
public figures in, 218-222
responsibility and, 226-230
social comparison, 217
sports and, 220
studies in, 234-240
values, as abstract structures, 222-225
view of cheating and, 238, 239
Trade-off reasoning, 41
see Value Pluralism Model
Trade-offs
accountability, 35, 36
boundaries, 37
denying/confronting, 36
forbidden, 38
posing questions, 39
weighing, 36

V

value blocking, 183
Value chains, 137
Value conflict, 2, 4-6, 33-35
avoiding blame, 40, 41
see Value trade-offs
Value congruence, 164
Value differences
see Values, cross-cultural view
Value discrepancies
see Value systems
Value Pluralism Model (VPM),
authoritarian personality theory, 29-31
cognitive style/political ideology relationship. 29-33
ideologue hypothesis, 29-31
limitations of, 29, 34, 35
propositions of, 25-32
revised, 34-36
slavery issue, 33, 34, 45
social-content postulate, 35-43

thought induced attitude polarization, 33
see Value Pluralism Model-Revised
Value Pluralism Model-Revised
application of, 47, 48
incommensurability, 37
moderator in decision making, 37
trade-offs and, 26
value-free pluralism, 44-47
Value relevance
commitment and, 210
Value systems
abortion studies, 1, 2, 53-67, 72
capital punishment, 53, 54
circular structure of, 72
competing, 4, 5
complementary, 4, 5
dynamic or rule bound, 55, 56
environmental study, 61-63
fluctuation of, 57
integrated, 22
List of Values, 55
memory distortion, 69,70
multiple vs. traditional systems approach, 55-57, 71
operation of multiple, 72, 73
Rokeach Terminal Values Survey, 57-63-67
sanctity of life value, 53, 54, 60
self-states and, 67-70
stability of, 54, 55
target issues as variable for change, 70, 71
value accessibility, 73
value self-confrontation technique, 66, 67
Value transmission in families
age and, 254
attitudes toward outgroups, 254
Bartholomew's Relationship Style Questionnaire (RSQ), 263
conservatism, 262
cultural similarity, 258
dedication to causes, 254
Fearful/Dismissing, Secure, Preoccupied patterns, 263

husband/wife similarity, 257-259
liberalism/conservatism, 254
materialist values, 254
mediating effects of parenting style,
    268-271
parent-child similarity, 253, 254,
    257, 271, 272
parenting style and, 265-268, 271
relating styles, 263
right-wing authoritarianism, 259-
    263, 265, 271
social convention and, 260
value measurement, 255-257
value of ingroup, 262
value system comparisons, 254, 255
Value types
  compatibility, 4
  openness to change, 16, 17
  self-enhancement, 17
  self-transcendence, 17
Value violation
  and racism, 183
Value-attitude-behavior relations, 77-
    100
  false memory syndrome, 80-83
  moderators of, 79
  morality, 84-88
  self-identity, 88-91
  study of, 78
  The Great American Values Test, 78
  value justification hypothesis, 79
  women's equality, 79-81
Value-behavior linkage, 136, 137
Value-choices, 277-296
  health care study, 282-286
  see Media
Value-expression attitudes
  abortion and, 107, 131, 132
  attitude-perception studies, 110,
    130
  dogmatism, 108
  high/low self-monitoring, 108, 109
  manipulation of value relevance,
    109, 110, 131
  value-attitude-behavior links,
    107, 108, 132

values bonding procedure, 109
  versus social-adjustive types, 110
Values
  accountability, 25, 35, 36
  child rearing, 303, 305
  commitment under adversity, 198
  consumer motivation and
  cross cultural view, 3, 4, 289-325
  effects on attitudes and behavior, 77
  family, 155
  motivational goals, 2, 4
  personal/societal trade-offs, 25
  self-affirmation and, 195, 196, 199
  self-respect, 89
  trade-offs, coping with, 25-27, 33, 35
  types of, 2, 3, 4, 7
  universal requirements of, 2
  variables in, 83, 84
  World Values Survey, 304-323
  see List of Values, Morality,
    Prejudice, Tall poppies research,
    Voting behavior
Values, cross-cultural view, 298-325
  Canadian-American differences,
    299-304, 310, 311
  latent class analysis, 316-321
  Latin America, 301
  qualities measured, 305-317
  regression analysis, 321-323
  World Values Survey, 304-306, 316
Volunteerism
  self-affirmation and, 198
Voting behavior, 9-15
  in Israel, 10-15

W

World Values Survey, 304-323
  Age, 306
  children, 306
  community size, 306
  education, 306
  gender, 306
  marital status, 306
  occupation, 306
  religious attendance, 306